OBRIEN'S ORIGINAL GUIDE TO

CAPE COD
AND THE ISLANDS

O'BRIEN'S ORIGINAL GUIDE TO
CAPE COD
AND THE ISLANDS

Edited by
GREG O'BRIEN

PARNASSUS IMPRINTS
Hyannis, Massachusetts

First Parnassus Imprints Edition 1996

First published as *An Insider's Guide to Cape Cod and the Islands* in 1988, revised in 1990, by The Stephen Green Press

Cover photographs © Jane Booth Vollers

Sketches and maps by Kathy Rolbein

Grateful acknowledgement is made for permission to reprint excerpts from the following works:

Early Cape Cod by Jean Fritz. By permission of Cape Cod National Seashore.

Shipwrecks of Cape Cod by William P. Quinn. By permission of the author.

Library of Congress Cataloging-in-Publication Data

Insider's guide to Cape Cod and the Islands
    O'Brien's original guide to Cape Cod and the Islands / edited by
Greg O'Brien.
        p.   cm.
    First published as: An Insider's Guide to Cape Cod and the Islands
in 1988, revised in 1990, by Stephen Green Press. This is the 3rd
revised, updated, and retitled edition--Publisher's info.
    Includes index.
    ISBN 0-940160-66-8 (trade pbk.)
    1. Cape Cod (Mass.)--Guidebooks.   2. Martha's Vineyard (Mass.)-
-Guidebooks.   3. Nantucket Islands (Mass.)--Guidebooks.   4. Elizabeth
Islands (Mass.)--Guidebooks.   I. O'Brien, Greg.   II. Title.
F72.C3I57   1996   96-1855
974.4 '92--dc20   CIP

Printed in the United States of America on recycled paper

To Virginia and Frank O'Brien, two Cape Codders at heart;
thanks for your many years of love and support, without which I could
never have pursued this road less traveled.

—Much love, your son, the editor.

Contents

PROVINCETOWN

THE ISLANDS: *Martha's Vineyard, Nantucket, Elizabeth Islands*

LIST OF MAPS

Foreword

(Editor's note: writer E. J. Kahn, Jr. passed away before publication of this revised edition. Considered among the finest writers in America, Kahn's love for Cape Cod and his sense of this fragile peninsula will endure forever, as will his words.)

In Wyoming last summer, staring in awe at the magnificent mountains of the Grand Teton National Park, I was asked by an indigene to name my favorite American scene. When I answered, "Cape Cod," she replied, not unkindly, "Ah, yes, one of your flat little islands back east."

Since the dredging and then bridging of the Cape Cod Canal, what many of us like to call the Cape is, of course, an island of sorts, but we Cape Codders think of this tiny (to a westerner) spit of earth as an indispensable, indeed quintessentially historic, part of the United States mainland. For was it not at the then unarguably continental Provincetown, after all, that the *Mayflower* Pilgrims first stepped ashore in 1620, when Plymouth Rock was still just another anonymous chunk of littoral stone?

I say "we Cape Codders" with some hesitation, if not outright gall. The fact that I have owned a Cape Cod house for some 35 years does not, by that hallowed realm's stern criteria, make me one of the select. My son Hamilton, whose reflections on Provincetown appear hereinafter (how often is one lucky enough to be able to use "hereinafter"?), has been permanently domiciled and gainfully employed on Cape Cod his entire adult life, but he is not a Cape Codder any more than I am. *His* sons, however, having been born on the Cape, enjoy that distinction. For my part, I am satisfied to assert, when I am asked by what right I presume to write or talk about Cape Cod, that I am grandparentally linked to as authentic a brace of Cape Codders—with all their causes—as you could hope to shuck an oyster with.

I should perhaps mention here that if a recently formed Provincetown lobbying group has its way—you never know what causes will next be spawned on the Cape—we'll have a second canal to cope with. Its advocates

want Cape Cod to be sliced in two, near Orleans, so that in the event of a
meltdown of the Plymouth nuclear plant there'll be a water escape route out
into the Atlantic—thanks to the good offices of the World's First Whale and
Human Evacuation Canal and Research Institute—in the general direction of
Nantucket and the Vineyard. How the inhabitants of those tidy enclaves might
react to such a massive influx I dare not speculate; I suspect, though, that
the whales might be more welcome than the humans.

Meandering through Wyoming and other foreign states, I tend to gravi-
tate toward national parks. My East Coast residence, you see, turned out,
when the boundaries of the Cape Cod National Seashore were drawn more
than a quarter of a century ago, to be cozily within them. A weekly newspaper that my three boys put out for several summers while they were growing
up was titled, accordingly, *Park Here*. When Hamilton was seven and was
merely known as Tony, he was its editor-in-chief. He was an easy-going boss.
He allowed me to do what no other editor of mine has ever tolerated: to
write a gossip column. Because the *Cape Codder*—a twice weekly country
newspaper where Tony was feature editor—had a resident year-round columnist, Thomas Kane, who would periodically inform his readers of the arrival
of seasonal folk by some such phrase as "Lights on at Palmer Williams'," it
amused me once to draft an item that went "Lights on at Tommy Kane's." A
small joke, but my own, and Tony and his brothers were kind enough to stet
it. They also first published one of the great but regrettably unsung classics of
Cape Cod literature, the late Arthur Kober's "On Getting Lost in the Wellfleet
Woods."

Cape Cod, Martha's Vineyard, Nantucket, and the Elizabeth Islands are
becoming crowded—more visitors each summer, more of them deciding
each fall to stay on. The Sagamore Bridge that spans the existing canal has
seen some awful hot-weather traffic jams. There are longstanding settlers
who wonder if the Cape might not do well to adopt a policy promulgated
some years back by Governor Tom McCall, of Oregon, who gave his blessing
to the circulation there of "ungreeting" cards, the sentiments of which invited visitors to go away. Maybe we Cape Codders—there I go again—should
encourage our real estate brokers to emulate one of their ilk on Nantucket,
who not long ago declared that thenceforth he would have no truck with
new construction but would traffic exclusively, in the interest of stabilizing
the population, in the selling or renting of extant buildings.

Perhaps the laws of supply and demand will come into helpful play.
There seem to be so few beds available to summer migrants on the Cape
nowadays that the prices for occupying those there are have gone up
dismayingly. One sad result of this is that something like a thousand seasonal
jobs—waiters, shop assistants, baby-sitters, lifeguards, and the like—have
gone abegging, because even though prospective employers are offering such
perks as free bicycles, the young men and young women who'd ordinarily be
filling those slots can't find affordable quarters. Nobody has yet figured out a
way to sleep comfortably on a bike.

Mind you, when one speaks of "Cape Cod," one is really talking, puny as
the whole territory may seem to a Rocky Mountaineer, about a great many

areas of near-infinite variety. The tourist strips around Hyannis—motels, fast food, cut-rate furniture, you get the picture—are remote in ambiance if not in measured miles, from, say, the Kennedy compound at Hyannis Port, the Oceanographic Institute at Woods Hole, Chatham's well-coiffed dowagers, the usually amiable convergence of fishermen and fops on Provincetown's raffish Commercial Street, or the culturally redoubtable Truro Center for the Arts at Castle Hill.

Truro is where my tribe has hunkered down. It is a town so small (population, at last count, around 1,000) that motorists barreling along Route 6 may not always be aware they've passed through it. Sure, Truro has its drawbacks. In July and August, a parking space is tough to find either at the ocean beach, a short walk from my home, or at the also nearby post office—our two principal way stations, churchgoers excepted, for encountering gossip and antinuke petitions. In more halcyon days, one could pick up at the post office mail bearing simply one's name and "Truro, Mass." Then "Mass." became "MA" and the postal service invented zip codes. Then it launched a nine-digit-code campaign that was about as ineffective as my backhand. Our zip is "02666" and my post office box number is "212." I undertook once to test the new modus operandi by sending myself from New York, first-class postage duly affixed, an envelope bearing no address other than "02666-0212." It never arrived, but that didn't matter, because I'd enclosed only a blank sheet of paper.

What is it about the Cape, anyway, that has meant so much, by now, to three generations of my family? (Four, actually, if you count my father's quondam visits.) I can't speak for my Cape Codder grandchildren, but to me it means, among other pleasurable things, blueberries and locust trees and sea-clam pies (can there be a better way to start a low-tide day than a clamming expedition?) and beach-plum brandy and the sound of the surf in the lull of a storm and the absolutely dazzling blue of the sky (ask any painter) and so many longtime neighborly friends and friendly neighbors and—I guess above all—serenity. Also, I can go to work in my study without taking a subway, putting a tie on, or, if I am infused with pioneer spirit, shaving.

To others, naturally, the many-faceted Cape and its guardian islands have different, if not altogether dissimilar, appeals; and in the pages that follow editor Greg O'Brien and his knowledgeable associates are poised to reveal to newcomers, and to remind old-timers, of many of this very special region's marvels and even some of its cherished secrets.

—E.J. Kahn, Jr.
Truro, Massachusetts

Acknowledgments

I need first to acknowledge my wife for 19 years, Mary Catherine McGeorge O'Brien. Without her hard work, dedication, and knowledge of Cape Cod and its neighboring islands, this revision would not have been possible. I also thank Nancy O'Malley and Matt Hunter for their assistance in this project—months and months of gathering information and checking and rechecking facts.

There were many other people, newspapers, and organizations that helped in putting together this guidebook and its revision, all of whom deserve my thanks. In addition to the writers whose bylines appear on these pages, I particularly wish to thank the Chambers of Commerce of Cape Cod, Martha's Vineyard, and Nantucket, which gave me invaluable assistance. The Allen House on the island of Cuttyhunk and the Cape Cod National Seashore also helped me in compiling the information for this book.

Special thanks are in order for the Martha's Vineyard Chamber of Commerce and the Nantucket Chamber of Commerce for their help. I also want to thank all of the Cape and Island town halls, local libraries, and boards of trade.

In addition, I thank Elizabeth Aldred, Ben Barnhart, Marianne Cacciola, Dennis and Therese Gordon of Sir Speedy of Orleans, Jan Cormier, Robert Cousins, Sonja Greenbaum, Mary Beth Hartung, Barbara Hollis, Joanna Kingsley, Katharine Lawrence, John LoDico, Lou McGeorge, Greg McGrath, Sue Orant, Sally Pearson, Kathy Piekarski, Eileen Sundby, Paula Vallie, and Janice Walford for their various contributions and encouragements.

I also want to thank E. J. Kahn III for his help on the Cape Cod National Seashore essay.

Special thanks are also long overdue to my publishers at Parnassus Imprints—Walter Curley, who handles the business side, and Wallace Exman, one of the finest book editors in the business. Your direction and encouragement have made this a better book. And to Kathy Rolbein for her splendid artwork and maps.

I also thank my three children, Brendan, Colleen, and Conor, for their patience with me this last year. On one particular Sunday afternoon in June, Brendan turned to me in frustration when I couldn't play whiffleball with him and said, "Daddy, this sure is a long book!" He was right.

—Greg O'Brien
Brewster, Massachusetts

About the Authors

This guidebook was compiled and edited by a team of local writers and researchers who have lived and worked on Cape Cod and the Islands for many years. These contributors know the region intimately and know of its secrets, which they share in the pages to come—insider suggestions on where to eat, sleep, shop, swim, play golf, hike, camp, enjoy a night on the town, and even where to do laundry.

GREG O'BRIEN is editor and president of Stony Brook Publishing & Productions, Inc., a publishing, multi-media and film production company in Brewster on Cape Cod that helped produce this revised edition. He is former editor and publisher of Cape Cod Publishing Company in Orleans on the Outer Cape. Born in Rye, New York, O'Brien first set foot on Cape Cod when he was three. He summered in Eastham on the Outer Cape all through high school and college and after graduation joined the staff of the *Cape Codder,* reporting on towns from Chatham to Provincetown, and on the Cape Cod National Seashore.

O'Brien left the Cape in 1976 to become a political and investigative reporter for the *Arizona Republic* in Phoenix. He also contributed to the *Associated Press.* In 1979 he returned to the East to take a job as a general assignment and political reporter for the old *Boston Herald American.* In 1982 he became senior writer for *Boston* magazine and wrote about politics and human interest. In 1983 he returned to the *Cape Codder* to pursue his dream of running country newspapers. He is also former editor-in-chief of the *Cape Cod Business Journal*, a co-author of two other books about the Cape, a member of the Board of Trustees of the Cape Cod Museum of Natural History in Brewster, a former member of the Board of Trustees of Trinity School of Cape Cod, and a member of the Nauset Regional School Committee.

O'Brien still writes for *Boston* magazine and has contributed to other regional and national publications; he is currently at work on a book about Cape Cod archaeology. He lives in West Brewster with his wife, Mary Catherine (McGeorge), and three children—Brendan, Colleen, and Conor.

MARY CATHERINE O'BRIEN, Greg's wife, is a freelance writer and former stockbroker. She was born and raised in Phoenix, Arizona, and is a regular contributor to Stony Brook Publishing and Productions.

SETH ROLBEIN, who served as an executive editor on this project, came to Cape Cod more than 20 years ago as a teenager, spending summers working in the Mid-Cape town of Yarmouth. His first full-time job in journalism upon graduation from Harvard College was covering the town of Dennis for the *Register* for three years, starting in 1976.

Rolbein returned to the Boston area late in 1978 and worked as a writer, reporter, and producer for public television station WGBH-TV, as well as for National Public Television. In 1981 he became the founding editor of the *Cape Cod Business Journal* and moved to Orleans. He is now a freelance writer and producer, and a regular contributor and columnist for *Boston* magazine. He has also contributed to many regional and national magazines and newspapers.

E. J. KAHN, JR., was a staff writer with the *New Yorker* from 1937 until his recent death. The author of 25 books, among them *The China Hands* and *The Big Drink* (a history of the Coca-Cola company), Kahn owned a house in Truro on the Outer Cape for 35 years.

HAMILTON KAHN, E. J.'s son, got his start in the newspaper business when he was seven years old. In the early 1960s, his father published a mimeographed summer newspaper from the family's Truro home. Kahn cut his teeth covering sailing races and little league games.

Born in New York City, Kahn, who now lives year-round in Wellfleet, was feature editor of the *Cape Codder* and now is editor of the *Provincetown Banner*. Kahn decided to make the newspaper business a career after a decade of trying to make a living as a musician.

BRIAN TARCY has been a reporter for the *Cape Cod Times*, covering Falmouth government and features about the town.

MARK ALAN LOVEWELL is a descendant of the original Pease family that settled the Vineyard. He is a reporter and photographer for the award-winning *Vineyard Gazette*, a country newspaper published in Edgartown and owned by James Reston of the *New York Times* and his wife, Sally Fulton Reston.

Mr. Lovewell also writes a fishermen's column for the newspaper and is a former merchant seaman.

As a year-round resident of the island, he spends his spare time collecting and singing sea chanties, among other things. He is coauthor of the book *Songs of South Street*, which was published in 1976.

JEAN FRITZ, noted writer and author of several children's books, wrote the essay on early Cape Cod as part of an "artists in residence" program at the Cape Cod National Seashore. It was published in booklet form and a condensed version is reprinted here with the permission of the Cape Cod National Seashore.

It is an excellent primer on the Cape's history and geology.

The detailed listings for the Martha's Vineyard section were compiled by Joanne Walker of the Martha's Vineyard Chamber of Commerce. The Nantucket listings were complied by Mary Patton and her staff at the Cliff Lodge on Nantucket, and the Elizabeth Islands listings were compiled with the help of Nina Solod on Cuttyhunk Island.

Introduction:
How to Use This Guidebook

by Seth Rolbein

Cape Cod and its sister islands of Martha's Vineyard, Nantucket, and the Elizabeths have a mystique, a romantic lure no amount of summertime rush and crush could ever diminish.

The first time I felt the tug of the Cape was as a teenager, when I was flipping through an atlas trying to conjure up some sense of all those places in the United States I had never seen. When my eye caught the little spike off the coast of Boston, a craggy defiant arm hooking into the ocean and just beyond it flecks of islands acting as a continental vanguard, I knew I wanted to go there.

And that is part of Cape Cod's charm (perhaps its ultimate ruination, too): that it is alluring in an exotic sort of way, yet accessible to a teenager in the Northeast wanting his first taste of travel. I came here for the first time that summer; now, nearly two decades later, Cape Cod has become my home.

When all is said and done, the heart of this region, its attraction to visitor and resident alike, is the sea. Playful in the summer, ferocious in the winter, the Atlantic dominates the life and character of these maritime communities almost as much today as it did when the Pilgrims first sought refuge here nearly 370 years ago.

Man since then has done his best to build buffers and conveniences against the whim of nature—creating, for instance, 15 towns out of this sandy peninsula, imagining distinctions between up-island and down-island on the Vineyard and Nantucket, and defining the difference between public and private properties.

Throughout all this the sea hasn't changed much, regardless of whether you're standing on Nauset Beach in Orleans, Lighthouse Beach on Martha's Vineyard, Steamboat Wharf on Nantucket, Jetty Beach on charming Cuttyhunk, or the wide open clam flats of Cape Cod Bay. The tide still courses in, and in the winter, a wicked northeast wind still scours the dunes. Ships, such as the mighty Maltese freighter *Eldia*, continue to be wrecked on shoals by a power we can hardly imagine.

Then in return for this harshness, summer rolls around and the Atlantic is inviting once again. Traffic jams may frustrate the weary, "No Vacancy" signs may dot the landscape, construction may abound, but the sea will never be subdivided. And prime beaches, meadows, and salt marshes, most notably those within the 27,300 acres of the Cape Cod National Seashore, will never be built upon—areas such as Great Island in Wellfleet Harbor, where oyster shells carpet the sand and the only building is the remains of a tavern that entertained sea captains and sailors 200 years ago, or the Province Lands of Provincetown, where Sahara-like sand dunes slope towards the shore.

The Cape and Islands have a feel, an identity, all their own, and yet each region within the region has its own personality, all of which are described in considerable detail in this guidebook, written by people who live here year-round and know the area's secrets intimately. Falmouth, for instance, is a world apart from Sandwich, and a universe apart from Truro. And it is entirely possible to meet someone from Wellfleet who hasn't been to Chatham in five years, let alone across the Cape Cod Canal to the mainland. Martha's Vineyard is also vastly different from Nantucket, and neither island bears resemblance to the Elizabeth chain.

First, a bit about the Cape and Islands in general; a quick overview is essential in understanding the sum total of the region's parts and will be a help in using this guide. In some ways, the region is a study of contrasts and contradictions.

Politically, the Cape and Islands are known as one of the last Republican strongholds in Democratic Massachusetts, a strongbed of conservative Yankee individualism. Yet the district's present Congressman is Gerry Studds, openly gay, openly liberal. People here seem to care more about the fact that he's a defender of the environment and pushed hard for the 200-mile fishing limit than his well-publicized indiscretion with a Congressional page.

Historically, the area has the deepest European roots you'll find in this country: the *Mayflower* sought the shelter of Cape Cod Bay near Provincetown before the Pilgrims settled in Plymouth. The Cape is also home to one of the oldest highways in the United States; many of the homes that line the route were built by early settlers from Britain. Much has been done to preserve the area. Yet just a few miles away, on commercial Route 28, developers have had a free hand, constructing one motel and pitch and putt after another.

Culturally, there are paradoxes, too. In Provincetown, for instance, hardworking Portuguese fishermen rub shoulders with prominent writers, poets, and photographers, as well as a flamboyant gay community. And in Mashpee on the Cape and in Gay Head on Martha's Vineyard, descendants of the original settlers coexist peacefully with members of the Wampanoag Indian tribe, whose ancestors lived here long before the *Mayflower*'s arrival. Disputes, however, over who owns the land continue.

As in most summer resorts, there is a cultural schizophrenia here. The difference between "the season" and the "off season" is dramatic, although less so in recent years. Tourists have found that autumn and late spring visits to the Cape and Islands sometimes offer more beauty with less hassle than trips during the height of summer.

And the ocean, not so fickle as the air, stays warmer through the cold months—extending fall and moderating winter. The combination of this climate and all the warm memories of vacations past also bring many retired people to the area, a major impetus for the population boom of recent years.

Even a casual visitor to the area might sense some of the conflict that development pressure has created in these coastal communities. The irony of the argument on the Cape and Islands is that many old-time local families whom you might expect to be most zealously protective of the place have by and large been in the forefront of the building boom. The newcomers, "wash ashores," as they are sometimes called, have provided the push toward conservation and strict zoning—just as soon as they have moved into their own new homes, that is.

But for the most part residents seem to be of one mind when it comes to preserving parts of this fragile land. In the past few years, just about every town on the Cape and Islands has voted to acquire land, setting it aside for conservation and passive recreation. Cape Codders care about their land and would like those who visit here to leave with the same respect for the sea, the land, and life. Our guidebook, a look at the Cape and Islands from the inside out, was prepared with this in mind.

In the first two parts, you'll find informative essays about the Cape's history and geology and the power of the sea, as well as travel tips and a survival guide.

This guidebook divides the Cape and Islands into five sections: the Upper Cape, which covers the towns of Sandwich, Bourne, Mashpee, and Falmouth (including Woods Hole, a village with a flavor all its own); the Mid-Cape, which covers Barnstable (a town with seven villages including Hyannis, the Cape's commercial hub), Yarmouth, and Dennis; the Outer Cape (or Lower Cape, as "wash ashores" call it), which covers Brewster, Harwich, Chatham, Orleans, Eastham, Wellfleet, Truro, and the Cape Cod National Seashore; Provincetown, actually considered a part of the Outer Cape but a town that deserves a special section; and the Islands: Martha's Vineyard, Nantucket, and the Elizabeth chain.

Each of these sections includes the most complete Cape and Island listings in one book to date: lodgings, restaurants, entertainment, museums, historic sites, seasonal events, tours, children's activities, art galleries, craft and specialty shops, antique stores, beaches, boat rentals, sports, churches, fish and farm markets, ice cream parlors, bakeries, laundromats, and other categories. We provide descriptions of the various places, price ranges (for restaurants and lodgings), and for your convenience give the telephone numbers when possible. The Cape's area code is 508. Boston's area code is 617. We also offer our recommendations on what we think is the best the Cape and Islands have to offer from an insider's point of view.

For lodgings, we designate prices in three *general* ranges, and given the fact that prices change, we stress the word *general:* inexpensive; moderate; and expensive. Many lodgings fall between categories; we've done our best to generalize. Please call the lodgings for details.

For restaurants, we also list three *general* price ranges: inexpensive; moderate; and expensive. Again, many restaurants fall between two categories, and we've tried to be fair in generalizing. Call for specific price ranges.

We will be updating this guide periodically; oversights, omissions, or additions should be directed to editor Greg O'Brien, 25 Stony Hill Road, Brewster, MA 02631. Given the nature of the tourist industry and the number of businesses involved, omissions and occasional mistakes are apt to appear in a guidebook. For this, we apologize in advance. Also, given the months between deadline and publication, we cannot be responsible for late changes in names, hours, addresses, phone numbers, or descriptions.

We hope you find this guidebook helpful and entertaining. It was written with you in mind. Oh, one final word of humble advice: don't leave home without us!

PART I

- *Early Cape Cod*

- *A Land By The Sea*

- *Historic Cape Lighthouses*

- *Travel Tips*

- *Survival Guide*

Early Cape Cod

by Jean Fritz

If you were to draw a map of North America as it looked, or probably looked, 70,000 years ago, you wouldn't even see Cape Cod. It was part of the mainland with low hills and flat stretches that reached far out into the Atlantic Ocean. But if you were to drill 500 feet down into the ground of the Upper Cape today, you would find the same bedrock of granite that covers the root of New England.

The geography of New England was changed by ice. The weather in Canada became so cold that snow didn't melt in summer, but instead, just piled up deeper and deeper and formed sheets of ice or glaciers that were hundreds of feet thick. Gradually dragging along everything they met in their path, these huge sheets of ice spread south.

In the course of millions of years, there were a series of Ice Ages. It was during the last one—about 20,000 years ago—that Cape Cod was formed. Covering what is now Cape Cod, Martha's Vineyard and Nantucket, the ice sheet (or glacier sometimes up to two miles thick) crept south. And then it stopped. For a long time it stayed there; then as the weather warmed, it receded to form a new line that ran along the north side of Cape Cod. Again it stopped until the weather warmed up about 15,000 years ago. This time the weather stayed warm enough for the ice finally to melt altogether in what is now the New England area. Eventually, so much ice melted that the ocean level rose 400 feet. Miles of land, that had been at the edge of the continent, were now underwater. Only the highest parts were above water. The glacier left behind so much clay, sand and gravel and so many rocks that Cape Cod stuck out of the water and soon became land.

The hills along the northern coast of the Cape (beside the mid-Cape highway east of the Canal) are made up of the debris which the glacier gathered in its long journey from the north and dumped here. (Hills made by glacial deposits are called moraines.)

The ice didn't melt evenly. When the ice sheet retreated, it left behind great blocks of ice (sometimes a mile wide). When these blocks finally melted, they left great hollows in the ground. Some were simply depressions in the

3

ground; some later became cranberry bogs; some filled up with fresh water and have become fresh water ponds; some are connected by channels with the sea and have become salt ponds.

There are hundreds of these ice-block lakes (or kettles) on Cape Cod. Round Pond, north of Wellfleet, is an example of a deep fresh-water kettle. The Visitor Center of the National Seashore off Route 6 in Eastham has been named for the salt pond (or kettle) beside it.

Other reminders of the Ice Age can be seen on Cape Cod. Every large boulder originally came from some place further north. It was picked up by the glacier, dragged down to the Cape and left here.

Doane Rock, off the road that leads from the Salt Pond Visitor Center to Coast Guard Beach, is the largest glacial boulder on the Cape.

Many pebbles, stones and rocks have scratch marks on their surfaces. These were made as the glacier, rolling and scraping the rocks against each other, moved south. At the Eastham Coast Guard Station there is a boulder covered with such scratch marks (or glacial striations). The Wellfleet Historical Society has placed a large stone with glacial scratches in the window of their museum.

The Changing Cape

Not only has ice shaped the Cape, but wind and waves are constantly taking land away from one place and adding it to another. Four thousand years ago, the southern and eastern shores of the Cape were not only rough and ragged, they also extended at least two miles farther into the ocean. Gradually, however, waves and winter storms have smoothed out the coastline and have dragged sand away from the cliffs of the Lower Cape. Three feet of Atlantic shoreline disappears every year. But not all the sand has left the shore forever. Much of it is returned farther north in an ever-lengthening beach. First, the sand forms a sandbar underwater, and as more sand is added, the sandbar is exposed and becomes what is known as a sandspit, new land that is a continuation of the old.

All of the Provincelands (in Truro and Provincetown) is new land. Glacial deposits end at Pilgrim Heights in Truro. From there the sand has been built up in ridges or dunes that may be seen from the observation platform on the Race Point Road.

Nauset Beach in Orleans, North Beach in Chatham and Nauset Spit in Eastham are perfect examples of sandspits.

On Cape Cod Bay south of Truro where once there were four islands, there is now one long beach known as Great Island. Sand has filled in between the islands, and linked the islands, including Wellfleet's Great Is-

land *(which stood alone as recently as 1831) to the mainland. On the other hand, nearby Billingsgate Island, which once was the home of many families, is now only a sandbar at low tide.*

Each year Cape Cod loses more land than it gains. While the ocean side of the Outer Cape loses five acres a year, it gains only two new acres. In other words, the Cape loses three feet of beach a year. The planting of beach grass on bare dunes has helped to make the sand more capable of resisting storms and waves than it was before. If people respect these fragile areas, the beach will have a better chance to survive, although the Cape will continue to be reformed by wind and water, just as it always has.

Native Americans and Early Explorers

Cape Cod first belonged to the Indians. In the 16th Century, natives of the Wampanoag Federation lived peacefully, for the most part, around the edge of Cape Cod. There were five tribes on the Cape, each with its own *sachem* (chief) and all ruled by a *Great Sachem* whose headquarters were near Providence, Rhode Island. Each of the local tribes was represented in the Federation's Council, which had to approve all major decisions, particularly the decision to go to war.

But the Wampanoags wanted little change in their lives; they enjoyed their routines. Each year at the same time, they planted corn, beans, squash and pumpkins. They also built traps to catch birds; they used nets to catch fish; they hunted with bows and arrows.

At the museum of the Salt Pond Visitors Center, there are Indian fishhooks, pottery fragments, a bone harpoon, and spearpoints. A rock on which Indians used to sharpen their knives can be seen on the Fort Hill Trail in Eastham. Historical Societies of Wellfleet and Truro also display arrowheads and wampum in their museums. Indian artifacts can also be seen at the Wampanoag Indian Museum in Mashpee off Route 130.

Just east of the Great Island parking area is a marker over the grave of an Indian woman whose remains were found a few years ago on Indian Neck and buried here by the Wampanoag Tribal Council.

The natives had many worries—the weather, disease and the availability of food. But none compared to the white man, who would come to their shores and become their greatest danger, their worst enemy.

The Coming of Strangers

No one is quite sure when the first white men came to Cape Cod, but certainly during the 16th Century, fishermen from many nations were fishing off the coast of New England.

When Bartholomew Gosnold, who gave Cape Cod its name, arrived in the Woods Hole-Hyannis area in 1602, he realized that the natives had seen white men before. As soon as they sighted Gosnold's ship, they gathered a supply of pipes, skins and handicrafts for a session of trading. Some of them spoke a few European words.

Most of the natives wore no clothing. Gosnold reported, "Except skins about their loins and over their shoulders . . . One had his face painted over and his head stuck with feathers in the manner of a turkey cock's train."

Others were to follow Gosnold. In 1604, a Frenchman, Samuel de Champlain, visited the Cape and wrote a description of native customs. Their houses were round, covered with thatch and corn husks. Inside were raised wooden platforms with mats on which they slept.

At the Salt Pond Visitors Center there is a large reproduction of an Indian settlement at Nauset Harbor. Champlain is shown, climbing the hill from the shore.

During his visit, Champlain landed at Barnstable, which he called "port aux Huistres" (Oyster Harbor). He scattered French names over the Cape, but the names didn't stick. In 1614 along came John Smith, looking for whales and determined to give English names to the land he called "New England." Smith drew one of the first maps of Cape Cod; only he called it Cape James. He called Cape Cod Bay "Stuart Bay." Provincetown was named Milford Haven. As it turned out, Smith's names didn't stick, either. Gosnold had given the Cape its proper and lasting name.

During the period of exploration, the natives and the white men were usually, but not always, friendly. Two of Champlain's men were killed in a fight; John Smith's men killed several natives. Yet the quarrels were not always taken to heart.

A more serious event occurred after Smith had left for England. Captain Thomas Hunt, who was to follow Smith after loading up with fish and furs, kidnapped 24 natives, many of them Nausets from the Cape. He took them to Spain and sold them as slaves. One of the natives was from the Plymouth area and was called Squanto. Fortunately, he made his way back to the Wampanoags several years later and became a friend of the Pilgrims.

Squanto is buried on the Cape in Chatham where he died. A commemorative stone at the Chatham Historical Society on Stage Harbor Road states that the grave is "within gunshots" of that site.

An act of kidnapping was hard for the natives to forget or forgive. Indeed, they were still remembering six years later when white men came off the *Mayflower* to explore their coast.

The cry went up at 7 o'clock on the morning of November 9, 1620. The land was Cape Cod, and for one hundred passengers who for 65 days had shared cramped quarters on the *Mayflower*, the cry came like an end to a nightmare. Beaten about by storms, confined below deck, sickly, coughing, dirty, the passengers crowded on to the deck and squinted over the water.

Yes, it was land, all right. Low, brown, weather-beaten, wild—but it was land. Of course, it was not where they were supposed to be. Their contract with the Virginia Company entitled them to land in the Hudson River area, which was still several days away, but when they found how dangerous the waters were along the eastern coast of the Cape, they decided that contract or not they would settle nearby.

So out to the tip of the Cape (off Provincetown) they sailed; but, before dropping anchor, the leaders drew up a compact for all male members to sign, committing them to cooperate in the new government which would be established. Now they were free to go ashore, a few at a time. First, just to feel land under foot, then to wash clothes that hadn't been washed since they'd left England, to cut wood so they could have a fire and a hot meal for a change, and to run, which is what the children did.

The *Mayflower* stayed in the bay for a month while three separate parties searched the Cape for a place to settle. In single file, dressed in armor, carrying muskets, the men marched up the coast and through the woods and looked for a river, a good harbor and a suitable area for planting crops.

What the explorers discovered first was five natives, but they ran away too fast to be questioned. Next, they found a spring of fresh water—their "first New England water," which tasted better, they said, than anything they'd drunk in all their lives.

Pilgrim Spring in Truro, a short drive from Route 6, is commemorated with a marker and a trail.

The following day, the Pilgrims found on the beach a large metal kettle (made in Europe) and a mound of dirt, which seemed to be freshly packed. With 13 men standing around the mound, muskets at the ready, the other three men dug up what turned out to be a treasure. They found corn—several baskets which held three to four bushels each. Since this was too much to carry back, they hung one basket on a pole for two men to carry between them. They filled the kettle with loose corn and stuffed what they could in their pockets and clothes. On their second trip, they came back for more (a total of 10 bushels) and found also a bag of beans and a bottle of oil.

Corn Hill Beach in Truro is the site of the Pilgrim's lucky find. It was this Cape corn which the Pilgrims planted the following spring and which saved so many lives.

Not everything turned out as well for the Pilgrims. There were days of grieving. Three passengers died while at the Cape. But also there was a day of rejoicing when Peregrine White was born, the first white child to be born in New England.

The chief worry, however, was the worsening winter weather. And still no place had been found for a settlement. Although some argued for settling then and there on Corn Hill, it was finally agreed that one more discovery trip would be made. Robert Coppin, the *Mayflower* pilot who had been in the area the year before, said there was a good river and harbor across the bay.

So on December 6, 19 men set out in their shallop, an open boat, for the Third Discovery. Because of the extreme cold, they followed the coastline and camped that night on the beach near the present site of Eastham. The next morning they were surprised by a wild cry and arrows flying around them. At the edge of the woods stood a band of natives. They didn't stay long. When the Indians saw the white men running toward them in their coats of mail, muskets firing, they ran away. The Pilgrims called this their First Encounter and were thankful no one was hurt.

A sign on Route 6 in Eastham directs motorists to what is still called First Encounter Beach. Also, at the reconstruction of the old Plymouth Plantation in Plymouth (where the Pilgrims traded with the Dutch), there is a recreation of a small Indian village, similar to one that existed in the area when the Pilgrims landed.

After their encounter, the explorers continued on their way, and at the end of a stormy week, they returned to the *Mayflower* with the report that they had indeed found a good area for a settlement. On December 15th, the *Mayflower* left the Cape and sailed for the place that would soon be called Plymouth.

Three Mayflower *passengers who later emigrated to the Cape are buried in Eastham. Constance Hopkins Snow was 15 when the Pilgrims first landed on the Cape in 1620. Giles Hopkins and Joseph Rogers were each 13. Their graves are in the Old Cove Burying Ground on the east side of Route 6 in Eastham.*

In Eastham's Schoolhouse Museum (across from the Salt Pond Visitors Center) there is a small stool made from the wood of the Mayflower. *(When the* Mayflower *ended its days at sea, much of its wood was used to build a barn in England.)*

At Provincetown, the Pilgrim Monument commemorates the landing of the Pilgrims. Dedicated in 1910 in the presence of President Taft, the tower rises 252 feet above a 100-foot hill and declares to all of New England, "They came here first. It was here they came!"

Dioramas which show the Pilgrims on Cape Cod are displayed in the Provincetown Museum where there is also a large scale model of the Mayflower.

As more settlers came to the Plymouth area, various groups decided, with permission from the Plymouth government, to move to the Cape. Farming and fishing (whaling and ground fishing) were the chief occupations. First to be settled were Sandwich, Barnstable, Yarmouth and Eastham where the marshes provided acres of wild salt hay, ready-grown fodder from the marshes for their animals. By this time, most families had cattle which roamed freely, and were branded as western cattle are today. A man in Falmouth, for instance, marked his animals with a picture of a mackerel at the top of each ear.

Pigs too were allowed to wander loose as long as each one wore a ring in its nose to keep it from rooting and causing damage. The new settlers planted orchards with seeds they'd brought from England, set out corn and vegetable plots, cut down trees and built small square houses made of planks with clay packed between the cracks. A fireplace ran along one side of the house with a chimney so large that a person could look up and see the stars at night.

The government (or General Court) in Plymouth taxed net fishing for mackerel, bass and herring on Cape Cod and required that the money be used towards the establishment and upkeep of schools. In the early days school was held for only a few months during the winter.

There is still an example of an old schoolroom at the Schoolhouse Museum in Eastham; another is at the Heritage Museum in Provincetown. Also the Wellfleet Historical Museum contains a collection of old fashioned sleds, single runner skates, clay marbles, dolls and other toys. An entire room in the Chatham Historical Museum is filled with toys of long ago.

Early Cape Codders, however, were concerned with more than making a living. They were strict about the way people behaved and what they believed. Each town and each church had its own rules as well as those made in Plymouth. Swearing was forbidden, for instance. A person could be put in stocks for three hours for using bad language. In Barnstable a man was dismissed from church membership because he made fun of people. A woman was dismissed for gossiping. Even laughing at the wrong time could be dangerous. Two girls in Sandwich were punished for laughing at a man who was chasing a dog out of church.

Though their laws were strict, early Cape Codders were quite independent. It is not surprising, therefore, that it was a man from the Cape, James Otis Jr. of Barnstable, who is credited in these parts with introducing the idea of American Independence as early as 1761. The British had made it legal for its agents to enter and search a house whenever they pleased without even a court order. In a brilliant four-hour speech delivered before the state legislature, Otis declared that this was tyranny. A man's home, he said, was his castle. At that point, the colonists began to oppose the British.

But as time marched on, Cape Codders quarreled about Independence. Patriots (those who opposed the British) put up liberty poles to show their support for revolution. No sooner did the poles go up, than Tories (those who favored a British rule) knocked them down. There was violence on the Cape even before the war broke out. In Truro, patriots, no matter how sick they were, refused to go to a Tory doctor. A Tory widow was tarred and feathered for drinking tea (and bragging about it) after tea had been taxed by Britain. In Sandwich, a Tory left the room when the Declaration of Independence was read aloud.

The news of battles at Lexington and Concord reached the Cape on a Sunday morning in the middle of church services. Cape Cod, exposed on all sides to attack, was in a particularly vulnerable position. There was little Cape Codders could do to protect their shores, other than organizing shore watches to keep small privateers from landing. Cape towns were also expected to furnish the Continental Army with recruits.

In April of 1779, Cape Codders repulsed a British attempt to invade Falmouth. Still, if a large British ship chose to send its men ashore for supplies, the local residents couldn't stop them. The British ship-of-war *Somerset* with 64 guns came in and out of Provincetown with regularity. Officers of the ship sometimes attended the local church. The *Somerset*, it should be noted, was the ship in Boston's Charles River that Paul Revere had to row past on the night of his Midnight Ride.

For Cape Codders, perhaps the most triumphant day of the war came in November of 1778 when the *Somerset* struck the outer bar at North Truro and was beaten helplessly onto the beach. The 480 survivors of the *Somerset* were immediately captured and marched through cheering Cape villages straight to Boston. By the time officials in Boston appeared to take possession of the ship, Cape Codders had picked it clean.

In the museum collection at the Salt Pond Visitor Center in Eastham, there are pieces of wood from the Somerset *and other articles taken from the ship: money, shoe buckles, a musket and other belongings. At the Provincetown Museum in front of the Pilgrim Monument, a cannon from the* Somerset *is on display.*

Since Paul Revere is so closely associated with the Revolutionary War, it is interesting to note that he made the bells that still ring in at least two Cape churches: The Congregational Church in Falmouth and the West Parish Church in Barnstable.

Jean Fritz first wrote this essay, originally entitled "Back to Early Cape Cod," for the Cape Cod National Seashore. It is used here, in part, with the National Seashore's permission.

A Land By The Sea

Cape Cod and the Islands are dominated by the beach—a majestic environment of dunes, marshes and shoreline. The following essays, written and compiled by the Cape Cod National Seashore as a guide to its staff and by noted naturalists and biologists, take a close look at salt marshes, the shoreline and dunes, tides and coastal erosion. Richard LeBlond's and Donald Zinn's contributions are excerpted from A Guide to Nature on Cape Cod and the Islands, *Revised edition, Parnassus Imprints, 1995.*

The Salt Marsh
by Richard LeBlond

Of all the magnificent ecosystems of the Cape and Islands, it is the wetland that is most difficult to define.

"What is a wetland?" visitors often ask. The somewhat working definition is any perpetually saturated or periodically flooded land where you can ruin a good pair of sneakers. Wetlands, on the Cape and Islands, can be classified into two distinct groups: coastal saltwater wetlands, namely salt marshes; and freshwater wetlands that form in isolated depressions and along the borders of lakes, ponds, and rivers—freshwater marshes, wet meadows, swamps, bogs, and pond shores.

Biologically, wetlands are the most productive natural ecosystems on the earth, rivaling even our most fertile agricultural lands. All wetlands offer food, nesting sites, and protective cover to hundreds of species of plant and animal life, from the white-tailed deer to rare migratory birds. Salt marshes function as prolific fish and shellfish nurseries and filter harmful wastes out of the water. It is estimated that two-thirds of our commercial fish and shellfish spend at least part of their lives in a salt marsh. Wetlands also buffer and absorb floodwaters and storm energy; they prevent erosion of adjacent uplands by holding soil sediments in place, by dampening wave energy, and by reducing the velocity of water currents.

Wetlands are essential to water quality. They remove phosphorus and harmful nitrogen from septic wastes and provide valuable storage sheds for

11

groundwater needed by plants and animals that inhabit these sanctuaries. Wetlands also act as a natural pipe, funneling surface waters into the subsoil.

The beauty of our coast is all horizontal—a thin, sleek shoreline that runs virtually uninterrupted for thirty miles from Chatham to Provincetown where land meets the Atlantic on the backside of Outer Cape Cod; the sandy south shore of Martha's Vineyard from Wequobsque Cliffs to South Beach; the straight shot of shoreline from Nantucket's Great Point to Sankaty Head Light. The sea sprawls endlessly and on hazy days melts into the sky before reaching the horizon. It is a landscape that evokes serenity and invites participation and discovery.

Nowhere is this more apparent than in our coastal salt marshes, where a seemingly monotonous expanse of meadow sways in the wind, then in the water. But a closer look—the beginning of participation—reveals that a salt marsh is more than dominant swaths of grass. Threading and charging through these marshes are tidal creeks and their tributaries, some of them carrying greater volumes of water than any of our brooks and streams. Pockets of pooling water collect in and around the acres of grass, and thick strips of brown mud contour the edges. Each season brings new colors, peaking with lavender and yellow wildflowers in late summer. There are distinctions even in the grasses, as different species grow in different parts of the marsh.

The essence of the Cape and Islands brims in its salt marshes where most of the basic shoreline elements are present and interact: salt and fresh water; sand and tides; marine and terrestrial plants and animals. But land and sea do not merely meet here, they are in constant conflict. Beneath the visual serenity is a pitched battle of life and death, of destruction and creation, riding in and out with every tide. The salt marsh is a product of that battle and a prolific example of the ability of life not only to exist but to thrive in such a harsh habitat.

Imagine yourself as one of the countless salt marsh inhabitants meandering the tidal creeks or climbing the stem of a lanky cord grass plant. Twice a day your home is inundated by the incoming tide and by groundfish in search of food. Then there is the outgoing tide. Twice a day you are exposed to the air—hot in summer, cold in winter. You have to avoid drying out or freezing, and you have to worry about predators—the gulls, sandpipers, ducks, and fiddler crabs.

Yet, despite these harsh conditions, the salt marsh is exceedingly productive. How can such a hostile environment produce so much life? The answer is found by looking at the dynamic processes that form and maintain a salt marsh, but it can be summed up in one word: adaptation.

HOW SALT MARSHES ARE FORMED

Salt marshes form in quiet coastal waters protected from erosive wave action. The typical protector is a barrier sand spit, and the typical quiet water body is an estuary: a bay, harbor, or river mouth behind the sand spit. Take Sandy Neck as an example. The large barrier spit facing Cape Cod Bay on the East Sandwich-Barnstable line blocks waves from the bay, allowing the Great

Marsh—the largest salt marsh on Cape Cod—to form behind its protective arm. Likewise, Nauset Marsh on the Orleans-Eastham line has built up behind the Nauset Spit barrier. Other good examples are the marshland that has formed along the shore of the Martha's Vineyard Felix Neck Sanctuary behind State Beach on the coastal road from Oak Bluffs to Edgartown and the salt marsh behind Eel Point at the west end of Nantucket. Even small barrier spits will produce pockets of salt marsh as long as the waves are kept out and the tide is let in.

But wave protection and tidal influence alone will not create a salt marsh. A suitable floor of sand is needed, one that is fairly flat and shallow to permit the growth of grasses that dominate, define, and nurture the marsh. The sand floor, known as substrate, is built up by a peculiarity of the tides. The rate of tidal flow into the estuary where a marsh is forming is greater during the incoming tide than during the receding tide. In other words, the incoming tide has an ocean pushing it, while the outgoing tide is propelled only by gravity. The incoming flow is strong enough to carry sediment (mostly sand and silt) into the estuary, but the outgoing flow is not strong enough to carry the sediment back out. This slow rise in the floor does two important things. First, it creates a habitat for the forming marsh. Second, this continuous addition of sand allows the marsh to keep pace with a worldwide rise in sea levels. The stability that results from these massive processes is formidable. The marsh deposits in the Great Marsh lying behind Sandy Neck reach a depth of at least thirty feet and represent 4,000 years of steady rise with the sea. It seems something of a miracle that one of the most dynamic and hostile environments in the world has created one of the most stable and uniform habitats.

Storm wash-overs—less frequent but more dramatic than tidal sedimentation—also supply sand to salt-marsh floors, as high-energy waves break through barrier spits and spew sand into the estuary. The marsh behind the breakwater at the west end of Provincetown Harbor near the Provincetown Inn is an example of a marsh that has benefited from this source. A great storm in the winter of 1978 broke through the protective Long Point barrier, pouring tons of sand into flats adjacent to the marsh. Since then, the break has healed and the marsh has expanded over this new floor space.

Beaches and Dunes
by Donald Zinn

When people think of the Cape and Islands, they generally think of the beach. Sand beaches make up the largest habitat here. Most of our sands were carried by currents and tides from the continental shelf and deposited on the beach by waves; some were carried by rivers and estuaries to their mouths and deposited along the shore by prevailing coastal currents; and the rest had glacial beginnings—gleaned from the broad floodplains of glacial meltwater streams. Sand beaches are unstable habitats whose surfaces are at the mercy of every storm, tide, and wave, which constantly stir, sift, and redistribute the sand, continually reshaping the beach. This repeated roiling grinds the sediments into smaller particles and scatters the lighter elements to the higher parts of the beach where the wind carries the powdery, drier sand away to form sand dunes, leaving the coarser, larger grains behind. Below the low-tide line, waves also sort the sand grains, sending the finer particles to the bottom and washing the other seaward.

Beach sands along our shores consist mainly of eroded granite or granite-type rocks, composed of quartz particles of various colors occasionally infiltrated with minerals such as biotite—a dark brown to black or dark green mica—and chips of semiprecious gems such as garnets. There are also shell fragments of mollusks and crustaceans, as well as bits of detritus from many sources. A handful of beach sand viewed under a microscope reveals an attractive granular landscape of many hues and variously rounded shapes.

Our quartz sand tends to be fine and hard packed, an observation readily attested by all beach strollers. It is the home of exciting and little-explored microscopic animals and plants that live in the water-filled spaces between the sand grains. This group of unique organisms that live within these spaces is known as meiofauna (pronounced may-o-fawna). They glide, swim, or crawl through these spaces without displacing the particles. Meiofauna can be found from the surface of the sand to a depth of several meters. The area is more extensive than you might think; although the sand grains touch each other, the space between their irregular shapes provides ample living room. For a given volume of Cape beach sand, about 80 percent is sand and 20 percent is space.

The only plants growing in this area are algae, yeasts, and bacteria that are attached to the sand grains or live between them. These microscopic plants provide food for tiny but far more varied animals: protozoa, flatworms, roundworms, segmented worms, mites, sea slugs, and sea squirts. Many species display an amazing structure, having withstood the rigors of tides, waves, storms, extremes in temperature, and changes in salinity.

Beaches that are exposed to the ocean tides, winds, and waves of the Outer Cape from Nauset Beach in Orleans to Race Point in Provincetown are particularly unstable habitats. For this reason only the larger animals are able to survive—those that can burrow into the sand or move up and down the beach with the tide.

From a biological perspective, the more protected bay beaches are far more interesting between the tide lines than ocean beaches. Here you can see ripples from currents and the readily recognizable tracks of gulls, sandpipers, and other small birds—sometimes even those of crows and starlings. Occasionally along protected bay shores, like Barnstable's Sandy Neck, you can detect the alternating scratches of the scarce diamondback terrapin turtle. In the wet intertidal area or tidal flats, you will find the tracks, burrows, and holes of hard clams, razor clams, trumpet worms, clam worms, and sandworms, to name a few.

Farther up on the beach you will find sand fiddlers and beach hoppers but very little else, since most of the plant and animal life here is on the surface of the sand. Often the most commonly encountered materials are rows of live, dying, or dead seaweeds, termed black wrack, along the upper part of the beach, each row left behind at the level of high water. The rows of wrack are usually composed of species found immediately offshore: eelgrass, Irish moss, sea lettuce, kelp, and sponge. In the rows of wrack live several kinds of flies, like the eelgrass fly and biting green head. If rotting wrack is disturbed, often many tiny beach animals will emerge, like sand fleas or beach hoppers. On some beaches you'll find thin, sand-colored collars, a few inches high. These are egg masses of the moon snail, whose eggs are embedded in jelly in the sand collars. Other strange-looking sights include empty black rectangular cases with curled or horn-shaped extensions at the corners. These are mermaids' purses, or egg cases of the common skate, which have cut loose from their underwater nursery and drifted to the beach. Do not expect to see all of these animals at once; the habits, appearances, and migrations of marine beach fauna depend on temperature, tides, time of day, wave action, and season.

Sometimes the perfect shells of molted crabs and horseshoe crab skeletons, cast during growth, are carried onto the beach by the tide. Of course, parts of dead crabs and other invertebrate animals are often scattered about. Mollusk shells are also found in all stages of fracture and decay—color may be bleached by the sun, chips and breakage are common, edges may be dulled by rolling in the surf and by abrasion. These factors often make positive identification difficult. Usually the best collecting in terms of variety is accomplished directly after an onshore storm.

SAND DUNES

Amateur geologists have often described the Cape and Islands as one big sand dune. While this is an exaggeration, sand dunes—along with sandy beaches—dominate the picture postcard image of our region. In many places along the shoreline, you will find clusters and ridges of great and small sand dunes—from the great dunes of Provincetown to the minor dunes of Waquoit on Nantucket Sound on the south side, to the complex of dunes of Sandy Neck in Barnstable on Cape Cod Bay and the small dunes of Black Beach bordering Great Sippewissett Marsh and Buzzards Bay in Falmouth on the north and west sides, to the rolling dunes of Chappaquiddick on the Vineyard.

In many cases small foredunes (as they are called) are backed by larger and more massive dunes that gradually merge into the typical pitch pine and scrub oak environment of the Cape and Islands. Often between the dunes are hollows or swales, which—if they cut below the water table—become brackish or freshwater ponds. The dune water table is highest in winter and lowest in summer due to greater evaporation and less rain.

The highest coastal dunes on the Cape and Islands occur where the coastline is at right angles with the prevailing winds, which carry sand landward from the beach and from the intertidal sand flats. The finer sand particles are carried farthest inland and become characteristic of inland dunes.

The growth rates of dunes are directly related to the density and growth of beach grass, which helps to hold the dunes in place, although this is often a losing battle. On the Cape and Islands, the vertical dune growth rate varies from twelve to eighteen inches a year, but erosion and dune migration often blunt this growth.

Your first trek through the dunes will reveal a physical environment severe in several respects—shifting sand, strong winds, salt spray, intense light, and nutrient-poor soils. This environment is virtually uninhabitable for most species of plants and animals; indeed, those few that do occur must be well adapted to weather the harsh conditions. Plants such as American beach grass grow best when they are buried by sand. This and other beach grasses, by trapping sand and stabilizing the surface on which they grow, play a major part in the development and maintenance of coastal dunes.

Tides

by Janet Cote

A hundred years ago, lives of the people of Cape Cod were inseparably connected to the sea. They relied on the ocean-going vessels for their food, travel and trade, making an understanding of the tides essential for their survival. In an age of mass transportation, our link to the ocean and our knowledge of its cycles has weakened with time.

Visiting a bayside beach during a low tide may cause some inconvenience to a summer vacationer. All in all, most people have little cause to think about the ebb and flow of the ocean's tide. Playing a small part in modern life, the tides are the driving force behind life on the coast.

GRAVITATIONAL PULL

Newton provided the first detailed explanation of tidal action when he introduced the theory of gravitation in 1687. He proposed that objects exert a force upon each other which pulls them towards each other. This force, known as gravity, keeps the speeding planets in orbit around the sun and the moon spinning around the earth. Larger objects, such as planets, produce a stronger pull on each other compared to smaller objects. In addition, the force of gravity between objects will decrease as the distance between them increases.

As the earth and moon spin around a central axis, the moon's gravitational force pulls up on the earth's surface. The force isn't strong enough to change the shape of the inflexible land masses. However, as the moon passes over the earth's oceans, a mound of water is created. As the earth spins, the bulge of water travels across the planet's surface. This mound causes an increase in the water level, thus creating the tide. The whole ocean undergoes the regular tidal changes, though they are easier to perceive near shore.

CENTRIFUGAL EFFECT

Newton described a second effect which is necessary for the explanation of why we have two tides per day, even though we have only one moon. Centrifugal effects tend to throw objects away from spinning bodies. On the side of the earth away from the moon, this action counteracts the gravitational pull, and creates a second, smaller mound of water on the earth's surface. We experience the second tide as the earth turns beneath it.

Cape Cod, like most places on the coast, experiences semidurnal tides, meaning two high and two low tides occur daily. Each tide, controlled by lunar movement, takes place fifty minutes later than the previous day. The moon completes a full circle around the earth every 24 hours and fifty minutes, causing the variation of tidal timing from day to day.

SPRING AND NEAP TIDES

The sun's gravitational pull on the earth, though 81 times weaker than the moon's pull because of its immense distance from us, still affects the tides. During each lunar month, two higher than normal tides and two lower than normal tides occur. Corresponding to the full and new moon when the sun, earth, and moon align with each other, this phenomenon is called a spring tide. The name originated from an old Saxon word meaning rising or rolling of water and has nothing to do with the spring season. The sun's gravitational force is added to the moon's pull. This extra pull creates an extra large mound of water, resulting in extreme high and low tides.

The sun's pull creates another interesting tidal variation called "neap tide." Occurring on the first and third quarters of the moon cycle, the moon, earth and sun are positioned in a 90-degree angle. The force of the sun and moon work against each other, counteracting their effects on the ocean. A smaller mound of water is formed, producing a less significant change in the water level between high and low tide.

Local factors, such as coastal geography, add an interesting twist to the already complicated story of the tides. Most areas have semidurnal tides (two high and two low). However, the Gulf of Mexico experiences diurnal tides, having only one high and one low tide a day. Tidal height is another factor which is produced by local differences. For example, New York City normally has a five-foot difference between the high and low tide marks; whereas, Rockport, Maine sees a change of ten feet between tides, and the Bay of Fundy has an incredible thirty-foot change in water level.

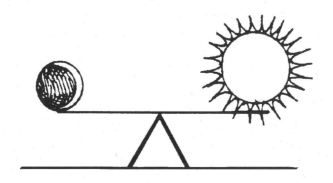

The tides are an essential life regulating force in and around the ocean. Bays, estuaries and marshes rely on the huge amount of water which is forced into these areas churning and distributing organic matter in its wake. Nutrients produced in the estuaries are then flushed into deeper water as the tides recede, fueling the food chains of the open ocean. The tides set the rhythm of life for the plants and animals of the ocean's edge. Horseshoe crabs and small fish called grunion are stimulated to mate by the change in tides.

Erosion on Outer Cape Cod
by Mike Whatley

Erosion is a natural thing on Cape Cod. In fact, much of what we enjoy about the Cape is a result of this natural process. The wide sandy beaches we walk on are made from sand that falls down from the glacial cliffs, or scarps, behind the beach. Waves, currents and wind then move much of this sand to other parts of Cape Cod. All of the Province Lands area, as well as Nauset Spit, and much of Great Island were created by the movement and relocation of sand. If erosion of the outer beach cliffs were somehow stopped, these formations would eventually disappear.

Human construction such as buildings and parking lots, however, often suffer severely from coastal erosion. The Highland and Nauset Lighthouses are in danger of falling over the cliff as a result of shoreline retreat. In 1977, the Old Harbor Life Saving Station had to be moved from North Beach in Chatham to Race Point Beach in Provincetown in order to save it. In the following year, a 300-car parking lot located at Coast Guard Beach in Eastham was completely demolished by the Great Storm of 1978. More recently, private home sites in Chatham have fallen into the ocean as a result of coastal erosion. We have now learned that it is better to build farther away from the shoreline, and to plan for regular replacement of buildings and features that need to be located close to the water's edge.

NATURE PREVAILS

We have also found that natural "systems" are often better at slowing and controlling erosion than human "solutions" (such as building sea walls, jetties, or placing boulders along the beach). Scientists have found that the natural movement and placement of sand (both up and down the coast, as well as on and off the shoreline) slows the erosion effect of waves. You can test this on your own. Try running on a sandy beach for a certain distance. Time yourself. Then try running for the same distance on a parking lot. Time yourself again. The sand on the beach will have slowed you down considerably. Likewise, the soft sandy beach slows down the power of storm waves much better than solid concrete barriers can.

Beach grass planting in the Province Lands dunes is another way in which natural restoration activities can help correct unnatural erosion rates. Beach grass traps the sand blown by the wind, and is actually responsible for forming all of the dunes that you see on Outer Cape Cod. When people or animals trample beach grass and kill it, the dunes in turn begin to fall apart. Before the Pilgrims arrived on Cape Cod, the beach grass in the Province Lands did such a good job of holding the dunes together that once a complete forest grew on top of them. Sometimes you can still see the remains of old trees poking through the sand!

The average natural erosion rate on the ocean side of Cape Cod has been calculated by scientists at three feet a year. This means that there may be no erosion for several years, and more than three feet other years. Thus, the Cape is gradually narrowing. Its natural life span still gives the Cape several thousand more years.

Human activities that increase erosion can upset the natural "give and take." While natural processes narrow the Cape, they also build it up in other areas. All of the Province Lands was created by sand being transferred from other parts of the Cape. The same is true of Nauset Spit, Monomoy, and Sandy Neck. These sandy streches can also grow upwards, due to windblown sand deposits forming into dunes, which in turn are stabilized further by native vegetation. Cuts in these features by trails created by humans can cause accelerated, unnatural rates of erosion. This is why it is important for people to learn not to take shortcuts through the dunes to get to the beaches. Beach grass can wthstand the most powerful winds, but can die if stepped on more than twice. Erosion is a natural process that has shaped much of Cape Cod as we see it today. It is important that this process be kept natural and not be upset by human interference.

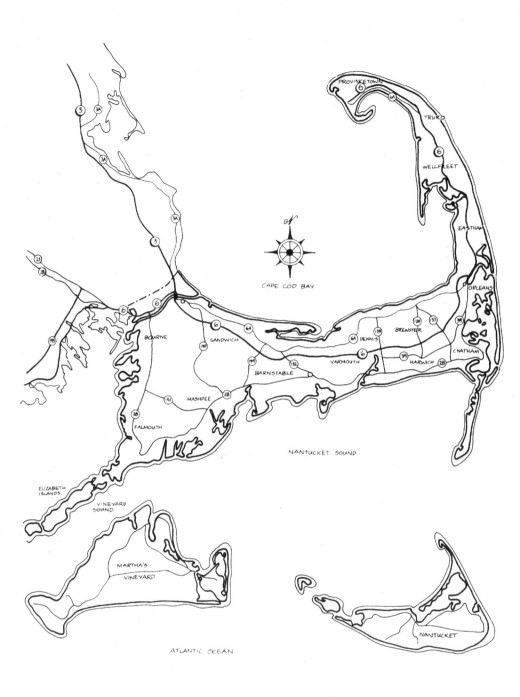

CAPE COD & THE ISLANDS

Historic Cape Lighthouses

compiled by the Cape Cod National Seashore Staff

Lighthouses are as much a part of Cape Cod as the sea. In fact, for centuries they have guided mariners to safety through treacherous shoals. There are eight working lighthouses on the Cape, mile-for-mile one of the largest concentrations of working lighthouses in the world. Cape Cod, indeed, is the sort of place you would expect to find lighthouses. Sweeping far out into the ocean, the Cape is a substantial obstacle to navigation. In the last 300 years, there have been more than 3000 documented shipwrecks along Cape shores. A tour of Cape lighthouses, courtesy of information written by the Cape Cod National Seashore, through Laurel Guadazno, will take you from Woods Hole to Provincetown. You can visit all of them; the lighthouses include:

• *Nobska Light*—located on Nobska Point overlooking Woods Hole harbor, the light warns mariners away from two dangerous shoals, the Hedge Fence and L'Hommedieu. The first light station was built here in 1828; it was a keeper's house with a light tower on top. In 1879, a new metal tower, the same one you see today, was built in Chelsea (outside Boston) and shipped in four sections to the Cape. The iron tower was lined with brick and a new keeper's house was added. Like all Cape lighthouses today, Nobska Light is unmanned. It was automated in 1985, and stands 87 feet above the sea. Its light flashes every six seconds and can be seen from 16 miles at sea. Mariners in safe water see a white light, while those near the shoals see a red light.

• *Bass River Lighthouse*—Bass River Lighthouse today forms the center section of an historic inn in West Dennis, the Lighthouse Inn on Nantucket Sound. The lighthouse was built in 1850 to mark the entrance to Bass River, once an important entrance to the Mid Cape for commercial boats; at one time, Bass River was considered as a site for the Cape Cod Canal. The lighthouse became a private residence in 1915 after it was de-commissioned. It is now one of the few privately-owned lighthouses on the East Coast.

• *Chatham Light*—The first lighthouse was established in Chatham in 1808. It consisted of two brick towers and a keeper's house. The two towers were built to help mariners distinguish the light from other lighthouses, a problem in early days before light technology created distinctive flashes. Ultimately, it was decided that Chatham's two lights were too costly to maintain because of the additional fuel, personnel and supplies needed. So one light—the north tower—was moved in 1923 to Nauset Beach in Eastham, and the south tower was moved back from the bluff to its present location next to the Chatham Coast Guard Station, near the mouth of Chatham Harbor.

• *Nauset Light*—Distinctive with its handsome red stripe around the top of its tower (called a daymark), Nauset Light off Ocean View Drive in Eastham can be distinguished during the day from other Cape Cod lighthouses. Today it is threatened by erosion and the Nauset Light Preservation Society is seeking to move it back from the edge of a sand cliff. Donations to the society are greatly appreciated; call Eastham Town Hall at 508-255-0333 for more information.

• *Cape Cod Light*—Cape Cod Light, or Highland Light, as it is sometimes called, also is perilously close to the sea. Off Route 6 in Truro (follow the signs), Cape Cod Light was established in 1798 and is the Cape's oldest lighthouse. For transatlantic sailors, Cape Cod Light was the first light seen on voyages from Europe. The present brick lighthouse and associated buildings were built in 1857. Standing 66 feet tall and located high on a clay cliff, the light's beacon shines 183 feet above the ocean and can be seen 20 miles out to sea. The beacon flashes a white light every five seconds, and can be seen by motorists at night from Truro to Provincetown.

• *Race Point Light*—Accessible on foot, four-wheel drive or by boat, Race Point Light is about two miles west of Race Point Beach in Provincetown. The light was built in 1816 to help ships navigate the dangerous knuckles of the Cape's fist on their way into Provincetown Harbor. Between 1816 and 1946, more than 100 vessels were shipwrecked on the beach and offshore shoals. So treacherous is the area that Race Point Light is equipped with a foghorn to warn ships in times of poor visibility. The keeper's house and lighthouse currently on the site were built in 1876; the 40-foot tower is 41 feet above the ocean and its white light, flashing every 15 seconds, can be seen 16 miles out to sea.

• *Wood End Light and Long Point Light*—The best spot to view Wood End Light and Long Point Light is from the breakwater by the rotary at the end of Commercial Street in Provincetown. It is a half hour walk to the tip of Cape Cod where Long Point Light marks the entrance to Provincetown Harbor. During the summer, a private shuttle in the town center offers service to Long Point.

Wood End Light, visible at the far end of the breakwater, is the twin of Long Point Light. Unlike other Cape lighthouses, Wood End Light is a squire white tower; built in 1873, it is now powered by the sun and flashes a red light every 15 seconds.

Travel Tips

Traveling to the Cape is simple. Driving south from Boston, take Route 3 south to the Cape Cod Canal. Follow signs for the Sagamore Bridge or for the Bourne Bridge depending on your destination. The Sagamore Bridge connects to Route 6, the Cape's main highway that runs from Sandwich to Provincetown at the Cape's tip. Running parallel to the main highway is historic Route 6A, far more scenic but a slower ride along the shores of Cape Cod Bay. The Bourne Bridge connects to the more commercial Route 28 for those heading to Falmouth, Bourne and Mashpee. You can also fly from Boston's Logan Airport to Barnstable Airport in Hyannis; Cape Air (1-800-352-0714) and USAir Express (1-800-943-5436) offer regular service to the Cape and Islands.

Driving north from Connecticut and Rhode Island, take Route 95 north to Route 195, then follow signs for the Cape. Newport, Rhode Island is about an hour and a half drive from the Cape; take Route 195 North to Route 25 and follow signs for the Cape.

It is difficult to get lost on Cape Cod; you're surrounded by water. And for that reason, you must take a ferry boat or fly to Martha's Vineyard and Nantucket.

You can take the Hyline Cruises from the Ocean Street docks in Hyannis to Martha's Vineyard and Nantucket (1-508-778-2602); the Steamship Authority transfers automobiles and passengers from Hyannis to Nantucket (1-508-540-2022) and from Woods Hole in Falmouth to Martha's Vineyard. You can also fly to both islands from Barnstable Airport. For a flight to Nantucket, call Island Airlines (1-800-248-7779). For a flight to the Vineyard, call USAir Express (1-800-943-5436) or Cape Air (1-800-352-0714).

Survival Guide
by Greg O'Brien

Now that we've told you how to get here and the best time to travel, we offer you a survival guide, of sorts—miscellaneous tips we hope you'll find helpful.

Important Public Information: all of our listings begin with a list of telephone numbers for town halls, police departments, fire departments, rescue squads, hospitals, clinics, vets and local chambers of commerce.

For quick reference, though, here are the names and phone numbers of local hospitals and clinics: Outer Cape Health Services in Wellfleet (349-3131); Cape Cod Hospital in Hyannis, a village of Barnstable (771-1800); Chatham Medical Offices in Chatham (945-0187); Cape Cod Medical Center in Dennis (394-7113); Falmouth Hospital in Falmouth (548-5300); Falmouth Walk-In Medical Center in Teaticket, a village of Falmouth (540-6790); Martha's Vineyard Hospital in Oak Bluffs (693-0410); Medi-Center Five Clinic in Harwich (432-4100); Mid Cape Medical Center in Hyannis (771-4092); Nantucket Cottage Hospital in Nantucket (228-1200); Orleans Medical Clinic in Orleans (255-9577); Outer Cape Health Services in Provincetown (487-9395).

Other important phone numbers to keep at the ready are the Cape Cod Chamber of Commerce, in Buzzards Bay near the Bourne Bridge (759-6000), and in Hyannis off Route 6 (362-3225); the Martha's Vineyard Chamber of Commerce in Vineyard Haven (693-0085); and the Nantucket Island Chamber of Commerce in Nantucket Center (228-1700).

Location: Cape Cod is a peninsula in southeastern Massachusetts, separated from the mainland by a man-made canal that connects Cape Cod Bay with Buzzards Bay. Thoreau once called the Cape, "the bared and bended arm of Massachusetts". . . a place where you can put America behind you. The peninsula, which begins at Bourne and Sandwich (the shoulder) and ends at the fist (Provincetown) is about 70 miles long. At the shoulder, the Cape is about 20 miles wide, and near its fist, it narrows to less than a mile.

The island of Martha's Vineyard, about 10 miles wide and about 24 miles long, is approximately 6 miles east of Woods Hole, a village of Falmouth that offers year-round ferry service to the island.

The island of Nantucket, about 31/2 miles wide and 14 miles long, is about 20 miles southeast of Hyannis.

The Elizabeth Islands, a chain of islands, begin just off Woods Hole and extend southwest for about six miles.

Weather: The weather here in the summer is about 10 degrees cooler than in Boston and about 10 to 15 degrees cooler than in muggy New York—primarily because of our soothing ocean breeze. Average daytime temperatures here range between 75 and 85 degrees, although there are a few hot, muggy spells (usually a week in late June and a week in early or mid-August) when the temperature hits 100. In general, the summer weather is delightful and helps the locals make it through the long, cold and gray months of January, February, and March.

Dress: For the most part, dress on the Cape and Islands is casual (the locals call it "beachy"), although some restaurants and night spots require jackets and a few insist on ties. Light clothing is recommended, but visitors should pack a sweater or sweatshirt because nights can get chilly.

Lodgings: For recommendations see our listings. Many lodgings accept credit cards; reservations are strongly recommended; off-season rates are offered. Many cottages, however, do not supply linens; you must bring your own or rent them. We suggest you check before you come.

Seasons: Most people come to the Cape and Islands in June, July, and August, but insiders will tell you the best time to visit is in September. The sun is still hot, the water is warm, and the crowds are mostly gone. You can find a parking spot at your favorite beach and a seat at some of the Cape and Islands' finest restaurants. And if you wait another month, you can even get a deal on a place to stay.

Once just a summer place, "the season" on the Cape and Islands, which begins in April or May, now extends into October and even into November (actually, it's pleasant, albeit cool, here right up until Christmas). There are year-round activities and festivities scheduled.

Beaches: Cape Cod and the Islands are blessed with beautiful beaches. You have your choice of beaches on the Atlantic, Cape Cod Bay, Nantucket Sound, Vineyard Sound, Buzzards Bay, Pleasant Bay, and numerous coves and ponds. Most require beach stickers; see our listings or telephone the respective town halls for more information. Many island beaches do not require stickers.

On bright sunny weekends in July and August, we suggest you get to the beach by 10:30 or 11 A.M. to get a parking spot. The lots fill up fast. No swimming is allowed in the Cape Cod Canal.

Boating: There are as many opportunities for boating on the Cape and Islands as for swimming. All towns have public landings—places where you can launch your boat free of charge. Access is available to the ocean and all bays and sounds that surround the area. For more information, check our beach and pond listings or call the town halls.

Fishing and Shellfishing: The Cape and Islands are noted for their great fishing holes and rich shellfish beds. Fishing and shellfishing licenses are required in most places. Again, we suggest you check our listings or phone the respective town halls. You should also take note of when the towns will allow you to scratch for quahogs, steamers, mussels, oysters, and the like. Most of the shellfish areas are posted. Ask if you're not sure.

Bicycling: On the Cape and Islands, particularly in July and August, often the best and least frustrating way to make your way around town is on a bicycle. Cape Cod and the Islands also have a number of fine bike trails that run by the shore, alongside ponds, and past marshes and bogs. We recommend you try the Cape Cod Bike Trail, which begins in Dennis off Route 134 and runs up to Eastham, where you can connect with a Cape Cod National Seashore Trail. We also recommend you try the shoreline trails on Martha's Vineyard and Nantucket.

Sports: If you're sunburned, tired of the beach scene, or if the weather is less than perfect, the Cape and Islands offer a wide range of recreational activities and spectator sports. There's golf and tennis (see Essentials sections) and also sailing races, road running, exercise classes, outdoor basketball, bowling, and much, much more. Check the sports pages of local newspapers for up-to-date specifics.

For those vacationing on the Cape who would rather sit than play, there's the NCAA-sanctioned Cape Cod Baseball League, the Cape Cod Amateur Soccer League, and the Cape Cod Summer Lacrosse League.

The Cape Cod Baseball League, now underwritten by major league baseball, is more than 100 years old and is considered one of the top summer college leagues in the country. The major leagues are filled with Cape Cod Baseball League graduates. There are teams in Harwich, Hyannis, Chatham, Falmouth, Brewster, Bourne, Wareham, Orleans, Cotuit, and the Dennis-Yarmouth area. The league plans to expand into other towns.

The soccer and lacrosse leagues attract the same caliber of players. The soccer league has teams in Chatham, Falmouth, Barnstable, West Barnstable, Brewster, the Orleans-Eastham area, and the Dennis-Yarmouth area. The lacrosse league has teams in Hyannis, Sandwich, Falmouth, and Orleans.

While team sports dominate the Cape summer athletic scene, road racing on the Cape and Islands is second to none. The biggest running event of the year is, of course, the world-famous Falmouth Road Race, held each August. There are many other races, though, worth running. For specific races and times, check the local newspapers or call the Chamber of Commerce. Here is a sampling: The Chatham Harbor Run, a 10-kilometer race held in June; the Chatham Harbor Walk, held the same day as the harbor run; the Brew Run, held in Brewster in August; the Wellfleet Five-Mile Race, held in July (children under 12 can compete in a shorter race); the Paul White Memorial Race, a 4.8-mile run held in North Falmouth in July; the 4.2-mile Osterville Run, held in Osterville in July; the Bobby Byrnes Pub 10-Kilometer Run, held in Mashpee in August; the Harwich Cranberry Festival Run, held in Harwich in September; the Bourne VFW 20-Kilometer Race (the oldest road race on Cape Cod), held in Bourne in September; the *Cape Codder* newspaper's John Gray Half-Marathon, held in Orleans in September.

For those looking for a tougher challenge, the Cape offers some great triathlons, among them: the Sprint Triathlon at Craigville Beach in June; the Seaside Triathlon in Barnstable; and the nationally-recognized Bud Light Endurance (Ironman) Triathlon held in September in Barnstable.

Police: The local police on Cape Cod are tough on speeders and drunk drivers. Our strong advice to you is don't speed on the highways and back roads and don't drink and drive. Why ruin your vacation?

Media: To keep informed of up-to-the-minute schedules and times of movies, shows, museums, art galleries, and other forms of entertainment, we suggest you read the local newspapers. On the Upper Cape, read the *Cape Cod Times*, a daily, and the *Enterprise* in Falmouth, which is published three times a week. On the Mid-Cape, read the *Cape Cod Times* and the weekly *Register.* On the Outer Cape, read the *Cape Codder,* a twice-weekly, the *Cape Cod Times*, and the weekly *Provincetown Advocate.* We also recommend you pick up a copy of the June issue of *Boston* magazine, which publishes a special section each year on the Cape and Islands.

The Locals: We're really not bad people once you get to know us. But you must understand that it's often trying for us in the summer when we can't get to the supermarket or the beach or into our favorite restaurant or to work on time. Most of us generally enjoy the tourists and want them to leave Cape Cod with some of the same feelings we share about this place. So if we seem at times impatient, don't take it personally. We're just having a bad day.

PART II

- *Upper Cape*

- *Mid-Cape*

- *Outer Cape*

- *Provincetown*

- *The Islands*

UPPER CAPE

Sandwich, Bourne,
Mashpee, Falmouth

Upper Cape: Viewpoints

by Brian Tarcy and Mary Catherine O'Brien

It's a grand entrance. As you make your approach to Cape Cod, the miles of monotonous highway, grueling traffic jams, and nauseating exhaust fumes you left behind are all but forgotten. Your attention is drawn, almost immediately, to the graceful, curving steel girders of the Bourne and Sagamore bridges, which span the Cape Cod Canal and link this narrow land with the rest of America.

In an instant, travelers are filled with a sense of exhilaration and anticipation. Locals call it "the magic of the bridges." On the other side await scores of pristine sandy beaches, freshwater ponds, hiking and bicycle trails, fishing holes, and shellfish flats, not to mention all the antique shops, gift shops, malls, and restaurants any visitor could ever want.

First you must get there. The Sagamore Bridge is 1408 feet long and has a vertical span of 136 feet. It links Boston and northern New England with the Upper Cape and connects with the Mid-Cape Highway. Also called Route 6, the highway runs the 70-mile length of the peninsula, parallel to the more rural Route 6A. The Bourne Bridge, by contrast, is 2384 feet long and has the same vertical span. It links the Upper Cape with Rhode Island, Connecticut, New York, and points beyond. The bridge feeds traffic to commercial Route 28, which runs south to Falmouth and Woods Hole, then east and north towards Orleans on the Outer Cape. And on a busy summer day, there is plenty of traffic. During June, July, and August, about 50,000 cars a day cross the Sagamore Bridge, and more than 40,000 cars a day head over the Bourne Bridge—creating at times traffic jams that a social scientist might use to test the nation's courtesy index. We advise you to avoid, if at all possible, crossing the bridges on weekends—especially Fridays (heading toward the Cape), between 3 P.M. and 10 P.M. Saturday mornings (heading toward the Cape), and Sunday afternoons (heading off Cape) from noon until late in the evening.

But, if you find yourself stalled in traffic on the bridges, take a moment to glance down at the spectacular Cape Cod Canal, a waterway between Buzzards Bay and Cape Cod Bay. The canal was built between 1909 and 1916 to reduce the number of shipwrecks on the backside of the Cape and to shorten the run from New York to Boston by avoiding the long and often hazardous trip around Provincetown. Originally, the 17.4-mile waterway was only 100 feet wide and 25 feet deep, but in later years it was widened to 540 feet and made 7 feet deeper. The canal actually turned the Cape into a man-made island. Natives here, in fact, refer to the other side of the bridge as "the mainland."

The need for a canal was first raised by Pilgrim Captain Miles Standish in 1623, and then by General George Washington 153 years later. Standish recognized the importance of expediting trade between the Dutch of New Amsterdam and Plymouth Colony. General Washington's interests were military; he thought a canal would provide greater security to commercial ships and naval vessels in time of war. Ironically, the very route Standish proposed was followed by engineers 286 years later in designing the canal. After several false starts, construction began in earnest in 1909; the canal was opened in 1914. At first, many found it difficult to navigate. Currents, given tidal variances between Buzzards Bay and Cape Cod Bay, change directions every six hours and reach speeds of up to four knots.

You can, by the way, take cruises along the canal. We suggest you try Cape Cod Canal Cruises ships, which depart from Onset Bay Town Pier off Buzzards Bay on the mainland; for more information, telephone 508-295-3883. The tours will give you a gull's-eye view of such landmarks as the canal traffic control center, the canal's vertical lift railroad bridge, the Sandwich Boat Basin, Bourne's Gray Gables (the site of President Grover Cleveland's summer White House), and the Aptucxet Trading Post, a replica of a trading post established in 1627 by the Pilgrims to trade pelts of otter and beaver with the Indians and Dutch of New Amsterdam (New York). The original post marked the start of efforts to settle Cape Cod.

Those hearty souls who first settled the Upper Cape in the 1600s were as pragmatic as they were religious—coming here, the history books tell us, "to worship God and make money." But, since the Pilgrim days, the Upper Cape's economy, like the tide itself, has had its ups and downs. Farming was the main occupation here in the early days; there weren't many choices. The region's fertile, but rocky, soil yielded a good harvest. So did the sea. Cape Cod Bay and Nantucket Sound were literally filled with cod, haddock, flounder, and lobster. In addition, the mud flats on Cape Cod Bay, where the tide runs out hundreds of yards, offered (and still does) a ready supply of shellfish—quahogs, steamers, littlenecks, mussels, and oysters. Pilot whales washed up on the shores (as they do today) with such regularity that beaches were designated "common areas" and profits from whale oil were parceled up among residents. The spoils were so enticing that adventuresome locals took their dories out into the bay to herd the whales in. It wasn't long before fishing replaced farming as the chief occupation, but the British blockade in the late 1700s and the War of 1812 almost put an end to the industry. The demand for fish, though, was greater than the supply, and in time the industry prospered again.

The arrival of the railroad in the mid-1800s (a narrow railroad bridge was built shortly after the canal was opened) did much to revive the fishing industry by offering a faster, more efficient way of getting fish to market. The railroad was also a help to farmers, cranberry growers, and local glassmakers, such as the old Boston and Sandwich Glass Company of Sandwich. But the Upper Cape's economy ebbed again in the late 1800s, a victim of hard economic times. There wasn't much here to keep the great-great grandsons and granddaughters of the original settlers, so they left in droves, seeking their fortunes in such cities as New Bedford, Boston, and New York. Soon the Cape's biggest export became its young, and for a while the future here looked bleak. Fortunately for the Cape, mainlanders at about this time had swifter means of transportation at their disposal and began exploring the peninsula. Thus the Cape Cod tourist was born.

First to be discovered, primarily because of its proximity to the mainland, was the Upper Cape—one of three distinct regions on this peninsula. The region consists of four towns: Sandwich, the Cape's oldest town; Bourne, which straddles both sides of the bridge; Falmouth, the Cape's second-biggest summer community; and Mashpee, the ancestral home of the Wampanoag Indians, a tribe of the Algonquin Nation. Each town is distinct. To the casual visitor, the region may all look the same, but if you take the time to explore some of its back roads—such as Shore Road (on the Cape side) in Bourne, Quisset Avenue in the Woods Hole section of Falmouth, Old Mill Road in Mashpee, and Sandy Neck Road in Sandwich—you'll notice the differences are striking.

Sandwich, for instance, has the feel of a New England farming village. Falmouth offers nightlife, convenient shopping, and some of the Cape's finest beaches. Bourne, particularly the village of Buzzards Bay on the mainland, has much in the way of old Yankee charm. Mashpee, the most remote of the four towns, is as rural as any of the Cape's 16 communities but is easily accessible.

Cape Codders are an independent lot, and residents of the Upper Cape are no exception, especially when it comes to mixing with other Cape communities. At a town meeting a few years back, the subject of school regionalization (sharing educational facilities with a Mid-Cape town) was brought up for discussion and a vote. At this point, a crusty Upper Cape native leapt to his feet, grabbed the microphone, and in a voice reminiscent of Daniel Webster, who once vacationed here, pleaded: "I don't want my children educated on foreign soil."

Needless to say, the proposal was struck down.

The Upper Cape, called "upper" because of its proximity to the mainland, is often called "the gateway to Cape Cod," but this is one gate you shouldn't just duck through. The region offers some of the Cape's finest natural resources and commercial amenities. We recommend you spend some time here to take them in.

If shops interest you more than beaches and you can't wait for your "fix," take the Sagamore Bridge entrance to the Cape, get off at exit 1, and follow signs for the Cape Cod Factory Outlet Mall (about a quarter mile from the exit ramp). Here you can browse through such discount stores as Carter's Children's Wear, where you can buy quality clothes for infants, toddlers, girls, and boys; the Corning Factory Store, where you can purchase fine houseware and cookware direct from the manufacturer; Bed N Bath for linens; Bugle Boy for boys clothing; Casual Corner or Bass Outlet for shoes; also Izod, American Tourister, Osh Kosh. For more information, call 800-772-8336.

Also worth a visit is the nearby Christmas Tree Shop. Don't let the name fool you. This general-merchandise discount chain sells everything from children's toys, to living room lamps, to Waterford crystal. Dollar for dollar, the Christmas Tree Shop is the best bargain on all of Cape Cod. You can't miss it once you get over the Sagamore Bridge. Its thatched roof and windmill are designed to grab your attention. Many of the locals see it as an architectural blunder, but for hard-core shoppers, the Christmas Tree Shop is a memorable shopping experience.

To get there, take exit 1, follow the road (past the Cape Cod Factory Outlet Mall) until you reach a set of lights. Turn right at the lights onto Route 6A. The road along the canal will lead you under the bridge to an entrance to the store. There is such a variety here to choose from, the store will keep even the most restless children and impatient spouses occupied for the better part of an hour. (There are six other Christmas Tree shops elsewhere on the Cape as well.)

After your spree, take your bags full of bargains and head back out to Route 6, the Mid-Cape Highway. Now save the rest of your money for things that are truly Cape Cod.

Sandwich

The first town we suggest you visit, if you haven't already stopped off in Bourne's Buzzards Bay, is Sandwich. Getting there is simple. Take exit 2 off the Mid-Cape Highway and turn left at the end of the ramp. That will put you on Route 130 (Water Street), which leads into the Sandwich Center (a right on Route 130 would take you to Mashpee and to Route 28, which leads to Falmouth).

Sandwich is thought to have been named after a seaport in East Kent, England, rather than the Earl of Sandwich, who was born 118 years after the town was incorporated. But there is no sure record of how the name was chosen. We do know this, though: the town had its beginnings in 1627 as a trading post. Ten years later, Plymouth Colony granted Edmund Freeman, then from Saugus, a town north of Boston, and nine others permission to establish a settlement for 60 families in the area. "Those tenn men of Saugust," the proclamation read in its old English, "shall have liberty to view a place to sitt downe & sufficient lands for three score famylies. . . ." The town was incorporated two years later.

Today, Sandwich comprises 42 square miles and has a year-round population of more than 10,000, many of whom commute to jobs in Boston or on Boston's South Shore. The town has seven villages, although not all have separate post offices: Sandwich, East Sandwich, South Sandwich, Scorton Neck, Forestdale, Wakeby, and Farmersville. Sandwich and East Sandwich are without a doubt the most interesting to visit and have the most to offer; the other villages are residential areas with a scattering of shops and restaurants. While in Sandwich make sure you visit the town center. The center hasn't changed much from the late 1800s; it is set off by rows of weathered clapboard homes and white Greek Revival houses, a pillared town hall, a common ringed by large old shade trees, the tall white spire of the First Church of Christ, and large well-groomed lawns.

Sadly, your introduction to Sandwich, if you take Route 130 into the center, is disappointing. The first town landmark you pass is the dump. But don't be discouraged. Continue on. Within a quarter of a mile you will pass the red brick Henry T. Wing School (on your right) and the picturesque Quail Hollow farm store on your left. Not far from here is the Hoxie House. Built in 1637, it is thought to be the oldest house on Cape Cod. The graceful saltbox sits on a high knoll overlooking willow-lined Shawme Lake. The home is named after one of its occupants in the 1800s—whaling Captain Abraham Hoxie. Open to the public from mid-June through September, the house is worth a visit. Admission is free.

Take time while you're here to view Shawme Lake, divided by nature into an upper and lower pond. On the shore of the lake you'll also find the Thornton W. Burgess Museum, the old Town Hall, and nearby Dexter's Grist Mill, a working grist mill open to the public from mid-June until September. You can spend the better part of a morning or afternoon in the area, taking in the sights or just sitting on the shoreline watching the geese, ducks, and swans.

Next to the Hoxie House is the Burgess Museum, established in honor of Thornton W. Burgess, the renowned children's author and naturalist. Born in Sandwich in 1874, the prolific Burgess, a conservation pioneer, wrote more than 15,000 stories and 170 books. He is best known for his Mother West Wind and Peter Rabbit stories. "Burgess drew on his childhood memories, especially of Green Briar, to create charming bedtime stories for his own young son," notes a brochure published by the Thornton W. Burgess Society, which runs the museum. "Animal characters came alive in habitats such as the Old Briar Patch, Smiling Pool, and Crooked Little Path." Burgess, as a young man, had worked as a messenger boy for a mail-order pond lily business and "roamed the woods surrounding Green Briar almost daily," according to the society, which was established in 1976 as a nonprofit educational organization "to inspire in youth a reverence for wildlife and a concern for the environment" and to perpetuate Burgess's accomplishments.

The museum, housed in a restored 1756 home once owned by Burgess's aunt, Arabella Eldred Burgess (it is now owned by the town), offers the largest known collection of Burgess's writing, original illustrations done for his books by Harrison Cady, and natural history exhibits relating to the life and work of the renowned author. The museum is open from April until Christmas, and during July and August, special children's story hours are held.

If you have time, we suggest you visit the old briar patch itself. It is located about two miles away in East Sandwich off Discovery Hill Road and is part of the Green Briar Nature Center and Jam Kitchen. The center offers natural history lectures, field trips, and special events year-round. The jam kitchen sells delicacies like beach plum jelly, cranberry conserve, and sun-cooked strawberries—all made in an old-fashioned kitchen that has been selling jams and jellies for more than 80 years. For more information, call the society at 508-888-6870.

While you're in the town center area, we recommend you also take in the Sandwich Glass Museum, across from Town Hall; the Yesteryear Doll Museum, next to the Dan'l Webster Inn on Main Street; and Heritage Plantation of Sandwich on Grove Street.

The Glass Museum, open almost year-round, is owned and operated by the Sandwich Historical Society and displays glassworks made in the 1800s at a time when Sandwich was home to one of the nation's largest early glass factories. "Although Sandwich is especially noted for its early pressed lacy glass with a stippled background . . . it also produced quality blown, cut, and engraved ware," boasts a museum brochure, noting all are on display here.

If you love dolls, don't miss the nearby Yesteryear Doll Museum, which offers an extensive doll collection from around the world. Some of the dolls are more than 500 years old. The museum is open from May 15 until October 31, Monday through Saturday, 10 A.M. until 4 P.M. , and on Sundays from 1 P.M. until 4 P.M.

The Heritage Plantation of Sandwich is also a sure bet; more than 100,000 visitors a year walk through its doors. It is located on 76 acres of gardens and woodlands about a mile from the town center at the intersection of Pine and Grove streets and offers an impressive collection of antique cars, military artifacts, including two fine firearms collections, and Americana. Lectures, educational programs, workshops, and craft classes are also offered here. The museum was founded in honor of Josiah Kirby Lilly, Jr., and "is dedicated to the presentation and preservation of the collections assembled by the Lilly family and many other contributors," according to a plantation pamphlet. In addition to antique cars, which include the first official White House car—a 1909 white Steamer, originally owned by President Wiliam Howard Taft—the plantation offers displays of military artifacts and exquisitely landscaped grounds. It also features an art museum, a windmill built in the 1800s, old barns, and a gift shop.

If you're still in the town center area and it's time for lunch or dinner, we recommend you consider eating at the Dan'l Webster Inn; but reservations are needed. The inn, which also provides elegant rooms and suites, is a reproduction of a parsonage turned tavern. The tavern was used as a meeting place for Patriots during the revolution.

If you just want to go to the beach, there's no better place than Sandwich Town Beach on the bay side off Freeman Avenue. The beach is wide, the view spectacular, and the water invigorating. The best time to go is at high tide or between tides; check local newspapers for tide charts. To get to the beach, take Town Neck Road off Route 6A, then turn right on Freeman Avenue. Behind the beach is Sandwich Marsh, a perfect spot for hiking. There's a boardwalk that runs from the beach and across the marsh. It's a favorite spot for photographers and artists.

While you're in the area, you might want to take in Sandwich Marina, one of the Cape's biggest boat marinas. It is located at the north mouth of the canal, not far from the Canal Electric plant. There are a number of good seafood restaurants in the area, too. Among them are Seafood Sam's (off Coast Guard Road, offers a striking view of the Sagamore Bridge), and a place called Horizons on Cape Cod Bay, on Town Neck Road (view of Sandwich Town Beach).

Before you leave Sandwich, you should also take time to see the Shawme-Crowell State Forest.

The Shawme-Crowell State Forest (there's an entrance at the intersection of Main Street and Swamp Road) offers clean, comfortable camping and travel trailer facilities on a first-come, first-served basis. Picnic tables, fireplaces, and showers are available. For more specifics, call 508-888-0351 or write for a Shawme-Crowell State Forest brochure (Box 446, Sandwich, MA 02563).

Part of the forest, we should note, is in neighboring Bourne—one of many things the two towns share in common. While you're in the Sandwich area, we suggest you visit Bourne.

Bourne

Bourne, the only Cape town to be split by the canal, was once a part of Sandwich. In the early days, there was much distrust and rivalry between residents of both areas over such things as what churches to attend and who would control the town's government. After a request to separate from Sandwich was rejected at a town meeting in the late 1800s, residents of the villages that now make up Bourne persuaded the state legislature to allow them to incorporate. Bourne, more industrial than Sandwich, prospered under the new arrangement, but has since had its share of economic problems and still seems to be searching for an identity—one that appropriately addresses the fact that the town is severed by the Cape Cod Canal. Bourne was officially incorporated in 1884, making it the last Cape town to do so.

There are some who suggest the town was named after Richard Bourne, an early settler who ministered to the Indians, but most agree the town bears the name of Jonathan Bourne, an early and affluent resident, a merchant who profited greatly from the whaling industry.

Once quite rural, the town of Bourne in the 1800s boomed with factories, mills, and wharves for fishing and shipbuilding. The town, with its magnificent shoreline, also attracted its share of summer visitors, including former President Grover Cleveland, who converted a fishing lodge on the Cape side of the canal into the summer White House. The home, called Gray Gables, no longer stands, but history buffs might enjoy viewing the site, which is not far from Monument Beach. To get to Gray Gables, take Presidents Road, which is off Shore Road. In all, there are seven villages within Bourne:

Buzzards Bay

This village, named after the body of water it abuts, is Bourne's commercial center. It offers much in the way of shops and restaurants; the center of the village, off Main Street, was renovated recently. In the summertime, traffic

headed for the Bourne Bridge often builds up here. Next time you find yourself in one of these gridlocks, park the car and spend some time exploring
Buzzards Bay. The Chamber of Commerce is located at the old train station,
which was reopened several years ago when summer rail service was restored to the Cape. During July and August, there are free band concerts in
Buzzards Bay Park off Main Street. Also at the end of each summer, the park
hosts a Scallop Festival, a crafts fair held under a circus tent. The three-day
festival usually attracts more than 50,000 people. Scores and scores of scallop dinners are served during the event. Check with the Chamber of Commerce for dates and times.

While you're in the Buzzards Bay area, you might also want to take in
the following: the 70-acre Bourne Scenic Park, located on the north bank of
the canal, just to the northeast of the village. The park offers campsites,
playgrounds, hiking, fishing, and an Olympic-sized, sea-level swimming pool.
Through a series of intricate valves, the water in the pool changes with the
tide; the Massachusetts Maritime Academy, the oldest maritime (merchant
marine) academy in the country. The 55-acre campus is located at the end of
Taylor's Point off Main Street; the Buzzards Bay Railroad Bridge, an engineer-
ing marvel built in the mid-1930s when the present Bourne and Sagamore
bridges were constructed. The railroad bridge, which spans the canal, is located off Taylor Road. You can't miss it; its medieval turrets can be seen for
miles. The 545-foot-long bridge has a single-track span that moves up and
down. When the bridge is not in use, the track is hoisted 135 feet above the
canal. The track can be lowered in a matter of minutes for the trains coming
in from Hyannis or down from the Boston area.

Bournedale

Located along the canal on the mainland, just south of the Great Herring
Pond, this residential village offers just a handful of shops and motels, but
the view of the waterway from here is spectacular. There is a large parking
area off the Cranberry Highway, a part of Route 6. We recommend you pull
off and take in the view. Across the road you'll find a cemetery called Burying Hill, an ancient burial ground of the Wampanoag Indians and a good
place for a summer walk.

Sagamore

This rural village, which faces Cape Cod Bay, is the only Bourne village that
straddles the canal. On the mainland, points of interest (all along the shoreline) include Sagamore Highlands, Sagamore Beach, and Scusset Beach, the
most accessible. Run by the state, this beach offers ample parking (at a nominal
fee), rest rooms, a snack bar, and a fishing pier (one of the best fishing holes
on the Cape for striped bass, bluefish, cod, and pollock). On the Cape side,
you'll find Sagamore Center, a collection of small shops and restaurants spread
out over a few square miles. Many people, including some of the locals,
mistakenly think Sagamore Center is part of Sandwich because of its proximity to Sandwich Center.

Bourne Village

On the Cape side of the canal, this sedate and residential village is located at the intersection of five roads (Sandwich Road, Trowbridge Road, Waterhouse Road, Perry Road, and Shore Road) less than a mile west of the Bourne Bridge Rotary. Worth a visit is the Bourne Library on Keene Street and the Aptucxet Trading Post, which overlooks the canal at the end of Aptucxet Road, not far from Trading Post Corners. Here in this replica of the original post you will find artifacts and displays that tell of the early Pilgrim days. The trading post was the start of American commerce and currency—the first organized business in the New World. Profits from the post were used by Pilgrims to repay a group of London merchants who had financed the trip aboard the *Mayflower*. The trading post museum is also a part of what is called the Free Enterprise Trail, a 35-mile loop throughout the Upper Cape that features a number of places visitors can shop, dine, and view historic sites.

Monument Beach

Off County Road on the Cape side, this residential, beachside community near the Buzzards Bay shoreline and south of Bourne Village offers a beautiful stretch of sandy beach between Phinneys Harbor and Wings Neck (see map). If you're looking for a nice drive, we suggest you take Mashnee Road (off Presidents Road) out to Mashnee Island or Wings Neck Road (off Shore Road). Formerly a summer colony, Monument Beach is a year-round community.

Pocasset

On the Cape side just south of Monument Beach and north of Cataumet off Shore Road, you'll find Pocasset. This residential village also has its share of fine harbors and beaches. Among them are Red Brook Harbor, Pocasset Harbor, and Hens Cove.

Cataumet

Located on the Cape side south of Pocasset and north of Falmouth, this is the smallest of Bourne's villages yet one of the prettiest. It is situated between Red Brook Harbor and Squeteague Harbor (squeteague, by the way, is a fish common to Buzzards Bay; the Indians used to make glue from it). To the west is a picturesque point of land in the shape of a blowfish called Scraggy Neck. From here you can see Cleveland Light, a lighthouse directing ships entering the canal. Another point of interest is Kingman Marina, a marina facility complete with a restaurant, the Chart Room, that overlooks Red Brook Harbor and Bassett Island. The Chart Room, which serves lunch and dinner, is housed in an old New Jersey Central Railroad barge built in the early 1900s. The barge was towed to the harbor in 1953 and was opened as a restaurant in 1966. It's a great place to eat; swordfish is the specialty. Call for reservations.

Another landmark worth visiting while you're in the Bourne area is the Massachusetts Military Reservation off Falmouth-Sandwich Road. The 14,700-acre reservation, called "Otis" by many, houses Otis Air Force Base, Camp Edwards National Guard Training Site, a Coast Guard air station and the Cape Cod Air Force Station. Parts of the reservation are in Bourne, Sandwich, Mashpee, and Falmouth. There are entrances to the complex in Bourne, Sandwich, and Falmouth. The reservation has been actively used since World War II when air force planes regularly patrolled the waters off the Cape in search of German submarines. There is also a national cemetery here.

Mashpee

Despite its size, Mashpee, which runs south from the Sandwich line all the way to Vineyard Sound, is one of the fastest-growing towns on the Cape and has one of the richest histories. The Massapee Indians, part of the Wampanoag tribe, lived here thousands of years before the Pilgrims ever dreamed of leaving England. The Massapees were friendly, and their influence is still felt in these parts. Each July, usually on a weekend near the Fourth, an authentic "Indian powwow" is held. The annual event, sponsored by the Wampanoag Indian Council of Mashpee, is held on a baseball field off Route 130 about a mile north (heading toward Sandwich) of the Wampanoag Indian Museum. Scores of Indians from tribes all over the country attend in full headdress. Ceremonies usually start in the afternoon with a tribal dance and are followed by Indian sports and a clambake or a ham and bean supper. A special prayer service is usually held Sunday morning; in previous years, part of the service was spoken in Wampanoag Indian dialect. More events are held that afternoon.

Mashpee, which encompasses about 24 square miles, was established as a Plymouth Colony community in the late 1600s, although it was not incorporated until 1870. In 1660, the Reverend Richard Bourne convinced the state legislature to set aside 10,500 acres for the Indians of Cape Cod. The settlement was called the Plantation of Mashpee. Bourne subsequently converted many of the Indians to Christianity; Frederick Freeman in his *History of Cape Cod*, published in 1858, calls Bourne's converts "the praying Indians."

The Reverend Bourne's first meetinghouse church was simple and slapped together quickly. It was replaced in the late 1600s by a new meetinghouse on the shore of Santuit Pond at Bryant's Neck. In the early 1700s, the Indians moved the church by ox cart to its present site on Route 28, east of Meeting House Road. It is open to the public, along with the Wampanoag Indian Museum, not far from the church off Route 130. Here you will see Indian artifacts and displays. For years now, the Indians have sought the return of land that makes up most of the town. Their efforts, to date, have been rebuffed by the courts.

There's not much to see in the center of Mashpee, which consists of a town hall, library, and a Baptist church, all located near the intersection of Route 130 and Central Avenue. Of more interest are nearby Attaquin Park, a town-run beach with a boat ramp on Lake Avenue, and the Lowell Holly Reservation, a 130-acre nature preserve donated by former Harvard president Abbott Lawrence Lowell. Both are off Route 130 on the shores of Wakeby and Mashpee ponds—the largest freshwater pond complex on the Cape. The Lowell Holly Reservation on Conaumet Neck, a peninsula that divides the two ponds, is perfect for hiking and picnicking. The area was once a favorite fishing spot of Daniel Webster and Grover Cleveland. The reservation is open from May until October, from 8 A.M. until sunset. A small parking fee is charged on weekends and holidays. To get there, take South Sandwich Road off Route 130 for about a mile. You'll see an entrance on your left.

Like Abbott Lowell, the residents of Mashpee are quite conservation minded. At a 1985 town meeting, they voted to preserve more than 200 acres along the scenic Mashpee River from development. The river runs from Pine Tree Corner to Popponesset Bay, a distance of about four miles. It's a great spot for hiking or canoeing. Trails are listed on maps that are available through a group called the Friends of Mashpee River or at Town Hall.

Another good spot for hiking, canoeing, or swimming is the 432-acre South Cape Beach State Park, located at the end of Great Oak Road, not far from New Seabury, a 2000-acre resort and residential development. To get to South Cape Beach, drive south along Route 151 to the Mashpee Rotary, then south on Great Neck Road, which will lead you to Great Oak Road. South Cape Beach is a barrier beach, much like North Beach in Chatham. It protects a salt marsh and a salt pond from the ravages of winter storms. There is no bathhouse or visitor center here and parking is limited, but we suggest you try it. The park also has a fine nature trail, the Great Flat Pond Trail—a mile-long hike around fresh- and salt-water marshes, across uplands and through forests. The fishing here is fantastic.

On your way out of the park, you might want to take a peek at New Seabury. It has everything a resort could offer—two 18-hole golf courses (one of them, the Blue Championship links, is considered among the best in the country), 16 all-weather tennis courts, a marketplace, fine restaurants, bike paths, jogging trails, and a beautiful stretch of shoreline. It's a "vacationer's dream" a New Seabury brochure exclaims. A second-home retreat, each of New Seabury's 13 villages has a unique style—from seaside New England architecture to contemporary California-style patio homes. Some call it one of the best-designed second home communities yet built in the eastern United States. Others cite it as yet another case of overdevelopment. Come see for yourself.

You don't have to stay here, though, to enjoy New Seabury. We suggest you take in the Popponesset Marketplace, where you can browse or dine in an outdoor cafe or eat oysters and cherrystones at a comfortable raw bar. For more formal dining, we suggest the nearby Popponesset Inn or the New Seabury restaurant. Special events are offered at New Seabury throughout the year. In the spring, there is an annual St. Paddy's Day golf package, as well as celebrations on Easter, Mother's Day, and Memorial Day. In the fall, a special Harvest Fair on Columbus Day weekend features hay rides, craft exhibits, and colorful foliage. Events are also scheduled for Thanksgiving, New Year's Eve, and Valentine's Day.

For more information about New Seabury, telephone 508-477-9111 or write: New Seabury, Box B-1, New Seabury, MA 02649.

Oh, if you're in the Mashpee area in late July, don't forget to duck over to East Falmouth for the Barnstable County Fair, held on fairgrounds off Route 151, about three miles from the Mashpee Rotary. The annual fair features livestock and agricultural exhibits, amusement rides, and great food. Don't miss it. Check the local newspapers, the *Falmouth Enterprise* or the *Cape Cod Times*, for dates and times, or telephone Mashpee or Falmouth Town Halls.

Falmouth

On a busy summer day, as many as 100,000 people crowd into Falmouth's eight villages, which cover 44 square miles. By contrast, the town's year-round population is about 27,000. The villages are Teaticket or Davis Straits, a mix of farmland, homes, and shops off Route 28 between Falmouth and East Falmouth; Falmouth Heights, an affluent summer and year-round community off Grand Avenue near Falmouth Harbor (a great place for a drive); Falmouth Center, a commercial stretch off Route 28 between Woods Hole and Teaticket; East Falmouth, an ethnic residential area where many Portuguese and Cape Verdean fishermen and workers live; Hatchville, a growing residential development off Route 151 between North Falmouth and Pine Tree Corner; North Falmouth, a coastal community off Buzzards Bay, not far from the Bourne-Falmouth line; West Falmouth, a quiet and exclusive area with a beautiful harbor off Route 28A near Chapoquoit Point; Woods Hole, a quaint and yet bustling village tucked away in the southeast corner of Falmouth.

As most Cape towns, Falmouth was settled by those fleeing religious repression—in this case, Quakers and Congregationalists from Barnstable and Sandwich, who were given permission by Plymouth Colony in 1660 to settle Succonessitt, the "place of black shells," as the Indians called it. Succonessitt was incorporated in 1686, and seven years later its name was changed to Falmouth—after the English port from which discoverer Bartholomew Gosnold and his crew of 32 sailed on March 23 of 1602. Gosnold, who is credited with discovering the Cape and Islands (although many suspect the Vikings were here first), landed at Woods Hole, not far from Nobska Point on May 31, 1602.

Falmouth, the Cape's first summer colony, a haven for the wealthy, has always attracted its share of "free thinkers"—independent-minded men and women who are ready to argue just about any point at any given time. This independence has become a part of the town's character. For example, during the American Revolution and midway through the War of 1812, fearless Falmouth residents beat back the British: first, by breaking through a blockade in 1778 to recover a Falmouth schooner; then about 34 years later, by recapturing a prized town cannon stowed away on a five-gun British privateer called *Retaliation*.

Today, Falmouth—"the handsomest place in these regions," as Daniel Webster once called it—has something to offer just about everyone, British included. Falmouth native Katharine Lee Bates, author of *America the Beautiful,* certainly agreed. Wrote Bates of her hometown, "Never was there a lovelier town than Falmouth by the sea."

Falmouth is dominated as much by its shoreline as by its hills and meadows. The town, which faces Buzzards Bay to the west and Vineyard Sound to the south, has more coastline than any other Cape town. There are 14 harbors, more than 30 freshwater and saltwater ponds, and 10 public beaches. The beaches are Bristol Beach in the Maravista section of town near Falmouth Heights; Chapoquoit Beach in North Falmouth; Falmouth Heights Beach in Falmouth Heights; Grews Pond, a freshwater pond in Goodwill Park; Megansett Beach in North Falmouth; Menauhant Beach in East Falmouth; Old Silver Beach in North Falmouth; Stoney Beach in Woods Hole; Surf Drive Beach in Falmouth and Wood Neck Beach in West Falmouth. You'll find bathhouse facilities at Surf Drive Beach and Old Silver Beach and food concessions at Surf Drive Beach, Old Silver Beach, and Menauhant Beach. Lifeguards, you'll be pleased to know, are on duty at all public beaches from 9 A.M. until 5 P.M., and windsurfing is allowed at the beaches before 9 A.M. and after 5 P.M.

As in all Cape towns, beach parking can be a problem. Limited parking is available at town beaches for Falmouth year-round and summer residents with stickers, which can be obtained at the Surf Drive Bath House. Parking for the general public is available only at Surf Drive, Menauhant, Falmouth Heights, and Old Silver beaches for a daily fee. Visitors can purchase weekly, monthly, or seasonal parking permits.

When it comes to entertainment, dining, shopping, hiking, science exhibits, museums, and sports, Falmouth ranks among the Cape and Islands' best.

Falmouth is blessed with some of the Cape's finest restaurants, among them the Regatta at the mouth of Falmouth Harbor. The Regatta, with its excellent harbor view, is located at the end of Scranton Avenue off Route 28. Patrons can even arrive by boat, tying up at a 90-foot dock owned by the restaurant. Reservations are needed. The Regatta specializes in Cape Cod and continental cooking and is open from mid-May until mid-October. For a more casual meal, we suggest you try the waterfront Fishmonger's Café in Woods Hole or the Black Duck, which overlooks Eel Pond. Sample the chowder here.

If you like to shop, Main Street in the center of town, with its shops, boutiques, and malls, will satisfy the strongest of cravings.

For hiking, we recommend you spend time at the 45-acre Ashumet Holly Reservation and Wildlife Sanctuary in East Falmouth, the 400-acre Beebe Woods near Falmouth Center, and 334-acre Washburn Island in Waquoit Bay.

The Ashumet Holly Reservation on Ashumet Road is managed by the Massachusetts Audubon Society "and is well known for its eight species and 65 varieties of holly trees and its barn swallow colony," according to an Audubon brochure. In the summer, the reservation hosts a Lotus Festival. In the fall, there are a Frankinia Festival and a holly sale at Christmastime. For more information, telephone 508-563-6390.

Beebe Woods off Depot Road near the town center offers some great hiking trails and has some magnificent stone fences. The park was donated to the town by Josiah K. Lilly III, the owner of the Lilly Drug Company. The Lilly family, as noted earlier, was involved with the creation of Heritage Plantation in Sandwich.

The hiking is equally as good on the state-owned Washburn Island in Waquoit Bay. There is overnight camping available here. The state paid $2.1 million for the island in 1983, preventing a group of developers from building 50 homes on it.

If you're looking for recreation, Falmouth has everything from sailing to windsurfing to road racing. Falmouth's inlets and coves are among the best places on the Cape to sail and windsurf. But if you want to keep your feet on high ground, there's always the world-renowned Falmouth Road Race, a hilly 7.1-mile race along the shoreline from Woods Hole to Falmouth Heights. The annual August race attracts world-class runners. If running exhausts you, you can always watch. It's a great spectator sport.

Another traditional spectator sport in Falmouth is watching the Commodores of the Cape Cod Baseball League. Recognized as one of the best summer college leagues in the country, the league has an impressive list of graduates—among them the late Thurman Munson of the New York Yankees; Carlton Fisk, formerly of the Boston Red Sox, now with the Chicago White Sox; Ron Darling of the New York Mets; John Tudor, formerly with the Red Sox, now with St. Louis; and Cory Snyder of the Cleveland Indians. Check local papers for times and places of the games.

Bring your bike to the Cape, too. Biking is a great way to beat the summer traffic or take in scenic back roads. We suggest you take a spin on the Shining Sea Bikeway. The 3.3-mile bike path runs from Falmouth Center to Woods Hole along magnificent shoreline and by peaceful marinas. The path begins on Locust Street in the town center and ends at the Steamship Authority dock in Woods Hole.

For street fairs and fireworks, you're in the right place, too. Falmouth's Fourth of July display, one of the Cape's most flamboyant, is launched from a barge off Falmouth Heights and can be seen for miles. For many, it's the highlight of the season, along with an annual street fair held on Main Street in early July. The arts and crafts show attracts close to 20,000.

The village of Woods Hole is a museum in itself. In addition to the world-famous Woods Hole Oceanographic Institution (WHOI), whose expedition team found the *Titanic* in July 1986 about 500 miles off the coast of Newfoundland, the village is also home to the National Marine Fisheries Service Aquarium, the Marine Biological Laboratory, and the Bradley House, a Woods Hole Historical Society museum.

At the Oceanographic Institution near Little Harbor, you'll find a scientific and historical exhibit on the *Titanic*, as well as other oceanic research exhibits. Just a few minutes' walk from the institution is the marine fisheries aquarium, which offers a variety of fish exhibits. You can even watch workers feed the seals in an outdoor pool. At the Marine Biological Laboratory, guided tours of the research areas are given. The laboratory is housed in the 150-year-old Candle House, which was used many years ago to store whale oil and make spermaceti candles. For more information, telephone 508-548-3705. Also keep in mind the Bradley House, an old sea captain's home that is now a museum run by the Woods Hole Historical Society. The museum has an impressive collection of turn-of-the-century paintings, photographs, and artifacts.

Woods Hole is also the place to catch a ferry to Martha's Vineyard and Nantucket. Boats run regularly out of the Woods Hole–Martha's Vineyard–Nantucket Steamship Authority dock. The trip to the Vineyard, a few miles off the Falmouth coast, takes about 45 minutes. The ride to Nantucket, much farther offshore, is three hours and 15 minutes. If you plan to take your car over in the summer, you must make reservations months in advance. The boat to Martha's Vineyard runs year-round, one every hour in the summer and at regular intervals in the off season. The boat to Nantucket runs only in the summer, but there are several ferries a day. In the off season, the only ferry to Nantucket runs out of the Steamship Authority's Hyannis dock on South Street. For current prices and schedules, call 508-540-2022.

There is also ferry service in the summer from Falmouth Harbor to the Vineyard on the privately owned *Island Queen*. The trip takes about 35 minutes. For more information, call the *Island Queen* office at 508-548-4800.

Whether you're taking a ferry or just browsing around, the Falmouth Center and Woods Hole area is a great place for the family on either a sunny or a rainy day.

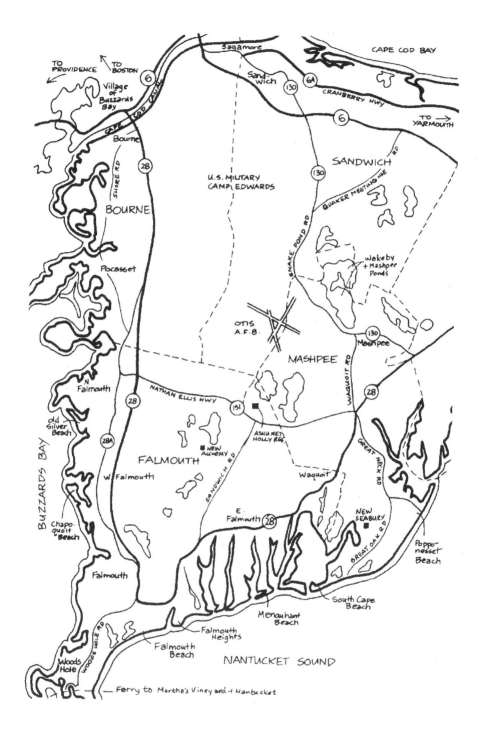

UPPER CAPE

Upper Cape: Essentials

 Important Public Information

MUNICIPAL SERVICES

- *Bourne Town Hall:* 759-0600
- *Bourne Police:* 759-4451
- *Bourne Fire and Ambulance:* 759-4411
- *Falmouth Town Hall:* 548-7611
- *Falmouth Police:* 548-1212
- *Falmouth Fire and Ambulance:* 548-2323
- *Mashpee Town Hall:* 477-1404
- *Mashpee Police:* 477-1213; 477-1212
- *Mashpee Fire and Ambulance:* 477-1234; 477-0411
- *Sandwich Town Hall:* 888-0340
- *Sandwich Police:* 888-1212
- *Sandwich Fire and Ambulance:* 888-2323

MEDICAL SERVICES

- *Cape Cod Hospital*, 27 Park St., Hyannis; 771-1800
- *Falmouth Hospital*, Ter Huen Dr., Falmouth; 548-5300
- *Falmouth Walk-In Medical Center*, 309 Rte. 28, Teaticket; 540-6790

VETERINARIANS

- *Anchor Pet Clinic*, 75 Davis Straits, Falmouth; 540-4323
- *The Animal House*, 3152 Cranberry Hwy., Buzzards Bay; 759-4522
- *Falmouth Animal Hospital*, Rte. 151, N. Falmouth; 563-7147
- *Forestdale Veterinary Clinic*, Rte. 130, Forestdale; 477-0206
- *Mashpee Veterinary Hospital*, Great Neck Rd., Mashpee; 477-9291
- *Sandwich Animal Hospital*, Rte. 6A, E. Sandwich; 888-2774
- *South Shore Veterinary Associates*, 230 Main St., Buzzards Bay; 759-2521

WEATHER

- *The Cape Codder Weatherphone*, 508-255-8500

Lodgings

B&Bs and Guest Houses

Major credit cards are accepted at most B&Bs and guest houses, and many places offer off-season rates. Call to inquire.

RESERVATION SERVICE & DIRECTORY

• *House Guests Cape Cod and the Islands* is the Cape and Islands' original and most varied bed and breakfast reservation service. More than 300 guest rooms are available; year-round service. Offers accommodations for singles, doubles, and families; water views and wooded locations. All accommodations have been inspected and approved; reasonable rates. For a directory covering Cape Cod and the Islands, write Box 1881, Orleans, MA 02653, or call 896-7053 or 1-800-666-HOST; Visa, MasterCard, American Express welcome.

• *Bed and Breakfast Cape Cod*, Box 341, West Hyannis Port 02672; 508-775-2772. Select from 60 host homes, country inns, and sea captains' houses on Cape Cod and the islands of Nantucket and Martha's Vineyard. Beaches, great seafood restaurants, whale watches, and summer theater are all a part of the local attractions. Modest/deluxe rates, private or shared baths. Write or call for free selection information.

BOURNE

• *Cape Cod Canalside Bed & Breakfast*, Box 536, Buzzards Bay; 759-6564. Moderate. Contemporary home abuts Cape Cod Canal. Off-season rates. Reservations required.

• *Oceanfront Bed & Breakfast*, 273 Phillips Rd., Sagamore Beach; 888-4798. Moderate. Offers a water view, private baths, continental breakfast. Off-season rates available.

FALMOUTH

• *Captains Inn,* Box 1448, N. Falmouth; 564-6424. Romantic Victorian estate in historic village. Elegant rooms, breakfast, convenient to Islands. Open year-round; off-season rates.

• *Captain Tom Lawrence House*, 75 Locust St., Falmouth; 548-9178 or 1-800-266-8139. Moderate. This guest house is open year-round and offers breakfast. Off-season rates; Visa and MasterCard.

• *Elm Arch Inn*, Elm Arch Way off Main St.; 548-0133. Moderate. Near center of village, 18th century inn, swimming pool.

• *Gladstone Inn*, 219 Grand Ave., Falmouth Heights; 548-9851. Moderate. Inn features water view, continental breakfast. Efficiency units available.

• *The Grafton Inn*, 261 Grand Ave., Falmouth Heights; 540-8688. Moderate. Offers a water view, private baths, continental breakfast, and efficiency units. Open year-round. Visa and MasterCard.

• *Grandview Guest House*, 197 Grand Ave., Falmouth Heights; 548-4025. Moderate. Offers a water view and continental breakfast. Seasonal.

• *Grey Whale Inn*, 565 Woods Hole Rd., Woods Hole; 548-7692. Expensive. This deluxe inn features a water view, private baths, continental breakfast. Seasonal.

• *Hastings by the Sea*, 28 Worcester Park Ave., Falmouth Heights; 540-2887. Inexpensive. Water view; continental breakfast. Seasonal.

- *Hawthorne Lodge*, 211 Grand Ave., Falmouth Heights; 548-0389. Inexpensive. Offering a water view, private baths, and continental breakfast.
- *Inn at One Main Street*, 1 Main St., Falmouth; 540-7469. Expensive. Deluxe year-round inn offers private baths, continental breakfast. Off-season rates.
- *The Marlborough*, 320 Woods Hole Rd., Woods Hole; 548-6218. Moderate. Features include private baths, pool, breakfast, and efficiency units. Year-round; off-season rates.
- *The Moorings*, 207 Grand Ave., Falmouth Heights; 540-2370. Moderate. Water view; private baths; continental breakfast. Off-season rates available.
- *Mostly Hall*, 27 Main St., Falmouth; 548-3786. Expensive. Private baths; breakfast. Year-round; off-season rates.
- *Old Silver Beach Bed & Breakfast*, 3 Cliffwood Ln., W. Falmouth; 540-5446. Moderate. TV and continental breakfast. Year-round; off-season rates.
- *Palmer House Inn*, 81 Palmer Ave., Falmouth; 548-1230. Expensive. Deluxe inn offers private baths and continental breakfast. Open year-round; off-season rates. Visa and MasterCard.
- *Peacock's, "Inn on the Sound,"* 313 Grand Ave., Falmouth Heights; 457-9666. Moderate. Overlooking Vineyard Sound, this inn has recently been renovated in country decor. Full breakfast.
- *Peterson's Bed & Breakfast*, 226 Trotting Park Rd., E. Falmouth; 540-2962. Moderate. Breakfast; year-round; off-season rates.
- *Scalloped Shell Inn*, 16 Mass Ave., Falmouth Heights; 548-8245. Moderate. Features a water view, private baths, and breakfast. Year-round.
- *Sjöholm Inn*, 17 Chase Rd., W. Falmouth; 540-5706. Moderate. Private baths; breakfast; efficiencies. Year-round; off-season rates.
- *Swan Point Inn*, 57 Main St., Falmouth; 540-5528. Private baths, TV, full breakfast. Children welcome. Off-season rates.
- *Village Green Inn*, 40 W. Main St., Falmouth; 548-5621. Moderate. TV; private baths; continental breakfast. Year-round; off-season rates.
- *Vineyard View Lodge,* 10 Worcester Ct., Falmouth; 548-2364. Moderate. Private baths and refrigerators, walk to beach, shops, ferry; pool. Off-season rates. Visa/MasterCard.
- *The Wildflower Inn B&B,* 167 Palmer Ave.; 548-9524 or 800-294-5459. Moderate. Located in Falmouth's historic district, full breakfast, some rooms with whirlpools. Separate Town House available with a full kitchen, living room and loft bedroom.
- *Woods Hole Passage B&B,* 186 Woods Hole Rd.; 548-9575. Moderate. One hundred year old carriage house and renovated barn on ample grounds, full breakfast.

SANDWICH

- *The Barclay Inn*, 40 Grove St., Sandwich; 888-5738. Walk to Sandwich Village. Year-round; off-season rates.
- *Bay Beach*, 1-3 Bay Beach Lane, Sandwich; 888-8813. Newly built. Suites with private bath, some whirlpools. Private beach. Nonsmoking adults only. Year-round; off-season rates.
- *Captain Ezra Nye House,* 152 Main St., Sandwich; 888-6142. Moderate. B&B, antique captain's house; private baths; in Sandwich Village; breakfast. Year-round.
- *The Dunbar House*, 1 Water St.; 833-2485. A 1741 colonial home; your British hosts bring a touch of England; tea room.

SANDWICH (CONTINUED)

- *Isaiah Jones Homestead Inn*, 165 Main St., Sandwich; 888-9115. Victorian atmosphere, private baths; continental breakfast. Year-round.
- *Ocean Front B&B*, 273 Phillips Rd., Sandwich; 888-4798. Moderate. Three decks with ocean view; private beach; seasonal; breakfast.
- *The Summer House*, 158 Old Main St., Sandwich; 888-4991. Moderate. Continental breakfast, Greek Revival architecture, built circa 1835, five bedrooms decorated in antiques, good location in Sandwich Village, credit cards accepted. May–October.
- *The Village Inn*, 4 Jarves St., Sandwich; 833-0363. In historic Sandwich Village; private baths. Nonsmoking.
- *Dan'l Webster Inn*, Main St., Sandwich; 888-3622. Expensive. Sandwich Center; Colonial atmosphere; restaurant; TV; 42 guest rooms and suites. Year-round.
- *Wing Scorton Farm Inn*, 11 Wing Blvd. (off Rte. 6A), E. Sandwich; 888-0545. Expensive. Restored 1758 farmhouse; seven acres of gardens, orchards; short walk to private beach; each room has private bath and working fireplace; full farm breakfast. Carriage house and cottage also available.

Resorts, Hotels, Motels, Inns, Condominiums, & Selected Cottages

Major credit cards are accepted at most of the following establishments, and many of them offer off-season rates. Call for more information.

BOURNE

- *Bay Motor Inn*, 223 Main St., Buzzards Bay; 759-3989. Moderate. Near shopping.
- *Cataumet Motel*, Rte. 28A, Cataumet; 563-6133. Moderate. Near beaches, shopping, and restaurants.
- *Mashnee Village*, 6 MacArthur Blvd.; 759-3384. Expensive. These deluxe cottages have a view of Buzzards Bay and feature a swimming pool and tennis courts.
- *Picture Lake Motel,* 790 MacArthur Blvd., Cataumet; 563-5911. Private baths, TV, pool. Near Otis AFB. Year-round.
- *Best Western Bridge Bourne Hotel*, 100 Trowbridge Rd., Bourne; 759-0800. Overlooking the canal. Heated indoor pool, whirlpools, restaurant. Weekly rates.
- *Yankee Thrift Motel*, Rte. 28; 759-3883. Inexpensive to moderate. Location and price are the drawing cards here. It also features indoor and outdoor swimming pools. Near the canal.

FALMOUTH

- *Admiralty Resort*, 51 Teaticket Hwy., E. Falmouth; 800-352-7153. Moderate. Offers a central location in Teaticket as its prime attribute, although on-premises dining and entertainment are other pluses. It also offers a swimming pool; TV in the room. Most major credit cards accepted.
- *Cape Colony Motor Lodge*, Surf Dr., Falmouth; 548-3975. Expensive. Across the street from Vineyard Sound, this deluxe motel includes a swimming pool. Major credit cards accepted.
- *Cape Wind Motel*, 34 Maravista Ave. Ext., E. Falmouth; 548-3400. Moderate. This deluxe motel on a saltwater inlet offers privacy, boats, and a dock. Kitchenettes. Major credit cards.

• *Carleton Circle Motel*, 579 Sandwich Rd., Falmouth; 548-0025. Moderate. Some kitchenettes; cocktail lounge, heated pool, near golf course and beaches. Year-round; off-season rates.

• *Ocean View Motel & Capers Restaurant*, 263 Grand Ave.; 540-4120. Moderate. Close to beach and shopping.

• *Coonamessett Inn*, corner Jones and Gifford Sts., Falmouth; 548-2300. Expensive. Although on a busy intersection, it is easy to get lost in the deluxe country inn atmosphere here. This old inn, near a par-3 golf course, has a restaurant, lounge with entertainment, and gardens. Major credit cards.

• *Falmouth Inn*, 824 Main St., Falmouth; 540-2500. Expensive. This deluxe motel was recently converted to a private motel from a Holiday Inn. Near the center of town and beaches. Features include a pool, game room, and cocktail lounge. Major credit cards accepted.

• *Falmouth Heights Motor Lodge*, 146 Falmouth Heights Rd., Falmouth; 548-3623. Moderate. Close to shopping.

• *Falmouth Marina Trade Winds Motel*, Robbins Rd., Falmouth; 548-4300. Moderate. Close to beaches and shopping.

• *Falmouth Ramada Inn on the Square*, 40 N. Main St., Falmouth; 1-800-676-0000. Moderate. Close to shopping and ferry; indoor pool. Value packages available year-round.

• *Flagship Motel*, 24 Scranton Ave., Falmouth; 548-1110. Moderate. Large rooms, AC, TV, walk to shopping and harbor.

• *Great Bay Motel*, Main St., E. Falmouth; 548-5410. Moderate. This motel has a location that is fairly central. Each room has color TV and parking at the door. Picnic tables. Major credit cards accepted.

• *Green Harbor Waterfront Motor Lodge*, Acapesket Rd., E. Falmouth; 548-4747. Expensive. Waterfront, pool, dock. Year-round; off-season rates.

• *Ideal Spot Motel-Efficiencies*, Rte. 28A, Falmouth; 548-2257. Close to beach and harbor. Visa/MasterCard.

• *The Inn at West Falmouth*, off Blacksmith Shop Rd., W. Falmouth; 540-7696. Expensive. Close to beaches and shopping; major credit cards. Year-round; off-season rates.

• *Mariner Motel*, 555 Main St., Rte. 28, Falmouth; 548-1331. Large rooms all on first floor, pool; walk to ferry and beaches. Major credit cards.

• *Nautilus Motor Inn*, Woods Hole Rd., Woods Hole; 548-1525. Expensive. This deluxe hotel features a beautiful view of Vineyard Sound and is adjacent to perhaps the finest restaurant in town, the Dome. The inn features tennis courts and a swimming pool and is very close to the village of Woods Hole.

• *Park Beach Motel*, Grand Ave., Falmouth Heights; 548-1010. Expensive. This deluxe motel features a dramatic view of Vineyard Sound, an outdoor swimming pool, and easy access to the center of town. Year-round.

• *John Parker Lakeside Resort*, off Andrews Rd., E. Falmouth; 548-5933. Expensive. Deluxe condos, near beaches. Year-round.

• *Quality Inn*, 291 Jones Rd., Falmouth; 540-2000 or 800-845-1507 in New England. Expensive. This deluxe hotel features a central location and many on-site amenities, such as a restaurant and lounge with entertainment. Open year-round; off-season rates available. Major credit cards accepted.

• *Red Horse Inn*, 28 Falmouth Heights Rd., Falmouth; 548-0053 or 1-800-628-3811. Expensive. Year-round deluxe accommodations including pool. Off-season rates available. Major credit cards accepted.

FALMOUTH (CONTINUED)

• *Sands of Time Motor Inn*, Main St., Woods Hole; 548-6300. Expensive. This deluxe motel overlooking Little Harbor in Woods Hole is minutes from all Woods Hole attractions. Private balconies. Open year-round. Visa and MasterCard.

• *Sea Crest Resort & Conference Center*, 350 Quaker Rd., N. Falmouth; 540-9400. Expensive. This deluxe hotel and conference center is on Old Silver Beach, considered by many the nicest town beach. Features include conference facilities, tennis courts, putting greens, and a game room. Year-round.

• *Sea Gull Inn*, 335 Grand Ave., Falmouth Heights; 540-7097. Moderate. Efficiency units; water view; continental breakfast. Visa and MasterCard.

• *Sea Shell Inn*, 88 Menahunt Rd., 548-6941 or 800-878-8024. Moderate. Oceanfront apartment units; private beach.

• *Shore Haven Motor Lodge*, 321 Shore St., Falmouth; 548-1765. Moderate. Close to beaches and shopping.

• *Shoreway Acres Motel*, Shore St., Falmouth; 540-3000 or 1-800-352-7100. Expensive. This deluxe motel features indoor and outdoor swimming pools, badminton, and croquet. Near downtown shops. Open year-round; off-season rates. Major credit cards.

• *Sleepy Hollow Motor Inn*, Woods Hole Rd., Woods Hole; 548-1986. Moderate. Close to beaches and shopping.

• *Sunset Motel*, Rte. 28A, N. Falmouth; 563-3661. Moderate. Close to beach; pool. Off-season rates.

• *Surfside*, 134 Menauhant Rd., Falmouth Heights; 548-0313 or 1-800-341-5700. Moderate. Close to beaches and shopping.

• *The Tides Motel*, Grand Ave., Falmouth Heights; 548-3126. Moderate to expensive. Close to water and shopping.

• *Town & Beach Motel*, 382 Main St., Falmouth; 548-1380. Moderate. Walk to all activities. Off-season rates. Visa/MasterCard.

MASHPEE

• *La Plaza Del Sol Motel*, Rte. 130, Mashpee; 477-0238. Moderate. Deluxe motel units and apartments; pool, tennis.

• *New Seabury Resort and Conference Center*, Box B-CC, New Seabury; 477-9111. Expensive. Located on a 2000-acre peninsula, this resort has 36 holes of golf, 16 tennis courts, private beaches, miles of walking and jogging trails. Each of the 13 "villages" in New Seabury is different—4 are private homes. Marina, restaurant, and lounge. Open year-round.

• *Popponesset Inn*, Box B-CC, Rock Landing Rd., New Seabury; 477-1100. Expensive. Rustic Cape Cod cottages located on the ocean; same amenities as the New Seabury Resort. Seasonal, open May to October. Cottages have fireplaces.

• *River Bend Motel & Cottages*, Great Neck Rd.; 477-1900. Moderate. Close to beaches and shopping.

• *Southcape Resort & Club*, Rte. 28, Mashpee; 477-4700. Moderate to expensive. Time-sharing condominiums with fireplace, washer/dryer, pools, tennis courts, barbecues, and saunas.

• *Town Line Motor Inn*, Rte. 28; 428-6433. Moderate. Close to shopping.

SANDWICH

• *The Cedars*, 19 Ploughed Neck Rd., E. Sandwich; 888-0464. Housekeeping cottages for 2–6 persons. Swimming pool, close to beach. Pets allowed.

• *Country Acres Motel*, Rte. 6A, Sandwich; 888-2878. Moderate. Close to beaches and shopping.

- ***Dun Roamin'***, 5 John Ewer Rd., S. Sandwich; 477-0541 or 477-0859. Moderate. Lakefront cottages, private beach, fishing, good for children.
- ***Earl of Sandwich***, Rte. 6A, E. Sandwich; 888-1415. Moderate. Close to shopping and beaches.
- ***Oceanside-Waters Edge Cottages***, North Shore Blvd., E. Sandwich; 800-886-4998. Moderate to expensive. Heated 1–4 bedroom cottages, many oceanfront. Private beach, picnic tables.
- ***Old Colony Motel***, Rte. 6A, E. Sandwich; 888-9716. Moderate. Close to beaches and shopping.
- ***Peters Pond Park***, Cotuit Rd., S. Sandwich; 477-1775. Modern 3- and 4-bedroom, heated cottages on one of Cape Cod's finest lakes. Trout and bass fishing, boating, swimming. No pets.
- ***Pine Grove Cottages***, Rte. 6A, Box 74, E. Sandwich; 888-8179. Private cottages, modern appliances, pool. Pets welcome. Major credit cards.
- ***Sandwich Lodge***, Rte. 6A, Sandwich; 888-2275 or 1-800-282-5353. Moderate. Close to beaches and shopping.
- ***Sandy Neck Motel***, Rte. 6A, E. Sandwich; 362-3992. Moderate. Close to beaches.
- ***Shady Nook Inn***, Rte. 6A, Sandwich; 888-0409 or 1-800-338-5208. Moderate. Close to beaches and shopping.
- ***Spring Garden Motel***, 578 Rte. 6A, E. Sandwich; 888-0710. Moderate. View of tidal creek, beach nearby. Year-round. Major credit cards.
- ***Spring Hill Motor Lodge***, Rte. 6A, E. Sandwich; 888-1456. Moderate. Close to beaches and shopping.
- ***Surfside Cottages***, 191A North Shore Blvd., E. Sandwich; 888-1731 or 888-5875. Two-bedroom waterfront cottages on private beach. Fully equipped, fireplace, picnic tables, grill. Great fishing and boating.
- ***Whaleback Hill Cottages***, 376 Rte. 6A, E. Sandwich; 888-0338. Efficiency cottages, heated, TV, linens included. No pets. Near beaches, shops, golf courses, fishing. Open April to mid-October.

Campgrounds

BOURNE

- ***Bay View Campgrounds Inc.***, MacArthur Blvd.; 759-7610.
- ***Bourne Scenic Park***, off Rte. 6, Buzzards Bay; 759-7873. Numerous campsites; modern rest rooms, swimming, picnic areas, playground; located along Cape Cod Canal.

FALMOUTH

- ***Cape Cod Camping Club***, off Landers Rd.; 548-1458. Fully equipped, modern facilities.
- ***Resort Camplands International***, off Landers Rd.; 548-1458. Modern facilities, fully equipped.
- ***Sippewissett Campgrounds***, Palmer Ave.; 548-1971 or 548-2542. Fully equipped, modern facilities.

MASHPEE

- ***Otis Trailer Village***, off Rte. 151, on John's Pond; 477-0444. Playground, private beach, boats rentals. Open April to October.

SANDWICH

- *Dun Roamin' Trailer Park*, 5 John Ewer Rd., RR #2, S. Sandwich; 477-0541 or 477-0859. Beach and play area.
- *Peters Pond Park*, Cotuit Rd., Box 999; 477-1775. Located on a freshwater lake, this 105-acre park has 500 sites and can take RVs as well as pup tents. There are also cottages, cabins, or teepees for rent. Amenities include adult recreation building, playgrounds, laundry, boats for rent, large playing field, sports equipment, store, and teenage recreation room. No pets. Open April to October.
- *Scusset Beach Reservation*, near Jcts. 3 and 6; 888-0859. At Scusset Beach, 98 tent and trailer sites, playground, fishing pier, no reservations. Open year-round.
- *Shawme-Crowell State Forest*, Rte. 130 off Rte. 6A; 888-0351. There are 250 sites for tents or trailers, but there are no water or electrical hookups. No reservations—first-come–first-serve basis; no swimming, but you can use Scusset Beach. Open April to November.

Dining

BOURNE

- *Chart Room*, One Shore Rd., Cataumet; 563-5350. Moderate. This excellent restaurant specializes in seafood. Water view; casual dress. Serves lunch and dinner. Accepts major credit cards. Reservations are needed.
- *The Dolphin Inn*, 11 Buttermilk Way, Taylor Pt., Buzzards Bay; 759-7522. Inexpensive to moderate. Varied menu.
- *Finnie's Place*, 618 MacArthur Blvd., Pocasset; 564-4464. Inexpensive to moderate. Varied menu.
- *Grandma's Pie Restaurant*, N. Bourne Rotary, Buzzards Bay; 759-1111. Moderate. Serves lunch and dinner. Seafood and chicken. Casual dress; major credit cards accepted; no reservations needed.
- *Graziella's Pizza*, 375 Barlow's Landing; 563-5541. Inexpensive. Pizza.
- *HollyBerry's*, 254 Shore Rd., Monument Beach; 759-8955. Moderate. Family restaurant overlooking Back River of Monument Beach. Homemade soups and pies.
- *Lindsey's Seafood Restaurant*, 3138 Rte. 6; 759-5544. Inexpensive to moderate. Fish-and-chips.
- *Lobster Pot*, 3155 Rte. 6; 759-3876. Inexpensive. Fish-and-chips.
- *Lobster Trap Fish & Chips*, 290 Shore Rd.; 759-3992. Inexpensive. Fish-and-chips.
- *Mezza-Luna*, 253 Main St., Buzzards Bay; 759-4667. Inexpensive. This Italian restaurant features fine food; it also has a fine prime rib. Serves lunch and dinner; casual dress. Accepts major credit cards. Reservations are suggested on weekends.
- *Mitchell's*, 570 MacArthur Blvd.; 563-1811. Moderate. Seafood, steaks, pasta. Live entertainment.
- *Port O'Call*, 57 Main St., Bourne; 759-2166. Lunch and dinner specials, full liquor license. Weekend entertainment, dancing.

• *Quintal's Inc.*, 343 Scenic Hwy., Buzzards Bay; 759-7222. Inexpensive. Serves breakfast, lunch, and dinner; casual dress. Accepts major credit cards; reservations are needed.

• *The Bridge Restaurant*, New Bridge St., Sagamore; 888-8144. Moderate. Serves lunch and dinner; casual dress. Accepts major credit cards; reservations are needed.

• *Sandy's Restaurant*, Bourne Bridge, Buzzards Bay; 759-3088. Inexpensive. This seafood restaurant is a deal at any price, but the low price is an extra. Large portions; serves lunch and dinner. Casual dress; major credit cards accepted. No reservations needed.

FALMOUTH

• *Black Duck*, 73 Water St., Woods Hole; 548-9165. Inexpensive. Breakfast and lunch; dinner on weekends. Water view; casual dress. No reservations needed.

• *Captain Kidd*, 77 Water St., Woods Hole; 548-8563. Moderate. Water view; serves lunch and dinner. Casual dress; major credit cards accepted. Reservations are needed.

• *Christopher's*, 105 Davis Straits, Falmouth; 540-7176. Inexpensive. Serves breakfast, lunch, and dinner; casual dress. Reservations are not needed.

• *Clam Shack Harbor View Salt Box*, 227 Clinton Ave., Falmouth; 540-7758. Inexpensive. Water view; serves lunch and dinner. Casual dress; reservations are not needed.

• *Coonamessett Inn*, corner Jones and Gifford sts., Falmouth; 548-2300. Moderate. This restaurant is for those with a discerning taste and serves American regional food in four dining rooms (lunch and dinner); semiformal dress. Major credit cards accepted; reservations needed.

• *D'Angelo's Sandwich Shop*, 650 Main St., Falmouth; 548-8980. Inexpensive. Serves lunch and dinner; casual dress. Reservations are not needed.

• *Domenic's Ice Cream & Sandwich Shoppes*, 50 Davis Straits, Falmouth, 540-0162, and 170 Main St., Falmouth; 540-5234. Inexpensive. Serves lunch and dinner; casual dress. No reservations needed.

• *Dome Restaurant*, Woods Hole Rd., Woods Hole; 548-0800. Moderate. This restaurant is a local favorite. A Buckminster Fuller geodesic dome with a view of Vineyard Sound, the Dome serves exquisite food, featuring seafood, steak, and prime rib. Serves lunch and dinner; casual dress. Major credit cards accepted; reservations are needed.

• *Executive Restaurant at the Admiralty*, 53 Teaticket Hwy., E. Falmouth; 548-4240. Moderate. Serves lunch and dinner; casual dress. Major credit cards accepted; reservations are needed.

• *Falmouth Inn*, 824 Main St., Falmouth; 540-2500. Moderate. Serves breakfast and dinner; casual dress. Major credit cards accepted; reservations are necessary.

• *Fishmonger's Café*, 56 Water St., Woods Hole; 548-9148. Moderate. Water view, great seafood, a local hangout.

• *Flying Bridge Restaurant*, Scranton Ave., Falmouth; 548-2700. Moderate. Another of Falmouth's many fine restaurants on the water with a dockside view of Falmouth Harbor. Serves lunch and dinner featuring seafood and roast beef; semiformal dress. Major credit cards accepted; reservations are needed.

• *Garden Room at the Quality Inn*, 291 Jones Rd., Falmouth; 540-2000. Inexpensive. Serves breakfast, lunch, and dinner. Casual dress; reservations are needed.

• *Golden Sails Chinese Restaurant*, 143-145 Main St., E. Falmouth; 548-3521. Inexpensive. Serves breakfast, lunch, and dinner; casual dress. Major credit cards accepted; reservations are needed.

FALMOUTH (CONTINUED)

- *Golden Swan*, 323 Main St., Falmouth; 540-6580. Moderate. Serves dinner in a European atmosphere; casual dress. Accepts all major credit cards; reservations are needed.
- *Grasmere Pub*, 327 Gifford St., Falmouth; 548-9861. Moderate. Serves lunch and dinner; casual dress. Accepts all major credit cards; reservations are needed.
- *Hearth 'n Kettle*, 874 Main St., Falmouth; 548-6111. Inexpensive. Serves breakfast, lunch, and dinner; casual dress. No reservations needed.
- *Landfall*, 2 Water St., Woods Hole; 548-1758. Moderate. Serves lunch and dinner; water view; casual dress. Accepts major credit cards; reservations are needed.
- *Lawrence's*, Nantucket Ave., Falmouth; 540-9600. Moderate. Serves lunch and dinner; casual dress. Major credit cards accepted. Reservations are needed.
- *Liam Maguire's*, 273 Main St., Falmouth; 548-0285. Moderate. Seafood, fish, steaks.
- *McMenamy's*, 70 Davis Straits, Falmouth; 540-2115. Inexpensive. This restaurant isn't fancy, but it is good for those who like fried seafood. Serves lunch and dinner; inside and outside dining; casual dress.
- *The Nimrod*, Dillingham Ave., Falmouth; 540-4132. Moderate. Charming old inn features small rooms with fireplaces. Continental cuisine and seafood; serves dinner. Casual dress; accepts all major credit cards; reservations are needed.
- *Papa Gino's*, Falmouth Mall, Falmouth; 540-4502. Inexpensive. Pizza.
- *Paul's Pizza & Seafood*, 14 Benham Rd.; 548-5838. Inexpensive. Serves dinner.
- *Peachtree Circle Farm Stand*, 881 Old Palmer Ave., Falmouth; 548-2354. Inexpensive. Serves lunch; casual dress; no reservations needed.
- *Peking Palace*, 452 Main St., Falmouth; 540-8204. Moderate. Serves lunch and dinner; casual dress. Accepts major credit cards; reservations are needed.
- *Pie in the Sky Café & Bakery*, 10 Water St., Woods Hole; 540-5475. Inexpensive. Water view; serves lunch and dinner; casual dress; no reservations needed.
- *The Quarterdeck*, 164 Main St., Falmouth; 548-9900. Specializes in seafood. Across from Town Hall.
- *Regatta of Falmouth by the Sea*, Scranton Ave., Falmouth; 548-5400. Expensive. This restaurant at the mouth of Falmouth Harbor features American and French food. Serves dinner, worth the expense. Formal and casual dress. Accepts all major credit cards; reservations are needed.
- *Seafood Sam's*, 350 Palmer Ave., E. Falmouth; 540-7877. Inexpensive. Fish-and-chips.
- *Shucker's World Famous Restaurant,* 91A Water St., Woods Hole; 540-3850. Inexpensive to moderate. Seafood, raw bar, lobsters, sandwiches.
- *Silver Lounge*, Rte. 28A, N. Falmouth; 563-2410. Inexpensive. Serves lunch and dinner. Casual dress; no reservations needed.
- *The Wharf*, Grand Ave., Falmouth Heights; 548-2772. Inexpensive to moderate. This restaurant, above the Casino-by-the-Sea nightclub in Falmouth Heights, features a fantastic view of Vineyard Sound. Sandwiches and seafood at lunch and dinner; casual dress. Reservations are needed.
- *Willow Field Tavern*, Rtes. 28A and 151, N. Falmouth; 564-5029. Moderate. Serves lunch and dinner; casual dress. Major credit cards accepted; no reservations needed.
- *Winston's*, 97 Spring Bar's Rd., Falmouth; 548-0590. Inexpensive. Serves lunch and dinner; casual dress. Accepts major credit cards; no reservations needed.

MASHPEE

- *Bobby Byrne's Pub*, Mashpee Commons, Mashpee; 477-0600. Inexpensive. Casual; burgers, sandwiches, full menu until midnight. Lunch, dinner. Credit cards accepted.
- *Cefalo's*, Mashpee Commons, Rte. 28, Mashpee; 477-5889. Serves breakfast and lunch.
- *Cherrystones Restaurant & Lounge*, Rte. 151; 477-4481. Inexpensive. Seafood, steaks. Open year-round.
- *The Flume*, Rte. 130, Lake Ave.; 477-1456. Inexpensive. Lunch, dinner. Year-round; take-out available.
- *Gone Tomatoes*, Mashpee Commons, Rte. 28, Mashpee; 477-8100. Italian cuisine.
- *New Seabury Restaurant*, Shore Dr. W., New Seabury; 477-9111. Expensive. Continental cuisine; lovely ocean view. Lunch and dinner served. Dancing and entertainment in the lounge. Seasonal.
- *Popponesset Inn*, Shore Dr. W., New Seabury; 477-1100. Expensive. Nice setting on Nantucket Sound. Lunch, dinner; seasonal. No reservations accepted. Entertainment and dancing.
- *Ratoli's Restaurant*, Rte. 28, Deer Crossing; 477-4011. Inexpensive. Casual; pizza, subs. Breakfast, lunch, dinner. Year-round.
- *Richard's Pub*, 100 Great Neck Rd., Mashpee; 477-1900. DJs and dancing Thursday–Sunday.

SANDWICH

- *The Bee-Hive Tavern*, 406 Rte. 6A; 833-1184. Moderate. Voted best family restaurant on Upper Cape; sandwiches, salads, breakfast on Sat. & Sun.
- *Bobby Byrne's Pub*, Rtc. 6A and Tupper Rd., Sandwich Village; 888-6088. Inexpensive. Publike atmosphere. General menu of burgers, sandwiches, soups. Open for lunch, dinner, year-round. Sunday brunch includes the *Boston Globe*.
- *Dan'l Webster Inn*, Old Main St., Sandwich Center; 888-3622. Moderate. A four-star country inn, fine wine list, award-winning menu. Entertainment offered nightly; 42 guest rooms available. Open year-round. Serves breakfast, lunch, and dinner.
- *The Deli*, Newman Village, Sandwich; 888-0568. Inexpensive. Good sub sandwiches.
- *Horizons on Cape Cod Bay*, Town Neck Rd., Sandwich Village; 888-6166. Inexpensive. Overlooks the mouth of the canal—watch boats coming and going on the outside deck. Decor is brass, wood, and cathedral ceilings; lots of glass to enjoy the view. Seafood menu with a specialty in crab salads. Open year-round for lunch and dinner (take a walk on the beach after dinner!).
- *Marshland Restaurant*, Rte. 6A, Sandwich Village; 888-9824. Inexpensive. Casual. Small booths and counter stools. Very popular spot for breakfast, and they are busy for lunch and dinner, too. A local favorite. Open year-round.
- *Meetinghouse Deli and Pizza*, Quaker Meeting House Rd., S. Sandwich; 477-4192. Inexpensive. Delivery.
- *Merchants Square Deli*, Merchants Row, Sandwich; 888-7717. Inexpensive. Deli.
- *Pizza by Evan*, 315 Cotuit Rd., New Village Square, Sandwich; 888-5944. Inexpensive. Pizza.

SANDWICH (CONTINUED)

• *Sandy Neck Restaurant*, 679 Rte. 6A, E. Sandwich; 362-2943. Inexpensive. On the way to Sandy Neck Beach. A popular, casual place with the locals. Breakfast, lunch, and dinner; grilled items, sandwiches, and soups.

• *Seafood Sam's on the Canal*, Coast Guard Rd., Sandwich Village; 888-4629. Inexpensive to moderate. Fried seafood; breakfast, lunch, dinner. MasterCard and Visa accepted.

• *Sweet Tomatoes*, 148 Rte. 6A; 888-5979. Inexpensive. Neapolitan style pizza, Greek salads, ice cream.

• *Tiki Hawaii*, 331 Cotuit Rd., S. Sandwich; 888-3543. Moderate. Chinese food.

Entertainment

Music & Stage

BOURNE

• *Bourne Choral Groupe*, Bourne Community Building; 759-3272. Frequent concerts; call for more information.

• *Bourne town concerts*, Buzzards Bay Park; call Town Hall (759-4486) or Chamber of Commerce (759-3613). Outdoor summer concerts. Free; usually held Thursday nights. Great for the family!

• *Theater on the Bay Inc.*, 1 Trowbridge Rd.; 759-0977.

FALMOUTH

• *Cape Cod Conservatory of Dance and Music*, Depot Ave.; 540-0611. Classes in art, music, dance; performances.

• *Falmouth Music Association,* 548-3863. Chamber music concerts; call for a schedule.

• *Falmouth Town Band*, 548-8500. Outdoor concerts; call for more information.

• *Highfield Theater*, Highfield Dr., Falmouth; 548-0668. Excellent local theater.

• *Woods Hole Folk Society*, Water St.; 540-0320. Excellent folk concerts, October–May.

SANDWICH

• *Cape Cod Chorale*, 888-1092. This Sandwich singing group offers a variety of concerts; call for more information.

• *Glasstown Players*, Sandwich Community Theater; 888-6300. Year-round performances.

• *Heritage Plantation,* at corner of Pine and Grove sts.; 888-3300. Outdoor jazz concerts throughout the summer months.

• *Let's Go! Theater*, Sandwich Community Theater; 888-5300. Focus is on children and instruction; performances given.

• *Sandwich Town Band*, 888-0157. Weekly summer performances.

Nightlife

BOURNE

• ***Chart Room,*** Shore Rd., Cataumet; 563-5350. Piano bar; nice atmosphere; spectacular view of Red Brook Harbor; restaurant and lounge.

FALMOUTH

• ***Admiralty Inn Executive Lounge***, Rte. 28, Teaticket; 548-4240. Nightclub; light rock.
• ***The Boat House***, Scranton Ave., Falmouth Harbor; 548-7800. Piano music, great view; perfect to just sit and relax.
• ***Brandy's at the Quality Inn***, Jones Rd., Falmouth; 540-2000. Top 40 music.
• ***Carleton Lounge***, Sandwich Rd., E. Falmouth; 548-0025. Comedy, dancing, live music.
• ***Casino-by-the-Sea,*** Grand Ave., Falmouth Heights; 548-0777. Top-notch live rock music.
• ***Century Irish Pub***, 29 Locust St., Falmouth; 548-0196. Live Irish music.
• ***Irish Embassy***, 734 Teaticket, E. Falmouth; 540-6656. Traditional Irish music.
• ***Liam Maguire's Irish Pub and Entertainment***, 273 Main St.; 548-0285. Live music.
• ***The Nimrod***, Dillingham Ave., Falmouth; 540-4132. Piano, trio on weekends.

MASHPEE

• ***New Seabury Inn***, Red Brook Rd., New Seabury (part of resort complex); 477-9111. Lounge with entertainment and dancing.
• ***Popponesset Inn***, Shore Rd., Popponesset (part of resort complex); 477-1100. Live music, sing-alongs and dancing.

SANDWICH

• ***Bobby Byrne's Pub***, Purity Shopping Center off Rte. 6A; 888-6088. Summer hangout for college students and a favorite among the locals; restaurant and bar.
• ***Captain's Chair***, Gallo Rd.; 888-6977. Piano bar; near the water.
• ***Dan'l Webster Inn***, Old Main St.; 888-3622. Dancing and popular music; restaurant and lounge.
• ***Horizons***, Town Neck Rd., on the beach; 888-6166. Water view; a favorite summer watering hole.
• ***The Wayside Pub & Eatery***, 79 Rte. 130, Forestdale; 539-0091.

Movie Theaters

BOURNE

• ***Buzzards Bay Theater,*** Main St., Buzzards Bay; 759-3212.

FALMOUTH

• ***Falmouth Mall Cinema,*** Falmouth Mall; 540-2169. Three movie theaters.
• ***Nickelodeon Cinemas,*** Rte. 151, Hatchville; 563-2208. Five movie theaters.

MASHPEE

• ***Mashpee Commons Cinemas,*** Rte. 28; 477-7333.

Museums & Historic Sites

BOURNE

- *Aptucxet Trading Post,* Aptucxet Rd., Bourne; 759-9487. Birthplace of American free enterprise. The first business contract in America was signed here. The village features Pilgrim Spring, the trading post, Solar Evaporation Salt Works, Jefferson Windmill, and the Gideon Ellis Tavern.
- *Buzzards Bay Train Depot*, Main St., Buzzards Bay. Built in 1914, this depot replaced the original one built in 1872.
- *Cataumet Pier*, 67 Redbrook Harbor Rd., Cataumet. The site of one of the nation's first labor strikes, in 1864. Demands were made to double wages from 15 cents to 30 cents per hour. This laid the foundation for trade unions.
- *Massachusetts Maritime Academy*, Buzzards Bay; 759-5761. Nation's oldest continuously operating maritime academy. Has a 55-acre waterfront campus and a library, with an exhibit. Open to the public 9 A.M. to 4 P.M. weekdays.
- *The Old House*, Head of the Bay Rd., Buzzards Bay. Built by the Gibbs family that settled the head of the bay in the 1600s.
- *Railroad Bridge*, Buzzards Bay. Erected in 1935; spans Cape Cod Canal.

FALMOUTH

- *Bradley House*, Woods Hole Rd., Woods Hole; 548-7270. Old sea captain's home now run by the Woods Hole Historical Society. Museum has impressive collection of turn-of-the-century paintings, photographs, and artifacts.
- *Falmouth Historical Society,* Palmer Ave., at Village Green, Falmouth; 548-4857. Two impressive historic homes and gardens; whaling items, portraits.
- *Friends Meeting House*, Rte. 28A, W. Falmouth. Built in 1775; cemetery on grounds.
- *Katharine Lee Bates House*, W. Main St., Falmouth; 548-7611. Open June–September. Birthplace of author of *America the Beautiful.*
- *Marine Biological Laboratory Tour*, Woods Hole; 548-3705, ext. 623. Call for reservations, mid June–July.
- *National Marine Fisheries Aquarium*, Woods Hole; 548-7684. Display tanks with fish and shellfish from the region, harbor seals during the summer months.
- *Oceanquest*, Water St., Woods Hole; 800-37-OCEAN. Ninety-minute trips out of Woods Hole with educators, scientists and mariners.
- *Woods Hole Oceanographic Institution*, Woods Hole. Scientific and historical exhibit on the *Titanic* and other oceanic research exhibits. Nearby is Marine Fisheries Aquarium on Water Street. Guided tours of the research areas at the Marine Biological Laboratory (548-1400), which is housed in the 150-year-old Candle House. Visit their Exhibit Center at 15 School St.; 289-2252 or 289-2663.

MASHPEE

- *Indian Museum*, Rte. 130, Mashpee Center; 477-1536. Located by the herring run, the historical museum contains Indian tools, artifacts, and clothing. Open May–October.
- *Old Indian Meeting House*, Rte. 28; 477-0208 or 477-1456. Built in 1684. Open June–October, weekends.

SANDWICH

- *Benjamin Nye House*, Old County Rd., E. Sandwich; 888-4213. Built in 1685, this house provides a good example of life in Colonial days, with displays of fur-

niture and household goods. Open June to October, 10 A.M.–4 P.M. weekdays, 1
P.M.–4 P.M. Sundays.
• *First Church of Christ*, Main St. Noted for its Christopher Wren's spire.
• *First Parish Meeting House*, corner of Main and River sts. Established by
the Pilgrims in 1638; famous for its bell and tower clock.
• *Green Briar Nature Center*, 6 Discovery Hill Rd., E. Sandwich; 888-6870.
This center is operated by the Burgess Society and has nature walks (Old Briar
Patch Trail is a self-guided one-mile trail), story times, herb festivals, and work-
shops. See adjacent Green Briar Jam Kitchen, which makes jams, jellies, and pre-
serves with turn-of-the-century cooking methods.
• *Heritage Plantation*, Pine and Grove sts.; 888-3300. A 76-acre landscaped
estate; open seven days a week from May to October. "A diversified museum of
Americana whose subjects range from military history to horticulture and folk
art"; a working carousel; classic collection of antique autos; more than 1000 varieties of trees, shrubs, and flowers on grounds; wooded trails; programs for children (see listing under Children's Activities).
• *The Hoxie House*, Rte. 130, Water St.; 888-1173. Open June–September; this
17th-century saltbox is thought to be Cape Cod's oldest house; restored to its
original condition with authentic dishes, furniture, and other household items.
• *Old Cemetery Point*, Grove St. Sandwich's first cemetery—oldest marker
dates to 1683.
• *Sandwich Glass Museum*, 129 Main St.; 888-0251. Sandwich is famous for its
19th-century glass factories, and this museum displays some of that glass manu-
factured between 1825 to 1888. Exhibits of glassmaker tools, photos, and other
historical artifacts. Open April to November, daily 9:30 A.M.–4:30 P.M.
• *Thomas Dexter's Grist Mill*, Old Main St., Sandwich Center. A restored
working mill—you can buy ground corn here and pick up some recipes, too.
Open daily during the summer.
• *Thornton Burgess Museum*, 4 Water St. on the edge of Shawme Pond; 888-
6870 or 888-4668. Established by the Thornton W. Burgess Society to "inspire in
youth a reverence for wildlife and a concern for the environment" (Burgess, a
children's author and naturalist, was born in Sandwich). Open April to December. The museum sponsors many special events and activities for children.
(There is a story time during July and August; look in the Seasonal Events section
for more information or call the museum.)
• *Wing Homestead*, Spring Hill Rd., E. Sandwich. Built in 1641, this house displays 17th-century antiques and artifacts. Open June to September on weekdays
10 A.M.–4 P.M.; 833-1540.
• *Yesteryear Doll Museum*, Old Main St.; 888-1711. An international collection of rare old dolls and dollhouses furnished in the style of early eras; open
May 15 to October 31, 10 A.M.–5 P.M., and Sundays, 1 P.M.–5 P.M.

Seasonal Events

BOURNE

• *Bourne Scallop Festival*, Buzzards Bay Park. Entertainment, tons of scallops,
gift booths; held on one of the first weekends in September. For more information, call 888-3300.

FALMOUTH

• *Barnstable County Fair*, Rte. 151, E. Falmouth. Last week in July; New England County fair, featuring rides, games, and agricultural events, 563-3200.

FALMOUTH (CONTINUED)

- *Christmas By the Sea,* a weekend of seasonal activities ending with a Christmas parade. Call Falmouth Chamber of Commerce at 548-8500 for more information.
- *Falmouth Road Race.* Third weekend in August; major running race (7.1 miles); 540-7000. Attracts such world-class runners as Olympic-medalist Joan Benoit.
- *Fireworks.* July 4, Falmouth Heights Beach. Typically a big day in town; fireworks blown off of barge in Vineyard Sound.
- *Band Concerts.* Each Friday night at the Margaret E. Noonan Park, Main St., 7-8:30 P.M. from June through August. Open Air Band Concerts on Thursday nights at 8 P.M., Scranton Ave., Falmouth Harbor, Marina Park.
- *Falmouth Street Fair*, on Main St. Sometime in the first two weeks of July.

MASHPEE

- *Annual Mashpee Wampanoag Pow-Wow*, Rte. 130, Mashpee Center. Held on the weekend closest to July 4. Native crafts, food, canoe races, clambake, Indian dances, and traditional dress.
- *Sandcastle Competition*, South Cape Beach. Held in August.
- *Christmas Parade.* December. Music, activities in stores.
- *New Seabury.* This 2000-acre peninsula has many seasonal events. Among them, Fourth of July parade, Harvest Fair in the fall with hay rides and arts and crafts, Popponesset Marketplace Heart Fund Day in June. Call New Seabury offices at 477-9400 for more information.

SANDWICH

- *Thornton W. Burgess Society*, 4 Water St.; 888-6870 or 888-4668. Society operates the Thornton Burgess Museum and the Green Briar Nature Center, which offer a variety of seasonal events; Spring Herb Festival, May Day Festival, Peter Rabbit's Egg Rolling Relay Race, Peter Rabbit's Summer Animal Fair, Whale of a Weekend; June Lawn Party, Farmer's Fall Market, and Fall Festival (hay rides, live music, and more), Thanksgiving Celebration, Victorian Christmas.
- *Historic House Tour.* Sponsored by the Sandwich Women's Club, usually in the fall.
- *Heritage Plantation*, Grove and Pine sts.; 888-3300. Annual June Antique Auto Show, Annual Antique Show in September, May Rhododendron Festival.
- *Christmas in Sandwich Village.* Tree lighting, special displays, and bellringers; early December; call Town Hall (759-6000) for more information.

Children's Activities

BOURNE

- *Bourne Kart Track*, 343 MacArthur Blvd., Rte. 28; 759-2636. Go-carts and other amusements.
- *Bourne Sports World,* MacArthur Blvd., Rte. 28; 759-5500. Bumper cars, kiddie rides, video games, miniature golf.
- *Water Wizz,* Rte. 6 & 28, East Wareham (just outside Bourne); 295-3255. If the kids get tired of the natural beauty of the Cape's beaches, there's always the commercial alternative of this water park.

FALMOUTH

- *Cape Cod Children's Museum,* 137 Teaticket Hwy.; 457-4667.

- *Cape Cod Coastal Canoeing,* 36 Spectacle Pond Dr., E. Falmouth; 564-4051. Half-day canoe adventures from the Upper Cape to Lower Cape, all equipment provided.
- *Oceanquest,* Water St., Woods Hole; 1-800-37-OCEAN. Ninety min. discovery voyages for children and adults of all ages; hands on marine education.
- *Ryan's Family Amusement Center*, 23 Town Hall Square; 540-4877. Bowling, video games.

MASHPEE

- *Playgrounds*, Rte. 130 behind the Recreation Center Building—basketball court and playground. Davis School behind Town Hall—playground and baseball field.
- *North American Soccer Camp*. Day camp held in August; call 477-2777 for registration and information.
- *Mashpee Recreation Department*. Summer program includes swimming lessons, tennis lessons, volleyball, and arts and crafts. The Recreation Department also lends out sports equipment such as rackets, balls, bats— a deposit and a two-week advance notice requested. Call 477-2777.
- *Herring Run*, on Rte. 130. Always a favorite with children in the spring when the herring are swimming upstream.

SANDWICH

- *Thornton W. Burgess Museum*, 4 Water St.; 888-4668. One of the best sources for educational and fun year-round activities for children on Cape Cod—from nature walks, story times with live animals, arts and crafts classes, and natural history programs to special events such as Peter Rabbit's Animal Fair in August and Egg Rolling Relay Races in April. All activities are planned with a creative flair. Call the museum for schedule of seasonal events and classes.
- *Green Briar Nature Center*, 6 Discovery Hill; 888-6870. This is also operated by the Thornton W. Burgess Society; programs include nature walks on Saturday mornings, story times, natural history classes, and special events.
- *Sandwich Library*, Main St.; 888-0625. Puppet shows and story hours; check at the library for times and dates or check local papers.
- *Heritage Plantation*, Grove and Pines sts.; 888-3300. Nature crafts classes, educational programs, a 1912 hand-carved, wooden merry-go-round that children can ride, nature trails.
- *Blueberry Picking*. Sandwich is one of the best places on the Cape for blueberries; there are several "pick your own" farms, but they have no phone numbers. Call the Chamber of Commerce for information or watch for signs along Route 6A.
- *Sandwich Community School,* 888-5300. Camp program that features a variety of sports, as well as dance, theater and computer workshops.

Shops

Art Galleries

BOURNE

Cataumet Art Center, 76 Scraggy Neck Rd. (off Rte. 28); 563-5434. Twenty area artists exhibited in various mediums: watercolors, oil, handwoven apparel, photography, ceramics, glass.

FALMOUTH

- *Falmouth Artists Guild*, 744 Main St., Falmouth; 540-3304. Continuous exhibitions.
- *Woods Hole Gallery,* 14 School St., Woods Hole; 548-7594. Assorted offerings.
- *Woods Hole Handworks*, 68 Water St., Woods Hole; 540-5291. Handworks.

SANDWICH

- *Beautiful Feet Books & Gifts*, 139 Main St., 833-8626. A store that not only offers a unique collection of books and gifts, it is owned and operated by the Berg family and their children.
- *Picture This!* 136 Merchants Row; 888-4600. Assorted offerings.
- *Sandwich Art Gallery,* 153 Main St.; 833-2098. Limited editions, folk art, originals, Cape artists.

Craft & Specialty Shops

BOURNE

- *Cape Cod Glass Works*, 845 Sandwich Rd., Sagamore; 888-9262. Assorted offerings.

FALMOUTH

- *Market Bookshop*, 15 Depot Ave., Falmouth; 548-5636. General bookstore specializing in New England and marine books.
- *Uncle Bill's Country Store*, Rte. 28A, N. Falmouth, 564-4355; and 606 W. Falmouth Hwy., Falmouth, 540-2489. Assorted offerings.
- *Woods Hole Handworks*, 68 Water St., Woods Hole; 540-5291. Handcrafts.

MASHPEE

- *Bosun's Marine*, 100 Falmouth Rd.; 477-4626. Sportswear, nautical gifts, marine supplies.
- *Cape Cod Book Center*, Rte. 28, Merry Meadow By-Way; 477-9903.
- *Factory Shoe Mart*, Rte. 28, Deer Crossing; 477-0017. Brand names at a discount; large selection.
- *Gold's My Bag*, Deer Crossing; 477-9613. Popponesset Marketplace in the summer. Jewelry.
- *Mashpee Commons*, at the Mashpee Rotary where Rte. 28 & 151 intersect. More than 60 shops and restaurants in a delightful shopping area similar to Quincy Market in Boston. Some of the stores you can find here are: Peach Tree Designs for unusual gifts and decorative items for your home; Write Choice for gifts and cards; Carroll Reed and Irresistibles for women's clothing; and The Gap for everyone.
- *Popponesset Marketplace*, New Seabury Resort; 477-9111. A collection of 20 shops, boutiques, and outdoor cafés. It is open weekends in June, September, and October, and the full season is from the end of June till Labor Day. There are lots of activities here, including free outdoor concerts every Friday and Saturday.
- *Puritan Clothing*, Mashpee Commons; 477-4333. Traditional men's and women's clothes.

SANDWICH

- *The Christmas Shop*, Rte. 6A, E. Sandwich; 888-4095. Assorted gifts, Christmas items.
- *Circles & Stems*, 4 Merchant Rd., Sandwich; 888-5111. Unique variety of gifts. Year-round.

• *Cranberry Craft Shop*, 385 Rte. 6A, E. Sandwich; 888-6338. Cranberry glass, jellies, craft supplies, souvenirs.
• *Giving Tree Gallery and Sculpture Garden*, 550 Rte. 6A; 888-5446. Over 70 artists concentrating on nature; jewelry, outdoor sculpture garden, nature walk on 4 acres overlooking Scorton Creek salt marsh, home accessories.
• *The Little Country Store*, 679 Rte. 6A, Sandwich; 362-8357. Country crafts and gifts.
• *Picture This*, 136 Merchants Row, Sandwich; 888-4600. Framing gallery.
• *Heather House*, 350 Rte. 6A, E. Sandwich; 888-2034. A special little shop with country gifts and antiques.

Antiques

BOURNE
• *Marketplace*, 61 Main St., Buzzards Bay; 759-2114. Assorted antiques, collectibles, and furniture.

FALMOUTH
• *Aurora Borealis Antiques*, 104 Queens Buyway, Falmouth; 540-3385. Assorted antiques, specializing in early glass, furniture, prints.
• *The Beach Rose,* 35 N. Main St.; 548-1012. Assorted antiques and collectibles.
• *Clipper Ship Antiques of Falmouth,* 79 Davis Straits, E. Falmouth; 540-1738. Assorted antiques, used furniture. Also estate and insurance appraisals.
• *Red Barn Antiques,* 681 W. Falmouth Hwy., W. Falmouth; 548-4440. Assorted antiques, furniture, glass and china.
• *Sophisticated Junk & Antiques Shop,* 108 Kind, Falmouth; 548-1250. Assorted antiques.
• *Uncle Bill's Country Store,* Rte. 28A, N. Falmouth; 564-4355. Assorted antiques.
• *The Village Barn Antiques Co-op,* Rte. 28A, W. Falmouth; 540-3215. Eight dealers in old barn, variety of antiques and collectibles.
• *Wingate Crossing,* 190 Rte. 28A; 540-8723. Country antiques featured in an 18th century barn.

SANDWICH
• *Heather House,* 350 Rte. 6A, E. Sandwich; 888-2034. Assorted antiques.
• *Heritage Antiques,* Maypop Lane, 151 Rte. 6A; 888-1230. Jewelry, sterling.
• *Old Kings Row Antiques,* 158 Rte. 6A; 833-1395. Paintings, clocks, 18th and 19th century furniture.
• *The Brown Jug Antiques,* 155 Main St.; 833-1088. Straffordshire china and authentic glass.
• *Paul Madden Antiques*, 146 Old Main St.; Sandwich Village; 888-6434. Appointment advisable; scrimshaw, Nantucket baskets, folk art, furniture.
• *Dunbar House and Homespun Garden,* 1 Water St.; 833-2485. Antiques, jewelry, gifts, and also a British tea room.
• *H. Richard Strand Antiques,* Town Hall Square; 888-3230. Antique furniture, china, lamps.
• *Madden & Company,* 16 Jarves St.; 888-3663. Antiques, folk art, garden accessories, gifts.

Sports & Recreation

Baseball

FALMOUTH

- ***Falmouth Commodores***: Cape Cod Baseball League. One of the best summer leagues in the country, this league has nurtured many major league stars. The Commodores play games at Guv Fuller Field. For more information, call the recreation department at 548-0090.

Biking

BOURNE

- ***True Wheel Cycles,*** 2 Williams Ave., Pocasset; 564-4807. Bike rentals.

FALMOUTH

- The ***Shining Sea Bikeway*** offers an excellent course between Falmouth and Woods Hole.
- Bike rentals are available at ***Holiday Cycles***, 465 Grand Ave., Falmouth Heights, 540-3549; ***Bill's Bike Shop***, 847 E. Main St., Falmouth, 548-7979; and ***Art's Bike Shop***, 75 Country Rd., N. Falmouth; 563-7379 or 800-563-7379.

MASHPEE

- ***Popponesset Bike Shop***, Mall Way, Popponesset Marketplace; 477-9111. Bike rentals.

SANDWICH

- ***Cape Cod Canal***. Access roads are clearly marked along the Cape Cod Canal bike trail; access in Sandwich is off Freezer Road on the west side of the boat basin near the U.S. Army Corps of Engineers Observation Station.
- ***East End Cycle Rental,*** 2 Freezer Rd.; 200 yards from the Cape Cod Canal Trail; 888-3444 or 800-675-6107.
- There is also biking at ***Scusset Beach State Reservation*** on Scusset Beach Road and at ***Shawme Crowell State Forest*** off Route 130 near the canal and Sandwich Marina.

Bowling

FALMOUTH

- ***Ryan's Family Amusement Center***, Town Hall Square; 540-4877. Candlepin bowling, game room.

Curling

FALMOUTH

- ***Cape Cod Curling Club***, Highfield Dr., Falmouth; 540-2414.

Fishing

BOURNE

Fishing tackle and supplies are available from the following:
- *Biff's Bait and Tackle Shop*, Rte. 6A, Sagamore; 833-2221.
- *Cape Cod Charlie's Bait & Tackle*, 340 Scenic Hwy., Buzzards Bay; 759-2611.
- *Cape Marine Inc.*, 304 Shore Rd., Monument Beach; 759-4455.
- *Kingman Yacht Charters*, Cataumet; 563-7136 or 800-732-2667. Sail and power boats for charter.
- *Maco's Bait & Tackle*, Cranberry Hwy., Buzzards Bay; 759-9836. Launching ramp, boats and motors, rod repair.
- *Red Top Sporting Goods*, 265 Main St., Buzzards Bay; 759-3371.

FALMOUTH

For fishing tackle and supplies, try these three stores:
- *Eastman's Sport & Tackle*, 145 Main St., Falmouth; 548-6900.
- *Green Pond Fish 'n Gear*, 366 Menauhant Rd., E. Falmouth; 548-2573 or 800-895-2573.
- *Gun and Tackle*, 56 Scranton Ave., Falmouth; 548-0143.

If you're interested in chartering a fishing boat, we suggest the following:
- *Patriot Party Boats*, 227 Clinton Ave., Falmouth; 548-2626 or 800-734-0088.

SANDWICH

- *Canal Marine Inc.*, 20 Freezer Rd., Sandwich; 888-0096. Fishing tackle and supplies.
- *Sandwich Ship Supply*, 68 Tupper Rd., Sandwich; 888-0200. Fishing tackle and supplies.

Golf

BOURNE

- *Pocasset Golf Club*, off County Rd.; 563-7171. 18 holes, par 72, 6200 yards.

FALMOUTH

- *Balleymeade Country Club,* 125 Falmouth Woods Rd., N. Falmouth; 540-4005. 18 holes, par 72, 6298 yards.
- *Cape Cod Country Club*, Theater Rd., Falmouth; 563-9842. 18 holes, par 71, 6500 yards.
- *Falmouth Country Club*, Carriage Shop Rd., E. Falmouth; 548-3211. 18 holes, par 72, 6535 yards.
- *Paul Harney Golf Course*, Rte. 151, Hatchville; 563-9800. 18 holes, par 60, about 3600 yards.
- *Woodbriar*, Gifford St., Falmouth; 540-1600. 9 holes, par 27, about 1450 yards.

MASHPEE

- *New Seabury Country Club*, Mall Way, New Seabury; 477-9111. There are two courses: **Championship**: 18 holes, par 72, 6909 yards, semiprivate. **Executive**: 18 holes, par 70, 5930 yards, public.
- *Quashnet Valley,* Old Barnstable Rd., off Rte. 151, Mashpee; 477-4412. 18 holes, par 72, 6302 yards.

SANDWICH

• *Holly Ridge*, Country Club Rd., off Race Ln., S. Sandwich; 428-5577. 18 holes, par 54, 3000 yards, public.
• *Round Hill*, Round Hill Rd., E. Sandwich; 888-3384. 18 holes, par 72, 6288 yards, public.

Hiking & Nature Trails

BOURNE

• *Bourne Scenic Park*, Rte. 6, Buzzards Bay. Located along Cape Cod Canal; swimming, camping, hiking trails.
• *Bourne Town Forest*, off County Rd., not far from Back River. Trails, hiking.

FALMOUTH

• *Ashumet Holly Reservation*, off Rte. 151, E. Falmouth. Imported holly trees; well manicured; hiking, trails; 40 acres.
• *Beebe Woods*, Depot Ave., Falmouth. Hiking and trails; 400 acres.
• *Goodwill Park*, off Rte. 28. Picnic areas, playgrounds, hiking, trails; 86 acres.
• *Falmouth Town Forest*, adjacent to Goodwill Park. Trails, hiking; area also known as Gifford Woods.
• *Washburn Island,* on Waquoit Bay. State-owned park, overnight camping.

MASHPEE

• *Gamefield Walking Course*, Central Rd., Senior Citizens Center. One-half-mile trail with 15 exercise stations for all ages and abilities.
• *Lowell Holly Reservation*, off S. Sandwich Rd. Picnic area, trails, swimming on 130 acres between Mashpee and Wakeby ponds.

SANDWICH

• *Old Briar Patch*, Green Briar Nature Center, Gully Ln. One-mile trail through Thornton Burgess country.
• *Talbot's Point Salt Marsh Wildlife Reservation*, Old County Rd., opposite E. Sandwich Post Office on Rte. 6A. Trail with marsh overlooks and views of cranberry bogs and the state game farm.
• *Wakeby Conservation Area*, off Cotuit Rd., S. Sandwich. Trails along Wakeby Pond that take you by cranberry bogs and holly trees.
• *Scusset Beach State Reservation*, Scusset Beach Rd., off Rte. 3. Hiking, picnicking, and biking.
• *Shawme Crowell State Forest*, Rte. 130, near Sandwich Marina and the canal. Hiking and biking.
• *Town Beach*, off Tupper Rd., off Rte. 6A. There is a boardwalk here that takes you over Mill Creek and marshland.

Sailing

FALMOUTH

Sailing lessons are offered through the Falmouth Recreation Center, 457-2567.

Sailboarding

FALMOUTH

- *Cape Sailboards*, Main St., Falmouth; 540-8800. Rentals and lessons available. Windsurfing is allowed on Falmouth public beaches before 9 A.M. and after 5 P.M.

Sporting Goods Stores

BOURNE

- *Red Top Sporting Goods Company*, 265 Main St., 759-3371.

FALMOUTH

- *Burt's Sports Specialty*, 850 Main St., Falmouth; 540-0644.

SANDWICH

- *Cape Cod Archery*, 14 Snake Pond Rd., Forestdale; 477-7023.

Tennis

BOURNE

Public town courts are in Buzzards Bay, Pocasset, and Monument Beach; for more information, call Town Hall, 759-6295.

FALMOUTH

- *East Falmouth School*, two courts.
- *Falmouth High School*, eight courts, reservations 457-2567.
- *Lawrence School*, three courts.
- *North Falmouth School,* one court.
- *Nye Park*, N. Falmouth, four courts.
- *Swift Park*, W. Falmouth, two courts.

For reservations on the above, call 540-0553.

- *Falmouth Sports Center*, six indoor and three outdoor courts; call 548-7433 for reservations and current rates.
- *Falmouth Tennis Club*, six courts; call 548-4370.

MASHPEE

- *Southcape Resort & Club*, Rte. 28; 477-4700. Three outdoor lighted courts and two indoor courts.
- *Mashpee Middle School,* Old Barnstable Rd. Town courts. 539-1446.

Southcape Resort sponsors the *Glenn Landers Memorial Tournament* in mid-September. All ages, call 477-4700.

SANDWICH

- *Holly Ridge Tennis Club*, Country Club Rd., S. Sandwich; 428-5577. Two courts.
- *Henry T. Wing Elementary School,* Rte. 130, Sandwich. Four courts; call 888-5300 for permit.
- *Sandwich High School*, Quaker Meeting House Rd., Sandwich. Eight courts; call 888-5300 for permit.

The Sandwich Tennis Association sponsors a *Sandwich Junior Tournament*; call 888-5785 for more information.

Beaches

BOURNE

All of Bourne's public beaches, with the exception of one, require town parking stickers, available at Town Hall. The exception is *Monument Beach*, off Shore Road in the Monument Beach section of Bourne. Parking here is free, and there are rest rooms and a snack bar.

The following beaches require town parking stickers:

- *Buzzards Bay Beach*, on Buzzards Bay.
- *Gray Gables Beach*, on Buzzards Bay at the mouth of the Cape Cod Canal.
- *Barlow's Landing*, in Pocasset.
- *Pocasset Beach*, in Pocasset.
- *Squeteague Harbor*, in Cataumet.

FALMOUTH

A parking fee is charged at all public beaches in Falmouth. All public beaches require town stickers (available at Town Hall), with the exception of *Old Silver Beach*, off Bay Shore Drive in North Falmouth (rest room, bathhouse, and snack bar facilities available at this Buzzards Bay beach); *Surf Drive Beach*, off Surf Drive in Falmouth (rest room, bathhouse, and snack bar facilities available at this Vineyard Sound beach); *Menauhant Beach* off Menauhant Road in East Falmouth (rest rooms and snack bar available at this Vineyard Sound beach); and *Falmouth Heights Beach* in Falmouth Heights on Vineyard Sound.

Beaches requiring town stickers are as follows:

- *Bristol Beach*, Falmouth Heights on Vineyard Sound.
- *Chapoquoit Beach*, W. Falmouth on Buzzards Bay.
- *Megansett Beach*, N. Falmouth on Buzzards Bay.
- *Wood Neck Beach*, W. Falmouth's Sippewisset section on Buzzards Bay.
- *Grews Pond*, a freshwater pond in Goodwill Park.
- *Stoney Beach*, Woods Hole between Buzzards Bay and Vineyard Sound.

MASHPEE

Beach stickers, required for all beaches, are available at the Mashpee Recreation Department on Route 130.

- *South Cape Beach*, on Vineyard Sound. This beach is owned by the town and the state. The town beach is open only to residents, but the state beach is open to all. Located at the end of Great Oak Road, the beach has a concession, rest rooms and lifeguards. The town's annual sandcastle competition is held here in August. This is also the site of a 432-acre state park, which has a nature trail—Great Flat Pond Trail—that goes through marshes and forest.
- *John's Pond Park Beach*, off Hoophole Rd. This is a freshwater beach with lifeguards, toilets, and a picnic area.
- *Attaquin Park*, off Lake Ave. This freshwater beach is on Mashpee/Wakeby ponds. There are bathhouses and a picnic area.

SANDWICH

Beach stickers, available at Town Hall, are required for all Sandwich beaches. There is a daily parking fee at *Sandy Neck Beach*. Visitor stickers are good for a week and are good for all beaches except Snake Pond. Notify local fire departments for permission for charcoal-cooking fires on beaches.

- *Town Beach*, off Tupper Rd., off Rte. 6A; Cape Cod Bay. Toilets; boardwalk provides a nice path over marshes and Mill Creek. There is a spit of land called Town Neck—on north side is Cape Cod Bay, perfect for fishing or swimming; on the other side (south side) is Mill Creek, great for canoeing or swimming. The water is warmer in the creek than it is in the bay.
- *East Sandwich Beach*, off Ploughed Neck Rd.; Cape Cod Bay.
- *Sandy Neck*, Sandy Neck Rd., Cape Cod Bay. Bathhouse, snack bar, toilets, beautiful high dunes, four-wheel drive vehicles allowed with permits.
- *Scusset Beach*, Scusset Beach Rd., on Cape Cod Canal near the Sagamore Rotary. State-run beach, bathhouse, snack bar, toilets, parking.
- *Wakeby Pond*, off S. Sandwich Rd., S. Sandwich. Surrounded by 145 acres of a conservation area. Freshwater beach.
- *Peters Pond*, Cotuit Rd., S. Sandwich. Freshwater beach.
- *Snake Pond*, Rte. 130, Forestdale. Residents only; freshwater beach.

 # Churches

BOURNE

- *First Baptist Church*, 298 Barlow's Landing Rd., Pocasset; 563-3164.
- *Church of Jesus Christ of Latter-Day Saints*, Old County Rd., Cataumet; 563-6974.
- *St. Peter's on the Canal Episcopal Church*, 165 Main St., Buzzards Bay; 759-5641.
- *Bourne United Methodist Church*, 37 Sandwich Rd., Bourne Village; 759-4898.
- *Cataumet United Methodist Church*, 1091 County Rd., Cataumet; 563-3555.
- *Swift Memorial United Methodist Church*, Old Plymouth Rd., Sagamore; 888-0170.
- *Grace Alliance Church*, Cypress St., Buzzards Bay (nondenominational); 759-5141.
- *St. Margaret's Church*, 141 Main St., Buzzards Bay (Roman Catholic); 759-7777.
- *St. John the Evangelist Church*, 15 Virginia Rd., Pocasset (Roman Catholic); Otis Air Force Base Chapel; 563-3121.

FALMOUTH

- *Church of the Nazarene*, Town Hall Square, Falmouth; 540-6432.
- *First Church of Christ Scientist*, 175 Palmer Ave., Falmouth; 563-2196.
- *Marantha Assembly of God*, 109 County Rd., N. Falmouth; 563-5191.
- *Falmouth Baptist Church*, 60 Central Park Ave., Falmouth; 548-3260.
- *First Congregational Church*, 68 Main St., Falmouth; 548-3700.
- *North Falmouth Congregational Church*, 155 Rte. 28A, N. Falmouth; 563-2177.
- *Waquoit Congregational Church*, 15 Parsons Ln., Waquoit; 548-5269.
- *St. Barnabas Memorial Church*, 91 Main St., Falmouth (Episcopal); 548-0892 or 548-3863.
- *Church of the Messiah*, Church St., Woods Hole (Episcopal); 548-2145.
- *Kingdom Hall of Jehovah's Witnesses*, 1255 Sandwich Rd., Hatchville; 563-7247.

- *Falmouth Jewish Congregation*, 37 Hatchville Rd., E. Falmouth; 540-8094.
- *Christ Lutheran Church*, 485 Brick Kiln Rd., Falmouth; 548-5689.
- *West Falmouth United Methodist Church,* Rte. 28A, Falmouth; 548-0011.
- *St. Anthony's Roman Catholic Church*, 167 Rte. 28, E. Falmouth; 548-0108.
- *St. Patrick's Church*, 511 E. Main St., Falmouth (Roman Catholic); 548-1065.
- *St. Elizabeth Seton Church*, 481 Quaker Rd., N. Falmouth (Roman Catholic); 563-3959.
- *St. Joseph's Church*, 33 Millfield Rd., Woods Hole (Roman Catholic); 548-0990.
- *Religious Society of Friends*, Rte. 28A, W. Falmouth; 540-0833.

MASHPEE
- *Mashpee Baptist Church*, Great Neck Rd.; 477-1330.
- *Christ the King Parish*, Mashpee Commons (Roman Catholic); 477-7710.

SANDWICH
- *Church of the Nazarene*, Rte. 6A, Sandwich; 888-8489.
- *Sandwich Community Church*, Marstons Mills (Assembly of God); 420-0081.
- *Corpus Christi Church*, 8 Jarves St., Sandwich (Roman Catholic); 888-0209.
- *First Church of Christ*, 136 Main St. (Congregational); 888-0436.
- *St. John's Episcopal Church*, 159 Main St.; 888-2828.
- *Covenant Baptist Church*, Kiah's Way, E. Sandwich; 888-7723.
- *Forestdale Baptist Church*, 110 Rte. 130; 477-1409.

Odds & Ends

Laundromats

BOURNE
- *Laundry Center*, 105 Trowbridge Rd., Bourne; 759-4966.

FALMOUTH
- *Falmouth Self Service Laundry*, Scranton Ave., Falmouth; 548-3911.
- *Towne Cleaners*, 383 Main St., Falmouth; 548-3232.
- *Village Laundromat*, 342 E. Falmouth Hwy., E. Falmouth; 540-0087.

Farm Stands

FALMOUTH
- *Jack in the Beanstalk*, E. Main St., Falmouth; 540-4191.
- *Peach Tree Farm Circle*, 881 Palmer Ave., Falmouth; 548-2354.

SANDWICH
- *Windstar Farm*, Country Farm Rd., Forestdale; 477-0051.
- *Blueberry Bob Farm*, off Spring Hill Rd. Pick your own blueberries.
- *Fleetwood Farms*, 10 Fleetwood Rd., E. Sandwich. Pick your own blueberries.

Fish Markets

BOURNE
- *American Lobster Mart*, S. Bourne Bridge Rotary, S. Bourne; 759-7844.

- *Cataumet Fish*, 1360 Rte. 28A, Cataumet; 564-5956.
- *Larry's Market*, 303 Barlow's Landing Rd., Pocasset; 564-4258.
- *Lobster Pot*, 3155 Cranberry Hwy., Buzzards Bay; 759-3876.
- *Lobster Trap Company*, 290 Shore Rd. (wholesale); 759-4928.

FALMOUTH
- *Coastline Seafoods*, Rte. 28, Waquoit; 540-6428.

MASHPEE
- *Cataumet Fish*, Deer Crossing and Rte. 28 ; 477-4116.
- *The Flume Fish Market*, Lake Ave.; 477-1456.

SANDWICH
- *Joe's Lobster Mart*, off Coast Guard Rd.; 888-2971.

Ice Cream Parlors

BOURNE
- *Betty Ann's Dairy Freeze*, 225 Main St., Buzzards Bay; 759-6653.
- *Whistle Stop Ice Cream*, 435 Shore Rd., Monument Beach; 759-8958.

FALMOUTH
- *Falmouth Dairy Queen*, 839 E. Main St.; 540-0669.
- *Peach Tree Circle*, 881 Palmer Ave.; 548-2354.
- *Whistle Stop Ice Cream*, 854 Rte. 28A; 540-7585.

MASHPEE
- *Ice Cream Scoop*, Popponesset Marketplace, New Seabury Resort; 477-9111.
- *Maggie's Ice Cream*, 681 Falmouth Rd. at the Mashpee Commons; 477-6442.

SANDWICH
- *Ice Cream Café*, 315 Cotuit Rd., Sandwich; 888-0300.
- *Ice Cream Sandwich*, 66 Rte. 6A; 888-7237.
- *Maggie's Ice Cream*, Cotuit Rd., S. Sandwich; 477-5711.

Bakeries

FALMOUTH
- *Marie's Bakery*, 410 W. Falmouth Hwy., W. Falmouth; 540-7406.
- *Pie in the Sky Dessert Café*, 10 Water St., Woods Hole; 540-5475.

SANDWICH
- *Doreen's Donuts & Baked Goods*, 31 Cotuit Rd., Sandwich; 888-6670.
- *MacNeil's Bakery*, Tupper Rd.; 888-3345.

Libraries

BOURNE
- *Jonathan Bourne Public Library*, 19 Sandwich Rd.; 759-0644.

FALMOUTH
- *Falmouth Public Library*, Main St.; 457-2555.

FALMOUTH (CONTINUED)

- *East Falmouth Library*, Rte. 28.; 548-6340.
- *North Falmouth Public Library*, Chester St.; 563-2922.
- *Woods Hole Public Library*, Woods Hole Rd.; 548-8961.
- *National Marine Fisheries Library*, Water St., Woods Hole; 548-5123.
- *Marine Biological Lab Library*, Water St., Woods Hole; 548-3705.

MASHPEE

- *Town of Mashpee Public Library*, Rte. 151; 539-1435. Great source of Wampanoag Indian history.

SANDWICH

- *Sandwich Public Library*, 142 Main St.; 888-0625. Puppet shows and story hours at library; check local newspapers for times.

Best of Upper Cape

BEST COUNTRY INNS

- *Grey Whale Inn*, 565 Woods Hole Rd., Woods Hole; 548-7692.
- *Wing Scorton Farm Inn*, 11 Wing Blvd. (off Rte. 6A), E. Sandwich; 888-0545.

BEST RESORT

- *New Seabury Resort & Conference Center*, New Seabury; 477-9111.

BEST BREAKFASTS

- *Bee-Hive Tavern,* 406 Rte. 6A, Sandwich; 833-1184.
- *Fishmonger's Café,* 56 Water St., Woods Hole; 548-9148.
- *Marshland Restaurant*, Rte. 6A, Sandwich; 888-9824.

BEST LUNCH

- *Popponesset Inn*, Shore Dr.W. (New Seabury Resort), New Seabury; 477-1100.

BEST CASUAL DINING

- *Bee-Hive Tavern*, Rte. 6A, Sandwich; 833-1184.

BEST FINE DINING

- *Regatta of Falmouth by the Sea*, Scranton Ave., overlooking Falmouth Harbor; 548-5400.
- *Chart Room*, Kingman Marina, Cataumet (overlooking harbor); 563-5350.
- *Dan'l Webster Inn*, Old Main St., Sandwich; 888-3622.

BEST FRIED SEAFOOD

- *Seafood Sam's*, Coast Guard Rd. (on the Cape Cod Canal), Sandwich; 888-4629; and Rte. 28, E. Falmouth; 540-3080.

BEST NIGHTLY ENTERTAINMENT (CASUAL)

- *Town Band concerts* in Sandwich, Bourne, and Falmouth; call Town Halls.
- *Century Irish Pub*, 29 Locust St., Falmouth; 548-6631. Live Irish music.
- *Irish Embassy,* Rte. 28, E. Falmouth; 540-6656. Live Irish music.

BEST MUSEUM & HISTORIC SITE

- *Heritage Plantation*, Pine and Grove sts., Sandwich; 888-3300.
- *Thornton W. Burgess Museum,* 4 Water St., Sandwich (on the edge of Shawme Pond); 888-6870.

BEST ART GALLERY

- *Falmouth Artists Guild*, 744 Main St., Falmouth; 540-3304.

BEST CRAFT, SPECIALTY, & ANTIQUE SHOP

- *Popponesset Marketplace*, New Seabury Resort area; 477-9111. Collection of about 20 shops.

BEST SEASONAL EVENT

- *Annual Mashpee Wampanoag Indian Pow-Wow*, Rte. 130, Mashpee. Held weekend closest to July 4. Call Mashpee Indian Museum for more information, 477-1536.

BEST PUBLIC BEACHES

- *Sandwich Town Beach*, off Tupper Rd., which runs off Rte. 6A.
- *South Cape State Beach*, at the end of Great Oak Rd., Mashpee.
- *Old Silver Beach*, on Buzzards Bay, N. Falmouth.
- *Surf Drive Beach*, off Surf Dr., Falmouth, on Vineyard Sound.
- *Falmouth Heights Beach*, in Falmouth Heights on Vineyard Sound.

BEST GOLF

- *New Seabury Resort*, New Seabury; 477-9111.
- *Cape Cod Country Club*, 48 Theater Dr., Hatchville; 563-9842.
- *Falmouth Country Club*, Carriage Shop Rd., E. Falmouth; 548-3211.

BEST HIKING OR NATURE TRAILS

- *Beebe Woods*, Depot Ave., Falmouth; 400 acres.
- *Sandwich Town Beach Boardwalk Trail*, Sandwich Town Beach. Trail takes you by Mill Creek and marshland.

BEST CAMPING

- *Bourne Scenic Park*, off Rte. 6, Buzzards Bay on Cape Cod Canal; 759-7873.

BEST FISH MARKET

- *Joe's Lobster Mart*, off Coast Guard Beach Rd., Sandwich; 888-2971.

BEST ICE CREAM PARLOR

- *Ice Cream Scoop*, Popponesset Marketplace, New Seabury Resort.

MID-CAPE

Barnstable, Yarmouth, Dennis

Mid-Cape: Viewpoints

by Seth Rolbein

When 75-year-old Reverend Stephen Batchelor led a band of followers to present-day Yarmouth to start a new settlement in 1637, he certainly had no idea that 350 years later many people of retirement age would have taken his example to heart.

Indeed, they've taken it one step further: most of the newer arrivals to the Mid-Cape, as the grouping of Barnstable, Yarmouth, and Dennis is called, have chosen to stay, while the good Reverend, an independent lout who delighted in making his own rules, departed two years after his arrival—shortly before being excommunicated by the Church of England for unchaste behavior.

In Batchelor's time the primary attractions of the Mid-Cape were good fishing, friendly Indians, and a rich but rocky soil. Today the Mid-Cape's attractions include many urban amenities without much urban hassle and comfortable, quiet suburban living with the bonus of the seashore near at hand.

This combination has changed the social complexion of the Mid-Cape in recent years in ways that the business community cheers but old Yankees might scorn. Younger professionals with families, particularly in Barnstable, have blended into both historic communities and new developments. Many live in West Barnstable, along pastoral Route 6A, in stately inns and farmhouses where home prices, for a time, were escalating 40 percent a year.

The mixture of "Yuppies," if you will, with "Orppies" (older, retired professionals), if you must, has brought a new level of year-round affluence to the Mid-Cape that compares with the opulence of summer mansions on Nantucket Sound. Suburban congestion caused by this growth has created its share of problems, but officials here are diligently searching for solutions.

The three towns of the Mid-Cape, about as old as any communities you'll find in New England, were once two: Barnstable and Yarmouth. Dennis (named after the Reverend Josiah Dennis, who pastored Yarmouth's East Parish and whose manse is north of the village proper and open to the public) broke off from Yarmouth and incorporated in 1793. But for 154 years Dennis was part of Yarmouth—a point Yarmouth old-timers never miss an opportunity to make. Dennis, however, draws civic pride from such achievements as the All-American Cities Award the town won in the mid-1970s for its conservation efforts and for opening up town government to more citizen participation.

Local history books tell us Yarmouth was probably named after a town in Norfolk, England, that bears the same name, but no one knows for sure. What we do know is that the area was settled in 1639 by three strong-willed men: Thomas Howes, Anthony Thacher, and John Crowe. The family names are still prominent in the area.

Another fact you should know about the Mid-Cape is that the towns are split up into villages, each offering visitors something different.

The town of Yarmouth, for example, has five villages: Yarmouth, along Route 6A near Centre Street; Yarmouth Port, just up Route 6A to the east and near Willow Street; South Yarmouth, along commercial Route 28 near Station Avenue; Bass River, along Route 28 near Bass River Beach; and West Yarmouth, also on Route 28 but near the Hyannis line.

The town of Dennis also has five villages: Dennis, along Route 6A near Beach Street; East Dennis, also on Route 6A but in the Sesuit Road and School Street areas; South Dennis, off Route 134, which runs between Routes 6A and 28; Dennisport, along Route 28 near the Harwich line; and West Dennis, along Route 28 near the Yarmouth line.

The town of Barnstable, the largest on Cape Cod, has seven villages, and this has confused summer visitors since they first began coming here in the early 1900s. First of all, Hyannis is not a town. It is a village of the town of Barnstable, located on the Route 28 side of the Cape. Secondly, in addition to the town of Barnstable, there is a village named Barnstable and a Barnstable County, which has its government seat in Barnstable Village but includes the entire Cape. Barnstable Village, we should also note, has three distinct sections: Cummaquid, to the east of the village center; Cobbs Village, at Barnstable Harbor northwest of the center; and Pond Village, a community off Route 6A to the east of Barnstable Village and not far from Hinckley Pond.

Confused? Don't worry about it: many year-round residents still can't get it straight. Now before we finish untying this Gordian knot, you should know that in addition to the villages of Barnstable and Hyannis, there are also West Barnstable on Route 6A and Centerville, Osterville, Cotuit, and Marstons Mills, all south and to the west of Hyannis.

To make up for all this confusion, Barnstable at least has the most fascinating history of the three Mid-Cape towns. Before the Pilgrims came here from Plymouth Colony, the area was inhabited by three tribes of the Wampanoag nation: the Cummaquids, the Mattakeese, and the Nobscusset Indians, all of whom befriended the early settlers. An example of this is the story of John Billingham, an adventurous and at times incorrigible Pilgrim boy who wandered off into the woods near Plymouth Colony and was lost. The incident is recounted in Edward Winslow's classic *Mourt's Relation*. Hoping to find the boy, Myles Standish led a search party of 10 to the Mid-Cape area, which had yet to be settled. There they met the Indian *sachem* (chief) Iyannough, whose warriors had found young Billingham. Iyannough gladly returned the boy, offered Standish and his crew fresh supplies and water, and sent them on their way. It was the start of a long friendship.

The first attempt to settle Barnstable was made by the Reverend Joseph Hull, who had been nudged out of a parish near present-day Weymouth on Boston's South Shore. Hull was to be pushed out of a parish again—this time by the Reverend John Lothrop, whose Congregationalist party settled along Barnstable's great marsh on Cape Cod Bay in the fall of 1639 and incorporated the area, which originally included Falmouth. Barnstable is named after a town in Devonshire, England, named "Barnstaple." The early settlers proved to be better farmers than spellers. And it's good they were; their survival depended on their ability to make a living off the land. Fishing, shore whaling, and trading were also required skills—as well as a knack for getting along with the Indians, who were more than willing to sell their land as long as they could hunt and fish on it. A case in point was the sale of a large parcel that now includes the villages of Hyannis, Centerville, and Osterville. According to Frederick Freeman's *History of Cape Cod*, published in 1858, a Barnstable man named Nicholas Davis traded an Indian sachem Yanno of the South Sea "20 pounds and two small pair of breeches" for the land. The area was later subdivided and settled.

In the years that followed, Barnstable gave birth to many a daring man, among them attorney James Otis, Jr., appropriately called "the Patriot." Otis's passionate speech before the state Superior Court in 1761, exhorting the Colonists to stand up to the British, is credited with lighting the flames of the American Revolution. "Let the consequences be what they will," Otis said, "I am determined to proceed and to the call of my country am ready to sacrifice estate, ease, health, applause and even life."

Freeman, in his history, calls Otis "a noble son of Cape Cod . . . an orator of superior power, of large heart, of enthusiastic daring, bred in the school of true patriotism."

That spirit of patriotism and independence can still be found today in many of the Mid-Cape's residents. Even the area's geography suggests strength. The Mid-Cape is best described as the Cape's muscle. The metaphor works geographically because the Mid-Cape is the flexing bicep of the craggy arm of this peninsula as it curves into the Atlantic Ocean. It also fits economically because the Mid-Cape is the commercial bull's-eye, the focus of commercial and industrial activity. And the metaphor works demographically because the Mid-Cape has the greatest concentration of people who live here year-round, who come here to their second homes in the summer, or who visit for a week or two at a time.

The Mid-Cape used to have all the ebb and flow of any tourist center, but in recent years it has evolved into more of a constant community, with a steady commercial and population base. Tourism remains a key element of the region's economy—and everyone certainly can tell the difference between winter and summer—but even an off-season visitor to this part of the Cape will find more businesses open than closed, and more things to do than walk on a deserted beach. It can fairly be said that this is where Cape Cod most clearly has lost some of its romance in the rush toward convenience and capital.

Hyannis in particular, one of Barnstable's handful of villages, has taken on the trappings of a rapidly developed suburb—with shopping malls, supermarkets, movie theaters, motels, and restaurants. The Cape's largest airport, bus depot, and ferry service to Martha's Vineyard and Nantucket are all found in Hyannis. This is Cape Cod's big city, although by the standards of much of the rest of the country it would still seem small; within only a few miles of the very heart of downtown can be found stately, secluded waterfront estates along Nantucket Sound, among them the Kennedy family compound in the Hyannis Port section of the village.

In terms of a quick overview, it is best to think of the Mid-Cape, like the Upper Cape and parts of the Outer Cape, as being divided by three main roads running parallel to each other from west to east.

On the south side is Route 28, which over the years has developed into a classic commercial and tourist strip. A rapid-fire succession of fast-food restaurants, motels and shops, nightclubs, resorts, and miniature golf courses line the road, particularly in the town of Yarmouth. It's where the action is on a hot summer night—and where stop-and-go traffic can do a very convincing imitation of a parking lot.

On the north side is Route 6A, also known as the Old King's Highway, and it is opposite Route 28. If there were one drive that best represents the best of Cape Cod, one automobile trip that a visitor could take to begin to understand why people find Cape Cod so special, that journey would begin and end on the Old King's Highway. Route 6A is perhaps the oldest road in the country, used from the very first days of the colony as the overland route to Boston. The highway winds through small villages that still live up to Cape Cod's quaint reputation. Commercial pockets are the exception rather than the rule, and many of the homesteads lining the road are authentically historic Colonial landmarks. Old King's Highway offers a living primer on the architectural styles of early America from one-story Capes with steeply sloping roofs to more grand Greek Revival manses and proud ship captains' homes with widow's walks aloft. For a glimpse of how the Cape used to be, for browsing in antique shops, and for avoiding the worst traffic even at the height of summer, Old King's is a superb alternative.

And between Routes 28 and 6A, right down the middle of the Cape's arm, Route 6 double-barrels its way through the landscape. When speed is of the essence, when sightseeing and exploring will have to wait for some other time, Route 6 is the highway.

The final thought in terms of an overview has to do with beaches.

The beaches along the Mid-Cape's south side all hug Nantucket Sound, fondly known as "the Pond" because the islands of Martha's Vineyard and Nantucket act as an offshore barrier and turn the Sound into a relatively calm body of water. Rare is the day when there is any kind of big surf along Nantucket Sound beaches. Tides are also temperate, running from four to five feet up and down, so there is a consistency to the beaches that may not be wild and exciting but is dependable (unlike bay side beaches) and pleasant. The water temperature, about 70 degrees in July, is also the warmest on the Cape.

Bay side beaches present a dramatic contrast to the Sound—indeed, bay side beaches present dramatic contrasts hour by hour, and day by day. Fourteen-foot tides regularly roll in and out. The shoreline is gently sloping, so at low tide long expanses of sandbars stand revealed—perfect for shellfishing and for children who want to explore marsh grass and hunt for hermit crabs. We suggest you equip them with nets and pails. The flats, as they're called, are great for long walks and for getting away from it all, but even after walking a good mile offshore at low tide the water in the bay might not be deep enough for anything beyond wading.

Wait a few hours, however, and the tide will cover the flats, lap the shore, and create an entirely different feeling. Within a dozen yards of shore, you can't put your feet down.

Although the tides run fast, the forearm of the Cape (like the islands on the south side) stop the waves from reaching any consistent size—surfers pass over the Mid-Cape altogether. The water on the north beaches tends to be colder than the water on the south, except on those days when the sun bakes the flats in the morning, and then the shallow water of a rising tide washes over in the afternoon and absorbs all that solar warmth.

South side beaches tend to be more crowded (as is the south side generally), with more parking facilities and more amenities such as snack bars and rest rooms. As far as the Mid-Cape goes, if you hear about a motel that's right on the beach, that will most likely be a south side beach; commercial development directly along the north shore is virtually nonexistent.

Barnstable

Barnstable is the flagship town of Cape Cod. Sometimes even born-and-bred Cape Codders forget that Barnstable is a collection of seven villages, each of which alone is as big as some of the smaller Cape Cod towns, each with interesting and unique personalities. The temptation is always to speak of Barnstable in hyperbole, as being the biggest and having the most of everything (including the kind of development that traditionalists deplore). And so long as you keep in mind the miniature nature of Cape Cod, the hyperbole rings true. All told, Barnstable is home to 27,000 people and comprises 60 square miles.

Hyannis is the most famous village of Barnstable, so well known that many people, as we have said, think it is a town of its own. Of course, it is the Kennedy connection that put Hyannis and Hyannis Port on the map, the memories of a summer White House in the 1960s, of touch football on the lawn, and the sweeping images of John Kennedy walking his daughter Caroline on the sandy beach, or the President at the tiller of a small sailboat in Nantucket Sound. The Kennedy compound remains, and the Kennedy influence remains, but these days Hyannis has come to mean something else to Cape Codders. It has come to define the commercial core of the entire peninsula.

To get to Hyannis from the Mid-Cape Highway, take exit 6 onto Route 132 south, which carries you smack into Cape Cod's suburbia. Competing shopping plazas line the road, but the granddaddy of them all is the Cape Cod Mall, built in 1970, with 80 stores and a 5000-car parking lot on almost 50 acres of land. When the mall was first built, everyone thought the owners were crazy; now they look at the full lot and use the word visionary. A visit will remind you of malls everywhere, from decor, to store selection (Filene's, Jordan Marsh, Sears, and so on), to packs of teenagers seeing and being seen.

The huge success of the modern mall threatened to turn Hyannis's older Main Street into a Cape Cod version of urban blight. Instead, Main Street pulled itself up by the bootstraps and remains a vital and interesting downtown. From Route 132, continue to what is known as the Airport Rotary (for obvious reasons; the runways are clearly visible) and swing around to the right onto Barnstable Road for three-quarters of a mile until you reach Main Street. Then take a right. Main Street is two lanes, one way, with parking on both sides and off-street parking lots on the north. On a summer night the effect is dramatic, like something out of a 1950s movie as cars rev side by side down straight lines.

This is a first-rate walking and browsing street, with a little bit of something for everybody. The east end tends to be more sedate and upscale. Puritan Clothing has been a Cape Cod retail favorite for decades. There are many good restaurants, like Alberto's Ristorante.

To the west, past Barnstable's old Town Hall and a village green that hosts occasional outdoor festivals (the popular Pops By The Sea concert among them), the road's pace quickens. Boutiques and ice cream stores mix it up with restaurants, T-shirt shops, art galleries, used-book stores, even miniature golf. The commercial concoction works in an eclectic way that no planner or architect could ever predict. Gringo's, a Mexican restaurant, has an outdoor patio right on Main Street, a place to have a drink and watch the show go by. Also visit the JFK Museum next to the Post Office; the museum documents Kennedy's love for the Cape.

The far west end of Main Street has an interesting cluster of restaurants, ranging from Harry's, small with surprisingly authentic Cajun cooking, to the ever-popular, more expensive Paddock on the West End Rotary.

Directly beside the Paddock is the Cape Cod Melody Tent, truly a class act, which every summer attracts top live entertainment to play under the big tent, in the round. It's always worth checking to see who's in town. Everyone from James Brown to Joan Baez, Rodney Dangerfield to the Temptations, have performed. The intimate setting is tough to beat.

North Street and South Street parallel Main Street on both sides, connecting with the main drag again at the west end. South Street is one way the opposite direction from Main Street, which makes it possible for drivers to loop around and cruise the action one more time. St. Francis Xavier Church, where Kennedys have married, is on South Street, as are signs to the various docks at Hyannis Harbor, where you can hop a ferry to Martha's Vineyard and Nantucket. Basically, you have a choice of two services, both have snack bars: the publicly owned Steamship Authority offers year-round service to Nantucket from the Authority's South Street dock. (The Authority offers year-round service to Martha's Vineyard from Woods Hole, just to the south and west of Falmouth proper.) The second option is the privately owned Hy-Line fleet, which offers spring, summer, and fall service to both islands from the Ocean Street dock (see maps). The Authority also offers service between Martha's Vineyard and Nantucket in the summer; you can take your car with you to both islands, but you must make reservations well in advance, either by telephone or through the mail. No reservations are needed for passengers.

If you don't like long boat rides we suggest you skip Nantucket or fly there from Hyannis or Chatham airports. The Steamship Authority trip from Hyannis to Nantucket takes two and a half hours. It takes two hours on the smaller, swifter Hy-Line. On a clear day it's a beautiful ride. The top decks of both vessels are great for sunbathing. The trip from Hyannis to Martha's Vineyard on the Hy-Line takes one hour and 45 minutes. By comparison, the Steamship Authority trip from Woods Hole to the Vineyard takes about 45 minutes (Woods Hole is much closer to the Vineyard than Hyannis). The trip from Woods Hole to Nantucket, however, takes three hours and 15 minutes (Woods Hole is farther from Nantucket than Hyannis).

While we're on the subject, ferry service in the spring, summer, and fall is also available from Falmouth Harbor to Martha's Vineyard on the privately owned *Island Queen.* The trip takes about 35 minutes.

It is possible to plan a relaxing day-trip to either island, but if you are headed there and don't care to linger on the Cape, you should know that Hyannis offers both plane and bus service to and from New York and Boston. Taxi service is available from the airport and bus terminal to the docks. Leave yourself plenty of time to make your connections. We recommend you get to the dock at least 45 minutes before your ferry leaves.

Continuing with our tour, we suggest you turn right onto Ocean Street which brings you along the harbor of Lewis Bay and Hyannis's busiest waterfront. A public park makes for a pleasant stroll, and at the end of Ocean Street is Kalmus Park Beach, the best oasis closest to downtown Hyannis for a picnic and swim.

You're now getting close to Kennedy compound country, along the shores of Hyannis Port. Driving along Gosnold Road to Ocean Avenue, around the quaint Hyannis Port Post Office and past the signs that order tour buses to turn around, you get a sense of the quiet, moneyed, summer home environment. But the best way (really the only way) to see the Kennedy compound itself is from the water; daily cruises leaving from the Ocean Street docks include the compound in their sightseeing. At sunset, the trip is spectacular.

But before leaving Hyannis proper, a few more places are worth mentioning:

• At the East End Rotary off Main Street is the home of the Cape Cod and Hyannis Railroad, Cape Cod's only railroad, which schedules daily tourist trips along old railway beds all the way across Bourne Bridge into Buzzards Bay and back. Crossing the canal is a real highlight. The ride is a marvelous combination of Cape Cod scenery and comfortable near-antique passenger cars that make the ride that much more enjoyable. Cape Cod Scenic Railroad offers two-hour scenic tours aboard a vintage train. Also available is an elegant Dinner Train and Ecology Discovery Tours.

• The section of Route 28 that connects the Airport Rotary to Yarmouth is a crowded thoroughfare usually worth avoiding. The town's biggest pickup night spot, Pufferbellies, is located on this stretch inside a huge old railroad roundhouse beside the tracks. Mildred's Chowder House, a favorite among summer visitors (and John F. Kennedy), is on Route 28 as well.

South of Hyannis is Hyannis Port, really only the beginning of the Barnstable shore, which includes the villages of Centerville, Osterville and Cotuit. Acre for acre, house for house, this is probably the wealthiest corner of Cape Cod.

But first there is Craigville Beach, a long sandy invitation to swim, which hugs Craigville Harbor. This is one of those beaches that are an integral part of many kid's memories of Cape Cod, one of those gentle Nantucket Sound beaches that people return to again and again. Lifeguards, snack bars, rest rooms, and fine sand are all easily found. Parking spaces can become precious by late morning on a hot day.

The road off the beach leads up to South Main Street, and at the corner is Four Seas, home of the best ice cream in town (this place had flavors such as cantaloupe and coconut more than 15 years ago, long before the rage). A left onto South Main Street leads toward Osterville; it is a very pleasant drive. The village of Osterville (it used to be called Oyster Land) has retained an upscale, quiet charm. Small stores line a well-defined village center. Here you'll find such classic clothing as Talbots, Mark Fore & Strike, and The Children's Shop, a unique but pricey children's shop. South of the village is prime meandering country: East Bay Road leads past East Bay Lodge, which in many ways personifies the ambience of Osterville. The road then jogs down to Crosby Yacht Yard and cozy Oyster Harbors, both of which are worth taking in. The Crosbys have been building wooden boats here for generations, including the famed Crosby catboat, an unusual sailing vessel used by fishermen in the early 1900s. The boat is still made there on special order.

We suggest you drive down Seaview Avenue also. It hugs the shoreline and wanders past imposing homes and such places as the Wianno Club, which looks like a scene out of the movie set of *The Great Gatsby*. Seaview Avenue dead ends at the mouth of West Bay after a journey through country estates. Backtrack and take Parker Road, which heads north, passing through a prefectly manicured golf course back to Osterville Center, thus completing a southern loop of the village.

Just down the road from Osterville Center is the village of Cotuit, a summer place that attracted so many Harvard professors and their families in the early 1900s it was nicknamed "Little Harvard." While Cotuit has no boutiques, or gift shops, its graceful clapboard homes framed by white picket fences make the drive through this village a high point of any tour. For a spectacular view of Cotuit Bay, head to the town landing off Oyster Place Road, which runs off Main Street. Cotuit, by the way, was once considered the oyster capital of New England. The Cotuit Oyster Company, founded in 1908, is still in business and located off Little River Road. Cotuit oysters, like Wellfleet oysters, have a distinct taste. You see them advertised as appetizers in restaurants throughout the world. Oyster connoisseurs say the taste has to do with the temperature, quality, and makeup of local waters.

On the north side of the Mid-Cape, the town of Barnstable has a separate personality. To get there from Osterville, follow Main Street north out of town, crossing busy Route 28 and connecting to Route 149. Passing through the village of Marstons Mills might feel more like visiting a New Hampshire town than a Cape village—this is one of the widest sections of the peninsula's arm, so tall trees and fertile farm land escape the ocean's bitter winter winds. Route 149 passes a grass-strip airfield—the oldest airstrip on the Cape—crosses over the Mid-Cape Highway, and leads all the way to Route 6A, the Old King's Highway, on the north side.

Probably the greatest attraction of West Barnstable is not the village center or winding Route 6A (pleasant though it is). West Barnstable is blessed to have Sandy Neck, one of the most magnificent beaches on Cape Cod, protecting its northern shore. To reach Sandy Neck, turn east on Old King's just over the town line into Sandwich, then turn north onto Sandy Neck Road. There is a large parking area at the dead end, with off-road access for four-wheel-drive jeeps (town stickers required at all times of year).

The adventurous pedestrian beachcomber who is willing to spend a day walking a stretch of Sandy Neck is more than rewarded with one of the Cape's most beautiful waterfront experiences. The neck stretches eight long miles, wide enough to have hidden dunes and hollows in its middle, laced with unusual beach growth, ringed by sandy beaches. Old bottles and even Indian relics testify to a long history of use; rare species of turtles and birds nest in the area, protected by dunes, and rangers. The long stretch of neck also protects fertile Great Marsh behind it; canoes and beetlecats can wind their way through the rushes at the right tides, disturbing giant blue heron who feed on abundant life in the water. For size, diversity, and sheer unspoiled beauty, Sandy Neck rivals any beach anywhere.

At the end of a beach day, back to the main road heading east, Route 6A is not too rude a shock. Old homes and old trees line much of the road. At the junction of Route 132 (which would take you back to Hyannis), both the Cape Cod Community College, with its 115-acre campus, and the Cape Cod Conservatory, which offers classes in dance, music, and art, are only a stone's throw up the road. The community college, which the locals call the "4Cs," houses what has been called the world's largest collection of Cape Cod books, charts, and research. You'll find this material in the William Brewster Nickerson Memorial Room, which is open to the public Monday through Friday. The room is open 8 A.M. to 4 P.M. Mondays, Tuesdays, and Wednesdays; on Thursdays and Fridays it is open about 8:30 A.M. until about 2:30 P.M. History buffs should check it out.

But if you're just in the mood for a drive, you should continue up Route 6A, perhaps with a detour onto Scudder's Lane or Rendezvous Lane, both of which yield nice views of Barnstable Harbor and Sandy Neck from town landings at the end of the street.

Just a mile or so up Route 6A from here you'll enter the village proper of Barnstable. The village center is dominated by the imposing columns of the Barnstable County Superior Courthouse. This is the seat of government and law on Cape Cod; the complex houses everything from courts, the Registry of Deeds, and the county planning commission to the county jail, a place you'll want to stay out of. Across the street from the courthouse, you'll find the Barnstable News Store, one of those places where you can buy almost anything. Next to the news store is The Village Landing where locals gather for breakfast and lunch. The deli has a great bakery. Another favorite eatery, and a watering hole for the courthouse crowd, is the Dolphin Restaurant.

Just past the village center, take a left turn at the lights down to Barnstable Harbor, filled with pleasure boats and fishing vessels when the season is right. A whale-watching operation has worked out of the harbor in recent years. Mattakeese Wharf, a seasonal restaurant beside the boat slips, has a deck from which you can watch activity in the harbor while eating lunch or dinner.

Continuing on our tour, drive back up Mill Way and turn east (left) on Route 6A and you will pass the Cape Cod Art Association, which exhibits and sells the paintings of local artists. Perhaps the biggest surprise along the way is to see a large working farm carved out from between the old Colonial homes. Visitors are not encouraged or allowed, however; this is the county prison farm, worked exclusively by inmates.

This is now Cummaquid, different from Barnstable more by state of mind and by virtue of a small post office than by anything very tangible. Just over the Yarmouth border, Willow Street turns south and leads directly back to Route 28 and the hustle of Hyannis. It's a world apart, yet only a few miles down the road.

Yarmouth

The town of Yarmouth has undergone such dramatic change and development over the past 20-odd years that it makes sense to refer to the town as two entities: Old Yarmouth and New Yarmouth. Eighteen thousand people live in the combination.

Old Yarmouth's bastion is on the north side, and nowhere is the Old King's Highway more authentic and interesting than here. Along a stretch of less than two miles are an eclectic collection of inns, restaurants, and shops, none of which is housed in a building built in this century. The Old Captain's Inn, the Village Inn, the Wedgewood Inn—all are small lodging houses. Abbicci is an upscale chic Italian restaurant, while the Old Yarmouth Inn has more of a Colonial feeling.

Local Yarmouth Port color isn't hard to come by, either. Directly on Route 6A is Hallet's Store, which looks and feels almost exactly as it must have looked and felt 100 years ago. The ice cream sodas at the fountain are not antique, however; they're the best in town, particularly if you drink one while swiveling on a stool.

Just a few yards away, directly behind Inaho, a great Japanese restaurant, and accessible by dirt driveways on either side of the restaurant, is Jack's Outback, open for breakfast and lunch. Aside from excellent short-order cooking, the main attraction here is Jack Smith, who manages to insult everyone in sight with such aplomb that they can't wait to come back for more. A sample of his odd humor: at the county's three hundredth birthday parade, Jack and cohorts constructed a makeshift float representing his restaurant that looked suspiciously like Jack's Outhouse, not Jack's Outback. "300 Years of Continuous Service," read the sign above. Joking aside, if you have a historical question about Yarmouth Port, collar Jack—he's a serious, well-read historian of the village.

Another 100-odd yards east on Route 6A is Parnassus Book Store, not a spot for claustrophobics but a heady discovery for any book lover. Parnassus is the kind of place where you walk in, start poking around and squeezing your way through the old racks, and next look up two hours later. Ben Muse is the proprietor, a fitting name for a man of books, and he holds court when he's not on a book-buying expedition to Central America. An outside awning protects some of Muse's collection from the rain; after hours just push the purchase price into the mail slot.

Still another few yards along the highway, on the south side of the street behind the Yarmouth Port Post Office, the town historical society maintains a handsome small botanical garden with accompanying nature walk. The hike leads through deep woods, near a secluded small pond, and is particularly satisfying because within moments it seems as though you're far away from civilization. In the winter, the trail is excellent for cross-country skiing on those rare days when the Cape gets enough snow.

Past the Yarmouth Port green another half-mile, on the left, a playground with swings and a basketball court is a good place to stretch. Even better, follow the road behind the court, along one of the oldest European cemeteries in North America (not bad for walking either, if old tombstones don't give you the creeps), past old homes and fields until the road opens into a small parking lot and picnic area at Grey's Beach. This is Bass Hole, where greenhead flies are much more plentiful in July than bass ever were at any time of the year. But the great attraction of Bass Hole, insects or no, is the Bass Hole boardwalk, which takes a straight line off the shore a quarter mile or more over the marsh. At the end of the plankway the marsh surrounds you; if the tide is right and you're adventurous, there is fun swimming in winding Chase Garden Creek.

Turning south, you can drive directly up Union Street from Route 6A, past the Dennis-Yarmouth Regional High School (where the D-Y "Dolphins" and "Dolphinettes" play sports), but a more scenic route is to take Setucket Road east of Union Street, passing over Crab Creek (which, unlike Bass Hole, still offers fishing for its namesake). Then turn right on North Main Street, which leads all the way to South Yarmouth at Route 28. A quick detour just before town onto Wood Road, then jogging to Kelley Road, is worth the trouble to find the simple, small South Yarmouth Quaker Meeting House, one of the oldest churches in the country, where Quakers still meet for a quiet hour of meditation and prayer on Sunday mornings. The public is welcome to attend.

At the Route 28 lights you have a choice: turn right again and begin the journey through New Yarmouth, or postpone that fate one last time and go straight down Main Street to see the part of town that the old-timers still call "Bass River" to distinguish it from the rest of South Yarmouth. This is a handsome, residential pocket of town. Main Street reconnects with Route 28 not too far to the west, but before that a left onto River Street will send you along the shores of Bass River, past Windmill Park to South Shore Drive and out to the Sound, where a handful of seasonal motels line the shore. Bass River Beach, at the head of the river, is public and includes a boat-launching ramp. Other small beaches, all with parking lots, nestle between motels. Among them are Parker's River Beach and Seaview Beach. South Shore Drive ends after a mile or so; Seaview Avenue passes through summer homes and cottage colonies to reconnect with Route 28.

And now, a few choice words about Yarmouth's Route 28: no self-respecting tourist trap can be without a road like this. On a rainy summer afternoon it can be a maddening snarl of stop-and-go traffic, but it also packs a virtual parade of businesses designed to cater to visitors. Motels line both sides of the road, upward of 1200 rooms available during the season, many of whose most compelling features are a swimming pool and cable TV. Fast-food restaurants abound. There's an amusement operation at the South Yarmouth end of the highway with pitch and putt and machine-pitch baseball; within a mile west is the most dramatic miniature golf course on the Cape (and probably the most expensive), known as Pirate's Cove. Near Parker's River, which roughly divides South Yarmouth from West Yarmouth, there is Aqua Circus and Petting Zoo, a commercial animal entertainment spot.

Sit-down dinner restaurants also proliferate on Route 28, although they are not inclined to be intimate eateries.

But Route 28's real claim to fame is its raucous clubs for college-age partiers and drinkers. The biggest is the Mill Hill Club, which has been known to handle 500 rowdy people on a Saturday night (not one of them over 35 years old). The Compass Lounge and the Planet Bar and Grill are also lively night spots. Their proximity encourages barhopping by car, but the location of the Yarmouth police department on the same stretch of road helps keep Saturday night activity within reason—usually.

For those who tend to find their fun in the sun, the best south side option in Yarmouth is Sea Gull Beach, found by turning onto South Sea Avenue and then following the signs on Sea Gull Road. This is one of the most representative of Nantucket Sound beaches, calm and sandy, with a fairly big parking lot that nevertheless overflows early and often. Unfortunately for the public, there isn't much beachfront open to explore as alternatives; a guard stands watch over the road near Sea Gull Beach, which leads to Great Island, a privately owned piece of paradise that stretches far into Nantucket Sound and protects the mouth of Lewis Bay.

One last bit of advice about Route 28: if it all gets to be too much, there are a few ways to sidestep the worst stretches of Yarmouth. Turning north at Camp Street, Higgins Crowell Road, or West Yarmouth Road, depending on where you are and where you're going, will connect you to Buck Island Road. It's not particularly scenic (although there are some nice cranberry bogs), but its main attraction is that it runs parallel to Route 28 through the heart of West Yarmouth, then connects back to the highway via Winslow

Gray and Forrest roads. In the worst of jams, the time saved could be as much as an hour.

Dennis

The town of Dennis has an hourglass figure that needs no diet to be maintained. Rivers and creeks corset the town, from Bass River and Chase Garden Creek on the west to Quivet Creek and Swan Pond on the east. The town is home to roughly 13,000 people.

The bridge over Bass River on Route 28 connects South Yarmouth with West Dennis. Aside from being a pretty good place to fish on a rainy day, it also serves as a commercial boundary; the strip development that marks Yarmouth begins to subside in Dennis, businesses tend to be housed in converted old homes rather than shopping malls, private residences reappear, and small villages are once again defined.

The first village along the south side is West Dennis, dominated by a large white church steeple so common to New England villages. The social scene is dominated by the Village Deli, on Route 28 in the middle of town, the stop of choice for a morning cup of coffee.

Turning south on Fisk Street or School Street near the center of the village, you'll find a nice mixture of old homes and summer cottages that characterizes West Dennis. The roads slide near Kelleys Pond and jog around Weir Creek. Keep pointing south, following your nose toward the sea. You'll soon reach Bob Stone's Lighthouse Inn, a West Dennis landmark for more than 50 years.

Then the road bellies into West Dennis Beach, the largest beach in Dennis. The parking lot is one mile long, tarred above a barrier beach that stretches into the mouth of Bass River. There is a fee to park during the season, and it's best to get there early on hot summer days. The West Dennis Beach crowd is classic Cape Cod in the summer, from families of four under umbrellas to teenagers with boom boxes hanging around the lifeguard stands.

Leaving West Dennis Beach, take Lower County Road, an alternative to Route 28 running parallel to the main highway but farther south and closer to the beach. The road passes over Swan River, reputed to have some of the most fertile oyster beds on Cape Cod, not to mention Swan River Fish Market—not fancy but excellent fresh seafood to stay or to go. Once past the river, you're in Dennisport.

This is the heart of Cape Cod as people envisioned it in the 1940s; small summer cottages on postage stamp lots along side streets with such names as Beachplum Lane and Captain Chase Road. In the winter this area is deserted, but in the summer it hustles—from the only remaining trailer park on Cape Cod with frontage on Nantucket Sound to the long row of low-rise motels built right on the beach in the 1950s and 1960s. Old Wharf Road, so named because there were indeed old wharves on the Sound that have long since washed away, hugs the shore off Lower County, and if you have a place to ditch the car, there are several small public beaches between motels. Glendon Road marks one, Sea Street marks another, and Raycroft Parkway marks a third.

In keeping with the territory, the best restaurants in Dennisport are not the fanciest. Bob Briggs' Wee Packet on Depot Street has been serving local seafood from a small kitchen for decades. The decor is nets and traps on the wall, Formica tables, plenty of food, and plenty of smiles. Up Sea Street at the corner of Route 28 is a fast-food mecca known as Kream 'n Kone, run by the same family since 1953. The fried food is a very big cut above the norm; unfortunately, this is not a well-kept secret, so go early or late to avoid the long line.

Dennisport Village, the last stop on Route 28 before Harwich, has undergone a face-lift in recent years; brick sidewalks (which certainly are not a part of Cape Cod tradition) nevertheless make the village a pleasant spot to shop and browse. For men who might need a haircut and shave, Cal's Barbershop takes care of business and offers the best chair in town to sit and watch the world go by.

Turning north in Dennis, the honky-tonk quotient drops immediately. The main north-south artery that slits the town down the middle is Route 134, which has been built up around the Route 6 highway exit into a Hyannis-like suburban shopping hub. Just past the highway is the Dennis Police Station, with its very strange display on the front lawn called "Curious Forms of Colonial Punishment." Stocks, a whipping post, and other "curious" relics were erected during bicentennial celebrations in 1976. Regardless of how it looks, it was not someone's idea of a joke—or a comment on the police force.

But there are better alternatives than Route 134 heading north. The best is Old Main Street off Route 28 in West Dennis, which almost immediately turns into a handsome tree-lined road past stately homesteads comparable to the best stretches of the Old King's Highway. The transition from commercial Route 28 to this quiet avenue is so abrupt as to be almost eerie, but dramatic change in short order is a Cape Cod characteristic.

As the road turns south and changes names (becoming Old Bass River Road), you enter South Dennis. Yes, it so happens that South Dennis actually is due north of West Dennis, which actually is west of nothing other then South Yarmouth. The names only make sense with the benefit of a long historical perspective and give but one inkling of how people's ideas of the center and focus of their community have evolved over the centuries.

South Dennis has no big commercial interest off Route 134, but Town Hall does attract a lot of traffic for everything from beach stickers to subdivision plans. The doors are open office hours; in the basement, somebody from the conservation commission could show you how to reach the beautiful hiking trails behind the building that lead on public lands through forests and marshes down to Bass River.

Over the highway, continuing north, a new and wide town bike path parallels the road for several miles on the right, while some unusual street names begin to crop up on the left: Viking Drive, Thorwald Drive, Leif Ericson Drive—all small roads that dead end near the head of Bass River along Follins Pond. Folklore has it that some of the earliest Viking explorers found their way into Bass River, a historical speculation fueled partly by Ericson's descriptions of his journeys, partly by unusual rocks and markings found in the area. Most people find more fancy than fact to the stories, but they explain Norse-named roads.

After the road passes over the ridge, which is the backbone of the Cape, it then begins dropping toward the bay. A sharp right turn onto Scargo Hill Road leads to Scargo Tower, an old stone circle about two stories high with stairs up the middle and a flat vantage on top. The tower offers what might be the nicest view of Dennis, with Scargo Lake below, the north side villages of Dennis beyond, and then the blue expanse of Cape Cod Bay.

In recent years Dennis taxpayers have invested an extraordinary amount of money in the public purchase of open lands, particularly on the north side. The most dramatic benefit for visitors is the town's bay side beaches, which are consistently superb.

Beginning at the northwest corner of Dennis, Chapin Beach can be reached from Route 6A by following signs from Dennis village at New Boston Road. You pass through "Little Taunton," or "Little Italy," as this part of town is known, because its summer homes were built and occupied mainly by Italian-Americans from the Massachusetts city of Taunton after World War II. Gina's, an Italian restaurant tucked behind a sand dune, is a local restaurant of choice for a moderately expensive meal among a younger crowd. Joe Mac's, in the same neighborhood, has more of the bar-and-tavern feeling. Rose's on Black Flats Road, also nearby, is the quintessential family Italian restaurant.

Chapin Beach has the largest parking lot in this part of town, and public land stretches all the way into Bass Hole and Chase Garden Creek. But to the east are a series of smaller beaches that hold similar attractions. Mayflower and Bay View beaches are the nearest. Corporation Beach is two miles east and can't be reached without returning to Route 6A and finding Corporation Road.

Tucked behind Dennis Village near Corporation Road are the grounds of the Cape Playhouse, which features live theater all summer, and the adjacent Cape Cinema, which is the handsomest movie theater on Cape Cod, replete with a big screen, cloth-draped seats, and a minor art classic of a ceiling mural. The historic buildings and grounds alone are worth a visit, and the Greenroom Restaurant offers a comfortable setting for dinner or a drink. Also on the Playhouse grounds visit the Cape Cod Museum of Fine Arts.

Next to the playhouse complex is a collection of shops called the Theater Market Place, which has a gourmet deli, an excellent bakery, and a gift shop.

Farther east along Route 6A, the road hooks around Scargo Lake, and there is a turnoff to a public beach for those who like fresh water rather than salt. The same turnoff leads into a pine forest up to Scargo Hill Pottery, the most interesting pottery studio in the area. The setting is rustic and creative, while Harry Holl, accompanied by daughters, apprentices, and admirers, turns out strong and functional works of art, much as he has above

Scargo Lake for more than 30 years. Usually someone is at work on a wheel in the open studio, so a visit can turn into an impromptu lesson in how to throw a pot.

Directly across the highway, Sesuit Neck Road branches off and leads all the way to Sesuit Harbor, the focus of boating activity on the north side of Dennis. Both charter boat fishing and whale-watching boats are available at Sesuit; their schedules depend entirely on the comings and goings of the tide. On the east side of Sesuit Harbor is yet one more small public beach and parking lot at the end of Cold Storage Road.

Sesuit Harbor roughly divides Dennis from East Dennis. East Dennis is probably the smallest of all the town's villages, but it is also perhaps the oldest, and least spoiled by new development. Turn off Route 6A onto School Street or South Street, and handsome old homes line the roads no matter which way you go. But the jewel of East Dennis is Crowe's Pasture, found at the end of South Street past the village cemetery. The road becomes dirt, then suitable only for four-wheel-drive vehicles that roll out to Quivet Creek in the summer. Acres of open upland parallel the beach, with town-maintained hiking trails that wind through low vegetation and offer changing vistas of the bay. Crowe Pasture is not marked on many maps, there are no signs directing people there, but once found it is a place to remember, and revisit.

For more information about the Mid-Cape area and for an up-to-the-minute schedule of activities, we suggest you pick up a copy of the *Register* newspaper, which recently celebrated its one hundred and fiftieth anniversary.

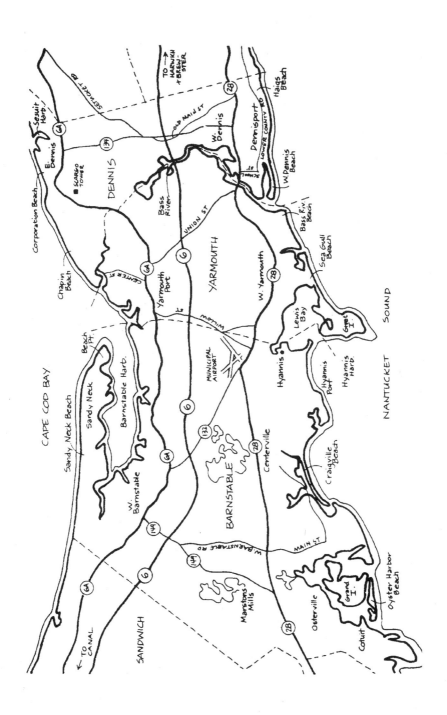

MID-CAPE

Mid Cape: Essentials

 ## Important Public Information

Municipal Services

BARNSTABLE

Barnstable Town Hall: 775-1120.
Barnstable Village: police (775-1212), fire (362-3131), ambulance (362-3131).
Centerville: police (775-1212), fire (428-9111), ambulance (428-9111).
Cotuit: police (775-1212), fire (428-6526), ambulance (428-6526).
Hyannis: police (775-1212), fire (775-2323), ambulance (775-2323).
Osterville: police (775-1212), fire (428-9111), ambulance (428-9111).
Marstons Mills: police (775-1212), fire (428-9111), ambulance (428-9111).
West Barnstable: police (775-1212), fire (362-3131), ambulance (362-3131).

DENNIS

Dennis Town Hall: 394-8300.
Dennis: police (394-1313), fire (398-2241), ambulance (398-2241).
Dennisport: police (394-1313), fire (398-2241), ambulance (398-2241).
East Dennis: police (394-1313), fire (398-2241), ambulance (398-2241).
South Dennis: police (394-1313), fire (398-2241), ambulance (398-2241).
West Dennis: police (394-1313), fire (398-2241), ambulance (398-2241).

YARMOUTH

- *Yarmouth Town Hall:* 398-2231
- *Bass River:* police (771-1212), fire (398-2211), ambulance (398-2211).
- *South Yarmouth:* police (771-1212), fire (398-2211), ambulance (398-2211).
- *West Yarmouth:* police (771-1212), fire (398-2211), ambulance (398-2211).
- *Yarmouth:* police (771-1212), fire (398-2211), ambulance (398-2211).
- *Yarmouth Port:* police (771-1212), fire (398-2211), ambulance (398-2211).

Medical Services

- *Cape Cod Hospital,* 27 Park St., Hyannis; 771-1800.
- *Mid Cape Medical Centers*, Rte. 28, Hyannis (771-4092); Rte. 28, Yarmouth (394-2151).

Veterinarians

- *After Hours Emergency Pet Care*, corner of Commonwealth Ave. and White's Path, S. Yarmouth; 394-3566.
- *Anchor Pet Clinic of Cotuit*, Cotuit; 428-2989.
- *Barnstable Animal Hospital*, 157 Airport Rd., Hyannis; 778-6555.
- *Cape Cod Animal Hospital*, Osterville Rd., W. Barnstable; 428-6393.
- *Dennis Animal Hospital*, 5 Beach Rd., Dennis; 385-8323.
- *Marianne McFarland*, 711 Yarmouth Rd., Hyannis; 775-4521.

Weather

- *WCIB Radio Weather Phone*, 540-7876.
- *Weather Phone Mid Cape*, 778-6262.
- *The Cape Codder Weatherphone*, 255-8500.
- *WQRC Radio Weather Phone*, 771-5522.

Tourist Information Services

- *Cape Cod Chamber of Commerce*, Rte. 6 at Rte. 132 Shootflying Hill Rd., Hyannis; 362-3225.
- *Hyannis Chamber of Commerce*, 319 Barnstable Rd., Hyannis; 775-2201.
- *Centerville Tourist Information*, 1698 Rte. 28, Centerville; 771-7509.
- *Town of Barnstable*, 397 Main St., Hyannis, 775-1120.
- *Dennis Chamber of Commerce Information Booth*, intersection of Rtes. 28 and 134, Box 275, S. Dennis 02660; 398-3568 or 398-3573.
- *Yarmouth Chamber of Commerce*, 911 Rte. 28, Box 479, S. Yarmouth 02664; 398-5311.

Lodgings

B&Bs & Guest Houses

Major credit cards are accepted at most B&Bs and guest houses, and many offer off-season rates. We suggest you call to inquire.

RESERVATION SERVICES & DIRECTORIES

- *House Guests Cape Cod and the Islands* is the Cape and Islands' original and most varied bed and breakfast reservation service. More than 300 guest rooms are available: year-round service. Offers accommodations for singles, doubles, and families; water views and wooded locations. All accommodations have been inspected and approved; reasonable rates. For a directory covering Cape Cod and the Islands, write Box 1881, Orleans, MA 02653, or call 896-7053 or 1-800-666-HOST; Visa, MasterCard, American Express cards welcome.
- *House Guest of Cape Cod*, Rte. 6A, Brewster; 896-7053. Offers accommodations in private homes, inns, and guest houses all over the Cape and the Islands.

• *Bed & Breakfast Cape Cod*, Box 341, West Hyannis Port 02672; 508-775-2772. Select from 60 host homes, country inns, and sea captain's houses on Cape Cod and the islands of Nantucket and Martha's Vineyard. Beaches, great seafood restaurants, whale watches, and summer theater are all a part of the local attractions. Modest/deluxe rates, private or shared baths. Write or call for free selection information.

• *DestINNations New England*, 420-3430 or 800-333-4667. This reservations service will book your Cape Cod B&B and then plan the rest of your New England tour as well.

BARNSTABLE

Village of Barnstable

• *Acworth Inn*, 4352 Old King's Hwy.; 362-3330. Moderate. A classic house; secluded; quiet and unhurried.

• *Anderson Acres*, 3885 Main St., Cummaquid; 362-4395. Moderate. Park like 2 1/2 acres of woods; lawns and gardens; within minutes of sandy stretches on the bay side of the Cape.

• *Ashley Manor*, 3660 Main St., Rte. 6A; 362-8044. Expensive. Hidden by tall boxwood hedges but worth finding; two acres of manicured lawns; gazebo; six bedrooms, most with working fireplaces; full breakfast. Garden cottage available. Off-season rates. Walk to beach and village.

• *Bacon Barn Inn*, 3400 Main St.; 362-5518. Victorian decor in a restored country barn. Located in Barnstable Village.

• *Beechwood*, 2839 Main St.; 362-6618. Expensive. Lovely Victorian Inn with a great wraparound porch; five large rooms with private baths; furnished with antiques. Rooms have either ocean views or garden views; afternoon tea on the porch; croquet on the lawn. Year-round. Lots of fireplaces and beech trees!

• *Charles Hinckley House*, 8 Scudder Ln.; 362-9924. Expensive. Private baths; year-round; English country breakfast.

• *Cozy Nest B&B*, 161 Maple St.; 362-4218. Romantic setting on a country lane, suites, full breakfast.

• *Crocker Tavern B&B*, 3095 Main St.; 362-5115. Moderate. Restored 1750s tavern that served as a meeting place for the Whigs during the Revolutionary War, furnished with antiques; waterviews and fireplaces; gourmet breakfast.

• *Fox Glen Manor Bed and Breakfast*, 4011 Main St., Cummaquid; 362-4657. Georgian colonial on five acres overlooking a pond, honeymoon suite available.

• *The Lamb & Lion*, Main St., Rte. 6A; 362-6823. Expensive. Four acres on salt marshes; pool; sun decks. Honeymoon suite, cottage, efficiencies available. Private baths; some fireplaces. Year-round; off-season rates.

Centerville

• *Adams Terrace Gardens Inn*, 539 Main St.; 775-4707. Moderate. Walk to Craigville Beach from this sea captain's house. Year-round.

• *The Inn at Fernbrook*, 481 Main St.; 775-4334. Moderate. B&B.

• *Long Dell Guest House*, 436 S. Main St.; 775-2750. Moderate. Sea captain's house; continental breakfast; studio apartment available.

• *Old Hundred House*, 1211 Craigville Beach Rd.; 775-6166. Inexpensive. Sea captain's house; 1500 feet from beach; continental breakfast.

Cotuit

• *Salty Dog Inn*, 451 Main St.; 428-5228. Moderate. Restored Victorian home; continental breakfast; walk to beach.

Hyannis

- *Mansfield House B&B,* 70 Gosnold St.; 771-9455. Walking distance to Hyannis and Island boats, private baths.
- *Physic Point,* 314 Ocean St.; 790-4720. Moderate. Lovely room with private bath; located near beaches, tours and Island ferries.
- *Salt Winds Bed & Breakfast,* 293 Sea St.; 775-2038. Moderate. Breakfast, walk to beach and town.
- *Sea Beach Inn,* 388 Sea St.; 775-4612. Moderate. Captain's home with private and shared baths, continental breakfast, some ocean views. Studio apartment available; one block from beach.
- *Sea Breeze Inn,* 397 Sea Street; 771-7213. Moderate. A/C; Canopy beds; private baths; close to ferries and restaurants.
- *Simmons Homestead Inn,* 288 Scudder Ave.; 778-4999 or 800-637-1649. Expensive. An 1820s Captain's home, full breakfast.

Osterville

- *East Bay Lodge,* East Bay Rd.; 428-5200 or toll-free 1-800-933-2782. Expensive. Country setting; close to beaches and shopping.

West Barnstable

- *Gentleman Farmer,* 886 Main St., Rte. 6A; 362-6955. Moderate. 19th-century farmhouse. Enjoy blueberry muffins made of fruit from their own blueberry patch; served on sun porch with the morning paper. Wine and cheese in the afternoon; croquet and badminton on spacious grounds. No credit cards.
- *Honeysuckle Hill,* 591 Main St.; 362-8418. Expensive. Victorian farmhouse; private baths. Afternoon tea; breakfast served on the front porch. Near Sandy Neck; complimentary transportation at train or airport. Credit cards accepted. Bicycles available for guests.

DENNIS

Village of Dennis

- *Captain Nickerson Inn,* 333 Main St.; 398-5966 or 800-282-1619. Moderate. Residential setting, Victorian home, bikes, children welcome, full breakfast.
- *Captain Judah Paddock House,* 1554 Route 6A, E. Dennis; 385-9959. Recently renovated sea captain's house, some rooms with fireplaces, continental breakfast.
- *Four Chimney's Inn,* 946 Main St., Rte 6A; 385-6317. Moderate. Lovely setting; walk to beach, Scargo Lake, Cape Playhouse; continental breakfast; porch; open March–December; fireplace in living room.
- *Isaiah Hall B&B,* 152 Whig St.; 385-9928. Moderate. Greek Revival 1857 farmhouse, walk to beach, lovely residential area. Some rooms with balconies, private and shared baths, open year-round, continental breakfast.
- *The Willows,* 79 Seaside Ave.; 385-3232. Moderate to expensive. Located in a charming residential area. Main house perfect for reunions—11 bedrooms, 7 baths, kitchen. Cottage available, walk to beach.

Dennisport

- *By-the-Sea Guests,* 57 Chase Ave. and Inman Rd.; 398-8685 or 1-800-447-9202. Moderate. On Nantucket Sound; private beach; rooms with ocean view; children welcome; continental breakfast; cottage available.
- *Ocean View Lodge,* Depot St., Box 676; 398-3412. Moderate. Continental breakfast; cottages available; barbecues; private and semiprivate baths.
- *Rose Petal Bed & Breakfast,* 152 Sea St.; 398-8470. Moderate. Walk to beach and village center, year-round, off-season rates.

West Dennis

- *The Beach House*, Oceanfront Bed & Breakfast, 61 Uncle Stevens Rd.; 398-4575. Expensive. Private beach on Nantucket Sound; private baths; decks; breakfast in sun room overlooking ocean, year-round.

YARMOUTH

Bass River

- *The Anchorage Bed & Breakfast*, South Shore Dr.; 398-8265. Inexpensive to moderate. Opposite Sea View Beach; continental breakfast; TV.
- *The Belvedere Guest House*, 167 Main St.; 398-1446. Inexpensive to moderate. 1820s sea captain's home. Breakfast; carriage house with studio apartment available; walk to beach.
- *Captain Isaiah's House Guests*, 33 Pleasant St.; 394-1739. Inexpensive. Sea captain's home; most rooms with fireplace; continental breakfast; studio apartments available. Open June to September.
- *Ocean View B&B*, South St.; 394-4939. Moderate to expensive. Private beach; full breakfast with homemade breads, refreshments in afternoon. Open year-round.
- *Wayfarers*, 186 Seaview Ave.; 771-4532 or 394-9981. Moderate. Only 600 feet to warm salt water beaches, family atmosphere.

West Yarmouth

- *Blasko's Guest House*, Rte. 28; 775-5356. Inexpensive. Private and shared baths; TV; some with refrigerators. Write: 68 E. Main St., Hyannis 02601.
- *The Manor House*, 57 Maine Ave.; 771-3433 or 800-962-6679. Moderate. Overlooks Lewis Bay; private baths; walk to beach and town; continental breakfast; fireplace in sitting room. Off-season rates.

Yarmouth Port

- *Captain Farris House*, 308 Old Main St.; 760-2818. Moderate to expensive. A nineteenth century sea captain's home located in a quiet residential neighborhood; includes a full breakfast.
- *Colonial House Inn*, Rte. 6A; 362-4348. Moderate. Sea captain's home built in 1730s; private baths; rates include dinner and continental breakfast; cribs or cots available; TV; air-conditioning.
- *Crook's Jaw Inn*, 186 Main St., Rte. 6A; 362-6111. Moderate to expensive. Sea captain's home; full breakfast; afternoon tea/coffee; picnic baskets available for daytrips; chauffeur service to and from airport and bus terminal; credit cards accepted; year-round.
- *Fisher's Net*, Rte. 6A; 362-8264. Moderate. Full breakfast is served every morning.
- *Liberty Hill Inn*, 77 Main St.; 362-3976 or 800-821-3977. Moderate to expensive. Charming, beautifully decorated 1825 Greek Revival home; breakfast in an elegant dining room or served in your room; private or shared baths. Year-round.
- *Old Yarmouth Inn*, 233 Rte. 6A; 362-8201. Oldest Inn on Cape Cod; breakfast included with room; family atmosphere.
- *One Centre Street Inn*, 1 Centre St. and Old King's Hwy., Rte. 6A; 362-8910. Moderate. Lovely area of Route 6A; breakfast; private and semiprivate baths; walk to beach; bicycles provided by inn; fireplace, library/sitting room.
- *Strawberry Lane*, One Strawberry Lane; 362-8631. A delightful antique sea captain's house. Small, friendly B&B ambiance with homestyle breakfast.
- *Village Inn*, 92 Main St., Rte. 6A; 362-3182. Moderate. Colonial sea captain's home; continental breakfast. Open year-round.

• *Wedgewood Inn*, 83 Main St., Rte. 6A; 362-5157. Expensive. All rooms with private baths; some with fireplaces; large rooms furnished with antiques; some four-poster beds; private porches; breakfast served on fine china and with fresh flowers. Year-round.

Resorts, Hotels, Motels, Condominiums, & Selected Cottages

Most of the following establishments accept major credit cards, and many of them offer off-season rates. Call for more information.

BARNSTABLE

Centerville

• *Centerville Corners Motor Lodge*, 1338 Craigville Beach Rd.; 775-7223. Moderate. Close to beach.

• *Coral Village*, 1006 Craigville Beach Rd., Box 537; 775-2971. Moderate. Cottages on Craigville Beach; heated; off-season rates; open May–October.

• *The Craigville Motel*, at the corner of Rtes 6 and 132; 362-3401. Moderate. Close to beach.

• *Trade Winds Inn*. Craigville Beach Rd. (Box 107); 775-0365. Expensive. Overlooks Craigville Beach and Lake Elizabeth. Private beach; lounge; putting green; TV; phone; heat; year-round.

Hyannis

• *Anchor-In Motel*, One South Street; 775-0357. Moderate. On the water, decks, refrigerators, walk to ferry.

• *The Angel Motel*, Rte. 132; 775-2440. Inexpensive. Pool, picnic area. Off-season rates.

• *Anric Oceanside Motel*, Ocean St.; 771-5577. Moderate. Close to water and shopping.

• *Bouchards Tourist Home and Apartments,* 83 School St.; 775-0912. Inexpensive to moderate. Private bath and entrances, garden patio. Walk to beach, town, and island boats. Cottages available.

• *The Breakwaters*, Sea Street Beach; 775-6831. Moderate to expensive. Water view.

• *The Cape Codder Hotel,* Rte. 132 and Bearse's Way; 771-3000 or 800-365-3207. Moderate. Close to airport and shopping.

• *Captain Gosnold Village*, 230 Gosnold St.; 775-9111. Moderate. Motel and cottage units, close to shopping.

• *Comfort Inn,* Rte. 28; 771-1700 or 800-771-7200. Newly renovated hotel with a Gold's Gym, indoor pool, free continental breakfast, Jacuzzis. Pepper's restaurant on premises.

• *Country Lake Lodge*, Rte. 132; 362-6455. Moderate. Close to shopping and scenic Route 6A.

• *Country Squire Motor Lodge*, 206 Main St.; 775-5225. Moderate. Close to shopping.

• *Days Inn*, 867 Iyanough Rd., Rte 132; 771-6100 or 1-800-325-2525. Moderate. Outdoor-indoor pool. Continental breakfast, exercise room, game room.

• *Glo-Min by the Sea,* 182 Sea St.; 775-1423. Cottages, efficiencies, and rooms. Pool, walk to beach, picnic area. Year-round.

• *Harbor House Motor Lodge*, Ocean St.; 771-1880. Moderate. Close to harbor.

BARNSTABLE (CONTINUED)

• *Harbor Village*, Marstons Ave., Hyannis Port; 775-7581. Moderate to expensive. One- to four-bedroom houses on 18 acres; fireplaces; private beach; canoes and fishing on property.

• *Heritage House*, 259 Main St.; 508-775-7000 or 1-800-352-7189 (in MA) and 1-800-528-1234 (outside MA). Moderate. Indoor-outdoor pools, Jacuzzi and saunas, 143 guest rooms.

• *Hi-Seas "By the Beach,"* 395 Sea St.; 775-8675. Inexpensive. Cottages, efficiencies, and rooms. Picnic area; close to beach and harbor.

• *Howard Johnson's*, Main and Winter sts.; 775-8600. Moderate. Close to shopping.

• *Hyannis Harborview*, 213 Ocean St.; 775-4420 or 800-344-2125. Moderate to expensive. Water view, close to harbor.

• *Hyannis Holiday Motel,* 131 Ocean St.; 775-1639 or 800-423-1551. Moderate. Close to shopping.

• *Hyannis Inn Motel,* 473 Main St.; 775-0255 or 800-922-8993. Moderate. Close to shopping.

• *Hyannis Motel*, Rte. 132; 775-8910. Inexpensive to moderate. Close to shopping.

• *Hyannis Ramada Regency Inn,* Rte. 132; 775-1153. Moderate to expensive. Pool, whirlpool, health club, six indoor tennis courts. Restaurant and lounge, some kitchenettes; loft suites for families; year-round.

• *Hyannis Sands Motor Lodge*, Rte 132; 790-1700. Moderate. Close to shopping.

• *Hyannis Travel Inn*, 18 North St.; 775-8200. Moderate. Close to shopping.

• *International Inn*, 662 Main St.; 775-5600. Moderate. Close to shopping.

• *Quality Inn*, 1470 Iyanough Rd., Rte 132; 771-4804. Moderate. Overlooks duck pond, on a golf course. Pool, whirlpool, sauna, game room, indoor tennis courts, playground; continental breakfast; some kitchenettes.

• *Jonah's Harborview*, Lewis Bay, Hyannis; 771-1784. Oceanfront cottage, master bedroom with full bath, cable t.v. and a fully equipped kitchen.

• *The Mains'l*, 535 Ocean St.; 775-5725. Inexpensive to moderate. Across from beaches and ferryboats. Seasonal.

• *Park Square Village*, 156 Main St.; 775-5611. Moderate. Private and shared baths; efficiencies and cottages. Pool; picnic area; walk to downtown; laundry room; swing set; shuffleboard; economical guest rooms.

• *Rainbow Resort Motel,* Rte. 132; 362-3217. Moderate. Close to shopping, close to pond.

• *The Rose Garden Cottage*, 256 Ocean Ave.; 771-7213. Moderate. A two minute walk to beach; fully equipped kitchen; most rooms have ocean view.

• *Sea Breeze Motel & Cottages*, 397 Sea St.; 771-4269. Moderate. Studio apartments and Cape Cod-style cottages available. Picnic tables and barbecues; swings; near beaches; TV. Some ocean views; honeymoon and family rates; year-round.

• *Sun & Surf Motel*, 503 Ocean St.; 771-1652 or 1-800-342-8022. Moderate. Close to harbor.

• *Tara Hyannis*, West End Circle; 775-7775 or 800-843-8272. Moderate to expensive. Resort and conference center. Indoor and outdoor pools, lighted tennis courts, health spas, saunas, game center. Various packages, leisure activity programs, information at hotel on events around Cape Cod, activities for children, video game room. Restaurant, golf course, year-round.

- *Traywick Homes and Cottages,* 648 Craigville Beach Rd., W. Hyannis Port; 775-3174. Expensive. Private homes; close to Craigville Beach.
- *Yachtsman Condominiums*, 500 Ocean St.; 771-5454 or 800-695-5454. Expensive. Townhouses at Lewis Bay and Nantucket Sound. Private beach; pool; two to four bedrooms; 2 1/2 baths. Many with fireplace; dishwasher; washer/dryer.

Osterville

- *East Bay Lodge,* 199 East Bay Rd.; 428-5200, toll-free 1-800-933-2782. Expensive. Well known in the area for its fine accommodations and setting; year-round; restaurant; tennis courts; near the water.
- *Michas Pond Summer Rentals,* 87 Oakville Ave.; 428-5152. Inexpensive to moderate. Pool, barbecue, lawn games. Studio, duplex, cottage, or a five-bedroom house available.

DENNIS

Village of Dennis

- *Bresnahan's Cottage*, 944 Main St., Rte. 6A; 385-3285. Moderate.
- *J. D. Starr Motel,* Rte. 6A; 385-9770. Moderate. Pool; air-conditioning; morning coffee; off-season rates.
- *Flax Pond Motel*, Rte. 6A; 385-3464. Moderate. Full breakfast (July–August); air-conditioning; play area for children; picnic area; pool, off-season rates; TV.
- *Ocean Vista on the Beach*, Mandigo Rd.; 385-3029. Moderate. One- to four-bedroom oceanfront units; TV; private beach; children welcome. Sun decks; outside showers; barbecue; picnic tables; volleyball; badminton; seasonal.
- *The Willows*, Seaside Ave. (off Rte. 6A); 385-3232. Moderate. Comfortable setting, near beaches.

Dennisport

- *Acorn Cottages*, 34 Longell Rd.; 394-6352. Moderate. Three to four bedrooms; outdoor showers; grills; picnic tables; walk to beach; fireplaces. Open April 15–October 15; off-season, call 617-769-0152.
- *Bambi Cottages*, 235 Division St. (Box 283); 385-5989. Inexpensive to moderate. Three-bedroom home with washer/dryer; TV; sleeps eight or more. Cottages sleep four to six; efficiencies available. Grills; picnic tables; walk to town center. Open May–October; off-season.
- *BayBerry Bluff*, Beach Hill Rd.; 398-3339. Moderate. One- to three-bedroom cottages on private beach; TV; picnic tables. Open May–October; off-season rates.
- *Beach Plum Motel*, Rte. 28, Box 693; 398-0080. Inexpensive. Efficiencies; rooms; grills; overlooks marsh; centrally located. Open year-round. Canoe and paddleboat rentals on premises.
- *The Breakers*, Chase Ave.; 398-6905. Moderate. Oceanfront; most rooms have balconies; private beach; pool; TV. Off-season rates; open April–October.
- *By The Sea,* Chase Ave. & Inman Rd.; 398-8685. Moderate. Oceanfront lodge.
- *Cape Haven Motel*, 75 Lower County Rd.; 398-5080. Inexpensive. Efficiency units; TV; walk to beach; picnic tables and grills. Year-round; off-season rates.
- *Captains Row*, 257 Old Wharf Rd.; 398-3117. Moderate. Cottages on ocean; private beach; seasonal.
- *The Club at Cape Cod Vacation Resort,* 177 Lower County Rd.; 394-9290. Efficiency units, walk to beach, grounds with picnic tables and grills, indoor/outdoor pools.
- *Colonial Village Motel & Cottages*, 420 Lower County Rd.; 398-2071. Moderate. Kitchenettes and four-room cottages; close to beach; pool. Off-season rates; open April to October.

DENNIS (CONTINUED)

- *Colony Beach Motel,* Old Wharf Rd.; 398-2217. Moderate. Rooms, efficiencies or two-bedroom apartments on Nantucket Sound, pool, continental breakfast.
- *Connie's Cabins*, 248 Main St., Rte. 28; 394-5145. Inexpensive. Close to beaches; seasonal.
- *Corsair Resort Motel*, 41 Chase Ave.; 398-2279. Moderate. Oceanfront; private beach; pool; rooms or efficiencies; sun deck; TV; refrigerator. Off-season rates; open April–October.
- *Cricket Court*, 130 Rte. 28; 398-8400. Inexpensive. 10 cottages near the beach; pets accepted with notice; open April–October.
- *Cross Rip Resort Motel*, 33 Chase Ave.; 398-6600 or 394-8985. Expensive. Oceanfront with private beach; pool; lounge; TV; refrigerator; rooms or efficiencies; children over four; seasonal.
- *Cutty Sark Motor Lodge & Inn*, Old Wharf Rd.; 398-9116 (winter, 617-767-2935). Moderate. Across the street from beach; pool; TV; air-conditioning; morning coffee; off-season rates.
- *Delight Cottages*, 125 Main St.; 394-4551. Moderate. Children's playground, yard games, and recreational field; grills; cribs and high chairs for rent. Open March 1–November 30.
- *Dennis Seashores*, Chase Ave.; 398-8512. Expensive. Two- to four-bedroom cottages; private beach; fireplaces; picnic tables and grills; off-season rates.
- *Dolphin Cottages*, 291 Lower County Rd.; 398-1551. Inexpensive. Walk to beach; barbecue; picnic tables. Write: R. Dauphinee, 139 Sea St., Dennisport 02639.
- *Doryman Motel,* Box 526, 73 Sea St.; 394-0000. Moderate. One block from beach; pool; TV; seasonal.
- *Ebb Tide Beach Club*, 88 Chase Ave.; 398-8733. Moderate. Two or three bedrooms; across from ocean; picnic area; gas grills; pool.
- *The Edgewater*, 95 Chase Ave.; 398-6922. Expensive. Oceanfornt; private beach; refrigerators; TV; indoor/outdoor pools; efficiency available; sauna; 18-hole putting green.
- *Gallivan Cottage*, near Old Wharf Rd.; 394-0616. Moderate. Three bedrooms; fireplace; 200 yards from private beach; sleeps eight. Write: J. Gallivan, 31 Ardmore Rd., Dedham, MA 02026; 617-329-0178.
- *The Garlands*, 117 Old Wharf Rd.; 398-6987. Moderate. Efficiency units on private beach; TV; open April–October.
- *Gaslight Resort*, Chase Ave.; 398-8831. Moderate. Across street from beach; refrigerator, TV; morning coffee; off-season rates.
- *Holiday Hill Motor Inn*, 352 Main St.; 394-5577 or 800-333-2569. Moderate. Pool; game room; air-conditioning; family units and efficiency available; seasonal.
- *Hurricane Pines*, Old Wharf Rd.; 398-2616. Moderate. One- to two-bedroom Cape Cod cottages; picnic area; across the street from beach. Seasonal.
- *Jonathan Edwards Motel*, Rte. 28, 393 Main St.; 398-2953. Moderate. Rooms, efficiencies, and apartments; TV; pool; game room; year-round.
- *The Lamplighter Motor Lodge*, Rte. 28 (Box 577); 398-8469. Moderate. TV; air-conditioning; pool; gym set for children; picnic area. Open April–October.
- *Marine Lodge Cottages*, 15 North St.; 398-2963. Moderate. One to four bedrooms in pine grove; some with fireplaces; screened porches; pool; tennis court; lawn games; picnic tables and grills; washer/dryer; childern's play area; cribs/high chairs available. Seasonal.

- *Murray Cottages*, 63 Lower County Rd.; 394-2114. Moderate. Homes or apartments near or on ocean; family rentals. Year-round.
- *Oceanside Condos*, 154 Old Wharf Rd.; 394-5359. Moderate. Across the street from Nantucket Sound, kitchenettes, pool overlooks the ocean.
- *Ocean Vista,* Mandigo Rd.; 385-3029. Moderate. Spacious villas, private beach, fully equipped kitchens, sundecks.
- *Old Wharf Inn,* 402 Old Wharf Rd.; 398-2804. Moderate. Apartments, cottages, efficiencies across the street from Nantucket Sound, seasonal.
- *"Old Landing,"* 301 Old Wharf Rd.; 398-3703. Moderate. Motel and cottages by the beach; TV; pool; snack bar. Open May–September.
- *Pelham House Resort*, 38 Sea St.; 398-6076. Moderate. On ocean; tennis courts; saltwater pool; TV.
- *Pilgrim's Haven*, 11 Pine St.; 394-0664. Moderate. Modern cottages; TV; picnic table; grills; walk to ocean.
- *Sea Lord Resort,* 20 Chase Ave.; 398-6900. Moderate. Across the street from beach; TV; pool; continental breakfast. Seasonal.
- *Sea Maples*, 138 Sea St.; 394-1885 or 800-732-1885. Moderate. One to three bedrooms; washer/dryer on premises; picnic tables; grills; play area; walk to beaches. Write: S.A. Capachin, 90 High St., Walpole, MA 02081; 617-668-8806.
- *Sea Shell Motel*, 45 Chase Ave.; 398-8965. Moderate. Private balconies overlooking Nantucket Sound; continental breakfast; TV; private beach; refrigerators in every room. Year-round.
- *Sea View Village*, Lower County Rd. and Chase Ave.; 398-9084. Moderate. One to five bedrooms; private beach.
- *Seawinds Condominiums,* Old Wharf Rd.; 398-6987. Moderate. Private beach; pool; sailboat rentals; rooms or efficiencies.
- *Shifting Sands Motel*, 9 Chase Ave.; 398-9145. Moderate. Oceanfront and private beach; every room with ocean view; no credit cards. Open June–October.
- *"The Skipper,"* Box 256, Captain Chase Rd.; 398-3952. Inexpensive to moderate. Efficiency units; TV; bike rentals; linens included.
- *Sound View*, 145 Old Wharf Rd.; 394-3313. Moderate to expensive. Private beach; oceanfront; deck overlooking beach. Open May–October.
- *The Soundings*, Chase Ave., Box 1104; 394-6561. Expensive. Oceanfront; private beach; indoor/outdoor pools; sauna; TV: putting green; efficiencies and suites available. Seasonal.
- *Spouter Whale Motor Inn*, 405 Old Wharf Rd.; 398-8010. Moderate to expensive. Oceanfront; pool; whirlpool; efficiency units; some ocean views; private beach.
- *Surf Motel*, Captain Chase Rd.; 398-8621. Moderate. Efficiencies; TV; grills; 500 feet to beach.
- *Three Seasons Motor Lodge*, Old Wharf Rd.; 398-6091. Moderate to expensive. Waterfront; private beach.
- *Uppvall Cottages*, Ocean Dr.; 398-0515 or 1-800-444-8801. Moderate. Two to three bedrooms; pool; TV; walk to beach; recreation area; off-season rates.
- *West Wind Motel & Guest House*, 15 Centre St.; 398-3015. Moderate. Efficiency; TV; guest rooms; picnic tables; grills.
- *Widow's Walk Motor Lodge*, 396 Lower County Rd.; 398-6800. Moderate. Some efficiencies; some with decks; TV; walk to beach. Open May–October; off-season rates.
- *William & Mary Motel,* 433 Lower County Rd.; 398-2931. Moderate. Units include kitchen; living room; patio.

DENNIS (CONTINUED)

- *Wooden Whale Cottages*, 58 Sea St.; 394-0621. Moderate. Two minutes to beach; picnic tables; fireplace.
- *Woody Glen Cottages*, Old Wharf Rd.; 398-3802. Moderate. Waterfront; private beach; one to three bedrooms; TV.

East Dennis

- *Sesuit Harbor Motel*, 1421 Main St. (Rte. 6A); 385-3326. Moderate. Close to harbor, beaches, and antique shops.

West Dennis

- *Ballast Motel*, 99 Main St.; 394-6603. Moderate. Forty-one units.
- *The Barnacle Motel*, Rte. 28; 394-8472 or 800-328-8812. Moderate. Pool, 35 units.
- *Cape House*, Shore Rd.; 518-489-5657. Moderate. Three bedrooms; washer/dryer; dishwasher; TV; gas grill; walk to beach; fireplace. Write: John Connors, 112 Fairlawn Ave., Albany, NY 12203.
- *Captain Varrieur's Cottages*, 18 Crowell Rd.; 394-4338. Moderate. Two to eight bedrooms; grills; outdoor furniture; some fireplaces; walk to beach. Thirteen-room house available for large gatherings.
- *Elmwood Inn*, 57 Old Main St.; 394-2798. Moderate to expensive. Elegant Victorian inn near Bass River.
- *Huntsman Motel Lodge*, 829 Main St.; 394-5415. Moderate. No pets.
- *Lighthouse Inn*, Lighthouse Rd., Box 128; 398-2244. Expensive. Resort on ocean; cottages; pool; play area; game room; tennis courts. Seasonal.
- *Pine Cove Inn & Cottages*, 5 Main St., Rte 28; 398-8511. Inexpensive to moderate. Waterfront accommodations; cottages and guest rooms; screened porches; free boats; private beach; sun deck. Seasonal.
- *Pines on Kelley's Pond*, 51 Pond St.; 362-2509. Moderate. Cottages close to beach; fireplace and screened porch with each. Pond good for swimming, fishing, and sailboats; grills; picnic tables. Seasonal.
- *Plantation Motel*, Rte. 28; 398-3868. Moderate. TV; pool; picnic tables.
- *Whip-o-Will Motel & Cottages*, 707 Main St., Rte. 28; 398-8649. Moderate. One-, two-, and three-bedroom cottages; efficiencies available. Picnic tables and grills. Seasonal.
- *Woodbine Village on the Cove*, Rte. 28; 881-1381. Moderate. Cottages with water view.

YARMOUTH

Bass River

- *Bass River Motel*, Rte. 28; 398-2488. Moderate. 20 units; some efficiencies. Pool; shuffleboard; picnic area; close to beach.
- *Beach House at Bass River*, 73 South Shore Dr.; 394-6501. Moderate to expensive. Continental breakfast; balconies overlooking ocean; TV; air-conditioning.
- *Best Western Blue Water Resort*, South Shore Dr.; 398-2288 or 800-367-9393. Moderate. Outdoor/indoor pool; saunas; whirlpool; shuffleboard; tennis; putting green. Efficiencies; private beach.
- *Brentwood Motor Inn and Cottages*, Rte. 28; 398-8812 (toll-free MA 1-800-742-2999; outside MA 1-800-247-3218). Moderate. Indoor/outdoor pool; whirlpool; sauna; game room. Efficiencies; TV; air-conditioning; year-round.
- *Cavalier*, 881 Main St.; 394-6575. Moderate. Located in a park like setting, heated pool, hot tub, and recreation facilities.

- ***The Dunes***, 170 Seaview Ave.; 398-3062. Inexpensive to moderate. Quaintness of Old Cape Cod combined with modern amenities; continental breakfast; a/c; heated pool; TV; coffee shop.
- ***Dawn Treader***, on the Bass River, 38 Charles St.; 394-3659. Moderate. View of Bass River; boat dock; picnic tables and grills; two-bedroom suites.
- ***Edge of the Sea Motel and Cottages***, 301 South Shore Dr.; 398-3332. Expensive. 14 units facing private beach; refrigerators; TV. One- and two-bedroom cottages; low off-season rates.
- ***Jolly Captain Condominiums on Bass River***, 41 Chase Ave.; 398-2279. Townhouse suites, kitchens, patios, river view, indoor/outdoor pools.
- ***Ocean Club on Smuggler's Beach***, South Shore Dr.; 398-6955. Moderate. Private beach, indoor/outdoor pools, fitness center, 63 rooms.
- ***Ocean Mist Resort***, 97 South Shore Dr.; 398-2633. Moderate. Oceanfront motel; private beach; rooms and loft suites; efficiencies available; TV.
- ***Pine Knot Motel***, 890 Main St.; 398-3315. Inexpensive. 20 pine-paneled units; efficiencies and family units; TV with HBO. Pool and children's area; refrigerators; grills and picnic tables; air-conditioning.
- ***Red Jacket Beach Motor Inn***, South Shore Dr.; 398-0500. Moderate. 1000 feet of private beach; 150 rooms with air-conditioning; TV; private balconies. Indoor/outdoor pools; sauns; whirlpool. Tennis court; putting green. Seasonal.
- ***Riviera Beach Motor Inn***, South Shore Dr.; 398-2273. Expensive. Private beach; whirlpool; indoor/outdoor pool. Game room; TV. Year-round.
- ***Windjammer Motor Inn***, 192 South Shore Dr.; 398-2370. Moderate. Pool; opposite beaches; TV; air-conditioning. Seasonal.
- ***Wayfarers All Cottages***, 186 Seaview Ave.; 771-4532. Moderate. Two-bedroom cottages. TV; patios; close to beaches.

South Yarmouth

- ***All Seasons Motor Inn***, 1199 Main St., Rte. 28; 394-7600. Moderate. New Motel with 114 rooms; indoor/outdoor pools; private balconies; whirlpool; saunas; air-conditioning; TV; game room. Open year-round.
- ***Ambassador Motor Inn***, 1314 Rte. 28; 394-4000 or 800-341-5700. Moderate. 90 units with heat, air-conditioning; TV; indoor/outdoor pool; whirlpool; saunas; game room. New motel; open year-round; off-season rates.
- ***Blue Rock Inn & Golf Course***, Todd St.; 398-6962 or 800-237-8887. Moderate. On Blue Rock Golf Course; Jacuzzi; private balconies or patios; pool; air-conditioning; TV; private beach.
- ***Captain Jonathan Motel***, 1237 Rte. 28; 398-3480 or 800-342-3480. Moderate. Picnic grounds and grill; pool; swings; continental breakfast; TV; air-conditioning; refrigerators. Open year-round; off-season rates.
- ***The Cove at Yarmouth Resort Hotel***, Rte. 28; 771-3666. Located on Mill Cove, two-room suites, indoor/outdoor pools and tennis courts, spa, restaurant, lounge.
- ***Four Winds***, 345 High Bank Rd.; 394-4182. Moderate. 1712 sea captain's home; guest house; cottages; efficiencies.
- ***Gull Wing Suites***, 822 Main St.; 394-9300 or 1-800-676-0000. Expensive. Each suite has a separate living room with a sleep sofa, refrigerator, and wet bar. Outdoor-indoor pools, Jacuzzi, coffee shop, game room. No charge for cribs.
- ***Pilgrim Acres Village***, 90 Seaview Ave.; 398-9202. Moderate. Located on Bass River; pool; one- to three-bedroom cottages; heat; private deck or patio; cribs and rollaways available; efficiencies; outdoor grills; picnic tables. Open June to October.

YARMOUTH (CONTINUED)

- *Riverview Motor Lodge*, 37 Neptune Ln.; 394-9801. Inexpensive to moderate. 110 units overlooking Parker's River; game room; private balconies; continental breakfast; pool; whirlpool; TV; air-conditioning. Off-season rates; year-round.
- *Seaside Village*, 135 South Shore Dr.; 398-2533. Moderate. Private beach; cottage units; efficiencies.
- *The Village Green Motel*, South Shore Dr.; 760-1266. Moderate to expensive. Forty-six studio and efficiency units with refrigerators; TV; pool; shuffleboard; badminton; beach opposite motel; grills; picnic tables; recreation room. Open April to October; off-season rates.

West Yarmouth

- *American Host Motel*, Rte. 28; 775-2332. Moderate to expensive. Close to Hyannis; indoor/outdoor pools; whirlpool; play area; picnic area; mini-golf on premises; TV; continental breakfast.
- *Americana Holiday Motel*, Rte. 28; 775-5511. Moderate. Close to Hyannis; continental breakfast; pool; sauna; whirlpool; game room; play area; shuffleboard; picnic tables; putting green; exercise room.
- *Cape Cod Irish Village*, Rte. 28; 771-0100. Moderate. Rooms, cottages, and efficiencies. Motel, pub, gift shop, and restaurant combination. Tennis courts; indoor pool; putting green; whirlpool; sauna; game room. Year-round; family specials.
- *The Cape Point*, 476 Rte. 28; 778-1500. Indoor corridors to all facilities; indoor and outdoor pools; whirlpool, sauna, game room; rooms with refrigerators; café. Open year-round; off-season rates.
- *Cape Sojourn Motel*, Rte. 28; 775-3825. Moderate. Indoor/outdoor pools; air-conditioning; whirlpool; putting green; picnic area; playground; game room; TV with HBO. Off -season rates and package plans.
- *Cape Traveler Motor Inn*, Rte. 28; 775-1225. Moderate. Pool; playground; shuffleboard. Seasonal.
- *Colonial Acres Resort Motel*, 114 Standish Way; 775-0935. Moderate. Ocean view; private beach. Seasonal.
- *Englewood Beach Condominiums*, 60 Broadway; 775-3900. Moderate to expensive. Private beach 100 yards away; some ocean views; indoor/outdoor pools; tennis court; shuffleboard; decks or patios. Seasonal.
- *Flagship Motor Inn*, 343 Rte. 28; 775-5155 or 800-676-0000. Moderate. Close to Hyannis; 136 new units; suites; balconies; TV with HBO. Indoor/outdoor pools; whirlpool; Jacuzzi; game room; coffee shop; playground.
- *Green Harbor on the Ocean*, 182 Baxter Ave.; 771-1126. Moderate. Villas, suites, or cottages; TV. Private beach; pool; rowboats; miniature golf; shuffleboard; bikes available.
- *The Holly Tree*, 412 Main St.; 771-6677. Moderate. New in 1987; 104 rooms with TV; air-conditioning, indoor/outdoor pools; whirlpool; restaurant and lounge.
- *Hunters Green Motel*, Rte. 28; 771-1169 or 800-334-3220. Moderate. 74 guest rooms with heat and air-conditioning; TV; indoor/outdoor pools; shuffleboard; game area; clay tennis courts nearby; free morning coffee. Package plans available.
- *The Mariner Motor Lodge*, 573 Main St., Rte. 28; 771-7887 or 800-445-4050. Moderate. Indoor/outdoor pool; game room; whirlpool; saunas; TV with HBO; clay tennis courts across the street; air-conditioning. Off-season rates.
- *The Mayflower Motel*, 504 Main St., Rte. 28; 775-2758. Moderate. Pool; air-conditioning; in-room coffee; TV.

• *Snug Harbor Motor Lodge*, Rte. 28; 775-4085. Moderate. 50 units with air-conditioning and TV; indoor/outdoor pools; whirlpool; game room; walk to Hyannis. Off-season rates.

• *Thunderbird Motor Lodge*, 216 Rte. 28; 775-2692; 1-800-247-3006 (outside MA), 1-800-443-8881 (in MA). Moderate. 140 large units with TV; HBO; air-conditioning; two pools; tennis court; saunas; putting green; game room; whirlpool; playground. Off-season rates.

• *Tidewater Motor Lodge*, 135 Main St., Rte. 28; 775-6322 or 800-338-6322. Moderate. Pool; sauna; playground; game room; picnic area; TV; decks or patios; air-conditioning; close to Hyannis.

• *Town 'n Country Motor Lodge*, 452 Main St., Rte. 28; 771-0212 or 800-992-2340. Moderate. Indoor/outdoor pools; kiddie pool; putting green; whirlpool; sauna; 150 units; air-conditioning.

• *Yarmouth Gardens*, 497 Main St.; 771-1998. Moderate. Pool; playground; game room. Open year-round.

• *Yarmouth Shores*, 29 Lewis Bay Blvd.; 775-1944. Inexpensive to moderate. Seven cottages with a private beach; fireplaces; children's play area. Seasonal.

• *Windrift Vacation Resort*, Rte. 28; 775-4697 or 800-354-4179. Moderate. Pool, wading pool for kids; cable TV; Heat/AC; continental breakfast.

Campgrounds

BARNSTABLE

There is no camping allowed in the town of Barnstable. There is, however, a nudist family camp to contact: *Sandy Terraces Nudist Family Camping Park*, Box 835C, Hyannis 02601; 428-9209. There are tent and RV sites, private beach, boating, tennis, volleyball, sauna, and clubhouse. Couples and families only. Must call or write before visiting.

DENNIS

• *Airline Mobile Home Park,* Paradise Ln., S. Dennis 02660; 385-3616. Trailer and tent sites; open June to Labor Day; reservations recommended; pool; no dogs allowed.

• *Grindell's Ocean View Park*, 61 Old Wharf Rd., RFD#1, Box 116, Dennisport 02639; 398-2671. Open Memorial Day–October; motor homes or trailers; no dogs.

Dining

BARNSTABLE

Village of Barnstable

• *Barnstable Restaurant and Tavern*, Rte. 6A; 362-2355. Moderate. Lunch and dinner year-round; nice atmosphere in the heart of Barnstable Village; tables outside; great bar.

• *Dolphin Restaurant,* Main St., Rte 6A; 362-6610. Moderate. View of marshes; seafood and varied menu; lunch and dinner; casual; music and dancing Saturday night. Reservations requested; year-round.

• *Harbor Point*, Harbor Point Rd.; 362-2231. Moderate. Beautiful views of Barnstable Harbor and Cape Cod Bay; fish and steaks, lunch and dinner. Casual; reservations advised; credit cards accepted; seasonal.

BARNSTABLE (CONTINUED)

- *Mattakeese Wharf*, 271 Mill Way, Barnstable Harbor; 362-4511. Moderate. Lunch, dinner, overlooks Barnstable Harbor; proper dress; seasonal; seafood and steaks; reservations suggested.
- *Village Landing*, Post Office Square, Rte. 6A; 362-2994. Inexpensive. Casual; nice atmosphere. Beer and wine; take-out.

Centerville

- *Centerville Pastry and Coffee Shop*, 23 Park Ave.; 775-6023. Inexpensive. Breakfast, lunch. Casual; no credit cards.
- *Four Seas*, 360 Main St., near Craigville Beach; 775-1394. Moderate. Sandwiches, famous spot for ice cream. Open May to September.
- *Hearth 'n Kettle*, 23 Richardson Rd.; 775-8878. Inexpensive to moderate. Casual family restaurant; year-round. Breakfast, lunch, and dinner.

Cotuit

- *The Regatta of Cotuit at the Crocker House*, 4631 Falmouth Rd.; 428-5715. Expensive. Old Colonial home; continental and American cuisine. Reservations only; proper dress; credit cards accepted; year-round.

Hyannis

- *Alberto's Ristorante*, 360 Main St.; 778-1770. Moderate. Northern Italian; lunch, dinner. Reservations suggested; credit cards accepted. Year-round.
- *The Backside Saloon*, 209 Main St.; 771-5505. Inexpensive. Pizza, grinders, pasta, take-out; casual; lunch, dinner; outside patio; credit cards accepted.
- *Barbyann's*, 120 Airport Rd.; 775-9795. Inexpensive. Family-style serving seafood, steaks; casual. Reservations not necessary; credit cards accepted. Year-round.
- *Barolo Ristorante*, 297 North St., 778-2878. Moderate. Italian cuisine at moderate prices, very good.
- *Baxter's Boathouse Club*, next door to Baxter's Fish n Chips (see below); 775-7040. Moderate. Casual; overlooks Hyannis Harbor, seafood. No reservations or credit cards; piano.
- *Baxter's Fish n Chips*, 177 Pleasant St.; 775-4490. Inexpensive. Great spot for children, on the harbor, deep-fried fish and seafood. No credit cards; no reservations; lunch, dinner. Open during the summer, closed Mondays.
- *The Benchmark*, 11 Ridgewood Ave.; 771-2822. Inexpensive to moderate. Family-style; lunch, dinner, sandwiches; credit cards accepted.
- *The Black Cat*, 165 Ocean St., 778-1233. Moderate. Overlooks Hyannis Harbor, outside dining, lunch, dinner and Sunday brunch, piano player some evenings, popular gathering spot.
- *Bobby Byrne's Pub*, 345 Rte. 28; 775-1425. Inexpensive to moderate. Pub atmosphere, burgers, sandwiches; no reservations necessary; credit cards accepted; lunch, dinner, Sunday brunch. Year-round.
- *Cape Cod Dinner Train,* 771-3788. Expensive. A unique dining experience aboard a train that takes you on a three-hour scenic tour of the Cape as you enjoy an elegant dinner. Proper dress required. Departs out of Hyannis.
- *Captain's Chair*, 116 Bay View St.; 775-5000. Moderate. Overlooking Lewis Bay; nautical atmosphere; seafood and steaks; lunch, dinner, Sunday brunch. Reservations recommended; credit cards accepted. Year-round.
- *Chef Urano's Restaurant*, 50 Sea St.; 771-7371. Moderate. Italian and continental cuisine; casual; dinner; credit cards accepted. Year-round.
- *Chili's Grill & Bar*, Airport Rotary, Rtes. 132 and 28; 790-0724. Inexpensive to

moderate. Southwestern cuisine comes to Cape Cod and it's a hit. Very popular; children's menu. Casual; no reservations; credit cards accepted.

• ***Cooke's***, Rte. 132; 775-0450. Inexpensive to moderate. Fried seafood, lunch, dinner. Casual; no reservations or credit cards. Seasonal.

• ***Copacabana***, 243 Stevens St., 790-8227. Foods with a Brazilian flair, nightly entertainment.

• ***Coyote's,*** Main St.; 778-4466 or Take-out 771-7427. Moderate. South Western and Texas style ribs, steaks.

• ***Craigville Pizza & Mexican***, 618 Craigville Beach Rd., W. Hyannis Port; 775-9534 or 775-2267. Moderate. Pizza, Mexican, subs, too; deliveries; casual; no reservations or credit cards.

• ***Dockside Inn***, 53 South St.; 775-8636. Moderate. On Lewis Bay Marina; varied menu but fish and chowders the specialty. Credit cards accepted; year-round. Breakfast, lunch, dinner; outdoor dining; raw bar.

• ***D'Olimpio's New York Deli***, 55 Iyanough Rd.; 771-3200. Inexpensive. Breakfast, lunch, dinner, take-out. Casual; reservations not necessary; credit cards accepted. Good bakery, too!

• ***Dragon-Lite Restaurant***, 620 Main St.; 775-9494. Moderate. Chinese food; credit cards accepted; reservations preferred; take-out available; lunch, dinner; open until 2 A.M. on Friday, and Saturday until 3 A.M.

• ***Duck Inn Pub***, 447 Main St.; 775-3000. Moderate. Light fare, sandwiches; casual.

• ***East End Grille***, 247 Main St.; 790-2898. Inexpensive. Pub atmosphere; lunch, dinner, late-night menu until midnight. Year-round.

• ***The Egg and I***, 521 Main St.; 771-1596. Moderate. Informal; egg specialties; open all night.

• ***Gourmet Brunch***, 517 Main St.; 771-2558. Moderate. Open 8 A.M.–3 P.M.; year-round. Casual; no reservations or credit cards.

• ***Gringo's***, 577 Main St.; 771-8449. Inexpensive. Mexican and American food, also sandwiches and seafood. Outside patio; casual; no reservations; credit cards accepted.

• ***Harbor House Restaurant***, Ocean Street Docks; 771-2770. Inexpensive. Informal atmosphere on Hyannis Harbor; breakfast, lunch, and dinner. Reservations not necessary; credit cards accepted. Dining on outside deck during summer.

• ***Harry's Cajun Restaurant & Bar***, 700 Main St.; 778-4188. Moderate. Small restaurant with a cozy atmosphere; good food; Cajun cooking. Casual; no reservations; credit cards accepted.

• ***Hearth 'n Kettle***, 412 Main St.; 771-3737. Inexpensive to moderate. Restaurant geared to the family; varied menu. Open 24 hours during the summer. Casual; no reservations.

• ***Heritage House Dining Room***, 259 Main St.; 775-7000. Moderate. Hotel restaurant; prime rib and seafood; candlelight; live entertainment. Reservations requested; credit cards accepted. Year-round.

• ***Holiday Inn***, Rte. 132; 775-6600. Moderate. Breakfast, lunch, and dinner. Restaurant; lounge (P.J. Wickers). Casual; credit cards accepted.

• ***Ramada Regency Inn***, Chappy's, Rte. 132; 775-1153. Moderate. Breakfast, lunch, dinner; seafood, beef.

• ***Sophie's Bar & Grill***, 335 Main St.; 775-1111. Moderate. Lunch, dinner, salad bar, seafood; casual; grilled pizza. Breakfast during summer. Year-round.

• ***Mainstreet Seafood & Grill and Shucker's Raw Bar***, 460 Main St.; 771-8585. Moderate. Seafood, clam bake, nightly entertainment, karaoke.

BARNSTABLE (CONTINUED)

• *Mallory Dock*, 477 Yarmouth Rd.; 775-9835. Moderate. Italian and continental cuisine; informal; no reservations; credit cards accepted.

• *Mildred's Chowder House*, 290 Iyanough Rd.; 775-1045. Moderate. Family dining; casual; reservations suggested; lunch, dinner; credit cards accepted. Year-round.

• *Mitchell's Steak & Rib House*, 451 Iyanough Rd.; 775-6700. Moderate. Across from the airport; sandwiches, steaks, seafood; children's menu; Sunday brunch. Year-round. Chowder has won chowder contests.

• *The Mooring,* 230 Ocean St.; 775-4656. Moderate. Overlooking Hyannis Harbor; seafood, Mexican food, burgers; outdoor dining; lunch, dinner; credit cards accepted.

• *Murph's Recession*, off Rte. 132 at Independence Park; 775-9750. Inexpensive. Sandwiches, quiches; informal; no reservations or credit cards.

• *The 19th Hole*, 11 Barnstable Rd.; 771-1032. Inexpensive. Sandwiches, beer, wine, lunch.

• *The Paddock*, W. Main St. Rotary; 775-7677. Next to Melody Tent. Expensive. Victorian-style restaurant; fresh flowers, linen tablecloths, and candlelight; outside dining in the garden café in the summer. A popular spot for dinner before the shows at the Melody Tent. Reservations suggested; lunch, dinner; credit cards accepted; jackets required.

• *Penguins Sea Grille*, 331 Main St.; 771-2023. Moderate. Italian food; casual; contemporary atmosphere; dinner. No reservations; credit cards accepted. Year-round.

• *Pepper's Café,* 287 Iyanough Rd. at the newly restored Comfort Inn; 775-1750. Moderate. Children's menu available. Opened here on the Cape by the owners of Rosalie's, a popular restaurant in Marblehead on the north shore.

• *The Red Lobster Restaurant*, 1095 Iyanough Rd.; 775-0755. Moderate. A recent addition to Hyannis by this national chain.

• *Roadhouse Café*, 488 South St.; 775-2386. Moderate. Small, cozy dining; seafood, veal, Italian specialties; lunch, dinner, brunch. Year-round; outdoor dining in summer.

• *Sam Diego's*, Rte. 132; 771-8816. Inexpensive to moderate. Mexican specialties with Cajun and Tex-Mex, too; casual; lunch, dinner; credit cards accepted. Year-round.

• *Sandy's Roast Beef & Seafood*, 225 Iyanough Rd.; 775-9799. Moderate. Casual; eat in or take-out. Year-round.

• *Shannon's*, 251 Iyanough Rd.; 775-9122. Inexpensive. Family-style, plenty of fish.

• *Shirdan's Country Kitchen*, Rte. 132; 775-8940. Inexpensive. Family restaurant; varied menu; breakfast served from 6 A.M. to noon; lunch and dinner.

• *Silver Shell Restaurant*, West End Circle at the Tara Hyannis; 775-7775. Expensive. Breakfast, lunch, dinner; reservations for dinner; seafood the specialty. Year-round.

• *Starbuck's*, Rte. 132; 778-6767. Moderate. Sandwiches, Cajun, Oriental, Italian, and a kid's menu. Credit cards accepted.

• *Steamers Grill & Bar,* 235 Ocean St.; 778-0818. Overlooks Hyannis Harbor, seafood, mesquite grill, open air deck, entertainment.

• *Sunnyside Restaurant*, 304 Main St.; 775-3539. Inexpensive. Family restaurant; breakfast served all day. Year-round.

- *Sweetwater's Grille & Bar*, 644 Main St.; 775-3323. Moderate. Southwestern.
- *Tiki Port*, Rte. 132 opposite Cape Cod Mall; 771-5220. Moderate. Chinese restaurant and Polynesian lounge; casual; take-out orders. Reservations accepted for large parties only.
- *Tugboats*, Hyannis Marina; 775-6433. Moderate. Overlooking the inner harbor of Hyannis, casual, great outside deck for dining, varied menu.
- *Up the Creek*, 36 Old Colony Rd.; 771-7866. Moderate. Steaks and seafood; lunch, dinner, and Sunday brunch; cozy atmosphere; reservations and credit cards accepted. Year-round.
- *Wack-a-Jacks*, Main St.; 775-8600. Moderate. Lunch; casual; credit cards accepted.
- *Windjammer Lounge*, Airport Shopping Plaza; 771-2020. Inexpensive to moderate. Lunch, dinner, Sunday brunch; lounge has video games, TV, pool table; casual.

Osterville

- *Wimpy's*, Main St.; 428-6300. Moderate. Seafood; snack bar, formal dining room as well as a family dining room; popular locally; credit cards accepted; casual.

West Barnstable

- *Old Village Restaurant*, Rte. 149; 362-9839. Moderate. Pizza, subs; casual; behind Old Village Store.

DENNIS

Village of Dennis

- *Captain Frosty's Fish & Chips*, 219 Rte. 6A; 385-8548. Inexpensive. Good spot to take the family after the beach or any time. A local favorite, it has outdoor seating and take-out service.
- *Dennis Inn & Restaurant*, 25 Scarsdale Rd.; 385-6571. Moderate to expensive. New England cuisine served in lovely dining rooms; a real country setting that is a bit out of the way; dinner and Sunday brunch; reservations suggested; major credit cards accepted.
- *Dennis Pizza*, Rte. 6A; 385-2487. Moderate. Pizza and hamburgers.
- *Gina's by the Sea*, 134 Taunton Ave.; 385-3213. Moderate. Casual; seafood and Italian food; lunch and dinner; family restaurant on the way to Chapin Beach, cozy. You'll return each summer!
- *Green Room Restaurant*, 36 Hope Ln.; 385-8003. Moderate to expensive. Recently redecorated, this restaurant provides a pleasant atmosphere with fresh flowers and a nice setting. Open April to December for lunch and dinner. Credit cards accepted. Reservations suggested; this is next to the Cape Playhouse and is a popular spot for dining before the theater.
- *Joe Mac's Family Restaurant*, 85 Taunton Ave.; 385-9040. Inexpensive. Casual dining with a varied menu; video game room for the kids; breakfast, lunch and dinner; no reservations; major credit cards accepted.
- *Margarites Restaurant*, 804 Main St., Rte. 6A; 385-3279. Moderate. Located in the Theatre Marketplace. Year-round. Lunch and dinner served in a cozy atmosphere; pasta, seafood; casual; credit cards and reservations accepted.
- *Red Pheasant Inn*, 905 Rte. 6A; 385-2133. Moderate to expensive. A restored 200-year-old Cape barn; candlelight dinners; year-round for dinner, lunch from June to October. Sunday brunch served; credit cards accepted; reservations recommended.

DENNIS (CONTINUED)

- **Rose's**, 27 Black Flats Rd., just off Rte. 6A at the Dennis Public Market; 385-3003. Moderate. Italian food served in a casual atmosphere; children's menu; dinner. Major credit cards accepted; reservations advised.
- **Scargo Café**, 799 Rte. 6A; 385-8200. Moderate. Casual; good place to stop before or after a play at the Cape Playhouse. Seafood, steaks, and some Cajun dishes; lunch and dinner served. Late-night menu available for the summer. Major credit cards accepted; reservations recommended.
- **Snowgoose Country Café**, 605 Rte. 6A; 385-7175. Inexpensive to moderate. Cute place for breakfast, lunch or dinner; casual. No credit cards. BYOB.

Dennisport

- **Bob Briggs' Wee Packet,** Corner Depot St. and Lower County Rd.; 398-2181. Moderate. Casual family restaurant; fried fish and seafood, beer and wine; children's menu; breakfast, lunch, and dinner; reservations not necessary.
- **Brother's Pizza**, Rte. 28; 394-2518. Moderate.
- **BZ's,** 862 Main St; 394-6247. Inexpensive. Very casual but very good pizza and Mexican food; beer and wine.
- **Captain Williams House**, 106 Depot St.; 398-3910. Moderate. Seasonal restaurant serving dinners by candlelight; reservations recommended; credit cards accepted.
- **Clancy's**, 8 Upper County Rd.; 394-6661. Moderate. Overlooking Swan River; casual; open-air deck; lunch and dinner served, varied menu; Irish music on weekends in the summer; credit cards accepted.
- **Coffee Cup**, 699 Main St.; 394-2037. Inexpensive. Breakfast and lunch served; take-out; picnics prepared.
- **Dennisport House of Pizza**, 481 Main St.; 394-5966. Moderate.
- **Dino's by the Sea**, 57 Chase Ave.; 398-8740. Inexpensive. Casual family dining with an ocean view; breakfast, lunch, and dinner, May–October; reservations recommended for dinner; no credit cards.
- **Ebb Tide Restaurant**, 88 Chase Ave.; 398-8733. Moderate. Old Cape Cod cottage across from the ocean; country breakfast and dinners served; reservations not necessary; credit cards accepted. Seasonal.
- **Joey's Pizza Palace**, 197 Lower County Rd.; 398-7437. Moderate. Pizza.
- **Michael Patrick's Publick House**, 435 Main St.; 398-1620. Inexpensive. Salads; sandwiches; kids' meals.
- **Ocean House**, Depot St. and Chase Ave.; 394-0700. Moderate to expensive. On the ocean; seafood served. Seasonal.
- **Rum Runner's Café**, 243 Lower County Rd.; 398-5673. Inexpensive. Casual; outdoor patio; lunch and dinner. Live entertainment starts around 9:00 P.M.— generally rock and roll; no reservations or credit cards.
- **Sea Breezes**, 17 South St.; 394-2100. Moderate. Casual; lunch and dinner; serving burgers, fish-and-chips, seafood; breakfast on the weekends. Reservations and credit cards accepted.
- **Swan River Seafood**, 5 Lower County Rd.; 394-4466. Inexpensive. Seafood restaurant with views of Swan River and marshes; casual; family-oriented; lunch and dinner; credit cards accepted. Seasonal.

East Dennis

- **Grumpy's**, 1408 Rte. 6A; 385-2911. Breakfast, lunch, gourmet coffee, homemade desserts, seafood.
- **Marshside Restaurant**, 28 Bridge St.; 385-4010. Inexpensive to moderate.

Cozy, comfortable restaurant located on the marsh; breakfast, lunch, and dinner; pleasant service. Coloring books, crayons, and some toys for itchy children; no reservations necessary; major credit cards accepted.

South Dennis

- *Box Lunch,* 3 Enterprise Rd.; 394-2202. Inexpensive. Healthy alternative to junk food.
- *D'Angelo's Sandwich Shop*, Rte. 134; 394-2030. Inexpensive. Casual; subs for take-out.
- *Jason's Tavern*, Rte. 134, Patriot Square; 394-3534. Inexpensive to moderate. Casual; seafood; mesquite-grilled chicken. Open year-round.
- *Jim's Pier 134*, 886 Rte. 134; 385-3367. Inexpensive to moderate. Seafood the specialty; casual; seasonal; lunch and dinner served. Reservations suggested for July and August.; credit cards accepted.
- *Red Cottage Store*, 36 Old Bass River Rd.; 394-2923. Inexpensive. Casual; breakfast, lunch, take-outs available.

West Dennis

- *Anthony's Italian Restaurant*, Rte. 134 & 28; 394-3531. Moderate. Italian and American cuisine and seafood; children's menu; major credit cards accepted.
- *Breakfast Room*, Rte. 28; 398-0581. Inexpensive.
- *Christine's Restaurant and Nightclub*, 581 Rte. 28; 394-7333. Inexpensive to moderate. Casual; pasta, seafood, steaks; no reservations; credit cards accepted.
- *The Lighthouse Inn*, Lighthouse Rd.; 398-2244. Moderate. Resort hotel overlooking the ocean; breakfast, lunch, dinner; reservations requested; MasterCard accepted. Seasonal.
- *Marathon Seafood Restaurant*, 231 Rte. 28; 394-3379. Inexpensive. Casual; breakfast, lunch, and dinner served year-round; no credit cards.
- *Royal Palace*, 369 Rte. 28; 398-6144. Inexpensive. Oriental cuisine; year-round; take-out service available.
- *Sir William's Café*, 85 School St.; 760-2727. Inexpensive Breakfast take-out.
- *Sundancer's*, 116 Main St., Rte. 28; 394-1600. Moderate. Overlooks Bass River; open deck; raw bar; casual; serving lunch and dinner; major credit cards accepted.
- *The Village Deli,* 296 Main St.; 394-6068. Moderate. Varied menu, a local hangout.

YARMOUTH

South Yarmouth

- *Bass River Golf Course Snack Bar*, Highbank Rd.; 398-1826. Inexpensive. Informal; breakfast and lunch served; reservations not needed; no credit cards.
- *Bass River Seafood Restaurant*, 15 Mill Ln., off Rte 28; 398-6434. Inexpensive to moderate. Informal seafood restaurant; nautical setting; lunch and dinner served year-round; major credit cards accepted.
- *China Inn*, 981 Rte. 28; 398-0141. Inexpensive to moderate. Polynesian and Cantonese food; casual; lunch and dinner. Reservations not required; major credit cards accepted.
- *Frontier Steak & Lobster House*, 769 Rte. 28; 394-8006. Moderate. Casual; serving dinner from April to Ocotober; credit cards accepted.
- *George's Pizza House*, 1311A Rte. 28; 394-0044. Moderate. Pizza.
- *Hearth 'n Kettle*, 1196 Rte. 28; 394-2252. Moderate. Family restaurant open year-round for breakfast, lunch, and dinner.

YARMOUTH (CONTINUED)

- **Kevin's Seafood**, 908 Rte. 28; 394-7610. Moderate. Casual; lunch, dinner; children's menu available; reservations and credit cards not accepted.
- **Longfellow's**, Old Townhouse Plaza; 394-3663. Inexpensive. Casual, pub atmosphere; no reservations; credit cards accepted.
- **Nikki's International**, 812 Rte. 28; 398-9440.
- **Pancake Man**, Rte. 28; 398-9532. Inexpensive. Casual; breakfast, lunch, and dinner; no reservations or credit cards.
- **Papa Gino's**, 940 Rte. 28; 398-1146. Inexpensive. Pizza and Italian food; casual.
- **Piccadilly Deli**, Rte. 28; 394-9018. Inexpensive. Casual; open 6 A.M. to 9 P.M.; breakfast, lunch, and dinner; take-out orders.
- **Red Jacket Beach Motel**, South Shore Dr.; 398-6941. Moderate. View of the ocean; breakfast and lunch; April–November; dinner in the summer. Reservations suggested; no credit cards.
- **Riverway Lobster House,** Rte. 28, at the Bass River Bridge; 398-2172. Moderate. Casual; dinner; credit cards accepted; reservations preferred. Year-round.
- **Riviera Beach Motor Inn**, 327 South Shore Dr.; 398-2273. Inexpensive. Casual; breakfast and lunch; outside patio available; reservations not necessary; no credit cards.
- **Skipper Restaurant**, 152 South Shore Dr.; 394-7406. Inexpensive to moderate. View of the water; breakfast, lunch, and dinner; April to October; reservations needed for five or more.
- **Skippy's Pier 1 Restaurant**, Rte. 28; 398-9556. Moderate. Casual; lunch, dinner; outdoor deck; varied menu; credit cards accepted, reservations not necessary.
- **Sugar 'n Spice Donuts**, 457 Station Ave.; 394-6057. Inexpensive. Breakfast and lunch to go.
- **Toly's House of Pizza**, 1020 Rte. 28; 398-6244. Inexpensive.
- **Union Station Restaurant**, Exit 8 off Rte. 6; 398-3883. Moderate. Seafood.
- **Windmill Kitchen**, 928 Rte. 28; 398-9728. Inexpensive. Breakfast specials; evening window service; yogurt, hot dogs, burgers.
- **Wok-n-Roll**, 1319 Rte. 28; 760-2060. Inexpensive. Chinese take-out.

West Yarmouth

- **Bagel Deli**, 594 Rte. 28; 771-7707. Inexpensive. Serves breakfast and lunch seven days a week; year-round; take-outs available.
- **Cape Point Breakfast Café**, 476 Rte. 28 (in hotel); 778-1500. Moderate. Breakfast served in casual atmosphere. Year-round; credit cards accepted.
- **Captain Parker's Pub**, 672 Rte. 28; 771-4266. Moderate. Sandwiches and seafood served in a pub atmosphere; lunch and dinner; casual; credit cards accepted; year-round.
- **Golden Boy Seafood**, 80 E. Main St., Rte. 28; 771-6232. Inexpensive to moderate. Casual; fried seafood and burgers; outdoor seating; breakfast, lunch, and dinner till 11 P.M. Seasonal; no reservations or credit cards.
- **Giardino's Family Restaurant**, 242 Rte. 28; 775-0333. Inexpensive. Casual, Italian food; breakfast, lunch, dinner; children's menu; take-out available.
- **Heavenly 2**, 194 Rte. 28; 775-4533. Breakfast and seafood. Open year-round; no credit cards accepted.
- **Lobster Boat**, 681 Rte. 28; 775-0486. Moderate. Located on Parker's River; dinner only; reservations suggested on weekends in summer.

- *Mama Angie's*, 416 Rte. 28; 771-6531. Inexpensive. Casual; Italian cuisine; outdoor patio; dinner only; reservations recommended; credit cards accepted.
- *Shirdan's Country Kitchen*, Rte. 28; 778-6844. Inexpensive. Casual; open 7 A.M. to 9 P.M. for breakfast, lunch, dinner.
- *Steve & Sue's Creamy Soft Serve*, 37 Main St. at Treasure Island; 775-4674. Inexpensive. Sandwiches served but mainly ice cream and candies. Open late February to November.
- *Takis Pizza*, 547 Rte. 28; 771-3331. Moderate. Pizza.
- *Tim's Roast Beef*, 198 Main St.; 775-9633. Inexpensive. Casual fast-food restaurant with indoor/outdoor seating; breakfast, lunch, and dinner served.
- *Yarmouth House Restaurant*, 335 Main St.; 771-5154. Moderate. Casual but proper dress; lunch, dinner; steaks, seafood; year-round. Major credit cards accepted; reservations preferred during the summer.

Yarmouth Port

- *Abbicci Restaurant,* 43 Main St., Rte. 6A; 362-3501. Expensive. Up-scale Italian cuisine, contemporary decor in an old inn. Lunch and dinner, reservations suggested.
- *Anthony's Cummaquid Inn*, Rte. 6A; 362-4501. Expensive. Nice views; dinner, seafood and steaks; popular restaurant in a large Colonial mansion; year-round.
- *Colonial House Inn*, Rte. 6A; 362-4348. Moderate. Lunch and dinner; meals served in dining room or on a veranda; casual; credit cards accepted; reservations preferred.
- *Dixon's Fish & Chips*, 559 Rte. 6A; 362-3228. Inexpensive. Fish and chips; sandwiches. Year-round; no credit cards.
- *Fearrington's*, Rte. 6A; 362-1499. The restaurant at King's Way serves lunch and dinner, mixed grille, pastas, seafood. Comfortable yet elegant setting.
- *Hallet's Store*, 139 Rte. 6A; 362-3362. Moderate. Casual, 1889 drugstore with a soda fountain; open 8 A.M. to 3 P.M.
- *Inaho*, 157 Rte. 6A; 362-5522. Great Japanese restaurant in a complimentary atmosphere.
- *Jack's Outback*, 161 Main St.; 362-6690. Inexpensive. Breakfast and lunch served in a casual atmosphere; known for good food and a good time; definitely worth a stop.
- *Old Yarmouth Inn*, 223 Rte. 6A; 362-8201. Moderate. Open year-round; lunch and dinner; casual; children's menu available; 17th-century inn; major credit cards accepted; reservations requested.

Entertainment

Music & Stage

BARNSTABLE

- *Cape Cod Melody Tent*, 21 West Main St., Hyannis; 775-9100 (box office). Variety of stars and groups appear—from Johnny Mathis to Sha Na Na. Wednesday mornings the theater presents children's plays.
- *Cape Cod Conservatory of Music and Art*, Rte. 132, W. Barnstable; 362-2772. Musical events held year-round.
- *Band concerts,* Village Green. Summer.

BARNSTABLE (CONTINUED)

• *Barnstable Comedy Club*, Rte. 6A, Barnstable Village; 362-6333. Year-round productions held, as well as workshops and special events.

DENNIS

• *The Cape Playhouse,* Rte. 6A, Box A, Dennis 02638; 385-3838 (business office), 385-3911 (box office). End of June to the first of September. Hollywood and Broadway stars perform in plays and musicals. Charming, small theater. On Friday mornings there is the Children's Theater Series. Performances are 9:30 and 11:30 A.M. Plays have included such childhood favorites as *Wizard of Oz* and *Sleeping Beauty.*

• *Dennis Band*, at the corner of Rte. 6A and Old Bass River Rd. Local groups plays on the Village Green in the gazebo. They play Monday nights in July and August.

YARMOUTH

• *Cape and Islands Chamber Music Festival*, Box 72, Yarmouth Port 02675; 255-9509. Cape-wide locations; young people's concerts and special events.

• *Cape Cod Performing Arts Association*, Box 205, Yarmouth Port; 362-3364 or 432-5951.

• *Cape Cod Symphony Orchestra*, 712 Main St., Yarmouth Port; 362-1111.

• *Annual Scottish Festival*, Dennis-Yarmouth High School, Station Ave., S. Yarmouth; 775-6896 (or write: Highland Light Scottish Society, Box 357, Yarmouth Port 02675). Pipe bands and highland dancing; usually held in June.

• *Band concerts*, off Higgins Crowell Rd., W. Yarmouth. Yarmouth Chamber of Commerce sponsors band concerts on Monday nights in July and August at 7:30 P.M. They are held at the Mattakeese Middle School gazebo.

Nightlife

BARNSTABLE

• *Mallory Dock Restaurant,* 477 Yarmouth Rd., Hyannis; 775-9835.

• *Baxter's Boathouse*, on the harbor, 177 Pleasant St., Hyannis; 775-7040. Popular; contemporary; piano.

• *Captain's Chair*, 166 Bay View, Hyannis. Piano. 775-5000.

• *East End Pub*, 247 Main St., Hyannis. Piano, contemporary. 790-2898.

• *Guido Murphy's*, 615 Main St., Hyannis; 775-7242. Live music, DJ.

• *Windjammer Lounge,* Airport Shopping Plaza, Hyannis; 771-2020. Guitar, contemporary.

• *Dolphin*, Main St., Barnstable Village; 362-6610. Piano.

• *East Bay Lodge*, East Bay Rd., Osterville; 428-6961. Dancing.

• *Wimpy's*, Main St., Osterville; 428-6300. Dancing, piano.

• *Heritage House*, Main St., Hyannis; 775-7000. Guitar.

• *Pufferbellies,* 183 Iyanough Rd., Hyannis; 778-2515. DJ, live bands, country line dancing, Top 40.

• *Laurels*, at Tara Hyannis, West End Circle, Hyannis; 775-7775. Disco.

• *The Paddock*, West End Circle, Hyannis; 775-7677. Piano.

• *The Mooring*, 230 Ocean St., Hyannis; 775-4656. Piano.

• *Harbor Point*, Harbor Point Rd., Cummaquid; 362-2231. Guitar.

• *Asa Bearse House*, 415 Main St., Hyannis; 771-4131. Live rock bands.

- *Mattakeese Wharf*, 271 Mill Way, Barnstable; 362-4511. Piano.
- *Roadhouse Café*, 488 South St., Hyannis; 775-2386. Piano bar.
- *Sophie's Bar and Grill*, 334 Main St., Hyannis; 771-1111. Live entertainment.

DENNIS
- *Christine's Restaurant*, 581 Main St., W. Dennis; 394-7333. Popular and rock music.
- *Improper Bostonian*, Rte. 28, Dennisport; 394-7416. Popular and rock music.
- *Jason's,* 228 Lower County Rd., Dennis; 398-9007. Popular and rock music.
- *Rum Runners Café*, 318 Lower County Rd.; Dennisport; 398-5673. Popular and rock music.
- *Sundancer's,* 116 Main St., Rte. 28, W. Dennis; 394-1600. Popular and rock music.
- *Lighthouse Inn*, Lighthouse Rd., W. Dennis; 398-2244. Folk music, variety.
- *Oceanhouse*, Depot St., Dennisport; 394-0700. Folk music, variety.
- *Clancy's*, 8 Upper County Rd., Dennisport; 394-6661. Irish music.

YARMOUTH
- *Mill Hill Club*, 164 Main St., W. Yarmouth; 775-2580. Popular and rock music.
- *Oliver's*, Rte. 6A, Yarmouth Port; 362-6062. Popular acoustic music.
- *Cape Cod Irish Village*, Rte. 28, W. Yarmouth; 771-0100. Irish music.

Movie Theaters

BARNSTABLE
- *Cape Cod Mall Cinema*, Cape Cod Mall, Hyannis; 771-1666.
- *Airport Cinemas*, Rte. 132, Hyannis; 771-4330.

DENNIS
- *Cape Cinema*, Rte. 6A next to the Cape Playhouse, Dennis; 385-2503. Foreign films and second-run movies. It's worth a trip just to see the theater.
- *Cinema at Dennisport*, Rte. 28, Dennisport; 394-7800.
- *Entertainment Cinemas*, Rte. 134, South Dennis; 394-1100; at Patriot Square Mall.

Museums & Historic Sites

BARNSTABLE
- *Centerville Historical Society Museum*, 513 Main St., Centerville; 775-0331. 19th-century Mary Lincoln House filled with antique dolls, quilts, Sandwich glass. Features a Colonial kitchen. Open June–September, Wednesday–Sunday; small admission fee.
- *Santuit and Cotuit Historical Society*, 1148 Main St., Cotuit Village. Museum and restored 18th-century Samuel Dottridge Homestead; early 19th-century American items. Open June–Labor Day, Tuesday and Sunday; no admission charge.
- *Cahoon Museum of American Art*, 4676 Falmouth Ave., Cotuit; 428-7581.
- *Osterville Historical Society and Museum*, corner of Parker and West Bay rds., Osterville; 428-5861. Captain Jonathan Parker House, built in 1798, features 18th- and 19th-century New England antiques, Sandwich glass. Open in the summer; small charge.

BARNSTABLE (CONTINUED)

• *Donald A. Trayser Memorial Museum*, Rte. 6A at corner of Phinney's Ln., Barnstable Village; 362-2092. Old Customs House has exhibits of Indian relics, Victorian furnishings, silver pieces by early Barnstable craftsmen, early farm and carpentry tools. Open in the summer, Tuesday–Saturday, 1:30–4:30 P.M.; small admission fee.

• *West Parish Meetinghouse*, Rte. 149, W. Barnstable. Dates from 1717; oldest congregational church in the United States; 1806 Revere bell. Open Memorial Day to Labor Day; no admission charge.

• *Sturgis Library*, Rte. 6A, Barnstable Village; 362-6636. Oldest public library in the nation—built in 1644. Good genealogical collection of early Massachusetts families and maritime history collection.

• *Lothrop Hill Cemetery*, Rte. 6A, Barnstable Village. Town's oldest cemetery. Rev. John Lothrop, a prominent man in the town's early history, is buried here.

• *Colonial Court House*, Rte. 6A and Rendezvous Ln., Barnstable Village. Built in 1772; contains items from the past. (Lectures on Cape Cod are held here.)

• *Cotuit Post Office*, 45 School St., Cotuit; 428-8094. First building in the United States built as a post office; built in 1821.

• *Cammett House*, Parker Rd., Osterville; 428-5861. This house shows what a household looked like in the mid-19th century; building dates to 1720s.

• *Herbert F. Crosby Boat Shop*, Parker Rd., Osterville; 428-5861. Emphasis is on the Crosby boat-building family who designed catboats.

• *JFK Museum*, 397 Main St., Hyannis; 362-5230. Museum honoring JFK and his ties to Cape Cod.

• *John F. Kennedy Memorial*, Ocean St., Hyannis. Fieldstone wall memorial and fountain.

• *St. Francis Xavier Catholic Church*, South St., Hyannis. Church where members of the Kennedy family worshipped during their visits to Hyannis, and where Maria Shriver was married. Plaque indicates President Kennedy's pew; open daily.

• *The Kennedy Compound*, Irving and Scudder aves., Hyannis Port. Best view is from the harbor or in the winter when all the bushes are bare.

DENNIS

• *Cape Museum of Fine Arts*, 60 Hope Ln., Dennis; 385-4477. Located in several buildings on the grounds of the Cape Playhouse, this recently formed group is gathering works of artists who have lived or worked on the Cape. The museum also offers educational programs, workshops for children, and other special projects. There is a Cinema Club that shows classic or unusual films.

• *Josiah Dennis Manse*, Nobscusset Rd. and Whig St., Dennis; Call 385-3528 for hours. The 1736 saltbox home of the minister for whom the town of Dennis was named. This house, situated on two acres of land, is listed in the National Register of Historic Places.

• *Scargo Hill Observation Tower*, off Rte. 6A. Views to Provincetown atop this 28-foot tower built in 1902. Open 6 A.M. to 10 P.M.

• *Town Indian Burial Ground of the Nobscusset Tribe*, Old King's Hwy., near Scargo Lake.

• *Curious Form of Colonial Punishment*, corner of Rte. 134 and Access Rd., in front of the police station. Permanent exhibit of stocks, whipping posts, and pillories.

• *Congregational Church of South Dennis*, Main St., S. Dennis. Oldest pipe organ in continuous use. Organ built in 1767; visitors welcome.

• *Jericho House*, corner of Old Main St. and Trotting Park Rd., W. Dennis; 398-6736. Headquarters for the Dennis Historical Society; open July and August.

YARMOUTH

• *The Captain Bangs Hallet House*, 2 Strawberry Ln., Yarmouth Port. Owned by the Historical Society of Old Yarmouth; parts of this house date to 1740. It is open Monday through Thursday in July and August.

• *1680 Thatcher House*, Rte. 6A, Yarmouth Port. Open Tuesday, Thursday, and Sunday, 1–5 p.m.; admission fee is charged.

• *The Winslow Crocker House*, located next to the Thatcher House on Rte. 6A. Like the Thatcher House, this house is owned by the Society for the Preservation of New England Antiquities. The house is a good example of Colonial architecture.

• *Baxter Grist Mill*, Rte. 28, W. Yarmouth. Built in 1710 to grind corn. Open daily.

• *Windmill Park*, site of *Judah Baker Windmill*, on the edge of Bass River in South Dennis. The windmill, built in 1791, is restored. There is a small swimming beach here.

Seasonal Events

BARNSTABLE

• *Hyannis Harbor Festival,* Bismore Park on Ocean St., next to the docks; 775-2201. Usually held in June; blessing of the fleet, art and crafts, sandcastle building, musicians.

• *WCOD Chowder Festival*, Cape Cod Melody Tent, Hyannis; 775-6800 (WCOD). Usually held in June. Sample offerings of chowder from more than 30 Cape restaurants—vote for your favorite; live entertainment; admission charge.

• *Hyannis Street Festival*, downtown Hyannis. Usually held in August.

• *Fourth of July*. Activities in the various villages include a parade in Hyannis and fireworks at the harbor in Hyannis.

• *Barnstable County Fair*, fairgrounds. Rte. 151, Falmouth; 563-3200. Late July.

• *Triathlons*. There are several: *Sprint Triathlon* and *Bud Light Endurance*, both at Craigville Beach, write DMSE, 430 C., Salem St., Medford, MA 02155, phone 396-3001 for further information; *Seaside Triathlon*, write Seaside Triathlon, Box 843, Barnstable 02630.

• *Hyannis Festival of Light*, Village Marketplace, North St., Hyannis; 771-4499. End of November; music, clowns, Santa, tree lighting.

• *"Pops By the Sea,"* Town Green, Hyannis. This concert has become a popular Cape Cod tradition as the Boston Pops visit Hyannis in August.

All of the villages of Barnstable have a variety of events, arts and crafts shows, festivals, and fairs throughout the year. Check local papers for calendars.

DENNIS

• *Dennis Festival Days*. Usually held in August, this festival has a wide variety of activities for all ages; kite-flying contest (at West Dennis Beach), arts and crafts, film festival, canoe races on Swan River, road race, moonlight cruises on Bass River and Cape Cod Bay, antique car parade, town barbecue on the Cape Playhouse grounds, clowns and other enterainment. For further information, contact the Dennis Chamber of Commerce at 398-3568 or 398-3573 or stop at their information booth at the corner of Rte. 28 and Rte. 134.

YARMOUTH

- *Yarmouth Seaside Festival*, at the John Simpkins School field across from Yarmouth Town Hall on Rte. 28 in South Yarmouth. This festival is held in October. Activities include canoe racing, sand sculpture, juggling acts, puppet shows, arts and crafts, a parade, and fireworks over Bass River. For information, call 394-0889.

Tours/Whale Watching

BARNSTABLE

- *Cape Cod Custom Tours*, 36 Ocean St., Hyannis 02601; 778-6933. Boat cruises to the Islands, around the harbor, or through the canal.
- *Cape Cod Adventures*, Cummaquid; 362-8001. Tours of Cape and the Islands.
- *Cape Cod Scenic Railroad*, 252 Main St., Hyannis; 771-3788. Climb aboard a vintage train for a historical and scenic tour of Cape Cod. Also available is the Dinner Train and the railroad's new Ecology Discovery Tour.
- *Hy-Line Harbor Cruises*, Ocean Street Dock, Hyannis; 775-7185. One-hour cruises, sunset cruises; good way to view Kennedy Compound; cocktails and snacks on board; seasonal.
- *Hyannis Whale Watcher Cruises*, Rte. 132, Hyannis; 775-1622 or 362-6088. April-October; food and beverage service; naturalist on board. Leaves from Barnstable Harbor.
- *Hyannis Aviation*, Barnstable Municipal Airport; 775-8171.
- *Cape Cod Flying Service*, Cape Cod Airport, 1000 Race Ln., Marstons Mills; 428-8732.
- *Hy-Line* (775-7185) and the *Steamship Authority* (540-2022 or 771-4000) both provide ferry service to the Islands from Hyannis. Call for schedules. Car space must be reserved well in advance.

DENNIS

- *Freya*, a 42-foot schooner sailing from Northside Marina in Sesuit Harbor, E. Dennis. The boat can accommodate up to six passengers. Call 385-3936 or 385-3937 for reservations and information.
- *Whale Watcher Cruises*, Northside Marina, Sesuit Harbor, E. Dennis. Besides whale watching, the boat also offers a sunset cruise on the Cape Cod Canal, a sunset cocktail cruise, and a lobster boil cruise. Call 385-7121 for reservations or information.

Children's Activities

BARNSTABLE

- *Cape Cod Miniature Golf*, 531 Main St., Hyannis; 778-6553.
- *Cape Cod Melody Tent*, West End Rotary Circle, Hyannis; 778-1322. During the summer children's plays are presented Wednesday mornings.
- *Cape Cod Storyland Golf*, 70 Center Street, Hyannis; 778-4339. One of the Cape's newest miniature golf courses, each hole gives a little history lesson on the Cape's towns. Bumper boats, too!

- *Merry-Go-Round*, West End Marketplace, 2nd floor, Hyannis.
- *Cotuit Library*, Main St., Cotuit; 428-8141. Preschool story hour on Tuesday mornings.
- *Kennedy Rink Skating Pond*, Bearses Way, Hyannis; 775-0379. Winter.
- *Barnstable Elementary School Playground*, Rte. 6A, Barnstable. An exceptional playground with a good variety of activities.
- *Pirate's Cove*, 728 Main St., South Yarmouth; 394-6200. 18-hole miniature golf course.
- *Cape Cod Potato Chip Factory*, Breeds Hill Rd., Hyannis; 775-3358. Self-guided tours, see popular potato chips being made, samples offered; open Monday through Friday 9 A.M. to 5 P.M.
- *Ryan's Family Amusement Center*, Cape Cod Mall; 775-5566.
- *Zoo Quarium*, Rte. 28, West Yarmouth; 775-8883. Moderate. Marine animals, New England wildlife, local pond and sea life, domestic animals from around the world.
- *Kidz Connection,* behind Cape Cod Mall, 771-8090. Video games, tunnel mazes, ball cages.

DENNIS

- *Sea View Playland*, Lower County Rd., Dennisport; 398-9084. Here you'll find a collection of 85 amusement devices, including miniature golf, Barn of Fun, and a snack bar.
- *Children's Theatre Series*, at the Cape Playhouse off Route 6A, Dennis. Performances on Friday mornings at 9:30 and 11:30 A.M. during the summer. Well-known children's favorites such as *Hansel and Gretel* and *Jack and the Beanstalk* are presented. Call the box office at 385-3911 for the schedule.
- *Cape Cod Gymnastics*, Hokum Rock Rd., Box 945, Dennis 02638; 385-8216. Gymnastics classes for preschool through high school.
- *West Dennis Public Library*, Main St., W. Dennis; 398-2050. There is a "read and sing" story hour for children.
- *Public park*, off Rte. 6A at the corner of New Boston Rd. and Nobscusset, across from the Dennis Market. Playground with a grassy area and sand, a good variety of playground equipment, well-kept.
- *Holiday Hill Miniature Golf*, Rte. 28, Dennisport; 398-8857. Game room, too.
- *Bass River Waterfront Mini Golf*, 30 Rte. 28, W. Dennis; 398-0937.
- *West Dennis Mini Golf*, Rte. 28, W. Dennis; 398-1606.

YARMOUTH

- *Aqua Circus*, Rte. 28, W. Yarmouth; 775-8883. Aquarium and petting zoo, sea lion and dolphin shows, pony rides, wild animal zoo, picnic area.
- *Bass River Sports World*, Rte. 28, S. Yarmouth; 398-6070. Miniature golf, baseball batting cages, video games, and driving range.
- *Ryan's Family Amusement Center*, 1067 Main St., Rte. 28, Yarmouth; 394-5644. Candlepin and tenpin.
- *Candy Company*, 975 Rte. 28, S. Yarmouth; 398-0000. Candies, nuts, fudge.
- *Pirate's Cove Adventure Golf*, 728 Main St., S. Yarmouth; 394-6200. Miniature golf.
- *Putter's Paradise*, Rte. 28, W. Yarmouth (between Windrift and Tidewater motels); 771-7394. Miniature golf and soft ice cream.
- *Camp Wingate*, White Rock Rd., Yarmouth; 362-6032. Summer camp.

Shops

Art Galleries

BARNSTABLE

- *Cape Cod Art Association Gallery & Studios*, Rte. 6A, Barnstable; 362-2909. Exhibits by Cape Cod artists, May–December.
- *Art Waves*, off Rte. 28, Cotuit; 428-7686.
- *S. Barber Antiques and Fine Arts,* 248 Stevens St., Hyannis; 775-0021.
- *Birdsey on the Cape*, 12 Wianno Ave., Osterville; 428-4969.
- *Chosen Arts Gallery of Fine Handcrafts*, 625 Rte. 6A, W. Barnstable; 362-8216.
- *Claire Murray,* 867 Main St., Osterville; 420-3562.
- *Gallery Under the Elms*, 4039 Rte. 6A, Cummaquid; 362-6069.
- *Harden Studios*, 3264 Main St., Barnstable; 362-7711.
- *Marjon Print & Frame Shop*, 51 Barnstable Rd., Hyannis; 775-1554.
- *The Paint Box Art Gallery*, 839 Main St., Osterville; 428-3823.
- *Richard's Galleries*, 337 Main St., Hyannis; 771-8350.
- *Spectrum*, 342 Main St., Hyannis; 771-4554.
- *Yankee Accent*, 23 Wianno Ave., Osterville; 428-2332.

DENNIS

- *Cape Museum of Fine Arts*, Theater Marketplace, Rte. 6A, Dennis; 385-4477.
- *Grose Gallery,* 524 Rte. 6A, Dennis; 385-3434.
- *Scargo Stoneware Pottery*, 30 Dr. Lords Road, S. Dennis; 385-3894.
- *Ruth Waite Studio Gallery*, 239 Main St., Dennisport; 394-5869.

YARMOUTH

- *Glotzer's Art Gallery*, 832 Rte. 28, S. Yarmouth; 398-8436.
- *Northside Craft Gallery*, 933 Rte. 6A, Yarmouth Port; 362-5291.
- *Oceanside Gallery*, 1198 Main St., Rte. 28, S. Yarmouth; 394-2822.

Craft & Specialty Shops

BARNSTABLE

Village of Barnstable

Barnstable Village is charming and a great place to browse in the shops and have lunch at the Village Landing or the Barnstable Tavern & Restaurant. Some of the shops in Barnstable are listed below:

- *Beautiful Things*, 3267 Main St., Rte. 6A; 362-3732. Hand-painted furniture, antiques and accessories.
- *The Crystal Pineapple*, Rte. 132; 362-1330. Gift shop, crystal and cranberry glass and Tiffany lamps.
- *The Whippletree*, 660 Main St.; 362-3320. Country items, dried flowers, antiques.
- *Salt & Chestnut*, Rte. 6A at Maple St.; 362-6085. Weathervanes, antiques.
- *Cape Cod Stencil Co.*, Rte. 149; 362-8294. Unique selection of stencils.
- *The Picket Fence*, 4225 Main St., Rte. 6A, Cummaquid; 362-4865. Craft store, quilting supplies.

- ***Tumbleweed Quilts***, Corner Rte. 6A and Rte. 132; 362-8700. Exhibits of quilts and fabric arts.

Centerville
- ***1856 General Store***, 555 Main St.; 775-1856. A country store.

Hyannis
Hyannis offers the Cape's widest variety of shops, outlets, shopping plazas, and boutiques. Several shopping areas and a mall are listed below. Be prepared for crowds on almost any day in the summer, especially if it's raining.
- ***Cape Cod Mall***, Rte. 132. This is the largest mall on the Cape, with over 80 shops, department stores, craft carts, and restaurants. At the central fast-food section you can get anything from a McDonald's hamburger to an Au Bon Pain croissant to a Taco Makers burrito. The mall has just been remodeled in mauves and teal greens, with brick walks and street lanterns. The improvements have made it even more attractive to those looking for something to do on a rainy day. Large department stores in the mall are Sears, Filene's, and Macy's. Some other well-known chains are The Limited, The Gap, Kay Bee Toys, and Thom McAn.

Some others worth looking at are Victoria's Secret, a lovely lingerie store; Crabtree & Evelyn, always a nice place to look for soaps and fragrances; The Gap Kids, The Gap's version for the younger set; Prints Plus, good variety of prints—from Monet to Disney posters; and Mrs. Field's Cookies, stop for a treat. Two marketplaces on North Street offer some upscale shopping in an area of brick walks and buildings.

At the factory outlet center on 540 Main St., you can find some of Hyannis's outlets.
- ***Other outlets around town***: Nevada Bob's, 30 Enterprise Rd., 775-9300, quality golf and tennis equipment, sportswear, accessories; Mass Bay Co., 595 Main St., 771-2114, Esprit, Lee, Oshkosh, all at discount prices; Cellar Door Discount Designer Shoes, Rte. 149, Marstons Mills, 428-0180; Dansk Factory Outlet, Rte. 132, 775-3118.
- ***Main Street*** is great for a shopping stroll. Some of the stores you'll find here are Black Swan, 211 Main St., 778-0177, quarterboard furniture; Buzzells Stained Glass, 18 E. Main St., 775-3488, gift shop; Brer Fox Woodcraft, 596 Main St., 775-4240, wooden products, toys, signs; Cotton Club, 575 Main St., 771-4588, cotton sportswear; Colonial Candle, 232 Main St., 771-3916; candles, silks, gifts; California Surf Co., 667 Main St., 790-0770; T-shirts, sportswear; Dancer's Pointe, 569 Main St., 775-2880, store for any budding ballerina or other talents; Far East Trading Co., 606 Main St., 771-2145, gift shop; The Jeanery, 595 Main St., 771-2114; Latienda Toys n Treasures, 624 Main St., 775-4429; From the Heart of Cape Cod, 569 Main St., 771-7544, gifts; Mole Hole, 448 Main St., 771-5424, gifts; Naked Furniture, 237 Main St., 771-8378, good quality unfinished furniture; Outermost Kites, 570 Main St., 775-7263, interesting and sophisticated collection of kites; Puritan Clothing, 408 Main St., 775-2400, classic men's and women's clothing; Shell Biz, 569 Main St.; Stephanie's Swimwear, 382 Main St., 775-5166, large selection of swimwear; Starboard Cargo, 580 Main St., 775-5470, gifts; Whistle Stop Gift Shop, 252 Main St., 775-8042; Where It's At, 569 Main St., 778-4066, gifts; Salty Roos, 602 Main St., 778-4522, skateboards, surf and water sport equipment.
- ***West End Marketplace***, corner of Sea and Main sts.; 771-0437. A collection of more than 30 shops and small eateries; upstairs is a wooden carousel, pinball machines, and other amusements for children.
- ***Christmas Crossing***, corner of Rte. 28 and Yarmouth Rd. Christmas Tree Shop, one of the most popular stores on Cape Cod—everything from toys to crystal at a discount.

BARNSTABLE (CONTINUED)

• *Southwind Plaza*, Independence Way, Rte. 132. This is a shopping plaza with the Super Stop & Shop supermarket and Bradlees (a general department store), its biggest stores, located at opposite ends of the plaza. But take time to browse through the shops in between.

This list of shops is not complete, so take your time and look around. There is a Marshall's behind the Cape Cod Mall. Also don't miss The Dancers' Place for exercise and dance clothing and accessories. A T.J. Maxx is across from the airport.

• *Festival of Hyannis*, Rte. 132, assortment of retail stores such as Toys R Us, Paperama, and Pier I.

• *Harvest of Barnstable*, 45 Plant Rd., Unit #104; 790-1010. Specializes in dried wreaths, centerpieces and other arrangements.

Osterville

• *Alpert's Art Inc.*, 843 Main St.; 428-7000. Gifts.
• *Appleseeds*, 1374 Main St.; 428-6081. Classic clothing.
• *The Children's Shop*, 27 Wianno Ave.; 428-9458. Beautiful children's clothing.
• *Horizons of Osterville,* Main St.; 428-8992. Gifts.
• *Joan Peters of Osterville,* 885 Main St.; 428-3418. Lovely decorator's shop, handpainted furniture, fabrics.
• *Mark Fore & Strike*, 21 Wianno Ave.; 428-2270. Men's and women's clothing.
• *Mulberry Corners*, 853 Main St.; 428-9547. Women's clothing.
• *Natural Image of Osterville*, 812 Main St.; 428-5729. Women's apparel.
• *Osterville Cheese Shop*, 29 Wianno Ave.; 428-9085. Gourmet shop.
• *Osterville House & Garden*, Main St.; 428-6911. Gifts.
• *Osterville Needlepoint Shop*, 891 Main St.; 428-4455.
• *Talbot's*, 32 Wianno Ave.; 428-2204. Classic women's clothing.

DENNIS

• *The Basket Shoppe*, off Rte. 28 near Rte. 134 intersection; 398-6850.
• *Basketville*, Rte. 28, W. Dennis; 394-9677. Variety of baskets and woodenware. They have a silk flower shop next door—great variety.
• *Bougainvillea of Cape Cod*, 774 Main St., Rte 6A; 385-3535. Furniture, home furnishings and specialties.
• *Cape Cod Braided Rug Co. Factory Showroom*, 259 Great Western Rd., S. Dennis; 398-0089. Custom-made rugs, chair pads, place mats.
• *Cape Cod Collection Ltd.*, 574 Rte. 6A, Dennis; 385-8367. Gifts.
• *Christmas Tree Shops*, Rte. 28, W. Dennis; 394-5557. A wide variety of items at discount prices.
• *Country Barn of Dennis*, Rte. 6A, Dennis; 385-4111. Country items.
• *Dennisport Dollhouse*, 497 Upper County Rd., Dennisport; 398-9356.
• *Emily's Beach Barn*, 708 Main St., Dennis; 385-8328. Sundresses, swimsuits (operated by Emily Lawrence).
• *Factory Shoe Mart*, Main St., Rte. 28, Dennisport; 398-6000. Family shoe store, name brands at discount prices.
• *The Glass Unicorn*, Rte. 28, S. Dennis; 394-5331. Imported gifts.
• *Holiday Hill Gift Shop*, Rte. 28, Dennisport; 394-4691. Woodenware, unfinished furniture, gifts.
• *Irish Items*, Rte. 6A, Dennis; 385-9231. Across from Cape Playhouse.
• *Ladybug Quilting Shop*, 612 Rte. 6A, Dennis; 385-2662. Quilts, fabrics, lessons.
• *Mill Stone Pottery*, corner of South and Sea sts. off Rte 6A, near Brewster/Dennis line, E. Dennis; 385-4214.

- *Paraffin-Alia Shop*, Post Office Square, Dennisport; 398-6763. Gifts.
- *Raspberry Thistle*, 259 Main St., W. Dennis; 398-8200. Fine fabrics.
- *The Steamer Trunk*, 608 Main St., W. Dennis; 394-0411.
- *A Touch of Glass*, 711 Rte. 28, W. Dennis; 398-3850.

A list of shopping plazas in Dennis follows:

- *Patriot Square*, off Rte. 134 (near Rte. 6 overpass); 394-4129. This center has Purity Supreme Supermarket and CVS Drugstore as the big tenants. Some other stores are Puritan Clothing, Strawberries (records and tapes), Royal Books (discounted books, some videos), Holiday Card and Gift Shop, and Marshall's.

YARMOUTH

- *Barefoot Trader*, 316 Main St., Rte. 28, W. Yarmouth; 394-4287. Gift shop.
- *The Bazaar of Cape Cod*, 367 Main St., Rte. 28, W. Yarmouth; 775-6760.
- *Christmas Tree Shop*, Rte. 28, W. Yarmouth; 775-8151, and Rte. 6A, Yarmouth Port; 362-3153. Probably the best bargains on Cape Cod—on everything from toys to Waterford crystal.
- *Little Bit of Love*, 807 Main St., S. Yarmouth; 394-1983. Gift shop.
- *Mill Store,* Rte. 28, W. Yarmouth; 771-1507. Unfinished furniture, wooden items for crafts.
- *Pewter Crafters of Cape Cod*, 927 Main St., Rte. 6A, Yarmouth Port; 362-3407. Complete line of pewter pieces; good quality.
- *Design Works*, 159 Rte. 6A, Yarmouth Port; 362-9698. Pottery, Scandinavian antiques, lace items.
- *Yarmouth Colonial Country Store*, 941 Main St., Bass River; 398-8785. Gifts.
- *Northside Craft Gallery*, 933 Main St., Yarmouth; 362-5291.
- *Union Station Plaza*, Station Ave., next to the A&P Future Store you will find Gotcha Covered Fabrics, a nice decorator's shop; Jewel Box; All Cape Sports; Silk Atrium; a Hallmark store; and a fish market.
- *Whale Feather Shop,* 1272 Rte. 28, S. Yarmouth; whale sculptures, jewelry, dried wreaths.
- *Wild Birds Unlimited,* Rte. 28 in the Hearth & Kettle Plaza, S. Yarmouth; 760-1996. Bird and garden accessories as well as crafts of local Cape Codders.

Antiques

BARNSTABLE

- *Back Yard Gallery*, off Rte. 28, Cotuit; 428-8623.
- *Stephen H. Garner Antiques*, 169 Main St., Barnstable; 362-8424. Furniture.
- *Harden Studios*, 3264 Rte. 6A, Barnstable Village; 362-7711. Art gallery along with other fine arts, accessories, antiques and furniture.
- *Hyannis Antique Co-op*, 500 Main St., 778-0512. Furniture, glassware, baseball, dolls, jewelry.
- *Maps of Antiquity*, 1022 Rte. 6A, 362-7169. Maps from all over the world dating from the 16th to the 19th century.
- *Plush & Plunder*, 605 Main St., Hyannis; 775-4467.
- *Rosemary's Antiques and Collectables*, 870 Main St., Osterville; 428-9025.
- *S. Barber Antiques and Fine Art*, 248 Stevens St.; 775-0900. Hand-painted furniture, country antiques and reproduction beds.
- *Salt & Chestnut*, Rte. 6A, Maple St., W. Barnstable; 362-6085. Weathervanes, crafts.

BARNSTABLE (CONTINUED)

- *Stone Antique Shop*, 659 Main St., Hyannis; 775-3913.
- *The Whippletree*, 660 Main St., Rte. 6A, W. Barnstable; 362-3320. Country antiques, folk art.

For information about auctions, call the Richard A. Bourne Corporation, Hyannis; 775-0797, or William Elkins Co., 20 Kent Lane, Hyannis, 771-2662.

DENNIS

- *Antiques*, 243 Rte. 6A; 385-6400. This 18,000-square-foot store features 135 dealers.
- *Village Antiques*, 601 Main St., Dennis; 385-7300. Specializing in clocks and repairing old clocks.
- *Curtis-Skylar Antiques*, 838 Main St., Rte. 6A at Corporation Rd., Dennis; 385-2921. Wicker, accessories.
- *Dennis Antiques*, 437 Main St., Rte. 6A, Dennis; 385-8091. Glassware, Waterford.
- *Dr. II*, 100 Centre St., S. Dennis; 394-8894.
- *Old Towne Antiques of Dennis*, 593 Main St.; 385-5202. Large selection of antiques and collectibles.
- *Red Lion Antiques*, 601 Main St., Rte. 6A, Box 749, Dennis; 385-4783. Furniture, antique linen and lace.
- *The Rose Victorian*, 485 Main St., W. Dennis; 394-1696. Antiques, collectibles, quilts, hand painted furniture and dried arrangements.
- *Staffordshire*, 1170 Main St., Rte. 6A, Dennis; 385-3690.
- *Trotting Park Antiques*, 803 Main St., W. Dennis; 398-3762.
- *Robert C. Eldred Co., Inc.*, Rte. 6A, E. Dennis; 385-3116. Auction house.

YARMOUTH

- *Collector's Corner*, 161 Main St., Yarmouth Port; 362-9540.
- *Cuffy's Factory Store,* 1 Reardon Circle, S. Yarmouth; 394-1371. Great buys on T-shirts, sweatshirts and shorts; off the beaten track but bargain hunters flock here.
- *Design Works*, 159 Rte. 6A, Yarmouth Port; 362-9698. Furniture, lace items, pottery.
- *1830 House Antiques*, 143 Main St.; 362-3820. Furniture, lamps, china, children's items.
- *Emerald House Antiques*, Rte. 6A, Yarmouth Port; 362-9508. Limoges, glass, silver, crystal.
- *Gilpin's Antiques*, 431 Main St., Yarmouth Port; 362-3090.
- *Constance Goff Antiques*, 161 Main St., Yarmouth Port; 362-9540 or 362-9928. Furniture, accessories, folk art.
- *Lil-Bud Antiques*, 161 Main St., Rte. 6A, Yarmouth Port; 362-8984 or 362-6675. Early American pattern glass, flint, nonflint silver.
- *Leona's Antiques*, 161 Main St., Yarmouth Port; 362-5169. Glass, porcelain, and antique dolls.
- *Nickerson's Antiques*, 162 Main St., Yarmouth Port; 362-6426.
- *Peach Tree Designs*, 173 Main St.; 362-8317. This lovely store used to be in Barnstable Village and recently moved to an antique house on Rtc. 6A in Yarmouth Port. Look for gifts, accessories, furnishings here.
- *The Prospector*, 18 E. Main St., Rte. 28, W. Yarmouth; 778-4116.
- *Rachels Antiques*, 797 Rte. 28, S. Yarmouth; 394-3183.

Sports & Recreation

Biking

BARNSTABLE

Bike rentals are available at the following:
- *Cascade Motor Lodge*, 201 Main St., Hyannis; 775-9717; one block from harbor, train, and bus.
- *Cove Cycle*, 11 Enterprise Rd., Hyannis; 771-6155.
- *Osterville Bicycle Service*, 846 Main St., Osterville; 428-5021.

DENNIS

Dennis Bike Path and *Cape Cod Rail Trail* are good bike paths. For information, on both trails, see listing under Hiking and Nature Trails in this section.
- *Idle Times Bike Shop,* 460 Rte. 134; 760-4515.
- *Hall Oil Co.*, Rte. 134, S. Dennis, 398-3831. Bike rentals.

YARMOUTH
- *The Outdoor Shop*, 50 Long Pond Dr., S. Yarmouth, 394-3819. Bike rentals.

Boating

BARNSTABLE
- *Cape Sailing Center*, 1-A Dock, Hyannis Marina; 771-9755. Boat rentals.
- *Peck's Boats*, 3800 Rte. 28, Cotuit; 428-6956. Rents sailboats, canoes, kayaks,sailboards.
- *Windsong Charters*, 10 Ocean St., Hyannis; 775-1630. Sailing charters.

DENNIS

Boat ramps are located at Rte. 28, W. Dennis, opposite Ferry St.; Cove Rd., S. Dennis; Uncle Freeman's Rd., W. Dennis; Sesuit Harbor, E. Dennis; Cove Rd., W. Dennis (Town Landing); Horsefoot Path, Dennis (Town Landing); Follins Pond, S. Dennis (Town Landing); Fisherman's Landing, off Rte. 6A, Dennis.
- *Cape Cod Boats*, Rte. 28 at Bass River at the bridge, W. Dennis; 394-9268. Boat rentals.
- *Karl's Boat Shop*, 47 Theophilis Smith Rd., S. Dennis; 394-9526 or 394-7368. Rentals and lessons by appointment.

Fishing

BARNSTABLE

If you're interested in chartering a boat, contact the following:
- *A-1 Sportfishing Charters*, from Barnstable Harbor; 888-6454 or 362-9719. 35- or 43-foot sportfisherman.
- *Kar-Nik Charters*, out of Lewis Bay, Hyannis; 775-2979 or 775-7812. 31- or 34-foot sportfisherman.
- *The Cygnet Fishing Charters*, Ocean St. Dock, Hyannis; 428-8628.
- *Helen H Deep Sea Fishing,* 137 Pleasant St., Hyannis; 790-0060. Year-round, bunks, full galley.
- *Hy-Line Deep Sea Fishing*, Ocean St. Dock, Hyannis; 790-0696.
- *The Wanderers*, Hyannis Harbor; 775-7361; 40-foot sportfisherman.

BARNSTABLE (CONTINUED)

- *Aquarius II*, Barnstable Harbor; 362-9617:
- *Barnstable Harbor Charter Fleet*, 186 Millway, Barnstable; 362-3908.
- *Captain Joe Eldridge*, 362 Millway, Barnstable; 362-3181.
- *Windward Charters Sport Fishing*, Hyannis Harbor; 362-4925. Also evening and sight-seeing cruises.

DENNIS

There are a number of fishing charters in Dennis:
- *Albatross Deep Sea Fishing*, Sesuit Harbor, E. Dennis; 385-3244; if no answer, 385-2063.
- *Champagne Charters*, Sesuit Harbor, E. Dennis; 800-810-2478. Variety of fishing adventures as well as sunset cruises, family beach picnics and private parties.
- *Day Breaker*, Sesuit Harbor, E. Dennis; 385-3571. 32-foot sportfishermen.
- *Captain George Maber*, 209 Setucket Rd.; 385-7265.
- *Champion Lines*, 44 Rte. 28, at Bass River, W. Dennis; 398-2266.
- *Innuendo Charters*, 43 New Boston Rd., Dennis; 385-2402.
- *East Dennis Charter Fleet*, E. Dennis; 385-5007.

Bait and tackle are available from the following:
- *Bass River Bait and Tackle*, 42 Main St., Rte. 28, W. Dennis; 394-8666.
- *Cotuit Bait and Tackle,* 4424 Rte. 28, Cotuit; 428-2111.
- *Riverview Bait and Tackle,* 1273 Rte. 28, Yarmouth; 394-1036.
- *Truman's,* 608 Main St., W. Yarmouth; 771-3470.

YARMOUTH

- *A-1 Sport Fishing Charters*, 72 South St., Bass River; 398-2486; if no answer, call 888-6454.

Golf Courses

BARNSTABLE

- *Oyster Harbors*, Oyster Harbor, Osterville; 428-9881. 18 holes, par 72, 6887 yards, private.
- *Cotuit Highground*, 159 Crocker Neck Rd., Cotuit; 428-9863. 9 holes, par 28, 1121 yards, public.
- *Cummaquid*, off Main St., Cummaquid; 362-2022. 18 holes, par 71, 6273 yards, private.
- *Hyannis Port Club*, Hyannis Port; 775-2978. 18 holes, par 71, 6203 yards, private.
- *Hyannis Golf Club*, Rte. 132, Hyannis; 362-4551. 18 holes, par 72, 6249 yards, public.
- *Tara Hyannis*, West End Circle, Hyannis; 775-7775. 18 holes, par 54, 2767 yards, public.
- *Wianno*, Parker Rd., Osterville; 428-9840. 18 holes, par 71, 6049 yards, private.

DENNIS

- *Dennis Highlands*, off Old Bass River Rd.; 385-8347. 18 holes, par 71, 6500 yards, public.
- *Dennis Pines*, Old Bass River Rd.; 385-8347. 18 holes, par 72, 7029 yards, public.

YARMOUTH

- ***Bass River***, High Bank Rd., S. Yarmouth; 398-9079. 18 holes, par 72, 6200 yards, public.
- ***Bayberry Hills***, off W. Yarmouth Rd. at Old Townhouse Rd.; 394-5597. 18 holes, par 72, 7170 yards.
- ***Blue Rock***, off High Bank Rd., S. Yarmouth; 398-9295. 18 holes, par 54, 2770 yards, public.
- ***King's Way***, Rte. 6A, Yarmouth Port; 362-8870. 18 holes.

Hiking & Nature Trails

BARNSTABLE

- ***Sandy Neck***, Sandy Neck Beach, W. Barnstable. About a 4.8-mile round-trip trail. There are several different ones. Orange markers point the way; the dunes and marshes here are spectacular.
- ***Otis-Atwood Conservation Area,*** West Barnstable. Off Rte. 6, Exit 5, take a left and then head west at the sign for the service road. Or from Race Lane, head north on the Crooked Cartway to reach this 1,224-acre parcel.

    Popple Bottom Road cuts across the parcel's middle. To the north, the land is described as knob-and-kettle topography typical of glacial moraines. White pine and holly grow in the southeast corner. Watch out for the shooting range north of the power lines.
- ***Arnold Property at Long Pond.*** This 37.5-acre parcel borders Long Pond in Marstons Mills. From Newtown Road follow Lakeshore Drive west. The land contains large open fields and a mature, mixed upland forest.
- ***Crocker Neck Conservation Area.*** This attractive parcel is on Popponesset Bay and is accessible from School Street to Crocker Neck Road, south to Cotuit Cove Road.

    By walking the length of its ninety-seven acres one can experience salt marsh on the eastern and southern borders and a freshwater marsh on the northeastern border.
- ***"1776" North and South.*** For the south parcel, travel from Route 149, then east on Church Street, and park across from the cemetery. The north parcel is located off Route 6A.

    The interesting south parcel is distinguished by old open fields and swamplands, as well as wet woodlands and scattered hummocks of upland forest. Wetlands and salt marsh are also included.
- ***Darby Property.*** For a good look at two kettle ponds side by side, the 103-acre Darby Property is the place to go.

    From Main Street in Osterville, head east on Pond Street, then take a quick right on Tower Hill Road to park.

    Joshua's and Micah's ponds lie side by side with trails around and between them. Pitch pine, oak, and holly mark the area.
- ***Hathaway's Pond Area.*** Off Phinney's Lane, a road leads to Hathaway's Pond Recreation Area. Two ponds actually share the same name. A typical array of pitch pine, oak, and small wetlands dots the area. The ponds are also known for their excellent trout fishing.

DENNIS

- ***Indian Lands and Conservation Nature Trails***. Signs from Town Hall parking lot point the way for the trail; 3/4 mile; views of Bass River and marshes;

DENNIS (CONTINUED)

level path. Blueberry, bayberry, swamp azalea, viburnum; watch out for poison ivy. Good fall, spring, and winter hike.

• *Fresh Pond Conservation Area*, Rte. 134, heading south, 6/10 of a mile from the intersection of Rte. 134 and Lower County Rd. There are four trails of various lengths for hikes. Level terrain; wild cranberry; wildlife, ducks on lake, and bluberries.

• *Whitfield Johnson Nature Trail*, end of Forest Pines Dr., off Rte. 134, E. Dennis. Mostly scrub pine; 3/4 mile; level and hilly areas.

• *Crow's Pasture*, end of Quivet Cemetery, E. Dennis. 2 1/2 miles round trip to Cape Cod Bay; wild apple and cherry trees, honeysuckle, beach plum and arrowwood.

• *Life Course*, off Access Rd. across from the Highway Garage, S. Dennis. 1 1/4 mile in length, this path has 20 exercise stations with exercise apparatus; it is a level trail and can be used for walking and jogging as well as exercising.

• *Dennis Bike Path*, Old Bass River Rd., Water District Building, S. Dennis. Four miles round trip. Good for jogging and walking as well as biking.

• *Cape Cod Rail Trail*, off Rte. 134 across from Hall Oil Company (where you can rent bikes), S. Dennis. This 11-mile trail begins in Dennis and winds through pines, lakes, and cranberry bogs all the way to Eastham where it hooks up with the National Seashore bike path to Coast Guard Beach. Used for walking and horseback riding as well as biking.

• *Scargo Beach*, off Rte. 6A. About 200 feet of beach on Scargo Lake; white cedars, wild azalea, bayberry as well as freshwater swimming.

• *Romig–Jacquinet Conservation Area*, off New Boston Rd., two houses past the Berrian Studio. Flat trail, about 1 1/2 miles round trip; tall cedars and oaks, marsh grasses, bayberry and bearberry.

• *Princess Beach*, off Scargo Hill Rd. 200 feet on Scargo Lake; facilities include grills, bathrooms, swings, and picnic benches.

• *Scargo Tower*, off Scargo Hill Rd.; view of Cape Cod Bay.

• *Hokum Rocks*, off Rte. 6A at the corner of Nobscusset and New Boston Rd., across from the Dennis Market. Nice playground with grass and sand and a good variety of equipment for children.

For a more complete description on the nature trails, refer to the Dennis Chamber of Commerce pamphlet, available at the Information Booth at the intersection of Routes 28 and 134.

YARMOUTH

• *Horse Pond Conservation Area*, Higgins Crowell Rd., W. Yarmouth, near Mattakeese School. A 3100-foot trail along Horse Pond.

• *Dennis Pond Conservation Area*, Willow St., Yarmouth Port. The trail winds through the woods with a side trail along the shore line.

• *Meadowbrook Road Conservation Area*, end of Meadowbrook Rd., W. Yarmouth. This is a short boardwalk that takes you through swamp and marsh to the edge of Swan Lake.

• *Raymond J. Syrjala Conservation Area*, Winslow Gray Rd., W. Yarmouth. A 3540-foot trail that goes in a loop.

• *Boardwalk*, at Bass Hole Beach, at the end of Centre St., Yarmouth Port. A 1000-foot boardwalk over water and marsh.

• *Yarmouth Botanic Trail*, off Rte. 6A, behind the Yarmouth Port Post Office; 362-3021. Parking available at the Gate House, which also has a map of the trail.

Fifty acres were donated to the Historical Society of Old Yarmouth. The sandy trail begins by an herb garden and will take you on to see lady's slippers, oaks, Miller's Pond, and possibly some turtles. Open June–October.
- *Picnic areas*: Long Pond, S. Yarmouth; Wings Grove, S. Yarmouth; Wilbur Park, S. Yarmouth, grills and rest rooms; Centre St., Yarmouth Port, grills and rest rooms.

Horseback Riding

BARNSTABLE
- *Holly Hill Farm,* 240 Flint St., Marstons Mills; 428-2621.
- *Sheriff's Youth Ranch,* 1445 Osterville Rd., W. Barnstable; 420-3505.

DENNIS
- *Dennis Riding School,* Airline Rd., S. Dennis; 385-3030.
- *Salt Meadow Farm,* 226 Great Western Rd., S. Dennis; 398-3644.

Sporting Goods Stores

BARNSTABLE
- *Eastern Mountain Sports,* Village Marketplace, Hyannis; 775-1072.
- *Butler Sporting Goods,* 815 W. Main St., Hyannis; 771-4595 or 800-698-4310.
- *Play It Again Sports,* 25 Iyanough Rd., Hyannis; 771-6979.
- *Sports Port*, 149 W. Main St., Hyannis; 775-3096. Bait, license, information, supplies, skin diving equipment.
- *Cape Cod Rod & Reel Repair*, 210 Barnstable Rd., Hyannis; 775-7543.

YARMOUTH
- *Truman's*, 608 Main St., W. Yarmouth; 771-3470.

Tennis

BARNSTABLE
- *Tennis of Cape Cod*, off Rte. 132, Hyannis; 775-1921. Six indoor courts. Membership not required; summer memberships available.

In Hyannis there are courts at Barnstable High School, off W. Main St.; Barnstable Middle School, Rte 28; and Old Barnstable Middle School, off South St. No charge; call the Recreation Commission for more information at 775-5603.

Centerville has courts near the Elementary School, off Bumps River Road. No charge.

There are two courts off West Bay Road in Osterville. No charge.
- *Kings Grant Racquet Club*, Main St., Cotuit; 428-5744. Seven courts available for rent.
- *Cape Cod Community College*, 2240 Rte. 132, W. Barnstable; 362-6925. Courts available for small charge.
- *Tennis at the Tara,* West End Circle, Hyannis; 775-7775.

DENNIS
- *Dennis Racquet & Swim Club*, off Oxbow Way, Dennis; 385-2221. Courts for rent; lessons available.
- *Marine Lodge*, 15 North St., Dennisport; 398-2963. Asphalt court.
- *Dennis Tennis Club*, 628 Main St., S. Dennis; 394-2262. Court fees lower in May, June, and September; slightly higher for July and August.

DENNIS (CONTINUED)

• **Dennis Public Courts**, Nathaniel H. Wixon School, Rte. 134, S. Dennis; 394-8300.

• **Sesuit Tennis Centre,** 1389 Rte. 6A, E. Dennis; 385-2200.

YARMOUTH

• **Mid Cape Racquet Club**, Whites Path. S. Yarmouth; 394-3511. In addition to nine indoor tennis courts, this club also has four racquetball courts, one squash court, a fitness center, health spa, and saunas. Lessons available in tennis and racquetball. The Mid Cape Racquet Club sponsors the *Mid-Cape Open* in mid-summer. Call 394-3511 for more information.

• **Bass River Athletic Club**, 1067 Rte. 28, S. Yarmouth; 398-0131. There are seven racquetball courts, aerobic and exercise classes, saunas, and whirlpools. Summer memberships available.

• **The Cove at Yarmouth,** 183 Rte. 28; 771-3666. Indoor courts.

Beaches

BARNSTABLE

Beach stickers are available at Barnstable Town Hall, South St., Hyannis, and are required at all public beaches. Visitors can purchase parking stickers $5 a day (in 1987) or $10 a week. Cape Cod Bay is on the north side (Route 6A) of Barnstable; Nantucket Sound is on the south side (Route 28) of Barnstable. There are no open fires permitted on the beaches. Major beaches all have lifeguards.

Centerville

• **Craigville Beach**, Craigville Beach Rd. Large beach with snack bars, bathhouses, rest rooms, showers, very popular with the college crowd.

• **Covell Memorial Beach**, next to Craigville. Sticker required.

• **Wequaquet Lake**, Shootflying Hill Rd. Large freshwater lake, boating, fishing, sticker required.

Cotuit

• **Lovell's Pond**, Newtown Rd., Santuit. Freshwater.

Hyannis

All three beaches can be reached from Main Street.

• **Kalmus Park**, end of Ocean St. Snack bar, bathhouse, and parking (board sailors allowed here west of jetty).

• **Veteran's Park**, Ocean St. Picnic area, snack bar, grills, playground, and showers.

• **Sea St. Beach**, Sea St. Showers and snack bar.

Marstons Mills

• **Hamblin's Pond**, Rte. 149. Freshwater.

Osterville

• **Joshua's Pond**, Tower Hill Rd. Picnic area and grills. Most beaches in Osterville are private.

West Barnstable

• **Sandy Neck**, off Rte. 6A. Rest rooms, snack bar, bathhouse. Four-wheel-drive vehicles allowed but require a permit. Call Town Hall at 775-1120 for information.

- *Millway Beach*, off Rte. 6A by Barnstable Village Harbor.
- *Hathaway's Pond*, Phinney's Ln. Freshwater.

DENNIS

In Dennis, there are 16 saltwater beaches and two freshwater pond beaches; 10 of the beaches are on the north side of town (Route 6A), and six beaches are on the south side (Route 28). Beach stickers, available at Town Hall, are required for parking at most town beaches.

North Side Beaches

- *Corporation Beach*, off Corporation Rd., which is off Rte. 6A. Rest rooms, snack bar, bathhouse.
- *Mayflower Beach*, off Dunes View Rd. Concession stand, lifeguards, rest rooms.
- *Bay View Road Beach*, off Beach St. Lifeguards, rest rooms.
- *Horsefoot Path Beach*, end of Horsefoot Path, which is off Beach St. This is a walk-on beach—no lifeguards, no parking.
- *Harbor View Beach*, end of Harbor Rd., which is off Sesuit Neck Rd. There is a small parking area.
- *Chapin Beach*, off Chapin Beach Rd. There are rest rooms but no lifeguards; four-wheel-drive vehicles are allowed on the back trail of Chapin Beach. Permits required; licenses available at Town Hall.
- *Crowe's Pasture*, off South St. on Quivet Neck. This beach is open to four-wheel-drive vehicles; no lifeguards.
- *Sea Street Beach*, off Sea St., E. Dennis. Parking and bathhouse.
- *Cold Storage Beach*, a beautiful beach at the end of Cold Storage Rd. For residents only. Go in June or September!
- *Scargo Lake Beach*, off Rte. 6A. Small parking lot, stickers required.
- *Princess Beach*, a freshwater pond on the south side of Rte. 6A, off Scargo Hill Rd., Dennis. Bathhouse, lifeguards.

South Side Beaches

All the beaches listed below can be reached from Route 28.

- *West Dennis Beach*, off Lighthouse Rd. Bathhouse, snack bar, lifeguards, and a large parking lot. Good place to view boats at the mouth of Bass River.
- *South Village Road Beach*, off Lower County Rd., at the mouth of Swan River. Small beach, rest rooms, small parking area.
- *Sea Street Beach*, off Rte. 28. Rest rooms, bathhouse, and parking.
- *Haigis Street Beach*, off Lower County and Old Wharf rds., Dennisport. Rest rooms and parking.
- *Inman Road Beach* and *Raycroft Parkway Beach*, both off Chase St., Dennisport. Rest rooms and limited parking. Inman has lifeguards.
- *Glendon Road Beach*, off Glendon Rd., Dennisport. Rest rooms and parking.

YARMOUTH

Most Yarmouth beaches are located on Nantucket Sound (Rte. 28), although the town does have shoreline on the bay. There are also some freshwater ponds to choose from. Beach stickers, available at Town Hall, are required at all public beaches. Summer visitors can purchase daily stickers ($7 a day in 1989), weekly stickers ($30), or seasonal stickers ($75). Most of the beaches have at least one lifeguard, and most have toilet facilities.

Nantucket Sound Beaches

- *Sea Gull Beach*, off South Sea Ave. Lots of parking, snack bar, and picnic area.

YARMOUTH (CONTINUED)

- *Smugglers Beach*, off South Shore Dr. Lots of parking and picnic area; mouth of Bass River.
- *South Middle Beach*, off South St.
- *Seaview Beach*, South Shore Dr. Picnic area.
- *Parker's River Beach*, off South Shore Dr. Picnic area.
- *Colonial Acres Beach*, at end of Standish Way. Small parking lot.
- *Englewood Beach*, end of Berry Ave. Small parking lot.
- *Thatcher Town Park*, off Seaview Ave. No lifeguard or toilets, small parking lot.
- *Bay View Beach*, end of Bay View St. Small parking lot.
- *Windmill Beach*, off River St. Weekend lifeguard, no toilets.
- *Wilbur Park*, Highbank Rd. No toilets or lifeguards, on Bass River.

Bay Beach

Yarmouth has only one bay beach:
- *Bass Hole*, also known as Gray's Neck Beach, off Center St., off Rte. 6A. Playground, toilets, and picnic area. Set inside a marsh; fairly small; more of a scenic beach than a swimming beach.

Ponds

- *Long Pond*, off Indian Memorial Dr. Playground, toilets.
- *Dennis Pond*, off Summer St., Yarmouth Port.
- *Flax Pond*, off N. Dennis Rd. Toilets.
- *Little Sandy Pond*, off Tom Brook Rd. No lifeguard.

Churches

BARNSTABLE

Centerville

- *Our Lady of Victory*, 230 South Main St.; 771-5035 (Roman Catholic).
- *South Congregational Church United Church of Christ*, 565 Main St.; 775-8332.

Cotuit

- *Cotuit Federated Church*, High St.; 428-6163.

Hyannis

- *Cape Cod Synagogue*, 145 Winter St.; 775-2988.
- *Faith Assemblies of God*, 154 Bearse's Way; 775-9049.
- *Federated Church of Hyannis*, 320 Main St.; 775-0298.
- *First Baptist Church*, 486 Main St.; 775-1846.
- *First Church of Christ, Scientist*, Bearse's Way at Stevens St.; 775-3521.
- *St. Francis Xavier Church*, 347 South St.; 775-5361.
- *St. George Greek Orthodox Church*, corner of Strawberry Hill Rd. and Rte. 28; 775-3045.
- *Salvation Army Community Center*, 100 North St.; 775-0364.
- *Unity of Cape Cod*, 435 Main St.; 775-8583.
- *Hyannis Bible Church,* Lincoln Rd.; 775-7018 (Baptist).

Osterville
- *Seventh-Day Adventist Church*, Rte. 28 and E. Osterville Rd.; 428-8921.
- *St. Peter's Episcopal*, Wianno Ave.; 428-3561.
- *Osterville Baptist Church*, Main St.; 428-2787.
- *Our Lady of the Assumption*, Wianno Ave.; 428-2011 (Roman Catholic).

West Barnstable
- *First Lutheran Church*, 1663 Main St.; 362-3161.
- *Our Lady of Hope*, Rte. 6A.
- *Presbyterian Church of Cape Cod*, Rte. 132; 362-2011.
- *St. Mary's Episcopal Church*, Main St.; 362-3977.
- *Unitarian Church*, 3330 Main St., Rte. 6A; 362-6381.
- *West Barnstable Laestadian Church*, Plum; 362-4623.

DENNIS
- *Dennis Union Church*, Village Green, Rte. 6A, Dennis; 385-3543.
- *East Dennis Community Church*, Center St., E. Dennis, 385-3989. The often-photographed white-steepled church that typifies old churches throughout rural New England.
- *Church of the Nazarene*, 209 Upper County Rd., Dennisport; 394-4854.
- *Cape Cod Pentecostal Assembly*, 29 Mill, Dennisport; 394-0963.
- *Mid-Cape Assembly of God*, Dennis; 385-6005.

YARMOUTH
- *Bass River Community Baptist Church*, Main St., Bass River; 394-4904.
- *Evangelical Baptist Church*, Rte. 28 at Pond St., S. Yarmouth; 398-3531.
- *First Congregational Church of Yarmouth*, Rte. 6A, Yarmouth Port; 362-6977.
- *New Testament Baptist Church*, Higgins Crowell Rd., W. Yarmouth; 771-3276.
- *Our Lady of the Highway*, Rte. 28, S. Yarmouth (Catholic). Memorial Day to Labor Day; 398-6623.
- *Religious Society of Friends*, 58 N. Main St., S. Yarmouth; 398-3773.
- *Sacred Heart,* Summer St., Yarmouth Port (Catholic); 771-3873.
- *St. David's Episcopal Church,* 205 Old Main St., Bass River; 394-4222.
- *St. Pius*, Station Ave., S. Yarmouth; 398-6623. (Catholic).
- *United Methodist Church*, 324 Main St., S. Yarmouth; 398-9482.
- *West Yarmouth Congregational Church*, Rte. 28, W. Yarmouth; 775-0891.

Odds & Ends

Laundromats

BARNSTABLE
- *Acme Laundry*, 1676 Falmouth Rd., Centerville, 775-6144; 428 Main St., Hyannis, 775-0020; 770 Main St., Osterville, 428-6698.
- *Bradley's Cleaners*, 242 Main St., Hyannis; 775-0564.
- *Clothesline Laundromat,* 71 Barnstable Rd., Hyannis; 778-1976.
- *The Laundry Room*, 497 W. Main St., Hyannis; 771-5022.

BARNSTABLE (CONTINUED)
- *Starbrite Laundromat,* 489 Bearse's Way, Hyannis; 778-1928.
- *Village Laundromat,* Rear 1380 Rte. 6A, Barnstable; 362-2938.
- *Washboard Coin Laundry*, 710 Main St., Hyannis; 771-1512.

DENNIS
- *Dennisport Automatic Coin Laundry*, 13 Hall, Dennisport; 398-8911.

Farm Stands

BARNSTABLE
- *Lambert's Rainbow Fruit*, 1000 W. Main St., Centerville; 771-1616.

DENNIS
- *Tobey Farm*, 352 Main, Rte. 6A; 385-2930. Fresh produce (let the kids look at the hens and roosters in the pen in back!).
- *Hart Farm*, 21 Upper County Rd., Dennisport; 394-2693.
- *Salt Air Farm*, 512 Rte. 6A, Dennis.

YARMOUTH
- *Barney's Farm,* 77 N. Dennis Rd., S. Yarmouth. Pick your own blueberries, in August.
- *Lambert's Fruit and Produce,* 325 Rte. 28; 790-5954.

Fish Markets

BARNSTABLE
- *Barnstable Harbor Fish & Lobster Co.*, 3176 Main St., Barnstable (on Barnstable Harbor); 362-3900.
- *Cotuit Oyster Co.,* Little River Rd., Cotuit; 428-6747.

The supermarkets also have good fish markets: Stop and Shop in Southwind Plaza off Rte. 132 in Hyannis andStar Market on Rte. 28 in Marstons Mills.

DENNIS
- *Swan River Fish Market*, Lower County Rd., Dennisport; 398-2340.
- *Northside Seafood Market,* 1408 Main, Rte. 6A, E. Dennis; 385-6676.
- *Jim's Pier 134,* Rte. 134, S. Dennis; 385-3367.
- *Sved's,* 608 Rte. 28, Dennisport; 394-7300. Fresh fish, lobsters, smoked fish, sandwiches and salads.

YARMOUTH
- *Bass River Fish Market*, 215A Mill Ln., S. Yarmouth; 398-5550.
- *Lobster Trap of Yarmouth,* White's Path (at Union Station Plaza); 398-8360.

Clambakes

- *Flying Lobster Clambake Co.*, 9 Old Main St., W. Dennis; 394-2866. Clambakes.

Ice Cream Parlors

BARNSTABLE

- *Ben & Jerry's*, 352 Main St., Hyannis; 790-0910.
- *Four Seas Ice Cream,* 360 S. Main, Centerville; 775-1394.
- *Ice Cream Scoop and Sandwich Shoppe,* 3261 Main, Barnstable; 362-5558.
- *Maggie's Ice Cream Patch,* 862 Main St., Osterville; 428-2648.
- *Sandy's Ice Cream & Food Shop,* 918 Main St., W. Barnstable; 362-3290.
- *Vanilla & Chocolate, Inc.,* 497 Main St., Hyannis; 778-4844.

DENNIS

- *Ice Cream Store & Muffin Shop,* Rte. 28, Dennisport; 394-7105.
- *Ice Cream Smuggler,* 716 Main St., Dennis; 385-5307. Near the Dennis Village Green, outdoor patio and indoor seating.
- *Lickety Split,* 1381 Rte. 134, near the Rte. 6A intersection; 385-8707. Ice cream and sandwich shop, also serves breakfast. Small miniature golf course next to it.
- *Sundae School Ice Cream Parlor,* 387 Lower County Rd., Dennisport; 394-9122. Homemade ice cream and a marble soda fountain.

YARMOUTH

- *Coffee Talk Café,* 975 Rte. 28, S. Yarmouth; 760-5200. Featuring Four Seas Ice Cream (a favorite among Cape Codders) this spot also offers lunch, espresso and other desserts.
- *Jerry's Dairy Freeze,* 654 Main St., W. Yarmouth; 775-9752.
- *Steve & Sue's,* 37 Main St., W. Yarmouth; 775-4674.

Bakeries

BARNSTABLE

- *The Bagel Port,* Airport Shopping Plaza, Hyannis; 790-8111. More than just bagels, excellent sandwiches too.
- *Centerville Pastry & Coffee Shop,* 23 Park Ave., Centerville; 775-6023.
- *Creative Baking,* 115 Corporation Rd., Hyannis; 775-8555 or 800-445-8556.
- *D'Olimpio's NY Deli & Bakery,* 55 Iyanough Rd., Hyannis; 771-3220.
- *H 'n K Bakery,* off Rte. 28, Centerville; 775-8878.
- *Mrs. Field's Cookies,* Cape Cod Mall; 771-6193.
- *Pain D'Avignon,* 599 Main St., Hyannis; 790-0468.
- *Valle Montilio's Cape Cod Bakery,* 294 Main St., Hyannis; 775-1658.

DENNIS

- *Dennis Village Mercantile,* 766 Rte. 6A, Dennis; 385-3877.
- *Woolfies Home Bakery,* 279 Lower County Rd., Dennisport; 394-3717.
- *Village Bakery and Creamery,* 311 Main, W. Dennis; 760-3316.

YARMOUTH

- *Bagel Deli,* 594 Main St., Yarmouth; 771-7707.
- *Piccadilly Deli,* 1105 Rte. 28, S. Yarmouth; 394-9018.

Libraries

BARNSTABLE

- *Hyannis Public Library,* 401 Main St., Hyannis; 775-2280. Summer reading program.
- *Sturgis Library,* Rte. 6A, Barnstable; 362-6636.
- *Centerville Library Assn. Inc.,* 585 Main St., Centerville; 775-1787.
- *Cotuit Library Assn.,* Main St., Cotuit; 428-8141.
- *Marstons Mills Public Library,* Main St., Marstons Mills; 428-5175.
- *Osterville Free Library,* Wianno Ave., Osterville; 428-5757.
- *Whelden Memorial Library,* Meetinghouse Rd., W. Barnstable; 362-2262.

DENNIS

- *West Dennis Public Library,* Main St., W. Dennis; 398-2050.
- *South Dennis Public Library,* Main St., S. Dennis; 394-8954.
- *East Dennis Public Library,* 23 Center St., E. Dennis; 385-8151.
- *Dennis Memorial Library,* 1020 Old Bass River Rd.; 385-2255.

YARMOUTH

- *South Yarmouth Library,* 312 Old Main St., S. Yarmouth; 760-4820. Story hour for preschoolers on Wednesday mornings.
- *West Yarmouth Library,* Rte. 28, W. Yarmouth; 775-5206. Shell crafts workshop for children in July.
- *Yarmouth Port Library,* 297 Hallet St., Yarmouth Port; 362-3717.

Kennels

BARNSTABLE

- *Bayview Kennels,* Main St., W. Barnstable; 362-6506.

 # Best of Mid-Cape

BEST BED & BREAKFAST INNS

- *Beechwood,* 2839 Main St., Barnstable; 362-6618.
- *Liberty Hill Inn,* 7 Main St., Yarmouth Port; 362-3976.
- *Wedgewood Inn,* Rte. 6A, Yarmouth; 362-5157.

BEST RESORT

- *Hyannis Regency Inn and Conference Center,* Rte. 132, Hyannis; 775-1153.

BEST BREAKFASTS

- *Jack's Outback,* Rte. 6A, Yarmouth; 362-6690.
- *Marshside Restaurant,* 28 Bridge St., E. Dennis; 385-4010.

BEST LUNCHES

- *Mattakeese Wharf,* off Rte. 6A, Barnstable Harbor; 362-4511.
- *Mildred's Chowder House,* near Airport Rotary, Hyannis; 775-1045.
- *The Mooring,* 230 Ocean St., Hyannis Harbor; 775-4656.

BEST DINNERS (FORMAL)

- *Abbicci Restaurant,* 43 Main St., Yarmouth Port; 362-3501.
- *The Paddock,* next to Melody Tent, Hyannis; 775-7677.
- *Regatta of Cotuit,* 4631 Falmouth Rd., Cotuit; 428-5715.

BEST DINNERS (CASUAL)

Lee + Snooky recommend

- *Baxter's Boathouse Club,* Hyannis Harbor; 775-7040.
- *Gina's By the Sea,* 132 Taunton Ave.; 385-3213.
- *The Roadhouse Café,* 488 South St., Hyannis; 775-2386.
- *Snowgoose Country Café,* 605 Main St., Dennis; 385-7175.

BEST SEAFOOD

- *Baxter's Fish 'n Chips,* Hyannis Harbor; 775-4490.
- *Captain Frosty's,* 219 Rte. 6A, Dennis; 385-8548.

BEST NIGHTLY ENTERTAINMENT (STAGE)

- *Barnstable Comedy Club,* Rte. 6A, Barnstable Village; 362-6333.
- *Cape Cod Conservatory of Music & Art,* off Rte. 132, Barnstable; 362-2772.
- *Cape Cod Melody Tent,* Hyannis Center; 775-9100.
- *The Cape Playhouse,* Rte. 6A, Dennis; 385-3838.

BEST MUSEUM & HISTORIC SITE

- *Donald A. Trayser Memorial Museum,* Old Customs House, Rte. 6A, Barnstable; 362-2092.
- *Sturgis Library,* Rte. 6A, Barnstable; 362-6636. Oldest public library in the country.

BEST ART GALLERY

- *Cape Museum of Fine Arts,* Rte. 6A, Dennis; 385-4477.

BEST CRAFT, SPECIALTY, & ANTIQUE SHOPS

- *Christmas Tree Shop,* Rte. 28, Yarmouth (775-8151); Rte. 6A, Yarmouth Port (362-3153); Rte. 28, Dennis (394-5557).
- *Peach Tree,* 173 Main, Yarmouth Port; 362-8317.
- *Whippletree,* Rte. 6A, Barnstable; 362-3320.

BEST SEASONAL EVENTS

- *Blueberry Picking,* farms off Rte. 6A. End of July and beginning of August; farms are posted.
- *Hyannis Harbor Festival,* Bismore Park on Ocean St., Hyannis. Usually held in June; check with Cape Cod Chamber of Commerce.
- *Hyannis Street Festival,* Hyannis Center. Usually held in August; check with Cape Cod Chamber of Commerce.
- *Pops By the Sea,* Hyannis Town Green, August.

BEST PUBLIC BEACHES

- *Corporation Beach,* off Corporation Rd., Dennis.
- *Craigville Beach,* Craigville Rd., Craigville.
- *Sandy Neck,* off Rte. 6A, W. Barnstable.

BEST GOLF

- *Dennis Pines,* Old Bass River Road; 385-8347. Public.
- *Hyannis Golf Club,* Rte. 132, Hyannis; 362-2606. Public.
- *Oyster Harbors,* Osterville; 428-9881. Private.

BEST HIKING OR NATURE TRAILS

• *Sandy Neck Trail,* at Sandy Neck Beach, off Rte. 6A, W. Barnstable.
• *Yarmouth Botanic Trail,* off Rte. 6A, Yarmouth behind Yarmouth Port Post Office; 362-3021.

BEST FISH MARKETS

• *Barnstable Harbor Fish & Lobster,* Barnstable Harbor; 362-3900.
• *Cotuit Oyster Co.,* Little River Rd., Cotuit; 428-6747.

BEST ICE CREAM

• *Ben and Jerry's,* 352 Main St., Hyannis Center; 790-0910.
• *Four Seas Ice Cream,* 360 S. Main St., Centerville; 775-1394.
• *Maggie's Ice Cream Patch,* 862 Main St., Osterville; 428-2648.

OUTER CAPE

Brewster, Harwich, Chatham, Orleans, Eastham, Wellfleet, Truro, National Seashore

Outer Cape: Viewpoints

by Greg O'Brien

If you're looking to blend in with the locals, if you want to sound like an insider, then we suggest you refer to the eight towns from Harwich to Provincetown as the *Outer Cape*, not *Lower Cape* as most "wash ashores" call it. Nothing so grates on a native's nerves than to hear an out-of-towner pipe up, "I'm spending the day on the Lower Cape."

It's called "outer" by the locals because it *is* outer: the towns of Brewster, Harwich, Chatham, Orleans, Eastham, Wellfleet, Truro, and Provincetown (discussed in detail in the next section) form Cape Cod's outermost land, its slender fist and forearm, the last relatively undeveloped stretch of this narrow peninsula.

We recommend you come here *not* for the malls, gift shops, and pitch and putts (although they rival the Cape's best), but *simply* for the view—for a look, a peek, at Old Cape Cod, especially if "you're fond of sand dunes and salty air," as Patti Page sang in her celebrated song.

Here on the Outer Cape, you'll find plenty of sand dunes, fresh salt air, and quaint, pastoral villages here and there. The region is less developed, less settled, and less hectic than the Mid-Cape and Upper Cape for two main reasons. The first is distance. It takes close to an hour, without traffic, to drive from the Sagamore Bridge to the Orleans Rotary, and two or three hours in heavy weekend congestion. A second, more fundamental, reason is the Cape Cod National Seashore (discussed later in this section). Part of Chatham, about half of Eastham, two-thirds of Wellfleet and Truro, and practically all of Provincetown (outside the town center) belong to the Seashore. Created in 1961 by legislation signed by the late John F. Kennedy, the Seashore includes 27,000 acres of upland, about 30 miles of ocean coastline, scores of fresh- and saltwater ponds, numerous trails and landmarks, and two visitor centers—the Salt Pond Visitor Center off Route 6 in Eastham and the Province Lands Visitor Center on Race Point Road in Provincetown. The centers, open daily from spring until early winter, offer exhibits, slide presentations, and advice (from rangers or in brochures) about what to do while in the Seashore. And don't worry about the cost; just about everything here but beach parking is free.

So despite the drive, which can be trying in the summer, a visit to the Outer Cape should be on every vacationer's itinerary; you'll still be only about a half hour from the shopping and nightlife of Hyannis. And you can't get lost here. At Eastham, the Cape narrows to about three miles wide, making it an easy bike ride for visitors to watch the sun rise on the ocean or set on the bay. At the Truro-Provincetown line, the bay and the ocean are less than a mile apart.

And relax while you're here; the pace is a bit slower. Give yourself time to discover the magnificent stretches of ocean beaches framed by mountainous sand dunes, the many self-guided walks and bicycle trails, and the clear, placid kettle ponds that are perfect for fishing and canoeing. On the Outer Cape you'll find what's been called the jewel of the Commonwealth's state forest system—Nickerson State Park off Route 6A in East Brewster—acres upon acres of working cranberry bogs, shellfish-rich marshes and mud flats, back road farm stands where you can buy the sweetest corn you've ever tasted, historic sites and museums, four-star restaurants, and great summer theater.

Every town, in fact, has something different to offer.

In Brewster, you'll find some of the Cape's finest and most historic sea captains' homes. Brewster, for its size, was once home to more deep-water sea captains than any other town in America. Many of these homes are now inns, such as the splendid 200-year-old Isaiah Clark House on Route 6A, which promises to pamper visitors with old New England hospitality and twentieth-century comforts. The owners of the inn also run the Cape's original bed & breakfast reservation service, called House Guests Cape Cod. For more information, telephone 896-2223 or 896-7053.

Brewster is also home to one of the oldest and most authentic general stores on the peninsula. The Brewster Store on Route 6A, about two miles up the street from the Isaiah Clark House heading toward Orleans, was once a church. Built in 1852 by Universalists, the building six years later was turned into a general merchandise store, selling many of the same items it still offers today; penny candy, hot roasted peanuts, oil lamps, books, cards, and newspapers. It also has a working nickelodeon.

Harwich, with its five well-protected harbors (Wychmere, Saquatucket, Allen Harbor, Round Cove, and Herring River) and more than four miles of shoreline on Nantucket Sound, is a boater's paradise. The town also has several fine restaurants, among them the Sea Grille at 31 Sea Street; L'Alouette at 787 Main Street (restaurant Francais); the Country Inn (seafood, beef, and chicken) at 86 Sisson Road; and Brax Landing (seafood and beef) on Saquatucket Harbor off Route 28.

Chatham is the quintessential Cape Cod town—with its picturesque center (a collection of closely knit shops, boutiques, restaurants, and galleries), grand lighthouse, stately summer homes, and commercial pier (on Aunt Lydia's Cove near the corner of Shore Road and Barcliff Avenue) where fishermen each day unload their catch. A visit to the Outer Cape is worth the trip, if only to see Chatham.

Orleans is the commercial hub of the Outer Cape, but don't be put off by the large supermarket shopping centers that sit, like bookends, at both ends of town—Skaket Corners at the intersection of Route 6A and West Road and Stop & Shop and Jeremiah Square near the Orleans–Eastham Rotary. Orleans, particularly the east part of town, has much charm. Also, on the bay side at Rock Harbor, about a mile from the center of town, you'll find the Cape's largest charter fishing fleet. Here they go after bluefish, striped bass, mackerel, and an occasional tuna.

Eastham, the main gate to the Cape Cod National Seashore, offers two of the Cape's best ocean beaches—Coast Guard Beach and Nauset Light Beach; both with bathhouse facilities and parking. A small parking fee is charged.

Wellfleet has the feel of an old fishing village, yet it's different from the more trendy and pricey Chatham. It is simple, but in an elegant way—from its Main Street to the town pier. Like an Andrew Wyeth painting, time seems to have stood still in Wellfleet, much as it has in Truro.

Truro is about as rural as Cape Cod gets. There is no center to speak of, only a post office, a small restaurant, a gift shop, and a convenience store. But here you'll discover some of the best back roads on the Cape (try North Pamet Road, South Pamet Road, Longnook Road, and Old Mill Pond Road), and one of the Cape's prettiest harbors, Pamet Harbor (at the mouth of the Pamet River) at the end of Depot Road on the bay side.

Provincetown is a mixed bag. The town is what you might call commercially quaint. Here you'll find fishermen, artists, writers, merchants—straight and gay—all living in relative harmony. The best way to understand this cornucopia is to see it.

The Outer Cape has a history as rich as its culture and natural resources. The area was first settled by Pilgrims, some of whom had come over on the *Mayflower*. At one point in the mid-1600s, Eastham, which then included parts of Orleans, Harwich, and Chatham, had almost as much political muscle as Plymouth. There was, in fact, some discussion about relocating Plymouth Colony's seat of government in Eastham. One of the Colony's longtime governors, Thomas Prence, had moved to the Eastham area and after some tough bargaining was allowed to remain, traveling to Plymouth only when duty beckoned. Prence died in 1673, about the time when small independent settlements began cropping up around Eastham. Eight towns, in all, would eventually be formed.

Brewster

Present-day Brewster was once the center of Old Harwich. The area was settled in 1656 as the north parish of Harwich and incorporated as the town of Brewster in 1803. It was named after Pilgrim elder William Brewster, who came to the New World aboard the *Mayflower*.

The north parish separated from the south parish (present-day Harwich) over religious disagreements—the focus of most discord in surrounding towns. There was plenty of bad blood between the north and south parishes. Men of the north parish, mostly sea captains who traveled the world and brought back great riches, were independent, outspoken, and a bit on the snobby side, often thumbing their noses at the farmers and mill workers of the south parish.

Most of these sea captains worshipped at the old First Parish Church at the corner of Route 6A and Breakwater Road. The white clapboard church, called the "Church of the Sea Captains," was first built in 1700 for fiery preacher Nathaniel Stone, rebuilt in 1722, then built again in 1834. Many of the pews are still marked with the names of famous Brewster sea captains. The church, now a Unitarian Universalist Church, is open to the public. Services are held each Sunday, and chowder suppers are offered Wednesday in July and August at 6 and 7 P.M. A Mimsy puppet show for children is held every Thursday from 10 A.M. until noon. For more information, call 896-5577.

Behind the church is an old burying ground; many of the town's notorious and famous sea captains are buried here, including Captain David Nickerson, who, according to local lore, was handed an infant in Paris at the time of the French Revolution and asked to bring the boy all the way to Brewster and raise him. According to the legend, the infant may have been the Lost Dauphin of France, the son of Louis XVI and Marie Antoinette. Captain Nickerson was told to name the boy Rene Rousseau and to give him a good home. Rousseau eventually followed in his foster-father's footsteps. A sea captain himself, Rousseau was lost at sea when he was 26. Nickerson died a few years later. Rousseau's name is inscribed on the back of Nickerson's headstone—as was customary in those days.

For a town with no harbors, Brewster has an impressive maritime past. In addition to the salty sea captains who lived here, Brewster in the early 1800s was the terminus of a Boston-Brewster packet cargo service, with a landing at the end of Breakwater Road. Packet boats, according to town history, carried salt, tannery goods and cloth to Boston and other ports. In 1865, the packet service was upstaged by the Cape's first railroad. The New York, New Haven and Hartford Railroad established a line from Boston to the Cape in the late 1800s. Eventually service was extended to Provincetown—bringing travelers, supplies, and daily newspapers to the Cape. The railroad was the chief manner of transportation to the Cape until the 1920s when steamer service began between Provincetown and Boston, and highways were improved.

The railroad bed, now a paved bike trail called the Cape Cod Rail Trail, follows the same route—starting from Route 134 in South Dennis and running through Harwich, Brewster, and on to Eastham. The trail winds through woodlands, beside lakes and kettle ponds, salt marshes, creeks, and sandy beaches. Just off the trail are picnic areas, shops, lodgings, and places to eat. One place you should try in Brewster is a lunch spot beside the trail called the Brewster Express. They have terrific ice cream, too. You don't have to be on a bike to go there; it's off Underpass Road, about halfway between Route 6A and Route 137. Another favorite lunch place among bikers is a place off Route 6A called Cobie's; it's near Nickerson State Park, not far from the bike trail.

While Brewster today differs greatly from the Brewster of Captain

Nickerson's time, the town has retained much of its seaside charm. Brewster today has about 7000 year-round residents and covers an area of about 22 square miles. There are three villages—Brewster, East Brewster, and West Brewster—but because the towns are much smaller on the Outer Cape, the villages are not as distinctive and separate as they are on the more heavily populated and developed Mid-Cape and Upper Cape.

Although Brewster has no harbors, it is blessed with plenty of shoreline and good fishing. There are seven public beaches on Cape Cod Bay and 25 freshwater ponds (most of them are stocked with game fish). At low tide, the town's shellfish flats yield plenty of steamers, quahogs, and razor clams—depending on the time of year. Licenses, available at Town Hall, are required for taking shellfish. A small license fee is charged.

Brewster is typical of towns on the Outer Cape—small, rural, and under great pressure for development. The town, like others in this region, has begun buying up large tracts of open land and setting them aside for conservation and passive recreation. In the spring of 1987, for instance, the town spent several million dollars to buy 500 acres near Upper Mill and Walker's ponds (perfect for canoeing!). There is a greater awareness on the Outer Cape of the fragile nature of this land.

Upon entering Brewster from East Dennis on Route 6A, one is struck by the rural nature of the town. You'll come across the Cape Cod Museum of Natural History, a nonprofit organization dedicated "to discovery, study, and protection of the natural world." The museum offers natural history classes, exhibits, and year-round workshops for adults and children. An addition doubling the size of the exhibit and classroom space was recently completed. The museum also has a fine gift shop where you can buy everything from bird feeders to books about the environment and a library that is considered one of the finest natural history libraries in New England. The museum is situated on the edge of a marsh in Stony Brook Valley, and it owns the surrounding 80 acres. "Three (museum) trails traverse this varied landscape," a museum brochure points out. "The North Trail is only about a quarter mile and introduces you to the salt marsh community. The South Trail is somewhat longer and leads through a brackish cattail marsh up into a mature stand of American Beech. The mile-long Wing Island Trail crosses town land and ends in an unspoiled stretch of beach bordering Cape Cod Bay. Because parts of the trail flood at high tide, it is wise to check at the reception desk before walking this trail."

Farther up Route 6A, about two miles, you'll find the New England Fire & History Museum, another sure bet for the children. The museum has a magnificent collection of historic hand-drawn and horse-drawn fire equipment; an eighteenth-century New England common; a fascinating display of firemarks (old cast iron plates that were attached to homes indicating residents had paid their fire fighting taxes), old-time helmets, speaking trumpets, and other fire history memorabilia; the old-fashioned Apothecary Shoppe; and an award-winning diorama showing the famous Chicago fire of 1871. The museum, a nonprofit, public educational organization, is open seven days a week in the summer.

Brewster also has some first-rate restaurants, most of them located along Route 6A. Among the ones we suggest you try are the Brewster Inn and Chowder House (don't miss the live entertainment at the adjoining Woodshed tavern); the Bramble Inn (awarded three stars by both the *Boston Globe* and the *Boston Herald*); the Old Manse Inn (the atmosphere here is as good as the food); Chillingsworth (rated four stars, classic and nouvelle French cuisine, expensive but worth the price if you can afford it); the Brewster Fish House (try the scallops and homemade chowder); the Tower House Restaurant (great food, reasonable price); and The Beechcroft Inn (good food at a reasonable price), for the money, one of the best meals in town; and High Brewster (near the corner of Stony Brook and Satucket roads, rustic but elegant, a favorite among locals; you can enjoy cocktails in a garden setting overlooking Lower Mill Pond).

Other points of interest in Brewster are Nickerson State Park, off Route 6A, Bassett Wild Animal Farm, off Tubman Road, and the Stony Brook Mill and herring run.

The 1750-acre Nickerson State Park offers a variety of facilities and activities. Among them, 420 campsites, hot showers, swimming, four trout-stocked ponds (fishing licenses are required), a public picnic area, numerous hiking trails, and seven miles of paved bicycle trail (part of the Cape Cod Rail Trail). For more information, telephone 896-3491.

Bassett Wild Animal Farm, on Tubman Road between Route 124 and Route 137 (Long Pond Road), has pony rides, hay rides, picnic areas, and a collection of wild animals that would keep even the most rambunctious child's interest.

While you're in Brewster, you should also visit the Stony Brook Mill and herring run near the intersection of Stony Brook and Satucket roads. The old mill is a restored nineteenth-century mill that served as a public museum in the summer. The mill sits beside Stony Brook, better known as the town's herring run. From March to June, spawning alewives (herring) run from Cape Cod Bay up the brook through a series of ladders to quiet Upper Mill and Lower Mill ponds above the mill site. The herring, like salmon, swim against the current. Take the children. It's a fascinating phenomenon of nature.

In addition to parks, animal farms, and museums, Brewster also has a wide assortment of country inns (see listings at the end of this section), but if you're interested in staying at a resort, we suggest the 380-acre Ocean Edge Resort and Conference Center off Route 6A. You can rent two- or three-bedroom villas with views of meadows, woodlands, ponds, or Cape Cod Bay. The resort has an 18-hole championship golf course, tennis courts, a private beach, and a swimming pool twice as large as an Olympic pool. There's also a Jacuzzi, a wading pool, a shaded picnic area, a deck for sunning, and a free shuttle that departs hourly to area beaches. For more information, telephone toll-free (outside Massachusetts) 1-800-221-1837; in Massachusetts, call 1-800-626-2688.

If you're a golfer, play both Ocean Edge Course (where the New England PGA Championship is held) and Brewster's public course, the Captain's Course, off Freeman Road, about halfway between Route 137 and

Route 39. When the Captains' Course opened in 1985, *Golf Digest* called it the best new public course in America.

Brewster doesn't have a monopoly on great golf courses; Harwich has some fine ones, too.

Harwich

Like Brewster, Harwich had its share of sea captains. A Harwich Historical Commission booklet, entitled *Harwich Men of the Sea*, counts 124. But religious disputes so dominated the town's early history that Harwich unfortunately is remembered by some today more for its spiritual discord than for its impressive maritime history.

The religious wounds, though, were healed in the 1860s, and the town turned its attention toward new ways of making a living. The first commercial cranberry bogs in the country were established in Harwich, which is still a leader in cranberry production—primarily because of its soil conditions and extended growing season. Cranberries grew wild on the Cape, but Harwich men devised a way to harvest them commercially. You can still watch them being harvested in the early fall—like the leaves, they change color with the season, from summer green to deep fall crimson contrasted against a dark blue sky. Some bog owners, for a small fee, will even let you pick a few bushels. To celebrate its cranberry heritage, Harwich each September puts on the two-week Cranberry Festival, which features a wide variety of activities for the whole family, including arts and crafts shows, a fireworks display, a parade, and even the Cranberry Ball. There are more than a hundred events, which are held all over town—in libraries, parks, at schools, and on beaches. Check the *Cape Codder* and the *Cape Cod Times* (two local newspapers) for a schedule of events.

There's plenty to do in Harwich in the summertime—sunbathing, fishing, boating, browsing, bicycling, and taking in such places as the Harwich Historical Society Museum, which is located on the top floor of Brooks Academy in Harwich Center. Founded in 1844 as one of the country's first schools of navigation, the Academy now displays sextants, old periodicals, children's toys, an 1800s parlor, and an old schoolhouse complete with a wood stove.

If you prefer the outdoors to indoors, the town band puts on regular concerts at Brooks Park on Main Street in Harwich Center in July and August.

Like Brewster, Harwich has two excellent golf courses: the 18-hole Cranberry Valley Golf Course off Oak Street near the center of town (its rolling fairways are surrounded by tall pines and old cranberry bogs), and the challenging nine-hole Harwich Port Golf Course on Forest Street in Harwich Port.

The town, though, is most famous for its five harbors. The best are Wychmere, Saquatucket, and Allen harbors—all three man-made.

Wychmere Harbor, the most picturesque, has a fascinating history; it used to be a salt pond with no access to Nantucket Sound. At first it was called *Annosarakumitt* by the Indians; then it was called *Oyster Pond* and *Salt Water Pond* by the early settlers. Many years later, summer residents who lived on its shores named it *Wychmere*.

For a time in the nineteenth century, a racetrack was laid out around the pond. But some of the townspeople disapproved of horse-racing and had a channel cut through to open water to put an end to the sporting event, noted a longtime Harwich resident in a history of the harbor that was printed in the *Cape Codder*. Since 1899, the state has maintained the channel, which requires regular dredging.

The other two harbors had less intriguing histories. Saquatucket Harbor, opened in 1970, was dredged out of a marsh near the Andrews River, and Allen Harbor was fashioned in 1926 out of an inlet named after a sea captain named Allen.

Today, Harwich has a year-round population of about 9500 and consists of seven villages: Harwich, East Harwich, Harwich Port, North Harwich, Pleasant Lake, South Harwich, and West Harwich.

As you drive from Dennis into West Harwich on commercial Route 28, you come across a stretch of restaurants, shops, and lodgings. A summer favorite is the Cape Cod Irish Pub, which offers a wide selection of food, drink, and Irish music. And you don't have to be an O'Brien, O'Neill, or an O'Malley to enjoy it. At night, it's a favorite college hangout, and one of the Cape's best watering holes.

Another favorite just up the street is the 400 Club. It's casual; the food is good, the price is right. Lunch and dinner are served here.

But if breakfast is your favorite meal, we suggest you eat at the Stewed Tomato on Route 39 in Harwich Center, not far from the Route 28 commercial strip. An easy way to get from Route 28 in Harwich Port to Harwich Center—where you'll also find Town Hall, the town library, and Whitehouse Field (home of the Harwich Mariners of the Cape Cod Baseball League)—is to take Bank Street. It runs perpendicular to both roads.

Chatham

The old name for Chatham was *Monomoyick,* a reference to a Wampanoag Indian tribe. Monomoy Island, at the mouth of Chatham Harbor off the southern tip of the town, still bears the name. The island, once a part of the mainland, is now the province of the Massachusetts Audubon Society and is a wildlife preserve.

Although the Vikings are thought to be the first white men to visit Chatham, we do know that French explorer Samuel de Champlain anchored in 1606 for a brief visit in what is now called Stage Harbor. He named the harbor Point Fortune. At nearby Taylor's Neck, Champlain encountered the Indians in a bloody fight—the first such encounter in the New World between Europeans and Indians.

Chatham, arguably the most attractive town on Cape Cod, was actually settled in 1656 by a handful of Pilgrims, among them William Nickerson, a farmer from Norfolk, England, who fled his country in 1633 with his wife and children and sailed to Saugus, just north of Boston, to escape religious persecution. The family moved to the Cape in 1650 and settled in Yarmouth, near Bass River. Within a few years, Nickerson bought 4000 acres from the

Indians—almost all of what is now Chatham. He paid just a little more for the land than the Dutch paid for Manhattan.

Nickerson was a contentious man. "He got into a fight—a long drawn out affair—with those who ran Plymouth Colony," family historian Joshua A. Nickerson, retired president of the Nickerson Lumber Company, once noted in an interview in the *Cape Codder*. "They claimed he didn't have the right to buy land from the Indians, and insisted he buy it from *them*. At one point, they fined him five pounds an acre (20,000 pounds), which was more money than there was in the whole damn colony at the time. He finally agreed to pay a total penalty of 95 pounds, and then invited others to come in and settle on his land. I guess you could say he was Chatham's first speculator."

Chatham was incorporated in 1712 and has grown to a town of about 6500 year-round residents; its population, as in most Cape towns, more than triples in the summer. The town now has four villages: Chatham, West Chatham, South Chatham, and North Chatham.

Called the Cape's "elbow," Chatham is bounded by water on two sides: the Atlantic to the east and Nantucket Sound to the south. The town also has numerous coves, harbors, and ponds worth exploring—such as Ryder's Cove off Pleasant Bay, and Stage Harbor, Mill Pond, Oyster Creek, and Cockle Cove, all off Nantucket Sound.

Because it's stashed away in the eastern corner of the Cape, Chatham has no direct access to Route 6. To get there from the Mid-Cape Highway, take Route 137 to Route 28 on the west side of Chatham, then turn left. If you're coming from the Hyannis area, drive up Route 28 if the traffic along this commercial strip isn't oppressive. Otherwise, use Route 6. If you're coming down from Orleans and you're in the mood for a scenic drive, take Route 28 south; it goes by Pleasant Bay and Ryder's Cove.

Chatham also has a municipal airport that serves private and charter planes. It's located on George Ryder Road, just northwest of Chatham Center. Taxi service to the town center is available from here. For more information, telephone 945-9000.

You could easily spend the better part of a day touring Chatham. A good place to start is the west end of town on Route 28. Just east of where Route 28 intersects with Route 137, you'll see Marion's Pie Shop on the left, which sells fantastic homemade fish, fowl, and dessert pies. About a quarter of a mile from here, you'll come to the George Ryder Road intersection (take a left to get to the airport). There's a deli and an A&P grocery store at the corner. On the other side of Route 28 is the West Chatham Shopping Plaza. Farther up Route 28 at the Vineyard Avenue intersection, you'll find the Chatham Jelly and Jam Shop and Fancy's Farm Stand (where many of the locals in the summer buy their fresh vegetables).

You really don't hit the town center until you reach the intersection of Crowell, Depot, and Queen Anne roads. Stay on Route 28 (Main Street) if you're looking for Chatham Center.

The town center itself is a cozy collection of shops, boutiques, theaters, galleries, and places to eat. Some suggestions: take in Monomoy Theatre (summer stock and chamber music); Spyglass Nautical Antiques (sextants, antique telescopes, barometers and writing boxes); Pentimento (unusual cards, plush toys, handicrafts, Futon furniture and decorating accessories); Impudent Oyster (seafood and international dishes in an elegant setting); Chatham Squire Restaurant & Lounge (varied menu, a favorite of fishermen); Tale of the Cod (gift shop, browser's paradise); Christian's (good food, great upstairs lounge).

At the end of Main Street, a right-hand turn will take you to Chatham Lighthouse and Coast Guard Station. A left will head you in the direction of Orleans.

For a scenic drive, turn right at the end of Main Street, drive by the lighthouse (there's a parking lot overlooking the inner and outer beach), and turn right on Bridge Road, which will take you by Mill Pond. A right at the end of Bridge Road (on Stage Harbor Road) will bring you back to the town center. A left will take you toward the mouth of Oyster Creek.

If you take a left instead of a right at the end of Main Street and head toward Orleans, you will pass the majestic Chatham Bars Inn, a resort hotel that offers full recreational and conference facilities. Built in 1914, the inn (set on a rise) has a commanding view of Chatham Harbor, North Beach (an eroding sand spit that runs south from Orleans), and the mighty Atlantic. Stop and have a drink on the sweeping veranda—the best view in town.

Just up the street from the inn is the Chatham Fish Pier, where fishermen unload catches of haddock, cod, flounder, lobster, pollock, and halibut. The fish is boxed in ice, then trucked to local restaurants and fish markets, and to markets in Boston and New York. You can watch from a visitor's balcony. Bring a camera.

At a traffic light about a mile beyond the pier, Shore Road leads into Route 28. Go straight all the way to Orleans. Within a few miles, you will pass on your right Ryder's Cove and then Pleasant Bay, a large protected body of salt water that laps up against low sand bluffs (it's a perfect area for sailing). The state recently placed more rigid restrictions on development in the area; the bay is rich in plant and marine life.

"Every year the bay changes; the barrier beach grows, an inlet forms, the marsh advances," William Sargent of Woods Hole wrote in his book *Shallow Waters: A Year on Cape Cod's Pleasant Bay*. "Somewhere among the billions of organisms born each spring are unique individuals imperceptibly more fit to survive the bay's changing environment. Molded through antiquity from the unity of all living matter, they carry on the greatest of all experiments, that of life itself."

If you can spare the time, pull off to the side and take in the view. From here, you should get to Orleans in about 15 minutes.

There are many other points of interest in Chatham. Here are a few more suggestions: the Old Atwood House, located on Stage Harbor Road and owned by the Chatham Historical Society; built in 1752, it is one of the oldest homes in Chatham. The Railroad Museum is located at the old Chatham Railroad Company station at Depot Road; the 100-year-old building displays railroad memorabilia and old equipment. Chatham's Old Grist Mill, located near Chase Park off Shattuck Place, was built in 1797 by Colonel

Benjamin Godfrey to grind corn using only wind power. It is open to the public in July and August. Migratory waterfowl stop at Monomoy National Wildlife Refuge on their way north and south. Nearly every bird species recorded from New England has been seen here. Boat liveries from Chatham Harbor are available to the island. Kate Gould Park, located on Main Street, is the site of perhaps the best show in town, on Friday nights in July and August the town band plays here. The band plays folk dances for children and waltzes for adults. Bring lawn chairs, beach blankets, and picnic dinners—it will be one of the highlights of your summer.

Orleans

Of the 15 towns on the Cape, the only one with a French name is the town of Orleans, which was named after Louis-Philippe de Bourbon, duke of Orléans, France, according to one version of the town's history. Louis-Philippe was king of France from 1830 until 1848 and is supposed to have visited this area in the 1790s when in exile during the French Revolution.

Orleans is a town that has always been willing to extend a helping hand. During the American Revolution, for instance, Orleans provided the Continental army with beef, shirts, stockings, boots, and blankets. To defray the cost of these supplies, each resident was asked to contribute; the donations in 1776 were generous enough to outfit recruits for the Second Barnstable Regiment.

Orleans residents have always been an industrious lot, too. In 1804 the townspeople rolled up their collective sleeves and helped dig a canal through the marsh between Town Cove and the ocean side and Boatmeadow River off Cape Cod Bay, a distance of about three and a half miles. The one-lane ditch was called Jeremiah's Gutter after landowner Jeremiah Smith. It was the first known canal across Cape Cod. "Except for a brief service in the War of 1812, Jeremiah's Gutter never actually functioned with success as a canal," a town history points out, noting the waterway was too narrow and shallow. Those boats that made the trip from Boatmeadow River to Town Cove has to sail around dangerous shoals once they reached the Atlantic. The canal was used during the War of 1812, though, by local ships trying to slip through the British blockade. Gradually after the war, the canal filled in. It is now no more than a ditch.

But before the war ended, Orleans residents gave the British even more fits, driving off a boatload of sailors from British warships anchored off Rock Harbor. The British had demanded a $1000 ransom from Orleans, but the townspeople sent them packing, never to return again.

Orleans (where Route 6A and Route 28 come together and connect with Route 6 at the Orleans Rotary—not far from Jeremiah's Gutter) was part of the original Eastham settlement. Called "Pochet" at first, Orleans had its beginnings in the early 1700s as the south parish of Eastham. The first meeting-house was built on what is now the corner of Main Street and Meeting House Road in East Orleans. It was replaced in 1829 by the Federated Church building, an impressive white, clapboard structure that still stands today. Services are held on Sundays; headstones in an adjacent cemetery date back to the 1700s.

As in most Cape towns, the early settlers scratched out a living from shellfishing, agriculture, shipbuilding, coastal trades, and deep-sea fishing. Then in the late 1800s, the Industrial Revolution brought the factory business to Orleans. In 1873, the Cummings-Howes clothing factory started up near Cedar Pond, then moved in 1888 to a skating rink next to the old Cummings Block, now the intersection of Main Street and Route 6A. In 1890, the factory employed 125 to 200 people, using 125 steam-powered sewing machines to manufacture trousers. In addition, there were more than 50 saltworks in the area, which processed salt from seawater for use as a preservative.

Orleans has grown much since those early days, at the expense of some of its charm. Today the town, the commercial center of the Outer Cape, has a year-round population of about 7000 and is divided into three villages, each with a center: Orleans, whose center is near the Main Street–Route 6A intersection; East Orleans, whose center is on Main Street about two miles from Nauset Beach; and South Orleans, whose center is near the Route 28–Route 39 intersection.

In the Orleans center, there is a mix of restaurants (try the Land Ho! Tavern, a local hangout); a great bookstore (Compass Rose); specialty stores such as Cape Cod Photo & Art Supply and the Moppet Shop for children; a health food store (Whole Foods); and a fantastic lunch place, Hole-in One; and one of the most unique gift shops on the Outer Cape (Oceana). We suggest you also try the Cheese Corner and Deli on Main Street.

At the South Orleans center, you'll find a general store and several specialty shops.

In East Orleans, you'll find a great delicatessen (East Orleans Deli); a good fish market and an outdoor fish-and-chips place (Kadee's Lobster & Clam Bar); Country Liquors (which offers one of the best selections of wines and gourmet items on the Outer Cape); two fine restaurants (the Nauset Beach Club and the Barley Neck Inn, which for the price and atmosphere offers one of the better dinners on Cape Cod).

Other restaurants we recommend in town are the Arbor on Route 28; Ardath's on West Road (try it for breakfast); the Brown Bag on the corner of Old Colony Way and West Road (another good breakfast and lunch place, great atmosphere); the Captain Linnell House on Skaket Road; the Lobster Claw on Route 6A; Off the Bay Café on Main Street; and the Old Jailhouse Tavern on West Road.

While you're in Orleans, you should also visit the French Cable Station Museum, the Orleans Historical Society, the Christmas Tree Shop, and Rock Harbor.

The transatlantic cable station (now a museum) is located at the corner of Route 28 and Cove Road. It was built in 1890 to support the weight of heavy equipment necessary to transmit and receive messages from France. From here the cable ran to New York. Many historic news bulletins—such as Charles Lindbergh's landing in Paris and the occupation of France by the

Germans in 1940—were received at the Orleans station and passed along. Operators were expected during the course of an eight-hour shift to send Morse code transmissions of about 40 words a minute, according to a town history. The museum is open from July to mid-September, Tuesday through Sunday. All equipment in use when the station was closed in 1959 is on display.

The Orleans Historical Society, housed in the Meeting House, a Greek Revival building at the corner of River Road and School Road opposite Orleans Town Hall, has displays of Indian arrowheads and artifacts. The town's official weights, scales, and measures of more than 100 years ago are on view, as well as period clothing, early photographs, and the town's bicentennial quilt, the society notes in its brochure. There is also a letter dated 1814 from a British captain to the town of Orleans, demanding a ransom of $1000 in return for guaranteed protection of the town's saltworks.

As already noted in the Upper Cape section, the Christmas Tree Shop, located at the intersection of Route 6A and Route 28, is one of the most interesting shops on the peninsula. You can buy everything—from toys to furniture to cookware—and at *bargain* prices.

Rock Harbor, on Cape Cod Bay about two miles from the town center at the end of Rock Harbor Road, is among the prettiest harbors in all of New England. It is home to one of the Cape's biggest and best charter fishing fleets. Orleans, as you might have suspected, is an excellent place to fish. Even if you're not a fishing buff, you'll enjoy a trip on one of the charter boats. All are manned by experienced captains, salty fishermen who can tell more tales about the sea than you'll read in a book.

Eastham

The town of Eastham—along with Wellfleet and Truro (see below)—offers more in the way of peaceful beaches, coves, and crystal clear ponds than other towns on the Outer Cape (with the exception, of course, of Provincetown). Eastham—like Wellfleet and Truro—is dominated by the Cape Cod National Seashore. Some parts of this region, especially the highlands of Truro and the plains of Nauset, haven't changed much since Thoreau walked these shores in the mid-1800s.

"Everything told of the sea," wrote Thoreau in his classic *Cape Cod*, "even when we did not see its waste or hear its roar. For birds, there were gulls, and for carts in the fields, boats turned bottom upward against the houses, and sometimes the rib of a whale was woven into the fence by the road-side."

Originally called Nauset, Eastham was settled by Pilgrims in 1644. Descendants of the original settlers still live in the area; you see their names on street signs and mailboxes—Doane, Snow, Cook, Higgins, Hatch, and Bangs. Eastham has a year-round population of about 5000 and consists of two villages: Eastham, with no real center, only a scattering of shops and stores along Route 6, and North Eastham, with a more defined center at the corner of Route 6 and Brackett Road. Here you'll find a general store; a great ice cream place (Ben & Jerry's); Rick's Outermost Bar (a favorite among locals, college kids, and surfers); Fleming's Donut Shack (arguably, some of the best donuts on the Outer Cape; good coffee, too); a liquor store; pharmacy; and bike shop. You'll also find a great athletic club, the Norsemen (255-6370).

There are several other restaurants in town you should try: the Eastham Lobster Pool near the Route 6–Brackett Road intersection (another editor's choice)—fresh lobster, homemade chowder, mussels, and buckets of local steamers; Mitchel's Bistro, and restaurants in Mercantile Plaza, all off Route 6; and Arnold's on Route 6 across from Kingsbury Beach Road (best big-belly fried clams on Cape Cod, very casual).

Eastham also has its share of historic sites. Three worth taking in are the Swift-Daley House, the Old Schoolhouse Museum, and the Eastham Wind-mill.

The Swift-Daley House, located on Route 6 next to the post office, tells much about the town's past. It is a restoration of a full Cape with a central chimney, pumpkin pine floors, and borning and mourning rooms. On the second floor, up a steep flight of ship's cabin stairs, you'll find a display of wedding gowns and trousseaus from the 1800s and early 1900s. The attic is notable for its handhewn beams and wide roof boards. The parlor has a rosewood melodeon, a unique double oil lamp, and pictures of Eastham's bleak, barren landscape of 100 years ago.

The museum is open during July and August on Wednesdays and Fridays from 1:30 until 4:30 P.M. or by appointment; telephone 255-3380.

You should also visit the Old Schoolhouse Museum, opposite the Cape Cod National Seashore Salt Pond Visitor Center off Route 6. The building was once a one-room schoolhouse. On display you'll find whale jawbones, an old toolshed, U.S. Life Saving Service records, as well as memorabilia from the old school. The museum is open Monday through Friday during July and August from 1:30 until 4:30 P.M.

No trip to Eastham is complete without a stop at the town's old wind-mill off Route 6 across from Town Hall. A good time to visit is Windmill Weekend, usually held the weekend after Labor Day. Events include a crafts fair, square dance, parade, and community cookout. The entire weekend is planned by a committee of volunteers; new members are always welcome.

Make sure you visit Eastham's beaches. As we've mentioned, two of them—Coast Guard Beach and Nauset Light Beach on the ocean and with bathhouse facilities are within the Cape Cod National Seashore. You can bike ride on a scenic trail from the Park's Salt Pond Visitor Center off Route 6 to Coast Guard Beach.

In addition, there are some fine beaches on the bay side and at many of the town's freshwater ponds. Four of the best bay beaches are Thumpertown Beach, Campground Beach, First Encounter Beach (toilet facilities available), and Cooks Brook Beach (toilet facilities available). For a freshwater swim, try Wiley Pond (toilet facilities available) or Herring Pond (both off Herring Brook Road), and Great Pond off Great Pond Road.

When you're at the bay beaches, you can't help but notice the grounded naval ship offshore, called "the target ship" by the locals. It's the *General*

James E. Longstreet, which was towed to the site during World War II to be used by the air force for target practice. The mock bombing runs, discontinued in recent years, were quite a sight to watch from the beach.

Wellfleet

When people talk of Wellfleet these days, they often have in mind pirate ships and recovered booty. The discovery a few years ago of the remains of the pirate ship *Whydah* and its riches, a few hundred yards off Wellfleet's outer beach, has put Wellfleet in the news. The *Whydah* went down in a wild storm on the night of April 26, 1717. It was the flagship of pirate Sam "Black" Bellamy, who seized the one-time slaver in the Caribbean. All but a few of the pirate crew drowned when the ship sank, but survivors, some of whom were later tried and hanged, testified that hundreds of pounds of silver, gold, and other treasure were aboard the vessel.

In 1982 an exploration team, led by salvager Barry Clifford, began the first serious attempt to find and recover the *Whydah* and its sunken treasure. After years of effort and enduring much skepticism (even after he had recovered some coins and other artifacts), Clifford converted his skeptics to believers. In the fall of 1985, a bronze bell was hoisted up from the excavation site. Inscribed clearly on the bell was the inscription: "The Whydah Gally 1716."

To date, Clifford's team has recovered more than 5000 coins, a cannon (with an iron ball still in the firing chamber), and other artifacts—treasure worth millions. Some of the *Whydah* artifacts are on exhibit in Provincetown.

Something, it seems, is always washing up on Wellfleet beaches—if it's not pirate treasure, it is a school of misguided pilot (or blackfish) whales. In recent years, hundreds of pilot whales have stranded, as they have for hundreds of years, on Wellfleet and Eastham bay side beaches. No one seems to know why the whales, some more than 20 feet long and as heavy as three tons, go ashore, although there are all sorts of theories, ranging from parasite infections, to pneumonia, to a bad case of follow-the-leader. Some of the whales are safely pushed out to sea by scientists and volunteers, but most die and must be buried on the beach—a sizable expense for the towns, one that has drained local coffers.

There was a time in the 1700s when nearly every man in Wellfleet was a whaler. "Whales were so plentiful here that they regularly appeared in Wellfleet Harbor," according to a brief Cape Cod National Seashore history of the old whaling days. "Lookout posts on high ground alerted the whalers who pursued the great mammals in small boats. Local tradition holds that whalers often retreated to a tavern on the secluded bluffs of [nearby] Great Island. Here they could recount their adventures, fortify themselves with toddy, and consort with sympathetic ladies, while whalewatchers kept vigil nearby."

In 1970 archaeologists excavated the foundation of a building on Great Island believed to be the tavern. More than 24,000 artifacts were uncovered— among them, a rat-tailed pewter spoon, a British clay smoking pipe, a Redware pudding pan, the neck of a wine or oil bottle, and a piece of a locally-made porringer. The artifacts indicate the building was used between 1690 and 1740.

There is a trail that leads to the site, although there are no visible remains.

Whether it be pirate ships, whales, or ground fishing, the sea has always played a central role in Wellfeet's history.

Three of the town's most distinctive features are its spacious marina (on Commercial Street), its deepwater ponds, and its rich shellfish beds and fishing grounds, from which come not only the world-famous Wellfleet oyster, but also tasty bay scallops, quahogs, mussels, razor clams, blue crabs and sea clams. Scallops, cherrystones (small quahogs) and oysters can be shucked and served on the half-shell, while sea clams and quahogs are the main ingredient for chowders, clam cakes and other delicacies.

Shellfish licenses are available at the town shellfish offices near Mayo Beach and inside Town Hall. The shellfish beds are productive year-round, but check to make sure your favorite spot is open.

The ponds have much to offer, too—for bathers and freshwater anglers (fishing is year-round). Great Pond, Gull Pond, and Long Pond are the most accessible and are stocked (along with smaller ponds) with rainbow, brown, and brook trout. Largemouth and smallmouth bass can also be caught, but we recommend you throw the smallmouth bass back because the state is trying to reestablish the species. Perch, pickerel, and sunfish swim in the ponds, too.

For onshore and offshore ground fishing, meanwhile, visitors have a choice of the ocean or the bay. They can take a small boat out in Wellfleet Harbor in search of bottom fish—tautog up to 14 pounds and winter flounder that come up from the mud in early May. Bass are scarce everywhere, but can occasionally be caught in May and October, according to the town's chamber of commerce. Bluefish may be found June through October—sometimes at Mayo Beach and Shirttail Point. Night fishermen looking for bass or blues may want to check Duck Harbor on the bay and Newcomb Hollow or "Four Mile" beach on the ocean off Ocean View Drive. Top water pluggers or fly-fishing anglers may get lucky with bluefish inside Jeremy's Point. Small boats are available for rent at Wellfleet Marina.

Even in the town center, you'll feel the influence of the sea. At the First Congregational Church on Main Street, high up on the steeple, you'll find "the only clock in the world that strikes ship's time."

Stories about the bell clock have been written up in newspapers, magazines, and even in books, such as *Ripley's Believe It or Not*. Ship's time is quite confusing. We offer you a quick primer here, courtesy of the Wellfleet Chamber of Commerce: "two bells" are struck at one, five, and nine o'clock; "four bells" are struck at two, six, and ten o'clock; "six bells" are struck at three, seven, and eleven o'clock; and "eight bells" are struck at four, eight, and twelve o'clock. Half hours are marked by adding one stroke to the corresponding even hours.

Still confused? You're in good company.

Wellfleet Center is a rustic mix of shops, restaurants, and boutiques, but on a less elaborate scale than Chatham. In many ways, Wellfleet Center has more to offer the visitor more interested in "local color" than the price of a *Lanz* sundress. If you're looking for local color, sit on the park bench in front of Town Hall or slide in next to a fisherman at the Lighthouse Restaurant and order a bowl of chowder.

For a town with about 3000 year-round residents, Wellfleet has a healthy number of art galleries (the town has an impressive summer art colony), museums, and fine restaurants. Among them: the Wellfleet Oyster House, the Tavern Room at Duck Creeke, Sweet Seasons, Aesops Tables, the Bayside Lobster Hutt and the Book Store restaurants, Billingsgate, Serena's, Captain Higgins Seafood, Rookie's Family Restaurant, and Van Rensselaer's Restaurant.

The town also has five indoor movie theaters (Wellfleet Cinemas on Route 6 at the Wellfleet-Eastham line), a drive-in theater, and a weekend flea market (same location).

When it comes to beaches, Wellfleet can match the best the Cape has to offer. Try Lecount Hollow (also called Maguire Landing, at the end of Lecount Hollow Road off Route 6 in South Wellfleet); Four Mile Beach (at the crest of Ocean View Drive, which runs off Lecount Hollow Road); and Cahoon Hollow and Newcomb Hollow (farther down Ocean View Drive). Parking is available.

On the bay side, the town maintains parking lots at Duck Harbor, Mayo's Beach, Power's Landing, and Indian Neck.

If you're just looking for a peaceful drive, consider the little-known (at least among visitors) back road from Wellfleet to Truro. Take Old County Road at the end of Main Street, not far from the town library. Once you pass the town garage and dump and a few residential subdivisions (High Toss Bridge Road, Coles Neck Road, and Old Stagecoach Road), the road winds through woodlands and past creeks and marshes. Before you know it, you'll be in Truro. Stay on this road; bear left at the intersection of Pamet Point Road, stay straight at the intersection of Prince Valley Road. You can take this road all the way to Pamet Harbor and Truro Center.

Truro

Truro, whose beginnings date back to the Pilgrims, comes closest to what Cape Codders nostalgically call "old Cape Cod," with its striking cliffs, moors, hills, and valleys. Mile for mile, Truro probably has more scenic back roads than any town on the Cape. They're not hard to find either, once you're off Route 6. We again suggest, as mentioned in the Wellfleet section, that you drive along Old County Road, which offers panoramic views of Cape Cod Bay. On a clear day, you can see all the way to Sandwich. While you're on Old County Road, you should drive down to Ryder Beach, take a side trip on Pond Road or a left on Depot Road to Pamet Harbor. On the ocean side, follow the Pamet River along North and South Pamet roads.

Besides a handful of shops, stores, and restaurants, there's not much commercial development in Truro, which has a year-round population of about 2000 and three villages: Truro, with its center off Route 6 near North and South Pamet roads; North Truro, with its center at the intersection of Route 6A and Grozier Square; and South Truro, a residential area off Bound Brook Island and Pamet Point roads.

Truro, however, has its own nine-hole golf course overlooking the Atlantic (Highland Golf Links on South Highland Road); it's not a championship course, but it may be more fun to play. Next to Highland Light (called Cape Cod Light by some), the golf course is under the jurisdiction of the Cape Cod National Seashore. The lighthouse, run by the U.S. Coast Guard, was established in 1797 to help prevent shipwrecks on the Outer Beach. The existing tower dates back to 1857.

"Originally, the light beam emanated from two tiers of whale oil reflector lamps, but in 1901 a more powerful system, using a 12-foot high cylindrical lens was installed," a plaque at the base of the lighthouse reads. "The dual electric beams used today are similar to those used at airports. Highland Light, one of four active lighthouses on Cape Cod, also houses a radio beacon, which helps ships to judge their position. Every six minutes a one minute signal is broadcast—the letters H and I are repeated 23 times in Morse Code, followed by a steady tone. During the silent intervals, adjacent stations broadcast *their* signals."

During the early days, Highland Light's lamp and lens required constant attention. "Lightkeepers trimmed the wicks of the oil lamp every four hours, and every day they polished the prisms of the huge lens until they shined like gems. Today, beacon light requires little maintenance. The light bulbs last up to six months. Ships 30 miles (48 kilometers) away identify Highland light by the flashing effect of its (dependable) revolving beacons—on four seconds and off for a second, repeated constantly."

Highland Light, by the way, is usually the first lighthouse seen by ships traveling from Europe to Boston. The lighthouse is located on the edge of a bluff, in a rural, picturesque setting. Visitors are welcome.

One reason Truro is so rural is because a good deal of the town belongs to the National Seashore—an insurance policy, of sorts, guaranteeing the town will remain one of the Cape's prettiest and one of the most pleasant to visit.

Cape Cod National Seashore

The Cape Cod National Seashore was established on August 7, 1961, to protect the Cape's outer arm, 40 miles of dunes, marsh, and coastline. The seashore park was the first of its kind in the country. Never before had Congress created a national park in a residential and commercial area, and it was not accomplished without opposition. The creation of the Seashore caused some local residents to square off with the National Park Service over such fundamental issues as home building and use of the beaches, particularly the tricky question of whether four-wheel-drive vehicles should be allowed on the beaches. Residents have opposed strict restrictions that limit their access to beach shacks and favorite fishing holes.

Six of the Cape's towns—Chatham, Orleans, Eastham, Wellfleet, Truro, and Provincetown—have part of their acreage within the National Seashore's boundaries, although much of it remains in private hands. About half of Wellfleet and 70 percent of Truro's developable land is under the Seashore's jurisdiction. Property owners here must comply with a set of zoning bylaws stricter than any others on Cape Cod. These bylaws, written by the government and approved by the towns, make private development more of a privilege than a right. "Needless to say, this is still hard for old-timers to swallow: they remember the days when their families threw up dune shacks wherever they pleased and drive wherever their ancient vehicles could avoid getting stuck," points out E. J. Kahn III, former editor of the *Provincetown Advocate* and former senior editor at *Boston* magazine.

There is a total of 44,600 acres within the legislated boundaries of the Seashore, and the federal government has acquired 27,300 acres of that land.

Today the Seashore includes, among other facilities, six protected ocean beaches with parking (nominal fee) and bathhouse facilities, two visitor centers with exhibits and amphitheaters (the Salt Pond Visitor Center in Eastham and the Province Lands Visitor Center in Provincetown), several restored homes, a working lighthouse (Nauset Light in Eastham), a golf course (Highland Links in Truro), a lifesaving museum, a white cedar swamp, a beech forest, a restored cranberry bog, the site of Guglielmo Marconi's wireless transmission station, and a headquarters open to the public off Route 6 in South Wellfleet, in addition to numerous marked trails for walking, biking, and horseback riding.

It's hard for some visitors, though, to get beyond the beaches, by far the most spectacular on the Cape—white sandy beaches surrounded by marshland and formed by tall sand cliffs. The protected beaches, all off Route 6, are Coast Guard Beach (at the end of Doane Rock Road) and Nauset Light Beach (at the end of Cable Road) in Eastham; Marconi Beach (off Route 6 beyond the Seashore's headquarters in South Wellfleet); Head of the Meadow Beach (at the end of Head of the Meadow Road in Truro); Race Point (at the end of Race Point Road); and Herring Cove (on Province Lands Road).

The Seashore has a number of self-guided and ranger-guided walks. All are worth the hike—particularly self-guided walks, such as the one-and-a-quarter-mile Atlantic White Cedar Swamp Trail at Marconi Station, the one-and-a-half-mile Fort Hill Walk off Governor Prence Road, and the eight-mile Great Island Trail on Wellfleet's Great Island (you don't have to take the entire walk), and ranger-guided walks such as the three-mile, three-hour Outermost House walk along Nauset Marsh and south of Coast Guard Beach in Eastham.

A memorial to the historic Outermost House, destroyed in the raging Nor'easter of 1978, stands in front of the old Coast Guard Station overlooking the beach. "Naturalist Henry Beston came to these shores in September of 1927 and on the dunes about a mile down the beach, he built a cottage with two rooms and a fireplace," a plaque reads. "He lived there a solitary year in the company of the ocean."

His encounter with nature was recorded in the classic *The Outermost House*. An excerpt is inscribed on the plaque: "Listen to the surf, really lend it your ears, and you will hear in it a world of sounds: hollow boomings and heavy roaring, great watery tumblings and tramplings, long hissing seethes, sharp rifle-shot reports, splashes, whispers, the grinding undertone of stones, and sometimes vocal sounds that might be the half-heard talk of people in the sea."

The sea has always dominated the area now within the National Seashore, as well as the lives of the people who have enjoyed its calm and felt its scourge. For more than 300 years, ships have been tossed upon the sands of the Outer Beach. There have been an estimated 3000 shipwrecks off Cape Cod, dating back to the first recorded wreck—the *Sparrowhawk*, which was bound from Plymouth, England to Jamestown, Virginia, but was driven off course by storms and foundered on the bars off Nauset Beach in mid-December of 1626. The survivors spent the winter in Plymouth Colony.

"Today, if you walk the ocean beach from Chatham to Provincetown you can still see evidence of by-gone wrecks, the sun-bleached bones of schooners and square riggers buried in the dunes. Scores of them were left to rot," local historian and shipwreck expert William P. Quinn wrote in his book, *Shipwrecks around Cape Cod*, which he published himself and sells in Cape bookstores.

Here are brief excerpts from his book, a local best seller:

In the early days, a sailor was in trouble when a storm kicked up. Navigational equipment left much to be desired. The mariner had only a compass, a leadline, a barometer, a chart, and if he was lucky a lighthouse to fix his position on.

"It's been said," wrote author Henry C. Kittredge in his book *Cape Cod—Its People & Their History*, published in 1930, "that if all the wrecks were placed bow to stern, they would make a continuous wall from Chatham to Provincetown."

Concerned about the number of deaths from shipwrecks, Congress established the U.S. Life Saving Service in 1871. Lifesaving stations were built along coastal areas (now within the National Seashore) to provide needed shelter to survivors of shipwrecks. In all, there were 13 lifesaving stations on the Outer Beach; four in Chatham (Monomoy Point, Monomoy, Chatham Village and Old Harbor); one in Orleans (Nauset Beach area); one in Eastham (Coast Guard Beach); one in Wellfleet (Cahoon's Hollow); four in Truro (Pamet River, Highlands, High Head and Peaked Hill Bars); and one in Provincetown (Race Point). [You can still walk the beach today and find remnants of these stations. For more information, call the Cape Cod National Seashore headquarters at 349-3785.] For 10 months each year, the stations were manned by seven men; one of them, a keeper, stayed year-round. Among the duties of the surfmen was, to patrol the beach every night from dawn to dusk in fair and foul weather. Author Beston wrote in his *Outermost House* of "twinkles and points of solitary light from the lanterns and electric torches of the Coast Guardsmen of the Cape walking the lonely night patrols."

Surfmen and beachcombers never knew what to expect on the beach. For instance, the morning after the British schooner *Jason* wrecked near Pamet River station in 1893, crew member Samuel J. Evans was found clinging to a bale of jute, clad only in his underwear. He was wrapped in heavy blankets and rushed to the station. He recovered soon after. The bodies of 20 other crew men were later found floating in the sea or washed up on the beach.

Freeman Mayo of Eastham was equally surprised on a foggy morning in April of 1852 when he was walking near the surf and discovered a broken mast from a shipwrecked schooner. Tied to the mast was a 12-year-old boy, still alive but quite cold. The youth was John Fulcher, a cabin boy aboard the British brig *Margaret*, which had been wrecked in a storm off the Cape. John lived with the Mayo family for a while, then took up farming. After his experience with the sea, he decided land was much safer than the deck of a boat. He married and settled in Eastham; his descendants still live in the town.

Today, ships no longer pile up on the backside of the Cape with the same nightmarish regularity. But occasionally they do come ashore, as the 471-foot Maltese freighter *Eldia* did during a driving nor'easter on March 29, 1984. Her crew of 22 was rescued by a Coast Guard helicopter that had to fight hurricane-force winds. For almost two months, the *Eldia* sat on the lip of Nauset Beach in Orleans, a few hundred yards south of the parking lot. The scene attracted more than 100,000 visitors and was a boon to local merchants. Finally, she was tugged off the shore and escorted to Newport, Rhode Island, where she was repaired.

Historian Quinn each summer gives lectures on the *Eldia* and other shipwrecks, usually at the Seashore's Salt Pond Visitor Center in Eastham. Call the center for more information.

Other historic Seashore sites worth seeing are the Marconi Wireless Station in South Wellfleet and the Captain Edward Penniman House at Fort Hill in Eastham.

Not much is left of the station behind the Seashore headquarters where Marconi transmitted the first wireless signal between the United States and Europe. The messages were sent on January 18, 1903. "Messages were broadcast in international Morse code, and with elation the official communiques of President Theodore Roosevelt and King Edward VII were exchanged by the two stations," according to a Seashore account. "Within months, the South Wellfleet station was regularly sending American news . . . to the *London Times*. And in return, a telegraph line connected Cape Cod's wireless station with the South Wellfleet telegraph office, which relayed European messages to the *New York Times*. The Cape Cod station served as the first 'Voice of America.' A few remains of the station are left, including concrete foundations of transmitter house and northwest tower and sand anchors that held guy wires." The ocean has eroded the cliff site. The Seashore has a model depicting the station as it appeared in 1903.

The Penniman House at Fort Hill near the mouth of Nauset Harbor, built by whaling Captain Penniman, is one of the most resplendent sea captain's homes on the Cape, Seashore brochures note. It was built in the Second French Empire style. Captain Penniman, who left Eastham in 1842 at the age of 11 to seek his fortune at sea, "made much money from the sales of whale oil, baleen, spermaceti, and ivory," Seashore historians say. At 29 Penniman was captain of his own whaling ship. When he built his home in 1867, it was the most expensive house in town. He even had a cupola on the roof so he could watch his family at play while he kept an eye on the sea. Penniman died here in 1913. He was 82.

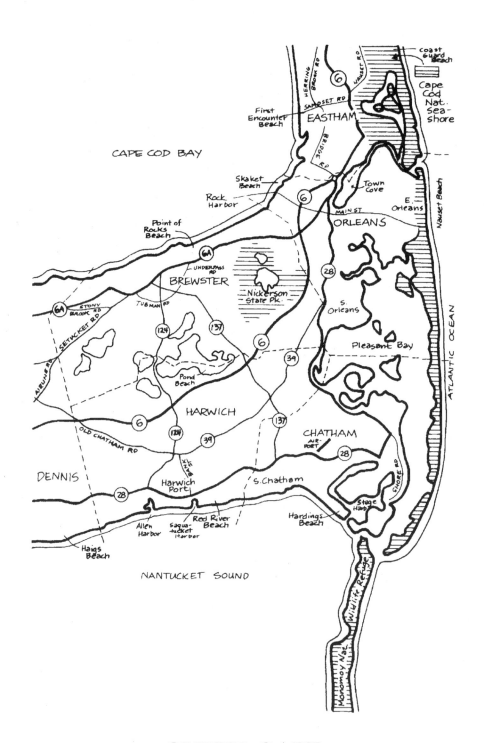

OUTER CAPE

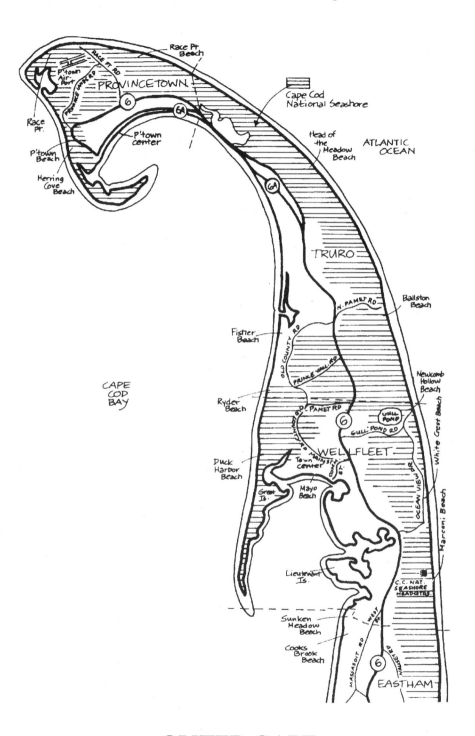

OUTER CAPE

Outer Cape: Essentials

 ## Important Public Information

Municipal Services

- *Brewster Town Hall:* 896-3701.
- *Brewster Police, Fire, Ambulance:* 896-3232.
- *Chatham Town Hall:* 945-2100.
- *Chatham Police:* 945-1212.
- *Chatham Fire and Ambulance:* 945-2323.
- *Eastham Town Hall:* 255-0333.
- *Eastham Police, Fire, Ambulance:* 255-2323.
- *Harwich Town Hall:* 432-0145.
- *Harwich Police:* 432-1212.
- *Harwich Fire and Ambulance:* 432-2323.
- *Orleans Town Hall:* 255-0900.
- *Orleans Police, Fire, Ambulance:* 255-1213.
- *Truro Town Hall:* 349-3635.
- *Truro Police, Fire, Ambulance:* 349-6711.
- *Wellfleet Town Hall:* 349-3707.
- *Wellfleet Police:* 349-2100.
- *Wellfleet Fire and Ambulance:* 349-3311.

Medical Services

- *Cape Cod Hospital,* 27 Park St., Hyannis: 771-1800.
- *Medicenter Five,* 525 Long Pond Rd. (Route 137 near Route 6 entrance-exit), Harwich; 432-4100. Walk-in medical clinic.
- *Outer Cape Health,* Rte. 6, Wellfleet; 349-3131.
- *Chatham Medical Offices,* 78 Crowell Rd. (off Rte. 28), Chatham; 945-0187.
- *Orleans Medical Center,* Rte. 6A (underground mall near Orleans-Brewster line), 255-8825; walk-in clinic, 255-9577.

Veterinarians

- *Animal Hospital of Orleans,* 65 Finlay Rd., Orleans; 255-1194.
- *Brewster Animal Clinic,* 463 Long Pond Rd., Brewster; 896-6344.
- *Animal Rescue League of Boston* (Brewster branch), Rte. 6A, near Brewster-Orleans line; 255-1030.
- *Eastham Veterinary Hospital,* Rte. 6, Eastham; 255-0149.
- *Pleasant Bay Animal Hospital,* Rte. 137, Harwich; 432-5500.

Weather

- *The Cape Codder* weatherphone: 255-8500.

Tourist Information Services

- *Cape Cod Chamber of Commerce,* Hyannis (just off Rte. 6): 362-3225.
- *Chatham Chamber of Commerce,* Main St., Chatham: 945-0342.
- *Eastham Information Booth,* Rte. 6, Eastham; 255-3444.
- *Harwich Chamber of Commerce,* town center; 432-1600.
- *Orleans Chamber of Commerce,* off Rte. 6A, Orleans; 255-1386.
- *Truro Chamber of Commerce,* Rte. 6, Truro; 487-1288.
- *Wellfleet Chamber of Commerce,* off Rte. 6, Wellfleet; 349-2510.

Lodgings

B&Bs & Country Inns

Major credit cards are accepted at most B&Bs and country inns, and many places offer off-season rates. Call to inquire.

RESERVATION SERVICES & DIRECTORIES

- *House Guests Cape Cod and the Islands* is the Cape and Islands' original and most varied bed and breakfast reservation service. More than 300 guest rooms are available; year-round service. Offers accommodations for singles, doubles, and families; water views and wooded locations. All accommodations have been inspected and approved; reasonable rates. For a directory covering Cape Cod and the Islands, write Box 1881, Orleans, MA 02653, or call 896-7053 or 1-800-666-HOST; Visa, MasterCard, American Express cards welcome.
- *DestINNations New England,* 420-3430 or 800-333-4667. This service will plan your Cape Cod B&B stay as well as plan the rest of your New England itinerary.
- *Orleans Bed & Breakfast Associates* is a year-round reservation service for the Outer Cape. Reasonable rates; more than 50 B&Bs available. Write Box 1312, Orleans, MA 02653, 617-255-3824 or 800-541-6226. Unique listings, great personal service, brochure available. MasterCard, Visa, and American Express accepted for deposit.
- *House Guest of Cape Cod,* Box 8 A-R, Dennis, MA 02638; 398-0787. Offers accommodations in private homes, inns, and guest houses all over the Cape and the Islands.

• **Bed and Breakfast Cape Cod,** Box 341, West Hyannis Port 02672; 508-775-2772. Select from 60 host homes, country inns, and sea captains' houses on Cape Cod and the islands of Nantucket and Martha's Vineyard. Beaches, great seafood restaurants, whale watches, and summer theater are all a part of the local attractions. Modest/deluxe rates, private or shared baths. Write or call for free selection of information.

BREWSTER

• **Beechcroft Inn,** 1360 Main St. (Rte. 6A); 896-9534. Moderate to expensive. Beautiful, old country inn at the corner of Route 6A and Tubman Road; full complimentary breakfast, recently renovated; beautiful grounds; call for more information.

• **The Bramble Inn and Restaurant,** 2019 Main St. (Rte. 6A); 896-7644. Moderate to expensive. 19th-century country inn; within walking distance to Cape Cod Bay, tennis, gift and antique shops; credit cards accepted; complimentary continental breakfast; candlelight prix fixe dinner by reservation; open year-round.

• **Brewster Farmhouse Inn,** Rte. 6A; 896-4232 or 800-892-3910. Expensive. Located across from the town-owned Drummer Boy property where Brewster holds its town band concerts and there is plenty of room for walking. Full gourmet breakfast, afternoon teas, heated pool and spa. You'll find attention to detail at this inn from terry cloth robes to turn down service.

• **High Brewster Inn and Restaurant,** Satucket Rd.; 896-3636 or 800-203-2634. Overlooking Upper Mill Pond, this inn offers a relaxing, enchanting setting. Rooms in the inn or enjoy one of the beautifully decorated cottages with fireplaces. Gourmet restaurant on premises.

• **Candleberry Inn,** Rte. 6A; 896-3300. Moderate. Lovely restored 1800s Federal home, beautifully maintained gardens, charming innkeepers, continental breakfast.

• **The Deck House B&B,** 72 Turning Mill Pond Rd.; 896-6396. Moderate. Overlooking Upper Mill Pond, this guest house offers canoeing, windsurfing and sailing in their backyard.

• **Captain Freeman Inn,** 15 Breakwater Rd. (off Rte. 6A); 896-7481. Moderate. An old sea captain's home with a large front sitting porch; close to bay and Brewster General Store; continental breakfast offered; swimming pool; credit cards accepted.

• **Isaiah Clark House,** 1187 Main St. (Rte. 6A); 896-2223. Moderate. A 1780 sea captain's estate restored to its original charm; offers all modern conveniences; five large bedrooms with private baths; full breakfast, complimentary pick up from Hyannis airport, many charming amenities, ask about the honeymoon package in the Rose Cottage; located on five lush acres; credit cards accepted; one of the Outer Cape's best country inns.

• **The Inn at the Egg,** Rte. 6A; 896-3123. Moderate. Across from the popular Brewster General Store, this is a historic home in a beautiful setting, breakfast included.

• **Ocean Gold,** off Rte. 6A in East Brewster near Nickerson State Park; 255-7045. Moderate. Full country breakfast, near bike trails and ponds.

• **Old Manse Inn,** 1861 Main St. (Rte. 6A); 896-3149. Moderate. An antique sea captain's home with nine guest rooms, all with private baths; complimentary breakfast. A four-course, prix fixe dinner is served by candlelight in sun room; call for reservations; credit cards accepted.

BREWSTER (CONTINUED)

- *Old Sea Pines Inn,* 2553 Main St. (Rte. 6A); 896-6114. Moderate. Turn-of-the-century mansion with 15 guest rooms; 9 have private baths; located on three acres; sitting porch and large deck; complimentary full breakfast; family suite available.
- *The Poore House B&B,* Rte. 6A; 800-233-6662. Moderate. Historic 1837 home, full breakfast, lawn games, private baths, air conditioning.
- *The Ruddy Turnstone,* Rte. 6A; 385-9871 or 800-654-1995. A 19th century Cape home with views of the marsh, full breakfast, secluded yard with gardens. Antique shop on premises.

CHATHAM

- *Bow Roof Guest House,* 59 Queen Anne Rd.; 945-1346. Moderate. Near beach, continental breakfast, linens available; year-round; call for more information.
- *Captain's House Inn of Chatham,* 371 Old Harbor Rd.; 945-0127. Moderate to expensive. Old sea captain's house on two acres, fireplaces, canopied beds, continental breakfast; open year-round; credit cards accepted; one of the Outer Cape's top country inns.
- *Chatham Guest House,* 49 Queen Anne Rd.; 945-3274. Moderate. Motel-style guest house with private baths, close to beach and center of town; call for more information.
- *Chatham Village Inn,* off Shore Rd. near Chatham Lighthouse; 945-0792 or 800-244-0792. Moderate to expensive. Water view; breakfast and dinner available at adjoining restaurant. Open year-round.
- *Cranberry Inn*, 359 Main St., Chatham village; 945-9232 or 800-332-4667. Expensive. Buffet breakfast, 18 guest rooms, charming inn in a convenient location.
- *Cyrus Kent House,* 63 Cross St.; 945-9104 or 800-338-5368. Moderate. Old sea captain's home, private baths, continental breakfast, close to town center; call for more information.
- *Inn at the Dolphin,* 352 Main St. (next to Dolphin of Chatham); 945-0070. Moderate to expensive. Eight elegant guest rooms, most with water views; heated pool, hot tub; near beach and town center; credit cards accepted.
- *The Moses Nickerson House Inn,* 364 Old Harbor Rd.; 945-5859 or 800-628-6972. Moderate to expensive. Recently renovated, charming and lovely gardens.
- *The Old Harbor Inn,* 22 Old Harbor Rd.; 945-4434 or 800-942-4434. Moderate to expensive. Private baths; breakfast; near beaches and town center; conference room and bridal suite available; major credit cards accepted.
- *Queen Anne Inn,* 70 Queen Anne Rd.; 945-0394. Expensive. Victorian inn with 30 elegantly furnished rooms, private baths, continental breakfast, tennis courts, fitness center, cribs and child care available; credit cards accepted.
- *Ye Olde Nantucket House,* 2647 Main St., South Chatham; 432-5641. Moderate. Greek revival style inn, 5 guest rooms, continental breakfast.
- *Wayside Inn,* 512 Main St.; 945-5550. Moderate to expensive. Recently renovated inn in the town center next to Kate Gould Park; credit cards accepted; call for updated information.

EASTHAM

- *The Over Look Inn,* Rte. 6; 255-1886 or 800-356-1121. Moderate. Inn is a restored Victorian sea captain's home in the center of Eastham's historic district, not far from Coast Guard Beach, the entrance to the Cape Cod National Seashore, and the Seashore's bike path. Located on one and a half acres, the inn has 10 bedrooms and three bathrooms, Visa and MasterCard accepted; afternoon tea served.

• *The Penny House,* Rte. 6; 255-6632. Moderate. This bed and breakfast was built in the 1700s and served as a sea captain's home. The house has traditional wide-planked pine floors, a ship builder's bow roof, and 200-year-old beams across the ceiling of the public room; continental breakfast served.

• *The Whalewalk Inn,* 169 Bridge Rd.; 255-0617. Moderate. An 1830 whaling captain's home located on a country road, beautiful grounds, gourmet breakfast, garden patio. This one is a sure bet!

HARWICH

• *Beach House Inn,* 4 Braddock Lane, Harwichport; 432-4444 or 800-870-4405. Expensive. Overlooks Nantucket Sound, breakfast buffet.

• *Blueberry Inn B&B,* 621 Main St., Harwichport; 432-6389. Ocean and harbor views from a 1789 house, country breakfast.

• *Camelot,* 525 Main St. (at the corner of Pilgrim Rd.); 432-0736. Moderate. Old captain's home; private baths; seasonal; call for more information.

• *The Country Inn,* 86 Sisson Rd.; 432-2769 or 800-231-1722. Moderate. Seven guest rooms with private baths, continental breakfast, pool, tennis courts, cozy atmosphere. MasterCard and Visa accepted; call for more information.

• *Dunscroft Inn,* 24 Pilgrim Rd.; 432-0810. Moderate. B&B; private baths; near private beach on Nantucket Sound; two efficiencies and cottage also available; call for more information.

• *The Gingerbread House,* 141 Division St.; 432-1901 or 800-432-1901. Moderate. Old English guest house, traditional teas served in gazebo in the afternoons.

• *The Grey Gull Guest House,* 547 Main St.; 432-0222. Moderate. Private baths; one block from the beach; located in the center of Harwich Port; call for more information.

• *Harbor Walk,* 6 Freeman St. (near Wychmere Harbor); 432-1675. Moderate. Cozy atmosphere, beautiful setting.

• *The House on the Hill,* off Rte. 28; 432-4321. Moderate. B&B; old New England atmosphere, deck, flower garden, continental breakfast, cots and cribs, patio with stone wall.

• *The Lion's Head Inn,* 186 Belmont Rd.; 432-7766 or 800-321-3155. Moderate. B&B; old 1800s half Cape house; cottages available; call for more information.

• *Sunny Pines B&B Inn,* 77 Main St.; 432-9628. Moderate. Near beaches, restaurants, and wildlife sanctuary; gourmet Irish breakfast; evening wine and cheese party served by candlelight; open year-round; call for more information.

• *The Tern Inn,* 91 Chase Rd.; 432-3714 or 800-655-5035. Moderate. Bed and breakfast inn with eight summer cottages for rent. Located in residential area, walk to the beach on Nantucket Sound.

• *Wedgewood B&B,* 115 Sisson Rd., Harwichport; 432-1378. Moderate. Private or shared baths, continental breakfast.

• *Wequassett Inn,* off Rte. 28; 432-5400 or USA 800-225-7125 or in MA 800-352-7169. Expensive. Luxury rooms, fine dining, tennis, overlooking Pleasant Bay. Great place to stay.

• *Willow House,* 23 Willow St.; 432-2517. Moderate. Attractive rooms, private baths, walk to beach.

ORLEANS

• *Academy Place B&B,* Rte. 28 & Main St.; 255-3181. Moderate. Historic sea captain's home in a central location.
• *Barley Neck Inn & Lodge,* Beach Rd.; 800-281-7505. Moderate. In East Orleans on the way to Nauset Beach, recently renovated old sea captain's home, pool, two new restaurants.
• *The Farmhouse,* 163 Beach Rd.; 255-6654. Moderate. 19th-century farmhouse, with ocean views; short walk to Nauset Beach; ocean view deck.
• *Hillbourne House,* Rte. 28; 255-0780. Moderate to expensive. Built in 1798, view of Pleasant Bay; private beach, dock, moorings; continental breakfast; cottages available; a sure bet; call for more information.
• *Ivy Lodge,* Main St.; 255-0119. Moderate. Guest house, 19th-century home, picnic area, close to beaches, beautiful setting.
• *Kadee's Gray Elephant,* 212 Main St., East Orleans; 255-7608. Moderate. Just one mile to Nauset Beach and set in lovely East Orleans, Kadee's has six studios with kitchen, a/c and cable TV.
• *Manor-by-the-Sea,* off Chatham Rd.; 328-5505. Moderate to expensive. Waterfront estate with private beach; ten bedrooms with six baths, game room, fireplaces; for more information, write 63 Crabtree Rd., Squantum, MA 02171.
• *Morgan's Way B&B,* 9 Morgan's Way; 255-0831. Two rooms with private baths, swimming pool, delicious breakfast.
• *Nauset House Inn,* Beach Rd.; 255-2195. Moderate to expensive. Small, cozy country inn; modern conveniences; a great place to stay.
• *The Parsonage Bed & Breakfast,* 202 Main St., near Nauset Beach; 255-8217. Moderate. Five rooms; efficiency apartment available; attractive area; breakfast in courtyard; call for more information.
• *Sea Sounds,* 9 Snow Goose Lane; 255-5855. This contemporary private home is located in East Orleans within walking distance to the ocean, private setting, one room has a Jacuzzi and a deck, full breakfast.
• *Ship Knees Inn,* Beach Rd. (near Nauset Beach); 255-1312. Moderate to expensive. Gracious old sea captain's home; private baths; short walk to beach, close to shopping, continental breakfast, year-round; another fine country inn.
• *Waterside Gardens,* 204 Barley Neck Rd.; 255-3823, winter 201-236-6300. Moderate. Lovely waterfront contemporary Cape on Pochet Inlet, full American breakfast. Enjoy the view, the gardens, the wildlife and easy access to all your favorite Cape Cod activities.

TRURO

• *The Gingerbread House,* Depot Rd.; 349-2596. Moderate. Inn with guest room and cottages; located on scenic, country road; walk to Pamet Harbor.
• *Parker House Bed & Breakfast,* Rte. 6A; 349-3358. Moderate. Attractive home, close to beach and shopping.
• *The Summer House Bed & Breakfast,* Pond Rd.; 487-2077. Moderate. Beautiful location, close to bay.

WELLFLEET

• *Aunt Sukie's Bayside B&B,* 525 Chequessett Neck Rd.; 349-2804 or 800-240-9999. Moderate. Antique home with water views, on Wellfleet bay beach, continental breakfast.
• *Cahoon Hollow Bed & Breakfast,* off Cahoon Hollow Rd.; 349-6372. One- and two-bedroom suites, private baths and sitting rooms; full breakfast, secluded setting with beautiful gardens; near beach.

• *The Holden Inn,* off Commerical St.; 349-3450. Twenty-six rooms available in two of Wellfleet's oldest sea captains' homes, views of Cape Cod Bay and Great Island.

• *The Inn at Duck Creeke,* Main St.; 349-9333. Moderate to expensive. One of the Outer Cape's great country inns; modern conveniences; fine restaurants nearby; close to beaches, harbor, and town center; continental breakfast; a sure bet!

Resorts, Hotels, Motels, Condominiums, & Selected Cottages

Most of the following establishments accept major credit cards, and many of them offer off-season rates. We suggest you call them for further information.

BREWSTER

• *Brewster Cottages,* Millstone Rd.; 896-3260. Moderate. Near scenic Route 6A.

• *Clipper Bay,* Ellis Landing; 896-5072. Moderate. Cottages near beach.

• *Dugan's Beach Apartments,* Robbins Hill Rd.; 896-3686. Moderate. Near Robbins Hill Beach.

• *Jolly Whaler,* Rte. 6A (Betty's Curve); 896-3474. Moderate. Cottages near beaches, shops, and hiking areas.

• *Lingerlonger by the Sea,* Linnell Landing Rd.; 896-3451. Moderate to expensive. Located on Cape Cod Bay, cottages and apartments, attractive setting.

• *Michael's Cottages in Brewster,* 618 Main; 896-3158 or 800-399-2967. Moderate. Nice setting right on Rte. 6A.

• *Ocean Edge Resort & Conference Center,* off Rte. 6A; 800-343-6074 or 896-9000. Expensive. Two- and three-bedroom villas offered, views of Cape Cod Bay; private beach, tennis courts, golf available; conference center run by Hilton. Kids programs, fitness room, indoor/outdoor pools, clay courts.

CHATHAM

• *Bradford Inn and Motel,* 26 Cross St.; 945-1030 or 800-562-4667. Located in town center; open year-round; complimentary breakfast served in nearby Captain Elijah Smith House; outdoor pool; TV; close to beach, golf, and tennis; credit cards accepted.

• *Chatham Bars Inn,* Rte. 28 (overlooking harbor); 945-0096 or 800-527-4884. Expensive. An American plan resort hotel; private beach, fine dining, outdoor heated pool, golf, tennis, sailing, fishing, spectacular views, recently redecorated and enhanced; credit cards accepted; call for more information. Housekeeping cottages also available.

• *Chatham Highlander,* 946 Main St.; 945-9038. Moderate. Close to beach, golf, and tennis; attractive setting; small but modern motel; 12 rooms with private baths; TV; managed by same people who own Bradford Inn; credit cards accepted.

• *Chatham Motel,* Rte. 28; 945-2630 or 800-770-5545. Moderate. Attractive setting, 20 rooms with private baths, playground, shuffleboard, picnic and barbecue area, no pets.

• *Chatham Seaside Cottages,* off Rte. 28 near Ridgevale Beach; 432-4421. Moderate. Close to shopping areas, well-equipped kitchens, fireplaces.

CHATHAM (CONTINUED)

• *Chatham Tides Motel,* 349 Pleasant St.; 432-0379. Moderate. Overlooking Nantucket Sound, private beach, efficiency kitchen units and cottages available, sun decks, TV, lawn games; credit cards accepted.

•*Chatham Town House Inn,* 11 Library Ln.; 945-2180 or 800-242-2180. Expensive. Sea captain's home with private baths and full breakfast, walk to beach and town center, beautiful gardens; call for more information.

• *Cranberry Inn at Chatham,* 359 Main St.; 945-9232. Moderate to expensive. 150-year-old inn, walking distance to beaches and shopping, public dining room, breakfast and dinner served; credit cards accepted; call for more information.

• *Dolphin of Chatham,* 352 Main St.; 945-0070 or 800-668-5900. Moderate. Resort motel close to beach, open year-round, some rooms with kitchenettes, heated pool, hot tub; TV; credit cards accepted; call for more information.

• *Fore 'n Aft,* Deep Hole Rd.; 432-9145. Moderate. Cottages near water.

• *Grassy Acre Cottages,* 1470 Main St.; 945-1976. Moderate. Fully equipped kitchenettes.

• *Harding House Motel,* at corner of Rte. 28 and Pleasant St.; 432-4535. Moderate. Open year-round, short walk to beach, comfortable accommodations, credit cards accepted.

• *Hawthorne Motel,* 196 Shore Rd.; 945-0372. Moderate. 16 rooms, modern conveniences, beautiful grounds overlooking Pleasant Bay and Atlantic Ocean, private beach; call for more information.

• *John B. Horne Cottages,* off Morris Island Rd.; 945-0734. Moderate to expensive. Located in private beach area, fully equipped, fishing and marina facilities nearby.

• *Lanterns Lane Cottages,* off Cockle Cove Rd.; 432-2145. Moderate to expensive. Two-, three-, and four-bedroom cottages available, fully equipped, fireplaces, walk to beach.

• *Mashpatuxett Village,* Cockle Cove; 432-0479. Moderate. Cottages close to water.

• *Master Mariner Motel,* Main St.; Rte. 28, W. Chatham; 945-2244. Moderate. Open year-round, off-season rates, restaurant and lounge, close to Hardings Beach; credit cards accepted; call for more information.

• *The Mooring Motor Lodge,* 326 Main St.; 945-0848. Moderate. Victorian guest house motel, efficiencies, cottages or coach house budget rooms available, walk to beach or town center; credit cards accepted.

• *Oyster Pond at Chatham,* Rte. 28; 945-1095. Expensive. Luxury townhouses overlooking Oyster Pond, pool, tennis courts, boating, private patios; credit cards accepted; call for more information.

• *Pilgrim Village,* off Rte. 28; 945-0041. Moderate. Family resort area on large freshwater pond, sandy beach, playground, picnic areas, one- to two-bedroom cottages.

• *Pine Oaks Cottages,* 314 Cockle Cove Rd.; 432-0892. Moderate. One- to three-bedroom units available, fully equipped, plenty of privacy, overlooking Nantucket Sound.

• *Pleasant Bay Village,* Rte. 28; 945-1133. Moderate to expensive. Luxury motel; suites, efficiencies, and cottages available. Beautifully landscaped, walking distance to beach, heated pool, gourmet breakfast, poolside lunch in season; credit cards accepted.

• *The Reliance Motel,* Rte. 28; 945-0710. Moderate. Near beach and restaurants, efficiencies available; heated pool, comfortable accommodations; credit cards accepted.

- *Seafarer Motel,* at corner of Rte. 28 and Ridgevale Rd.; 432-1739. Moderate. Open year-round, attractive rooms (some with kitchenettes), close to the beach; call for more information.
- *Surfside Motor Inn,* Holway St.; 945-9757. Moderate. Panoramic view of the Atlantic, private beach, comfortable accommodations, walk to town center; golf, tennis, boating, and fishing nearby; family units, continental breakfast.

EASTHAM

- *The Anchorage on the Cove,* off Rte. 6; 255-1442. Moderate. Two-bedroom cottages, overlooking cove; call for more information.
- *Aspinet Resort Motel & Cottages,* off Rte. 6; 255-2835. Moderate. Rooms and housekeeping cottages; near beaches, Cape Cod National Seashore, and shopping; comfortable accommodations.
- *Atlantic Breeze Motel & Cottages,* Rte. 6; 255-1076. Moderate. Comfortable accommodations; close to beaches, National Seashore, and shopping; call for more information.
- *Bayberry Hill Cottages on Ministers Pond,* 255-7738. Located on freshwater pond, one to three bedrooms, grills, screened-in porches, near National Seashore and bike trails.
- *Best Inn of Eastham,* Rte. 6; 255-1132 or 800-862-5550. Moderate. Comfortable rooms with all modern conveniences, large pool, tennis and health spa, close to beaches and shopping.
- *Blue Dolphin Inn,* Rte. 6; 255-1159 or 800-654-0504. Moderate. Two-bedroom suites, private patios, bikes, tennis, restaurant on premises.
- *The Captain's Quarters Motel,* Rte. 6; 255-5686 or 800-327-7769. Moderate. 34 rooms, pool, picnic tables, close to shopping and beaches, conference facilities.
- *Cove Bluffs Motel,* off Rte. 6; 240-1616. Moderate. Housekeeping suites; pool; near shopping, National Seashore, and beaches; call for more information.
- *Cranberry Cottages,* off Rte. 6; 255-0602 or 800-292-6631. Moderate. Pretty setting, rollaways and cribs.
- *Deschamps Cottages on Herring Pond,* Crosby Village Rd.; 255-8555 or 609-768-0970. Moderate. Private beach, close to shopping.
- *Eagle Wing Motel,* Rte. 6; 240-5656. Moderate. Open year-round; pool, picnic area, playground, close to beaches and shops.
- *Eastham "Ocean View" Motel,* Rte. 6; 255-1600 or 800-742-4133. Moderate. Comfortable accommodations, view of Atlantic and Nauset Marsh, private baths; call for more information.
- *Gibson Cottages,* off Rte. 6 behind the Eastham Windmill; 255-0882. Moderate. Wooded setting, private beach on lake, free row-boats and sailboats, one to three bedrooms.
- *Good Luck Cottages,* Ridge Rd.; 255-0434. Inexpensive. Comfortable accommodations, picnic areas, close to beaches and shopping, year-round.
- *Gull Cottages,* off Rte. 6; 255-4644. Moderate. Close to beach and shopping.
- *Hidden Village,* off Rte. 6, Bridge Rd.; 255-1140. Moderate. Contemporary cottages; call for more information.
- *Laskowski Cottages,* off Rte. 6 (between Thumpertown and Kingsbury beaches on the bay); 255-8677. Moderate. Private beach, beautiful setting.
- *Midway Motel & Cottages,* Rte. 6; 255-3117. Inexpensive to moderate. Located in a pretty grove; near beaches and shopping, children's playground, grills.

EASTHAM (CONTINUED)

- *Nauset Haven Lakeside Cottages,* Rte. 6; 255-0490. Moderate. Private beach, play area, fireplaces, screened-in porches, April to October.
- *Oak Grove Cottages,* off Rte. 6; 255-3284. Moderate. Comfortable accommodations, patio area, grills, lawn furniture, cribs, and play area.
- *Pine Tree Cottages,* Rte. 6; 362-2509. Moderate. Recreation room, close to beaches and shopping.
- *St. Aubin's Bayside Cottages,* Turnip Field Rd.; 255-3895 or winter, 203-644-1242. Moderate. Close to bay, picnic area, fireplaces.
- *Saltaway Cottages,* Aspinet Rd.; 255-2182. Moderate. Picnic and play areas, close to beaches and shopping.
- *Sheraton Ocean Park Inn & Resort Spa,* Rte. 6; 255-5000 or 800-533-3986. Moderate to expensive. Deluxe rooms, pool, tennis, spa, and dining; call for more information.
- *Shore Garden Cottages,* on Town Cove (off Rte. 6); 255-4795. Moderate. Private beach, dock, use of rowboats, near boat and canoe rentals.
- *Smith Heights Cottages,* off Rte. 6A; 255-5895. Moderate. Waterfront, beautiful setting, close to shopping.
- *Smith's First Encounter Village,* on First Encounter Beach; 255-0864. Moderate. Private beach, porches, sun decks overlooking bay.
- *Starfish Cottages,* off Rte. 6; 255-2356 or 362-2509. Moderate. Recreation room, TV, children's play area, swings.
- *Town Crier Motel,* Rte. 6; 255-4000. Moderate. Open year-round; 32 rooms, two suites, one efficiency, recreation room, outdoor-indoor pool, near beaches and shopping.
- *Viking Shore Motor Lodge,* Rte. 6; 255-3200 or 800-242-2131. Moderate. Pool, tennis courts, continental breakfast; seven-acre wooded resort; close to beaches, shopping, and bike trail.
- *Wheel In Cottages,* off Rte. 6; 255-2588. Moderate. Cottage complex borders Cape Cod National Seashore, picnic and grill areas, playground for children, cribs available.

HARWICH

- *Bayberry Motel,* Old County Rd.; 432-2937. Moderate. Close to beaches, located in residential setting.
- *Blue Anchor Inn,* Shore Rd.; 432-0703. Moderate. Close to water.
- *Cape Winds,* Shore Rd.; 432-1418. Moderate. Cottages close to water.
- *Cranberry Country Cottages,* 584 Main St.; 432-5627. Moderate. Fully equipped cottages with decks. Five minutes to beach.
- *The Coachman,* Rte. 28; 432-0707. Moderate. Close to shopping and restaurants.
- *The Commodore Inn,* 30 Earle Rd.; 432-1180 or 800-368-1180. Moderate to expensive. Full breakfast, 300 yards to Nantucket Sound, pool.
- *Handkerchief Shoals Motel,* Rte. 28; 432-2200. Pool, 26 units, lawn games, 1/2 mile to beach.
- *Harbor Breeze,* 326 Lower County Rd., Harwichport; 432-0337 or 800-272-4343. Moderate. Walk to beach, continental breakfast, family suites, pool, barbecue area.
- *Moby Dick Motel,* Rte. 28; 432-1434. Moderate. Close to shopping and restaurants.
- *The Sandpiper Inn,* 16 Bank St.; 432-0485 or 800-433-2234. Expensive. Continental breakfast, private beach, gas grills, and refrigerators in rooms.

- *Seadar Inn by the Sea,* Bank St. (overlooking Nantucket Sound); 432-0264. Moderate. Resort motel; water view, beach nearby, breakfast served, TV lounge.
- *Wequassett Inn,* Rte. 28 (overlooking Pleasant Bay); 432-5400. Moderate to expensive. A spectacular waterfront resort with a renowned chef; excellent restaurant; entertainment offered; credit cards accepted.
- *West Harwich Lodge,* Rte. 28; 432-2100. Moderate. Overlooks Herring River; close to shopping and restaurants, pool.
- *West Pines Cottage,* 207 Division St.; 432-1931. Inexpensive. On five acres, two to three bedrooms.
- *Wishing Well Motel & Cottage,* Rte. 28; 432-2150 or 800-432-4345. Moderate. Close to shopping and restaurants, pool.

ORLEANS

- *Cape Homesteads,* in East Orleans and near Pleasant Bay. Moderate. A collection of antique cottages and homes. For more information, call Bob or Claire Chiarello, 255-5083 or 255-1193.
- *Cottontail Cottages,* near Nauset Beach; 255-2176. Moderate. Close to shopping and restaurants.
- *The Cove,* Rte. 28; 255-1203 or 800-343-2233. Moderate to expensive. Water view of Town Cove; pool, comfortable accommodations, modern conveniences, within walking distances to shops; credit cards accepted.
- *Cove House Cottages,* off Rte. 6A; 255-1312. Moderate. Two year-round cottages available with kitchen, baths, and deck facing Town Cove; call for more information.
- *Governor Prence Motor Inn,* at corner of Rte. 6A and Rte. 28; 255-1216. Moderate. Comfortable accommodations; deluxe rooms and suites available; near Town Cove; indoor pool; coffee shop; located on five acres; credit cards accepted.
- *Lakecrest Cottages,* 225 Cranberry Hwy.; 255-3334. Moderate. Waterfront cottages, private beach, decks, fireplaces and grills; call for more information.
- *Nauset Beach-Side Motel & Apartments,* Beach Rd.; 255-3348. Moderate to expensive. Overlooking Nauset ocean beach, comfortable accommodations, spectacular views, close to shops.
- *Nauset Knoll Motor Lodge,* Beach Rd.; 255-2364. Moderate. Oceanfront motel, private baths, view of the marsh, close to shops.
- *Nauset Village Cottages,* off Rte. 28; 362-2509. Moderate. Comfortable, well-furnished cottages in the Pleasant Bay area, some with fireplaces, all with private docks. Cottages sleep two to eight people.
- *Ocean Bay View Housekeeping Cottages,* Portanimicut Rd.; 255-3344. Moderate. Cottages on Little Pleasant Bay with private beach, playgrounds, tennis, swings for the children.
- *Old Tavern Motel,* Rte. 6A; 255-1565. Moderate. 18th-century sea captain's inn attached to 25-room addition; comfortable accommodations, close to beaches and shopping, adjacent restaurant, continental breakfast; call for more information.
- *Orleans Holiday Motel,* at the corner of Rte. 6A and Rte. 28; 255-1514 or 1-800-451-1833. Moderate. Year-round, attractive rooms, across from Town Cove; near town center. The motel has a "Flote Bote" to take guests on a 15-minute trip through creeks and marshes to the barrier beach.
- *Packet Landing & Sea Breeze Motel,* Beach Rd.; 255-1550 or 800-899-1550. Moderate. One mile from Nauset Beach, continental breakfast, pool, other conveniences.

ORLEANS (CONTINUED)

• *Pleasant Bay Estate,* Towhee Ln.; 255-3670. Expensive. Waterfront accommodations with private beach, one- to three-bedroom units; call for more information or write Box 323, S. Orleans 02662.

• *Pleasant Bay Waterfront Compound,* off Rte. 28; 203-288-9291. Moderate to expensive. Spectacular water views, comfortable accommodations, cottages and beach houses, private beach, May to October.

• *Ridgewood Cottages and Motel,* at intersection of Rte. 28 and Rte. 39; 255-0473. Moderate. Open year-round, close to beaches and shopping, large outdoor pool, grill, patio, swings, comfortable rooms, quiet location.

• *Seashore Park Motor Inn,* off Rte. 6 near Orleans Rotary; 255-2500 or 800-772-6453. Moderate. Comfortable accommodations, 62 deluxe rooms and efficiencies, large indoor pool, saunas, Jacuzzi, near beaches and shopping.

• *Skaket Beach Motel,* at corner of Rte. 6A and West Rd.; 255-1020 or 800-835-0298. Moderate. Comfortable rooms, pool, close to beaches and shopping, continental breakfast, just off Shore Road exit on Route 6.

TRURO

• *Anchorage Motel, Apartments & Cottages,* Rte. 6A; 487-1068. Moderate to expensive. Water view, private beach, comfortable accommodations.

• *Big Fisherman Apartments,* Rte. 6; 487-0250. Moderate. Walk to beach, fully equipped apartments.

• *Braemar "House on the Hill,"* off Shore Rd. in North Truro; 487-2207. Moderate. Motel sensibly priced for a family vacation, water views, private decks, outdoor pool.

• *Cape Breeze,* Rte. 6A (Beach Point); 487-9110. Moderate to expensive. Cottages on bay, spectacular water views and view of Provincetown; call for more information.

• *Cape View Motel,* Rte. 6; 487-0363. Moderate to expensive. Water view, close to Provincetown, comfortable rooms, complimentary coffee and donuts.

• *Crow's Nest Motel,* on Cape Cod Bay; 487-9031. Moderate to expensive. Rooms and efficiencies all with water views, sun decks.

• *East Harbor Motel & Cottages,* Rte. 6A; 487-0505. Moderate. Comfortable two-bedroom cottage with 240 feet of private beach and spectacular views of Cape tip dunes.

• *Ebb Tide on the Bay,* off Shore Rd. in North Truro; 487-2122. Moderate to expensive. Luxury rooms adjacent to the beach, close to Provincetown.

• *Habor View Motel,* Rte. 6A; 487-1087. Moderate to expensive. Water view, private beach; tennis, golf, restaurants, and Provincetown nearby.

• *Horizon's,* Rte. 6A; 487-0042. Moderate to expensive. Water view, private beach, outdoor pool, decks, efficiencies, close to Provincetown.

• *Outer Reach Resort,* off Rte. 6; 487-9090. Moderate to expensive. Water views, close to beach, hiking, bike trails, and shopping.

• *Pilgrim Beach Village,* Rte. 6A; 487-3418. Moderate to expensive. Cottages, apartments, and efficiencies available; private deck; private beach.

• *Pilgrim Colony,* off Rte. 6; 487-0455. Moderate to expensive. Water view, private beach, two-bedroom cottages with sun decks.

• *Pilgrim Spring Motel,* Rte. 6; 487-9454. Moderate. Large rooms, pool, private baths, restaurant, deli, close to beach.

• *Prince of Whales,* Rte. 6A; 487-0567. Moderate. Close to beaches and shopping.

- *Sea Gull Motel,* Shore Rd. (Rte. 6A); 487-9070. Moderate to expensive. Two-bedroom apartments, private beach.
- *Sea Song,* Rte. 6A; 487-9227. Moderate. Comfortable cottages; conveniently located.
- *Sea Surf Motel,* on Cape Cod Bay; 487-0343. Moderate to expensive. Cottages and efficiencies, pool, beach.
- *The Seascape Motor Inn,* Rte. 6A; 487-1225. Moderate. Private beach, pool, close to Provincetown, continental breakfast.
- *Seaside Village Motel,* Rte. 6A; 487-1215. Moderate to expensive. Water view, private beach, two-bedroom efficiencies and cottages, great views of Provincetown and the bay.
- *Seascent Pines Cottages,* Castle Rd.; 487-0509. Moderate. Located in a peaceful grove near the bay; shopping nearby.
- *Shady Rest Cottage Colony,* Rte. 6; 349-9410. Moderate. One- and two-room efficiencies, outdoor grill, picnic tables, close to beach and shopping.
- *Sunnyside Cottages,* Shore Rd. (Rte. 6A); 487-9198. Moderate. Spacious, close to beach, five-minute drive from Provincetown.
- *The Topmast,* Rte. 6A; 487-1189. Moderate to expensive. On the bay; efficiencies, pool, private beach, sun decks and balconies.
- *Truro Motor Inn & Efficiencies,* Rte. 6; 487-3628. Moderate. Rooms, apartments, cottages, and efficiencies available; close to beaches and Provincetown.
- *White Villages,* off Rte. 6A; 487-3014. Moderate. Cottages on the beach, great water views.
- *Whitman House,* off Rte. 6; 487-1740. Moderate to expensive. "Authentic Cape village"; modern two-, three-, and four-bedroom units, two pools, restaurant and gift shop, near beach.

WELLFLEET

- *Brownies Cabins,* off Rte. 6; 349-6881 or 349-3453. Moderate. One- and two-bedroom cottages.
- *Brown's Landing,* at Indian Neck, 3 King Phillip Rd.; 548-4540 or 349-6923. Moderate. Cottages look out over a marsh, short walk to the beach, fireplaces and decks, April to November.
- *Chateau in the Woods,* Pilgrim Spring Rd.; 201-801-0864. Moderate to expensive. Four-bedroom house with deck, fireplace, wooded area; golf, tennis, and swimming nearby; attractive accommodations.
- *Colony of Wellfleet,* Chequessett Neck Rd.; 349-3761. Moderate. Close to beaches, marina, and town center.
- *Drummer Boy Condominiums and Apartments,* Cannon Hill Rd.; 349-3514. Moderate to expensive. Located by a picturesque cove, beautiful gardens, decks, everything from studios to penthouse apartments available; close to beaches and shopping.
- *Drummer Cove Cottages*, off Rte. 6; 349-2022. Moderate to expensive. Overlooks cove on the bay, screened-in porches; beautiful grounds; call for more information.
- *The Even' Tide,* off Rte. 6; 349-3410 or 800-368-0007. Moderate. Open year-round; rooms available as well as two- and three-bedroom cottages, picnic and playground areas, close to beaches and shopping.
- *Friendship Cottages,* Chequessett Neck Rd.; 349-3390. Moderate. Open year-round; water view, close to beach and shopping.
- *The Gold's Ocean View Drive Home,* Ocean View Dr., off Lecounts Hollow Rd.; 314-469-0692. Private home on high bluff overlooking Atlantic, spectacular

WELLFLEET (CONTINUED)

view; for more information, write J. Gold, M.D., 574 Conway Village Dr., St. Louis, MO 63141.

• *Green Haven Cottages,* off Rte. 6; 349-1715. Moderate. Comfortable accommodations, close to beaches and shopping, half mile from entrance to the Cape Cod National Seashore's Marconi Beach, open April to October.

• *The Mainstay Motor Inn,* Rte. 6; 349-2350. Moderate. Spacious rooms, near beach and shopping, continental breakfast; call for more information.

• *Massasoit Hill Trailer Park,* on Massasoit Rd. opposite Wellfleet Drive-In; 349-2469. Call for more information.

• *The Moorings,* near Wellfleet town pier; 349-3379. Moderate. Rooms and cabins, water views, seasonal.

• *Ocean Pines Motel,* off Rte. 6; 349-2774. Moderate. Near entrance to Cape Cod National Seashore's Marconi Beach, cottages available.

• *Ocean View Cottages,* Ocean View Dr.; 349-3111. Moderate to expensive. Spectacular views, comfortable accommodations, beaches and shopping nearby.

• *Pilgrim Acres,* Pilgrim Spring Rd.; 349-9324. Moderate. Fireplaces; porches; close to beach, golf, tennis, and shopping.

• *Pilgrim Spring Cottages,* off Rte. 6; 349-6000. Moderate. Pool, children's play area, family atmosphere.

• *Southfleet Motor Inn,* Rte. 6; 349-3580. Moderate. Sauna, indoor and outdoor pool, game room, restaurant, across from Marconi Beach entrance.

• *Surfside Colony,* Ocean View Dr.; 349-3959 or 255-3334. Moderate. Fireplaces, screened-in porches, ocean view; beach, golf, and tennis nearby.

• *Wellfleet Motel,* Rte. 6; 349-3535 or 800-852-2900. Moderate. Large family units, indoor and outdoor pool, picnic area, close to beaches and shopping.

Campgrounds

For more details, call campgrounds or Cape Cod Chamber of Commerce at 362-3225.

BREWSTER

• *Shady Knoll Campground,* Rte. 6A near Rte. 137 intersection; 896-3002. Reasonable rates; wooded sites for tents or RVs; offers playground, laundry, walk to food store, close to beaches, easy access for bicyclists; modern rest rooms, free hot showers. Open May 15 through Columbus Day; reservations requested; pets not recommended.

• *Sprawling Hills Park,* off Tubman Rd. (between Rte. 6A and Rte. 124); 896-3939. Offers 300 trailer and tent sites, family camping, freshwater pond, private beach, close to bay beaches and Route 6A shopping, located on 25-acre forested site, hot showers, rest room facilities, playgrounds, children's beach, pets and barbecues permitted; reservations recommended.

• *Nickerson State Park,* off Rte. 6A; 896-4615. Full facilities; pond and beaches; 1750-acre site; no reservations; considered top state park in the Commonwealth *(see Outer Cape:Viewpoints).*

• *Sweetwater Campground Resort,* off Rte. 124; 896-3773.

EASTHAM

• *Atlantic Oaks Cottages & Camping,* Rte. 6; 255-1437 or 800-332-2267. Shaded sites for tents or RVs; hot showers; full facilities; offers store, laundry, game room, movies; one mile from ocean and bay. Open May 15 until October 15; pets not recommended.

TRURO

- ***North Truro Camping Area,*** Highland Rd.; 487-1847. Family camping; full facilities; close to beaches and shopping; wooded area; no dogs from June 15 through Labor Day. Open year-round.
- ***North of Highland Camping Area,*** off Head of the Meadow Rd.; 487-1191. 237 campsites on 60 wooded acres; family campground; full facilities; close to beaches and shopping; also offers laundromat, store, and recreation building. Open May 23 through September 8; reservations by the week; no pets, motor-cycles, or motor homes.
- ***Horton's Park,*** S. Highland Rd.; 487-1220 or 800-252-7705. Half mile from Highland Lighthouse (also called Cape Cod Light); 200 campsites; wooded area; full facilities; no pets; reservations advisable.

WELLFLEET

- ***Maurice's Family Campground,*** S. Wellfleet (opposite drive-in theater); 349-2029. Tent and trailer sites in wooded area; family facilities and atmosphere; no pets; general store.
- ***Paine's Campground,*** Old County Rd., S. Wellfleet; 349-3007. Wooded tent and trailer sites; not far from ocean and bay; full facilities; no pets July and August; no campfires; bring camp stove or grill.

Youth Hostels

EASTHAM

- ***Mid-Cape Youth Hostel,*** Goody Hallett Rd., off Bridge Rd.; 255-2785 or 255-9762. Advance reservations are recommended; membership in American Youth Hostel Inc. is required.

TRURO

- ***Little America Youth Hostel,*** N. Pamet Rd. (Box 402); 349-3889 or 349-3726. Advance reservations are recommended; membership in American Youth Hostel, Inc. is required.

Dining

BREWSTER

- ***Beechcroft Bistro & Pub,*** 1360 Main St.; 896-9534. Moderate. Casual dining in a lovely old inn on Rte. 6A, afternoon tea starting in Sept. Tue.– Thurs. 1–4 P.M., featuring a variety of teas, homemade scones and other pastries.
- ***The Bramble Inn,*** Rte. 6A; 896-7644. Expensive. Continental dining, four-course fixed-price dinner; praised in the *Boston Globe*; year-round; major credit cards accepted; reservations required; proper dress.
- ***Brewster Coffee Shop,*** Rte. 6A; 896-8224. Inexpensive. Breakfast and lunch.

BREWSTER (CONTINUED)

• **Brewster Express,** Underpass Rd., by the bike path; 896-6682. Inexpensive. Great sandwiches.

• **The Brewster Fish House,** 2208 Main St.; 896-7867. Moderate. Comprehensive menu featuring fresh local seafood selections; seasonal lunch and dinner; MasterCard, Visa, and American Express are welcome.

• **The Brewster Inn and Chowder House,** Rte. 6A; 896-7771. Moderate. A renovated inn with a cozy atmosphere, homemade soups and chowders; live entertainment in adjacent tavern—the Woodshed; seasonal; no credit cards; casual dress.

• **Brewster Italian Deli,** Rte. 6A, next to the general store. Inexpensive. Great sandwiches!

• **Brewster Pizza House,** Rte. 6A, next to Cumberland Farms; 896-3341. Inexpensive. Pizza and subs.

• **Café Alfresco,** 1097 Main St.; 896-1741. Moderate. Breakfast, lunch, afternoon tea, and light supper at this café that features specialty foods such as: pastries, deli, gourmet pizzas, Espresso and fresh breads.

• **Chillingsworth,** Rte. 6A; 896-3640. Very expensive. French cuisine praised by *Esquire* magazine; elegant dining served in two seatings: 6–6:30 P.M. and 9–9:30 P.M.; lunch served in greenhouse setting; open most of the year; major credit cards accepted; reservations required; proper dress.

• **Cobie's,** 3260 Main St. (Rte. 6A), near Nickerson State Park entrance; 896-7021. Inexpensive.

• **High Brewster,** 964 Satucket Rd.; 896-3636. Expensive. Original paneling and beamed ceilings help to maintain the atmosphere of an old country inn. The terrace overlooks tranquil Lower Mill Pond. American cuisine, four-course price-fixed menu served year-round; reservations required; lodging available too.

• **Kate's,** Rte. 6A and Paines Creek Rd.; 896-9517. Inexpensive. Fried seafood and gourmet ice cream.

• **Laurino's,** Rte. 6A (near Orleans line); 896-6135. Inexpensive. Italian cuisine, pizza and subs; lounge with entertainment; year-round; no credit cards; no reservations; casual dress.

• **Longfellow's Pub,** Rte. 6A; 896-5413. Inexpensive. Varied menu, weekend entertainment; year-round; major credit cards accepted; no reservations.

• **The Old Manse Inn,** 1861 Main St.; 896-3149. Expensive. Enjoy prix fixe dining in a sea captain's home; dine by candlelight in the sun room with flowers gathered from the gardens. Year-round; credit cards accepted; proper dress.

• **Reef Café,** 1 Village Dr.; 896-7167. Moderate. Varied menu, gourmet pizza, live music during summer.

• **Tower House Restaurant,** 71 Main St.; 896-2671. Moderate. All menu offerings are homemade, from the breads to the desserts; enjoy casual dining with a creative flair, cozy lounge; open most of the year; credit cards accepted; no reservations.

• **Zontini's Café,** 2689 Main St.; 896-3355. Italian food, take out ice cream.

CHATHAM

• **Beach House Grill at Chatham Bars Inn,** Shore Rd.; 945-0096. Right on the water, best setting in town for lunch.

• **Campari's at the Dolphin,** 352 Main St.; 945-9123. Cozy Italian restaurant with the kitchen set in the middle of the restaurant, working fireplaces. Also Bittersweet Café serves breakfast in the morning—same restaurant.

• *Champlains at the Bradford Inn,* 26 Cross St.; 945-9151. Moderate to expensive. A few steps off Main Street in Chatham Center at the rear of the Captain Elijah Smith House; breakfast, lunch, and dinner served; known for its Sunday brunches and evening gourmet dinners. On Fridays in July and August try the old-fashioned New England clam chowder, baked bean and ham supper before the band concert. Seasonal, and year-round for functions; MasterCard, Visa, American Express, and Discover cards accepted; reservations needed; a three-star restaurant.

• *The Bistro,* 595 Main St.; 945-5033. Varied menu, comfortable setting upstairs at The Gallery, overlooks Main St.

• *Chatham Bars Inn,* Rte. 28 (overlooking harbor); 945-0096. Expensive. Great atmosphere and view; continental and American food; credit cards accepted; call for reservations; new grill also available, called the Tavern.

• *The Chatham Squire,* 487 Main St.; 945-0945 (restaurant), 945-0942 (lounge). Moderate. Fresh seafood dinners in a casual atmosphere; fishermen hang out in the lounge. Open most of the year for lunch and dinner; credit cards accepted; reservations aren't needed.

• *Christian's & Upstairs at Christian's,* 443 Main St.; 945-3362. Moderate to expensive. Housed in an old Colonial inn; excellent seafood, duck, and beef; classic upstairs lounge; open most of the year; major credit cards accepted; reservations needed.

• *Cranberry Inn,* 359 Main St.; 945-9232. Moderate. Wide variety of meats and seafood offered in 19th-century inn; seasonal; credit cards accepted; call for reservations.

• *The Garden Café at the Swinging Basket,* 483 Main St.; 945-4081. Moderate. Great lunch place, variety of soups, salads, and sandwiches offered; open a good part of the year; credit cards accepted; no reservations.

• *High Tide,* 1633 Main St., Rte. 28; 945-2582. Moderate. Varied menu, sun deck for cocktails; brunch, lunch, and dinner; open year-round; credit cards accepted; reservations not needed.

• *Impudent Oyster,* 15 Chatham Bars Ave.; 945-3545. Moderate to expensive. Good atmosphere, great seafood; credit cards accepted; reservations accepted.

• *Lou's Dugout Deli,* 155 Crowell Rd.; 945-DELI. Serves breakfast, lunch and specializes in deli sandwiches, soups, and desserts.

• *Northport Seafood House,* Rte. 28; 945-9217. Moderate. Lunch, dinner, and children's menu, varied offerings; open most of the year; call for more information.

• *Sea in the Rough,* Rte. 28, 1077 Main St.; 945-1700. Moderate. Family-style restaurant; fried clams, steamers, mussels, casseroles, beef, chicken; orders to go; reservations not needed.

• *Two Turtles at Chatham Townhouse Inn,* 11 Library Ln. (next to Eldredge Library); 945-2180. Moderate. Dining and lodging in old sea captain's home; Scandinavian breakfast specialties; seasonal; call for more information.

• *The Wayside Inn,* 512 Main St.; 945-4550. Moderate to expensive. Lunch and dinner; seafood and meat; great atmosphere; newly refurbished; next to Kate Gould Park; outdoor patio; credit cards accepted; call for reservations.

EASTHAM

• *Arnold's,* Rte. 6; 255-2575. Moderate. Offers the best fried clams on the outer Cape; family atmosphere; seasonal; no credit cards; no reservations.

• *Jimmy D's Restaurant,* Rte. 6; 255-9913. Moderate. Varied menu of fish and beef, Greek food offered, too; open year-round; credit cards accepted; reservations not necessary.

EASTHAM (CONTINUED)

- *Eastham Lobster Pool,* Rte. 6; 255-3314. Moderate. One of the most popular family places for seafood; open most of the year; credit cards accepted; no reservations.
- *Fairway Pizzeria*, Rte. 6; 255-3893. Inexpensive.
- *The Red Barn Restaurant,* Rte. 6; 255-4500. Inexpensive. Family atmosphere, menu selection includes fried seafood, pizza, hamburgers, and sandwiches.
- *Lobster Shanty,* Rte. 6; 255-9394. Directly across from the National Seashore Visitor Center and just off the bike path, this is a restaurant, game room, ice cream shop, gift shop all in one.
- *Lori's Family Restaurant,* Town Center Plaza off Rte. 6; 255-4803. Inexpensive. Varied menu, breakfast and lunch.
- *Mitchel's Bistro,* Main Street Mercantile, Rte. 6A; 255-4803. New fine dining restaurant, continental fare.
- *Poit's Family Seafood Restaurant,* Rte. 6; 255-6321. Inexpensive. Family atmosphere; breakfast, lunch, and dinner; no credit cards; no reservations.
- *Tumbleweed,* 4100 Rte. 6; 255-1661. Southwestern food, game room, nightly entertainment.
- *Warner B's,* Rte. 6; 255-0600. Inexpensive. Breakfast, lunch and dinner, family restaurant.

HARWICH

- *The Barnaby Inn,* 36 Rte. 28; 432-6789. Moderate. 1796 Cape home; American cuisine with an accent on freshly caught local seafood, fresh veal, beef, poultry; all entrée offerings include complimentary shrimp bowl; year-round; reservations required.
- *Bishop's Terrace,* Rte. 28; 432-0253. Expensive. Restored captain's house, entertainment in the Tavern garden room in season; year-round.
- *Brax Landing,* on Saquatucket Harbor, Rte. 28; 432-5515. Moderate. Waterfront dining, outside patio and deck open in the summer; something for everyone on the extensive menu; year-round; credit cards accepted; no reservations; casual dress.
- *Casa Barbi,* 383 Rte. 28; 432-9192. Italian cuisine, water views.
- *Country Inn,* 86 Sisson Rd., Rte. 39; 432-2769. Moderate. Guests enjoy warm hospitality, good food, and attentive service in a candlelit dining room, American and continental cuisine; year-round; MasterCard, Visa, and American Express accepted; reservations required.
- *The 400 Club,* 429 Main St., Rte. 28; 430-0404. Inexpensive. Casual atmosphere and a menu with something for everyone; for the sports enthusiasts, the "Sports Bar" is a must! Year-round; American Express, Visa, MasterCard accepted; no reservations.
- *The 400 East,* 1421 Rte. 39, across from the Stop & Shop Plaza; 432-1800.
- *Jake Rooney's,* Rte. 28 and Brooks Rd.; 430-1100. Seafood, steaks, sandwiches, good family restaurant, live entertainment.
- *The Mason Jar,* Rte. 28; 432-3293. Inexpensive. Deli and gourmet foods.
- *Raspberries at the Commodore Inn,* 30 Earle Rd.; 432-3103. Moderate. Breakfast buffets, clambakes.
- *The Sea Grille,* 31 Sea St.; 432-4745. Casual, but with a superb menu. Rave reviews on this one.
- *Seafood Sam's,* Rte. 28; 432-1422. Inexpensive to moderate. Fried seafood.

- *The Stewed Tomato,* Harwich Center; 432-1203. Inexpensive. Serving from 6 A.M., breakfast and lunch; year-round.
- *The Weatherdeck Family Restaurant,* Rte. 28; 432-8240. Moderate. Breakfast, lunch, and dinner; year-round.
- *Wequasett Inn,* Pleasant Bay Rd., Rte. 28; 432-5400. Moderate to expensive. Waterfront restaurant; overlooks Pleasant Bay; seasonal; proper dress required.
- *The Wheelhouse Restaurant and Lounge at the Commodore Motel,* 30 Earle Rd.; 432-1180. Moderate. A small quaint restaurant just a short distance from the beach; breakfast, lunch, and dinner served; open April through January.

ORLEANS

- *Australian Chicken Shop,* Rte. 6A; 240-3282. Charcoal roasted chicken, gourmet salads, take out only.
- *The Arbor,* Rte. 28; 255-4847. Moderate. Creative cuisine in an old sea captain's home; decorated with memorabilia throughout five cozy dining rooms; fresh seafood, duck, beef, and pasta. For more casual meals, try the downstairs Binnacle Tavern (255-7910), which serves Cajun, along with barbecue, Italian, and seafood specialties. Open most of the year; MasterCard, Visa, and American Express accepted; call for reservations at the Arbor.
- *Ardath's,* West Rd.; 255-9779. Inexpensive. Breakfast and lunch, varied menu; open year-round; no credit cards; no reservations; supper Friday nights, old-fashioned New England cooking.
- *Barley Neck Inn,* at the intersection of Main St. and Barley Neck Rd.; 255-0212. Moderate. Housed in an 18th-century sea captain's home near Nauset Beach, recently renovated. Open year-round. Also, Joe's Beach Road Bar & Grille for a more casual setting.
- *The Binnacle Tavern,* Rte. 28. *See listing for the Arbor;* 255-7901.
- *The Brown Bag,* at the corner of West Rd. and Old Colony Way; 255-4431. Inexpensive. Housed in a restored cottage; homemade soups, sandwiches, salads, desserts from its bakery; a great place for breakfast and lunch; no credit cards; no reservations.
- *Capt'n Elmer's Restaurant,* 18 Old Colony Way; 255-3350 (restaurant), 255-7221 (fish market). Inexpensive. Breakfast, lunch, and dinner; family restaurant; varied menu—from fresh eggs, to fresh fish, to hamburgers. Open year-round; no credit cards accepted; no reservations.
- *Captain Linnell House,* Skaket Rd. (turn left at the end of West Rd.); 255-3400. Moderate. Housed in an old sea captain's home; seafood and international cuisine; lunch and dinner. Open most of the year; credit cards accepted; reservations suggested.
- *Ciro di Pasta,* Rte. 6A; 240-0747. Moderate. Italian specialties for lunch and dinner, take-out menu, bright, cheery decor.
- *The Double Dragon Inn,* at corner of Rte. 6A and Rte. 28; 255-4100. Inexpensive to moderate. Located on boardwalk overlooking Town Cove; offers authentic Cantonese, Polynesian, and Szechuan cuisine; open year-round; lunch and dinner served; credit cards accepted; no reservations
- *Hearth 'n Kettle,* at corner of West Rd. and Route 6A; 240-0111. Inexpensive. Family restaurant; breakfast, lunch, dinner; varied menu; open year-round; casual dress; MasterCard, Visa, American Express accepted; reservations not required.
- *Homeport,* Main St. (town center); 255-4069. Inexpensive. Family restaurant; breakfast, lunch, and dinner; open year-round; no credit cards; no reservations.
- *Hunan Gourmet III,* off Rte. 6A in Underground Mall; 240-0888. Chinese food.

ORLEANS (CONTINUED)

• *Kadee's Lobster & Clam Bar,* 212 Main St., on the way to Nauset Beach; 255-6184. Moderate. Fish market next door; open-air café or indoor dining; seafood menu, family place; seasonal; no credit cards; no reservations.

• *Land Ho!* at the corner of Rte. 6A and Cove Rd. (town center); 255-5165. Moderate. One of the Cape's great drinking pubs and eating places; no trip to Outer Cape would be complete without a stop at this local hangout. Lunch and dinner; open year-round; no credit cards; no reservations.

• *The Lobster Claw,* Rte. 6A (near Orleans Rotary); 255-1800. Inexpensive to moderate. Lunch and dinner; great family place; seafood menu, children's menu; seasonal; credit cards accepted; no reservations; as is the Land Ho! worth a visit.

• *Lo Cicero's,* Rte. 6A (in Orleans Shopping Plaza);255-7100. Inexpensive to moderate. Varied menu, take-out orders; open year-round; credit cards accepted; reservations not required.

• *Nauset Beach Club,* Main St. near intersection with Beach Rd.; 255-8547. Moderate. Northern Italian food, popular, excellent.

• *Noonies Country Kitchen,* Rte. 6A (town center); 255-1415. Inexpensive. Breakfast and lunch, varied menu; open year-round; no credit cards; no reservations.

• *Off the Bay Café,* Main St.; 255-5505. Moderate. Varied menu for lunch and dinner; open year-round; credit cards accepted; reservations accepted.

• *Old Jailhouse Tavern,* West Rd. (off Rte. 6A); 255-JAIL. Moderate. Located in old stone house, formerly owned by Constable Henry Perry, once served as town jailhouse. Varied menu, great atmosphere; open year-round; credit cards accepted; no reservations.

• *Orleans Lobster Pound,* Rte. 6A; 240-1234. Casual family dining inside or on cheerful outside deck, kids' meals, clambakes.

• *Orleans Villa Pizza,* Rte. 6A; 255-5111. Inexpensive. Great food and prices!

• *Rosina's Café,* 54 Main St.; 240-5513. Italian cuisine, lunch, dinner; eat in or take out.

• *Sir Cricket Fish & Chips,* Rte. 6A; 255-4453. Inexpensive.

• *The Wheelhaus Café,* 2 Academy Place, Rte. 6A; 240-1585. Charming restaurant that serves breakfast, lunch and dinner; delicious desserts and an outside deck for dining.

• *The Yardarm,* Rte. 28; 255-4840. Inexpensive to moderate. Varied menu; open year-round; no credit cards accepted; no reservations.

TRURO

• *Adrian's at the Outer Reach,* off Rte. 6A; 487-4360. Moderate. Varied menu; breakfast, lunch, and dinner; Italian dishes, gourmet omelettes, woodfired oven pizzas, takeout available.

• *The Blacksmith Shop,* off Rte. 6A (town center); 349-6554. Moderate. Varied menu, good atmosphere; seasonal; call for more information.

• *Paparazzi,* Rte. 6A; 487-2658. Inexpensive to moderate. Seafood and Italian specials; reservations not required; call for more information.

• *Whitman House,* off Rte. 6; 487-1740. Moderate. Varied menu, country inn atmosphere; seasonal; credit cards accepted; call for reservations.

WELLFLEET

• *Aesop's Tables,* Main St.; 349-6450. Moderate. Varied menu, nouvelle New England cuisine; good atmosphere; lunch and dinner; seasonal; credit cards; call for reservations.

• *The Bayside Lobster Hutt,* Commercial St.; 349-6333. Moderate. Fresh fish and shellfish; waterfront atmosphere; dinner daily and lunch on weekends; seasonal; no reservations.

• *The Beachcomber,* off Ocean View Dr. (Cahoon Hollow Rd. overlooking ocean, spectacular view); 349-6055. Moderate. Varied menu, raw bar, gourmet pizza, children's menu, live entertainment (mostly folk and rock); call for more information.

• *The Book Store Restaurant,* Kendrick Ave.; 349-3154. Moderate. Varied menu, view of harbor; breakfast, lunch, and dinner; great place for the family; call for more information.

• *Box Lunch,* Briar Ln.; 349-2178. Inexpensive. Great sandwiches, breakfast also!

• *Captain Higgins Seafood Restaurant,* on the town pier; 349-6027. Moderate. Fresh seafood, also chicken and steak dishes; seasonal; call for more information.

• *Depot Café,* Commercial St.; 349-9533. Moderate. Café-style restaurant on the banks of Duck Creek; varied menu, homemade clam chowder; bring your own beer and wine; seasonal; hours vary; lunch and dinner.

• *Eric's Seafood Restaurant,* Rte. 6; 349-9373. Moderate. Varied menu; family restaurant; take-out; seasonal; no reservations needed.

• *Flying Fish Café,* Briar Ln.; 349-3100. Breakfast, lunch, dinner; ethnic and vegetarian specialties, in-house bakery & deli.

• *Gutsy Benders,* Rte. 6; 349-0800. Inexpensive. Take-out food; pizza, subs, stews and chili.

• *The Lighthouse,* Main St.; 349-3681. Inexpensive. Varied menu; breakfast, lunch, and dinner; year-round local hangout, worth a visit; no credit cards; no reservations.

• *Moby Dick's,* Rte. 6; 349-9795. Inexpensive. Family restaurant overlooking marsh; varied menu; seasonal; no reservations required.

• *Painter's,* 50 Main St.; 349-3003. Moderate. Seafood, pastas, salads. Upstairs has a lighter fare and entertainment.

• *A Pizza My Heart,* Commercial St.; 349-1400. Subs, salads, "eclectic" pizza.

• *PJs Dari Burger,* Rte. 6; 349-2126. Inexpensive. Seasonal.

• *Rookie's Family Restaurant,* Rte. 6; 349-2688. Inexpensive. Family restaurant; varied menu, lunch and dinner; no reservations required.

 • *Serena's,* Rte. 6; 349-9370. Moderate. Family restaurant, varied menu, children's plates; seasonal; MasterCard and Visa accepted; no reservations.

• *Sweet Seasons,* E. Main St., next to the Inn at Duck Creeke; 349-6535. Moderate to expensive. Cozy atmosphere with view of Duck Pond; varied menu includes seafood, beef, and fowl; seasonal; major credit cards accepted; call for reservations.

• *The Tavern Room Restaurant & Lounge at the Inn at Duck Creeke,* E. Main St.; 349-7369. Moderate. Housed in historic 1800 building; oldest pub in the village; varied menu; dinner starts at 6 P.M., light fare until midnight. Entertainment (folk, jazz, or blues) offered; seasonal; major credit cards accepted; call for more information.

• *Van Rensselaer's Restaurant,* also called VRs, Rte. 6; 349-2127. Moderate. Varied menu, nice atmosphere; open year-round; credit cards accepted; no reservations required.

• *The Wellfleet Oyster House,* E. Main St.; 349-2134. Moderate to expensive. Housed in a home built in 1750; quality menu of seafood and meat, 20 entrees to chose from; entertainment on weekends; seasonal; MasterCard and Visa accepted; call for reservations.

Entertainment

For more information about entertainment in the Outer Cape region, check the Tuesday and Friday editions of the *Cape Codder.*

Music & Stage

BREWSTER

• *Brewster Band Concerts,* Old Drummer Boy Museum property, Rte. 6A. Every Sunday night during the summer. Band plays in a gazebo while you enjoy the spacious grounds overlooking Cape Cod Bay. Bring a picnic.

• *Cape Cod Repertory Theatre,* Rte. 6A; 896-6140. Plays, also features children's plays in an outdoor theater.

CHATHAM

• *Band concerts,* Kate Gould Park, Chatham Center. Every Friday night in July and August, starting at 8 P.M. Town band plays marches and waltzes.

• *The Chatham Drama Guild,* 134 Crowell Rd.; 945-3563 or 945-0510. Good summer theater, call for more information.

• *Monomoy Theatre,* Main St.; 945-1589. Run by Ohio University; popular musicals and Broadway hits; one of the Cape's best summer theaters.

EASTHAM

• *First Encounter Coffee House,* Samoset Rd. Readings, music, and plays; check newspaper for schedule.

HARWICH

• *Band concerts,* Brooks Park, Harwich Center. July and August, 8 P.M.; for dates of concerts, call Harwich Chamber of Commerce at 432-1600.

• *Harwich Junior Theatre,* off Division St.; 432-2002. See listing under Children's Activities.

ORLEANS

• *Academy of Performing Arts,* Main St.; 255-1963. Good summer theater, call for more information.

• *Meeting House concerts*, July and August; for details, call Information Booth at 255-1386.

WELLFLEET

• *First Congregational Church.* Summer music series; for more information, call church at 349-6877.

• *Wellfleet Harbor Actor's Theatre,* off Kendrick Ave. (next to town pier); 349-6835. Drama, comedy.

Nightlife

BREWSTER

• *Laurino's,* Rte. 6A; 896-6135. Music from '40s and '50s, dancing.

• *Longfellow's Pub,* Rte. 6A; 896-5413. Live music (guitar and vocals); usually offered Wednesday through Saturday.

• *The Woodshed,* Rte. 6A; 896-7771. Live music (folk-rock); varied schedule.

EASTHAM
- ***First Encounter Coffee House,*** Samoset Rd. Folk and other entertainment; varied schedule.
- ***Sheraton Ocean Park Inn,*** Rte. 6, 255-5000. Live jazz, folk and rock bands; varied schedule.

HARWICH
- ***Bishop's Terrace,*** Rte. 28; 432-0253. Jazz, piano classics; varied schedule.
- ***The Irish Pub,*** Rte. 28 (near Bass River Bridge); 432-8808. Irish music, other offerings; varied schedule (a favorite among the college crowd and the Irish).
- ***Wequassett Inn,*** Rte. 28 (overlooking Pleasant Bay); 432-5400. Dinner, music, dancing; varied schedule.

ORLEANS
- ***The Barley Neck Inn,*** Main St. (at Main St. and Barley Neck Rd. fork); 255-6830. Varied schedule (another sure bet; also try the restaurant).
- ***Land Ho! Tavern,*** Rte. 6A; 255-5165. No live music, but come here for the "local color"; good food, too.
- ***Off the Bay Café,*** 28 Main St.; 255-5505. Guitar and vocals in the bar area; varied schedule.

WELLFLEET
- ***Aesop's Tables,*** Main St. (town center); 349-6450. Guitar, piano, jazz in upstairs lounge; varied schedule; also a restaurant.
- ***The Beachcomber,*** Ocean View Dr. (off Lecounts Hollow Rd.); 349-6055. Rock music; varied schedule.
- ***Bookstore and Restaurant,*** Mayo Beach; 349-3154. Live music, call for schedule.
- ***Painter's,*** 50 Main St.; 349-3003. Jazz, reggae, blues, rock; call for schedule.
- ***The Tavern Room at the Inn at Duck Creeke,*** E. Main St.; 349-7369. Jazz, piano, contemporary guitar; varied schedule.
- ***Wellfleet Oyster House,*** E. Main St.; 349-2134. Music and other entertainment in lounge; fine restaurant.

Movie Theaters

- *Harwich Port Cinema,* Main St.; 432-0072.
- *Wellfleet Cinemas,* Rte. 6; 349-2520; Orleans, 255-9619.
- *Wellfleet Drive-In*, Rte. 6; 349-2520.
- *Interstate Harwich Cinemas,* Rte. 137; 430-1160.

Museums & Historic Sites

Admission to museums and historic sites listed below is free, or a nominal fee is charged. For more information, telephone local chambers of commerce or town information booths.

BREWSTER
- ***Cape Cod Museum of Natural History,*** Rte. 6A; 896-3867. Exhibits, trails, lectures, workshops, children's activities; newly completed addition; open year-round.

BREWSTER (CONTINUED)

• *New England Fire & History Museum,* Rte. 6A; 896-5711. Old firefighting equipment on display, including early fire engines, authentic New England village with apothecary shop and common; open Memorial Day to Labor Day, off season by appointment. Good for children.

• *Stony Brook Mill,* Stony Brook Rd., across from herring run. Old grist mill grinds corn, upstairs museum with exhibit on early Brewster and a weaver; open July and August.

CHATHAM

• *Old Atwood House,* Stage Harbor Rd. One of oldest houses in Chatham, owned by town's historical society; open June–September.

• *Chatham's Old Grist Mill,* also called Godfrey Windmill, near Chase Park off Shattuck Place. Built in 1797; occasionally grinds corn using wind power; open July and August.

• *Chatham Winery,* Rte. 28; 945-0300. Open for tours by reservation. Picnic area, wine tasting.

• *The Mayo House,* just east of Cape Cod Five Cent Savings Bank on Main St. Example of a traditional Cape Cod house built in 1820; serves as headquarters for Chatham Conservation Foundation; furnished with period furniture; open Memorial Day to Columbus Day, hours posted at town information booth in town center.

• *Railroad Museum,* Dept Rd. Old Chatham Railroad Company station; railroad artifacts, including 73-year-old caboose; open last week in June until Labor Day.

EASTHAM

• *Old Schoolhouse Museum,* across from Cape Cod National Seashore's Salt Pond Visitor Center off Rte. 6. Displays of town history, shipwrecks, and old school; open July and August.

• *Swift-Daley House,* Rte. 6 next to Eastham Post Office. Displays of town history, excellent restoration of old Cape home built in 1700s; open July and August.

• *Eastham Windmill,* off Rte. 6 across from Town Hall. Believed to be oldest windmill on Cape; still grinds corn. Windmill Festival held weekend after Labor Day, see essay on Eastham in *Outer Cape: Viewpoints.* Windmill open July and August.

HARWICH

• *Historical Society Museum,* Brooks Academy in Harwich Center. Displays on early Harwich; open summers; 432-8089.

• *Old Powder House,* Harwich Center (next to Brooks Academy). Gun powder was stored here between 1770 and 1864.

ORLEANS

• *French Cable Station,* corner of Rte. 28 and Cove Rd. Built in 1890 to house on-land extension of transatlantic cable; among messages transmitted through the station were Charles Lindbergh's landing in Paris and the German occupation of France in 1940; open July–September; 240-1735.

• *Jonathan Young Windmill,* Town Cove Park across from Stop & Shop. Open July and August, weekends off-season.

• *Orleans Historical Society Museum,* corner of Main St. and River Rd. Housed in 1833 meeting house; formerly a Unitarian-Universalist Church; displays of Indian artifacts and town history; open July and August.

TRURO

- *Historical Society Museum,* Highland Light Rd., N. Truro. Indian artifacts on display, 17th-century firearms, old lifesaving equipment, shipwreck exhibits; open June–September; 487-3397.
- *Highland Light,* also called Cape Cod Light, off Highland Lighthouse Rd. Old, working lighthouse (see Truro section of *Outer Cape: Viewpoints*).

WELLFLEET

- *Historical Society Museum,* Main St. Displays of town history and Indian artifacts. Each summer historical society holds two fund-raising events: Strawberry Festival in June and summer cookout in August. Museum open late June until early September; 349-9157.
- *Samuel Rider House,* Gull Pond Rd. Displays of town history and Indian artifacts; open late June until early September.

Seasonal Events

BREWSTER

- *Bird Carver's Exhibit,* held each summer at the Cape Cod Museum of Natural History, on Route 6A. For times and dates, call 896-3867.
- *Arts & Crafts Fairs,* held at Brewster Community Center off Route 6A and at Brewster Elementary School on Underpass Road. Check the *Cape Codder* for listings or call Town Hall (896-3701).
- *Brewster in Bloom Festival.* Held in April, a weekend full of activities, including a parade.

CHATHAM

- *Band concerts,* Kate Gould Park, Chatham Center. Every Friday night in July and August; town band plays marches and waltzes; bring lawn chairs or beach blanket to sit on. Great fun for the children; concerts start at about 8 P.M.
- *July Fourth festivities.* Parade (one of the best on the Outer Cape), Main Street in town center. Starts in the morning; come early. For more information, call Chatham Chamber of Commerce at 945-0342.
- *Village Arts & Crafts Fair,* Chase Park. Held during the summer; for more information call Chamber of Commerce at 945-0342.
- *"Under Chatham Blue,"* held at Chatham Elementary School. Summer arts and crafts fair; for more information call Chamber of Commerce (945-0342).
- *Old Fashioned Christmas Stroll,* in Chatham, town center. Mid-December; hay rides, open houses (stores), Santa; for more information, call Chamber of Commerce (945-0342).

EASTHAM

- *Windmill Weekend,* at town windmill off Route 6 across from Town Hall. Held the first weekend after Labor Day; parades, cookout, craft shows, contests. For more information, call Chamber of Commerce at 255-3444.

HARWICH

- *Band concerts,* Brooks Park in Harwich Center. July & August, 8 P.M. For dates of concerts, call Harwich Chamber of Commerce at 432-1600.
- *Harwich Cranberry Harvest Festival.* Held in September; a week and a half of arts and crafts shows, contests, exhibitions, fireworks, clambakes, and a

HARWICH (CONTINUED)

parade; highlight of the season for Harwich. For more information about times and places, call 432-0145 or 432-9754.

• *Annual Harwich Professional Arts & Crafts Festival,* Brooks Park in Harwich Center. Held in early June; for more information, telephone Harwich Chamber of Commerce at (432-1600).

• *Annual Downtown Harwich Port Arts & Crafts Festival,* School House Parking Lot. Held in early August; for more information, call Chamber of Commerce (432-1600).

• *Harwich Fourth of July festivities.* Includes parade and arts & crafts fair; for more information, call Chamber of Commerce (432-1600).

• *Annual "Harwich Happening,"* First Congregational Church in Harwich Center. Sponsored by the Society for the Preservation of the Historic Harwiches; held in mid-August; the event depicts life in Harwich over the years; for more information, call Chamber of Commerce (432-1600).

• *Christmas House Tour.* Mid-December, sponsored by the Society for the Preservation of Historic Harwiches; for more information, call Chamber of Commerce (432-1600).

ORLEANS

• *Annual Artist and Craftsmen's Guild of the Outer Cape Show,* Nauset Regional Middle School, Route 28. One of the best fairs of the summer; for more information, call Orleans Chamber of Commerce at 255-1386.

• *Nauset Painters outdoor arts shows.* On weekends throughout the summer on the front lawn of Nauset Middle School.

• *July Fourth festivities.* Parade down Main Street in the morning; for more information, call Chamber of Commerce (255-1386).

• *Pops in the Park,* Eldredge Park; 255-1386. Cape Cod Symphony Orchestra plays in August for this wonderful outdoor concert.

WELLFLEET

• *July Fourth festivities.* Parade in the morning; along with Chatham's, one of the Outer Cape's better parades if you like a small town touch! For more information, call Wellfleet Chamber of Commerce at 349-2510.

• *Arts and crafts shows.* Held during the summer; for more information, call Chamber of Commerce (349-2510).

Children's Activities

BREWSTER

• *Bassett Wild Animal Farm,* 620 Tubman Rd. (between Rtes. 124 and 137); 896-3224. Children's zoo, picnic areas, pony rides, hay ride. Mid-May through mid-September.

• *Cape Cod Museum of Natural History,* Rte. 6A; See listing under Museums & Historic Sites.

• *Brewster Whitecaps,* Community Center on Rte. 6A; 896-3913. Brewster's team in the Cape Cod Baseball League holds weekly clinics for boys and girls ages 7–14.

• *Cape Cod Repertory Theatre,* 3379 Rte. 6A. Summer children's theatre on an outdoor stage. Call for reservations.

- *Moby Dick Farm,* Great Field Rd.; 896-3544. Hay rides, trail rides, horseback riding lessons.
- *Namskaket Farm,* off Rte. 6A (not far from entrance to Nickerson State Park). Pick your own strawberries. Opens 8 A.M., June and early July.
- *New England Fire & History Museum,* Rte. 6A. Old firefighting equipment, other displays (see listing under Museums & Historic Sites).
- *Woodsong Farm,* Lund Farm Way; 896-5555. Horsemanship program, pony camp.
- *Stony Brook Mill,* Stony Brook Rd. (off Rte. 6A). Herring run and old mill that grinds corn, other exhibits (see listing under Museums & Historic Sites).

CHATHAM

- *Chatham A's,* Veteran's Field. Weekly baseball clinics during the summer for boys and girls given by Chatham's local Cape League team.
- *Creative Arts Center,* 154 Crowell Rd.; 945-3583. Children's art classes, also classes in pottery, photography.

EASTHAM

- *Eastham Recreation Program,* Town of Eastham; residents and visitors; late June–mid-August; boys and girls 6–16; archery, arts and crafts, tennis, other sports and activities.
- *Family Sports Center,* Rte. 6; 255-5697. Golf driving range, pinball machines and video games; miniature golf, ice cream.

HARWICH

- *The Club House Mini Golf and Bumper Cars,* 1470 Rte. 39; 432-4820.
- *Grand Slam,* 322 Main St.; 430-1155. Bumper boats, arcade, batting cages, gyro gym.
- *Harwich Junior Theatre,* off Division St. Produces four plays every summer for children from age 5 and up. The theater also offers classes in creative dramatics for children 6 and older and in technical theater for children 10 and older. For more information, call 432-2002.
- *Harwich Recreation Program.* Town of Harwich; eight-week comprehensive program of sports for boys and girls during the summer—baseball, softball, basketball, tennis, diversified games and activities; offered to residents and summer visitors. At Sand Pond, swimming classes for those six and older are held daily; boating, sailing and lifesaving courses also offered; for more information, call Harwich Town Hall at 432-0145.
- *Harbor Glen Miniature Golf,* 168 Main St., W. Harwich; 432-8240.

ORLEANS

- *Summer Recreation Program.* Town of Orleans; extensive summer program for residents and visitors; Monday through Friday, 9 A.M. until noon; games, track and field events, junior olympics; field trips, arts and crafts, other recreational activities. Boys' playground is at Eldredge Field (corner of Route 28 and Eldredge Parkway); girls' playground is at Orleans Elementary School. Registration is held daily. For more information, call Town Hall at 255-0900.
- *Apple Grove Miniature Golf,* 212 Main St. (next to Kadee's Lobster & Clam Bar, on the way to Nauset Beach); 255-6184.
- *Cape Escape Miniature Golf,* near Orleans Rotary; 240-1791.
- *Charles Moore Arena,* O'Connor Way; 255-2971. Roller skating or rollerblading in summer, ice skating the remainder of the year. Rock Night on Fridays for 9-14 year-olds. Call for information on activities.

WELLFLEET

- *Summer Center,* Chequessett Neck Rd.; 349-7456. Music, arts and crafts, children age four to nine, weekly enrollment.
- *Wellfleet Bay Sanctuary,* off Route 6; 349-2615. Massachusetts Audubon Society trails, exchibits (excellent facility).

Shops

Art Galleries

BREWSTER

- *Aries East Gallery,* Rte. 6A at Ellis Landing; 896-7681. Artist-owner Geoffrey Smith specializes in landscapes and sports scenes, featured artist for the Head of the Charles Regatta; also features other artists.
- *Maddocks Gallery,* 1283 Main St.; 896-6223. Beautiful gallery with works by Jim Maddocks.
- *The Ruddeforth Gallery,* 3753 Main St.; 255-1056. Watercolors and oils by Debra Ruddeforth and color photographs by Tom Ruddeforth.
- *Struna Gallery,* 3873 Main St.; 255-6618. Original watercolors and pen and ink by T.J. Struna.
- *The Spectrum of American Artists and Craftsmen,* 369 Old King's Hwy. (Rte. 6A); 385-3322. A wide selection from the work of more than 400 American artists and craftsmen.
- *Underground Art Gallery,* 673 Satucket Rd.; 896-3757 or 896-6850. One of Brewster's most popular artists, Karen North Wells has a unique gallery designed by her husband and architect, Malcolm Wells. Also includes furniture, books and puzzles.
- *Winstanley-Roark Fine Art,* 2759 Main St.; 896-1948. Features work by Robert K. Roark, Anita Winstanley Roark and others.

CHATHAM

- *Admiral's Gig,* 409 Main St.; 945-5338. Marine and coastal paintings, ship models, handcarved birds and fish.
- *Afterhouse Gallery,* at the Swinging Basket Shop, 483 Main St.; 945-7670. Antique and contemporary prints and posters, nauticals a specialty.
- *Paul Calvo Art Gallery,* 490 Main St.; 945-3932. Contemporary fine arts.
- *Cape House Pottery,* 17 Balfour Lane (behind Pate's Restaurant on Rte. 28 in West Chatham); 945-1027. Decorative pottery, paintings of local area, handcrafted mirrors.
- *Creative Arts Center,* 154 Crowell Rd.; 945-3583. Photographs and prints.
- *Hearle Gallery,* 488 Main St.; 945-2406. Variety offered.
- *Tom Johnson Photography,* Gallery at Old Scrimshaw Leather Shop, 616 Main St.; 945-1911. Splendid photographs of the Cape.
- *Falconer Art Studio,* 492 Main St.; 945-2867. Watercolors and oil paintings.
- *Lighthouse Gallery,* 3 Main St. (next to Chatham Light); 945-9295. Cape Cod scenes in watercolors and oils; lighthouse paintings.
- *Munson Gallery,* in an old barn on Main St.; 945-2888. Prints and paintings.
- *Odells,* 423 Main St.; 945-3239. Artist-owned-and-operated gallery, original jewelry and fine metal work by Tom Odell, paintings and mixed media drawings by Carol Odell.

HARWICH
- *Guild of Harwich Artists,* 49 Lower Bank St., Harwich Port Library; 430-0410. Art is shown every fair Monday in Wheeler Park at Harwich Post Office; works by artists of the guild are on exhibit.
- *Just Africa Gallery,* 586 Main St., Harwich Port; 432-8098. Stone sculpture.
- *Roberta Ann Hogan Gallery,* 517 Rte. 28; 432-0435. Watercolors, oils, gifts, jewelry.
- *Private Collection Gallery,* 515 Rte. 28; 430-0303. Watercolors, photography, ceramics.

ORLEANS
- *Academy Gallery,* Academy of Performing Arts, Main St.; 255-1963. Variety offered.
- *The Artful Hand Gallery of American Artists and Craftsmen,* Main Street; 255-2969. Contemporary arts and crafts.
- *Exposure,* 46 Main St.; 255-6808. Photographs of Cape Cod, variety offered.
- *New Horizons,* Rte. 28; 255-8766. Crafts from all over the country are exhibited regularly.
- *Orleans Art Gallery,* intersection of Rock Harbor and Namskaket (Myrick) rds.; 255-2645. Contemporary realism; works by lesser-known American masters of the 19th and 20th centuries; other paintings, prints, and woodblocks are exhibited. Great gallery!
- *Orleans Town Hall Gallery,* basement of Town Hall off Main Street heading to Nauset Beach; 255-0900. Shows given by members of the Orleans Art Association.
- *Peacock's Pride Art Gallery,* Peacock Alley, Rte. 28; 255-6396. A collection of paintings, on exhibit are the works of Judy Knowles, Marilyn Chace Schofield, Sara Young-Pennypacker, Angela Zoni Mault, and Rosalie Stambler Nadeau. Don't miss it!
- *Pott's Gallery,* Rte. 28 and 6A; 240-3934. Specializing in limited editions of wildlife and nature prints.
- *Spindrift Pottery,* Rte. 6A; 255-1404. Watercolors, photography and pottery.
- *Tree's Place,* Rte. 6A and Rte. 28 intersection; 255-1330. A collection of contemporary New England artists' work and imported arts and crafts. Another sure bet!

WELLFLEET
- *Blake Gallery,* Main St.; 349-6631. Jewelry, paintings, pottery, blown glass, woven clothing, and accessories.
- *Blue Heron Gallery,* Bank St.; 349-6724. A fine art gallery representing more than 30 artists.
- *Cape Impressions Gallery,* Main St.; 349-6479. Over 100 crafts-people represented; oils, watercolors and prints.
- *Cherry Stone Gallery,* E. Commercial St.; 349-3026. Photographs and variety offered.
- *Cottontail Gallery,* Rte. 6; 349-2462. Cape Cod artists.
- *Cove Gallery,* Commercial St.; 349-2530. Variety offered.
- *The Hopkins Group Gallery,* Main St. and Holbrook Ave.; 349-7246. Variety offered.
- *Jacob Fanning Gallery,* Bank Square on Bank St.; 349-9546. Variety offered.
- *Kendall Art Gallery,* E. Main St.; 349-2482. Variety offered.
- *Left Bank Gallery,* Commercial St.; 349-9451. Variety offered.

Crafts & Specialty Shops

BREWSTER

- *The Brewster Bookstore,* Rte. 6A; 896-6543. Books, cards, puzzles, toys.
- *The Brewster Store,* at intersection of Rtes. 6A and 124; 896-3744. Authentic general store—everything from crafts to newspapers and candy. Worth a visit, even if you don't buy anything. Enjoy morning coffee with the locals on the front sitting porch.
- *Brewster Gift Shop,* Rte. 6A; 896-3466. Dinnerware, crystal, and china.
- *Bayview Gallery,* Rte. 6A; 896-6920. Special gifts, antiques, and floral design (silk flowers).
- *Brewster Pottery,* at corner of Rte. 124 and Tubman Rd. (look for sign); 896-3587. Assorted pottery.
- *Countree Sampler,* 84 Underpass Rd.; 896-4330. Country furnishings and home decor.
- *The Cook Shop,* 1097 Main St. (Rte. 6A); 896-7698. Kitchen things, especially for the gourmet.
- *Clayton's Clay Works,* 3820 Main St., Rte. 6A. Assorted potters, works in porcelain, stoneware and terra cotta.
- *Handcraft Shop,* Rte. 6A at Vesper Pond Rd.; 240-1412. Watercolors, pottery, candles, jewelry. Features artist-owner Eileen Smith's work, as well as a gallery for fine artisans in New England and throughout the country.
- *Heart Pottery,* 1145 Rte. 6A; 896-6189. Porcelain, raku pots, seaweed-fixed pots.
- *Hesperus Pottery,* 1603 Main St.; 896-4440. Assorted pottery.
- *Hopkins House,* 2727 Main St.; 896-9337. A delightful shop with an Americana and folk art emphasis. Special touches by artist and owner Mary Beth Baxter. The garden leading into her shop is an enchanting and award-winning entrance. Don't miss her bakery on premises.
- *Linda's Originals,* Rte. 6A; 385-2285. Hand-crafted gifts, country furniture, lace curtains, good variety.
- *Lemon Tree Village,* Rte. 6A. Although Brewster doesn't have the main street shopping advantage of a Chatham or Osterville, the shopping along 6A is worth the stops. But if you want to park the car in one spot, this shopping village is a good one. Included here are: La Bodega, a unique clothing and jewelry store; Cook's Shop, with everything for the kitchen and more; Blue Heron Bookshop, Hayley's Hideout, a children's clothing store, Artisan's Window, a cooperative gallery featuring works of 10 varied artists; Sola Gallery II, art work by Cape artists, sculptures, and Lavender Lady for some different gifts. Across the street is Period Antiques and next door is Café Alfresco where you can have a cappuccino, pastries or a light snack.
- *The Strawberry Patch,* Rte. 6A; 896-5050. Handmade gifts, great for kids, too. Run by the same family that owns the Brewster Store.
- *The Spectrum of American Artists and Craftsmen,* Rte. 6A; 385-3322. Crafts, paintings, graphics, photography, and sculpture.
- *Sydenstricker Galleries,* Rte. 6A; 385-3272. Assorted offerings, unique glassware.
- *TC Mullin Glassworks,* 2005 Rte. 6A; 896-2434. Unique glassworks by owner-artist Tom Mullin. Stop next door at the Wobbly Barn Gallery to see paintings and custom furniture.

- *Town Ho Needleworks,* at the corner of Rtes. 6A and 124; 896-3000. Needlepoint, other offerings (worth a visit).
- *Yankee Craftsman,* Rte. 6A; 385-4758. Next door to Linda's Originals, their new addition. Country furniture and crafts.

CHATHAM

- *The Artful Hand,* 459 Main St.; 945-4933. Contemporary arts and crafts, stores in Orleans and Boston, voted "Best of Boston" by *Boston* magazine. A unique shopping adventure.
- *Blumen Laden,* 612 Main St.; 945-9263. Assorted crafts.
- *Cabbages and Kings Bookstore,* 628 Main St.; 945-1603. A delightful bookstore at the end of Main St. near the rotary. Specializing in children's literature, toys and cards. A great spot to browse or to get help from the knowledgeable owners.
- *Calico Cat,* 193 Main St.; 945-1192. Unique and assorted crafts.
- *Cape Cod Craftsman,* 610 Main St.; 945-2474. Assorted crafts.
- *Chatham Nature Shoppe,* 637C Main St.; 945-7700. Gifts, nature themes, great store for kids.
- *The Children's Shop,* 515 Main St.; 945-0234. Attractive clothing for children, infants to 16.
- *Christmas Joy of Cape Cod,* 2624 Main St. (Rte. 28); 432-3810. Christmas ornaments, gifts, and crafts.
- *Coach & Four of Chatham,* 645 Main St.; 945-2335. Gifts, fudge, candy.
- *The Duck Blind,* 483 Main St.; 945-2626. For shore bird and waterfowl enthusiasts.
- *Foster's,* 400 Main St.; 945-1485. Decorator fabrics, other offerings, good prices.
- *Frillz,* 484 Main St.; 945-4054. Unique hand-painted women's clothing.
- *Gallery at Chatham,* 595 Main St.; 945-5449. Fine arts and crafts.
- *Lion's Paw,* Main St.; 945-4729. Beautiful gifts, variety of unique items.
- *The Mayflower,* 475 Main St.; 945-0065. Boston, New York newspapers, gifts, and souvenirs.
- *Noel, Noel,* 400A Main St.; 945-3547. Unique gifts.
- *Old Scrimshaw Leather,* 616 Main St.; 945-1911. Handcrafted leather goods.
- *Palais Royal,* 471 Main St.; 945-5562. Clothing, antiques and fine linens.
- *The Peddler's Porch,* 1238 Main St.; 945-7601. Over 200 local artisans display their crafts.
- *Pentimento,* 584 Main St.; 945-0178. Assorted and unusual crafts and goods.
- *The Sail Loft,* Bridge St. (near Mill Pond); 945-0555. Distinctive clothing for men and women.
- *Simpler Pleasures,* 433 Main St.; 945-4040. Fabrics and antiques.
- *The Rose Cottage Shop,* 1281 Main St.; 945-3114. Antiques, marine art, European country pine.
- *Tale of the Cod,* 450 Main St.; 945-0347. Considered one of the Cape's best and most unique gift shops, family run.
- *Wayside Gallery,* 512 Main St.; 945-0749. Located at the Wayside Inn, a fun and eclectic shop, lots of whimsical gifts, jewelry. You should find something memorable here!
- *Wee Three,* 2334 Main St.; 432-7464. Dolls, doll houses, accessories.
- *The White Unicorn,* 216 Orleans Rd.; 945-1730. Quilts, needlework, art, other.

EASTHAM

- *Collector's World,* Rte. 6; 255-3616. Unique gift shop.
- *Colonial Stoneware Trading Company,* 2390 Rte. 6; 240-7687. Reproductions of colonial pottery of the 1740–1800's period, visitors can listen to these owner-artists who wear colonial dress and tell the history behind the pottery they make.
- *Fabric Basket,* Rte. 6; 255-8909. Fabrics.
- *Glass Eye,* Rte. 6; 255-5044. Stained glass.
- *Grandmother's Attic,* 4205 Rte. 6, N. Eastham; 255-7789. Children's books, workshops.
- *Kate's Klassics,* off Rte. 6; 255-3733. Assorted crafts.
- *Ship's Lantern Village,* 655 Massasoit Rd., N. Eastham; 255-3843. Gifts, handcrafts.
- *Sunken Meadow Basketworks and Pottery,* North Sunken Meadow Rd., N. Eastham; 255-8962. Handwoven baskets and wall hangings; stoneware.
- *Tory Hill III,* corner of Massasoit and Oak Rd., just off Rte. 6; 240-0026. Antiques.

HARWICH

- *Adventures in Knitting,* 557 Main St., Harwich Port; 432-3700. Everything for the knitter.
- *Allen Harbor Nautical Gifts,* 335 Lower County Rd.; 432-0353. Wind and weather indicators.
- *Arleese,* 121 Main St., W. Harwich; 430-2159. Gifts, antiques, "all things cranberry."
- *Cinnamon Stick,* 537 Main St., Harwich Port; 432-3071. Country items, pottery, dolls.
- *Harwich Commons,* Rte. 137 & 39, at the Stop & Shop plaza, there is a collection of shops, including Talbot's and Orvis.
- *Pleasant Lake General Store,* Rte. 124; 432-5305. General merchandise, just off the bike trail.
- *The Port-O-Call Gift House,* 520 Main St., Harwich Port; 432-1525. Assorted offerings.
- *The Potted Geranium,* 188 Main St. (Rte. 28); 432-1114. Assorted offerings, handicrafts.
- *Southwest Trading Post,* Rte. 28; 430-5128. For those who didn't make it to the southwest last winter, here's your chance to find those Kachina dolls, Indian jewelry and pottery.

ORLEANS

- *Ania Home & Garden Boutique,* 80 Rte. 6A; 240-3446. Accessories, gifts, floral arrangements.
- *Artful Hand Gallery,* Main Street Square; 255-2969. Crafts and art.
- *Bird Watchers General Store,* Rte. 6A; 255-6974. Equipment and information for bird-watchers.
- *Brushstrokes,* 37 Main St.; 255-3355. Tile tables, clocks, painted furniture, fine arts and crafts.
- *Cape Cod Photo & Art Supply,* 38 Main St.; 255-0476. Stores in Chatham and Provincetown; complete line of art supplies, cameras, film, and other accessories.
- *Cape Light,* 46 Main St. (next to whole foods store); 255-5202. Custom and fine art photographic printmaking (excellent, stop by!).

- ***Christmas Tree Shop,*** at corner of Rtes. 6A and 28; 255-8494. Something for everyone, crafts, gifts, toys, furniture.
- ***Compass Rose Book Shop,*** Main St.; 255-1545. Great selection of books, cards, games, and stationery.
- ***Duck Soup,*** 50 Main St.; 240-3620. Gifts, folk art, collectibles.
- ***Goose Hummock,*** Rte. 6A (overlooking Town Cove, next to Orleans Inn); 255-0455. Marine and sporting goods store, boat rentals.
- ***Head & Foot,*** 42 Main St.; 255-1281. Stores in Chatham and Provincetown; men's and women's clothing at discount prices (some good buys here).
- ***The Herbary and Potpourri,*** Childs Homestead off Namskaket Rd.; 255-4422. Herbs, spices, vinegars, plants, teas.
- ***Maglebee's,*** Main St.; 255-3004. Women's clothing, accessories.
- ***Nauset Sports,*** off Rte. 6A (Jeremiah Square); 255-4742. Complete line of sporting goods and rentals, from softball to sailboarding.
- ***New Horizons,*** Rte. 28; 255-8766. Assorted crafts.
- ***Oceana,*** One Main St. Square; 240-1414. Located behind Off the Bay Café, this is a shop you should not miss. Gifts are exquisitely displayed, the emphasis is on ocean life and nature—a natural for Cape Cod.
- ***Orleans Carpenters,*** Commerce Dr.; 255-2646. Shaker reproductions.
- ***Puritan Clothing,*** off Rte. 6A in Orleans Shopping Plaza; 255-2800. Stores in Hyannis, Dennisport, Chatham, Falmouth, Wellfleet, and Mashpee; quality clothes for men and women, good selection.
- ***Ragg Time, Ltd.,*** 46 Main St.; 240-0925. Women's casual, comfortable clothing.
- ***Anne C. Ross Glass,*** Commerce Drive and Finlay Rd. (behind Daniel's Car Wash); 240-0510. Gifts and tableware.
- ***Spindrift Pottery,*** Rte. 6A; 255-1404. Assorted pottery.
- ***Through the Looking Glass,*** Rte. 6A; 240-0401. Quality children's clothing, toys, and books; they hold story hours for children during the summer.
- ***Tree's Place,*** at corner of Rtes. 6A and 28; 255-1330. Pottery, ceramic tile, artwork, jewelry, gifts (worth a look).
- ***Watson's Clothing,*** Main St.; 255-3003. Complete line of quality clothes and shoes.
- ***Westie's Shoe Outlet,*** 30 Main St.; 255-7137. Yes, shoes.
- ***Wheel Haus Nautiques & Gifts,*** 2 Academy Place; 255-1586. Ship models, nautical theme gifts, hand-knit sweaters and a children's corner.

TRURO

- ***Whitman House Gift Shop,*** Rte. 6; 487-1740. Quilts, assorted gifts.

WELLFLEET

- ***Abiyoyo,*** Main St.; 349-3422. Artistic T's, creative toys amd unique gifts.
- ***Blake Gallery Contemporary Arts & Crafts,*** Main St.; 349-6631. Contemporary arts and crafts.
- ***The Boathouse,*** Holbrook Ave.; 349-6417. Summerwear.
- ***The Corner Cape,*** 1 Bank St. (Bank Square); 349-9694. Jewelry, crafts, antiques.
- ***Higgins House Ltd.,*** 3 Main St.; 349-7405. Women's clothes.
- ***Jules Besch Gallery,*** 275 Main St.; 349-1231. Stationery, cards, decorative arts.
- ***Living Arts,*** Main St.; 349-9803. Assorted crafts.
- ***Ragg Time, Ltd.,*** Bank Square; 349-2122. Women's casual clothing.

WELLFLEET (CONTINUED)

- *Salt Marsh Pottery,* E. Main St.; 349-3342. Assorted crafts.
- *The Secret Garden,* Main St.; 349-1444. Accessories for home and garden, bird feeders, eclectic variety—a great store.
- *Wellfleet Flea Market,* Rte. 6, at the Wellfleet Drive-In; 349-2520 or 800-696-FLEA. A seasonal adventure from April through the fall. Those who go, rave! Snack bar and playground too.
- *Wellfleet Pottery,* Commercial St.; 349-6679. Country china, assorted pottery and crafts.

Antiques

BREWSTER

- *Barbara Grant Antiques & Books,* 1793 Main St. (Rte. 6A between Rte. 137 and Rte. 124 intersections); 896-7198. Books, furniture, antiques.
- *Baxter Antiques,* Rte. 6A; 896-3998. Assorted antiques.
- *Breton House,* 1222 Stony Brook Rd. (off Rte. 6A); 896-3974.
- *William Brewster Antiques,* 2912 Main; 896-4816. Antiques include a wide variety of items that includes furniture, clocks, mirrors.
- *Countree Sampler,* 84 Underpass Rd.; 896-4330. Slightly off the antique path of 6A, this shop is worth the stop for new, used or antique furniture.
- *Donald B. Howes,* Rte. 6A (opposite Fire Museum); 896-3502. Paintings, books, assorted antiques; appointment recommended.
- *Huckleberry's Antiques,* 2271 Main St.; 896-7189. Accessories, rugs, furniture, linens.
- *Kingsland Manor Antiques,* Rte. 6A; 385-9741. Beautiful antique store. You can't miss the impatiens here in the summer!
- *King's Way Antiques,* 774 Main St. (opposite windmill); 896-3639. Assorted antiques, quilts, fur.
- *Monomoy Antiques,* 3425 Main St. (Rte. 6A and Crosby Ln.); 896-6570. Assorted antiques.
- *Packet Antiques,* Stony Brook Rd. (near Our Lady of the Cape Catholic Church); 385-3189. Assorted antiques.
- *Pepper House Antiques,* Rte. 6A; 896-3304. Assorted antiques.
- *The Pflock's Antiques,* 598 Main St.; 896-3457. Furniture, copper, brass, nautical antiques.
- *Pink Cadillac Antiques,* 3140 Main St.; 896-4651. Specializes in Depression era glass, pottery, china and other collectibles from the 20's to the 50's. Look for the pink Cadillac out front!
- *Rocking Chair Antiques,* 1379 Main St.; 896-7389. Assorted antiques, doll house miniatures; appointment recommended.
- *The 1661 House,* 2727 Main St.; 896-6565. Assorted antiques.
- *Edward Snow House Antiques,* 2042 Main St.; 896-2929. Early American antiques, formal furniture, collectibles.
- *Sunsmith House Antiques and Books,* 2926 Main St. (across from Ocean Edge); 896-7024. Country furniture, toys, books.
- *Tymeless Antiques and Art Gallery,* 3811 Main St.; 255-9404. Native American items, country pine and oak, baskets, pottery and watercolors by Tom Stringe.
- *Van Gogh's Chair,* 1215 Main St.; 896-1969. French country arts, kitchenware, tools.
- *Yankee Trader,* 2071 Main St. (Rte. 6A); 896-7822. Assorted antiques.

CHATHAM

- *The Afterhouse & Garden Café*, at the Swinging Basket, 483 Main St.; 945-7670. Assorted antiques.
- *Bayberry Antiques,* 300 Orleans Rd.; 945-9060. Americana, toys, folk art.
- *Chapdelaine Antiques,* 400 Main St.; 945-1511. Folk art, country furniture, crystal, quilts.
- *Chatham Antiques,* 1409 Main St.; 945-1660 or 398-2561. Assorted antiques.
- *House on the Hill Antiques,* 17 Seaview St.; 945-2290. Toys, assorted antiques, nostalgia.
- *The Little House,* 2523 Main St.; 432-4411. Assorted antiques, furniture.
- *Old Harbor House,* 402 Main St.; 945-4669. Assorted antiques.
- *Simpler Pleasures,* 433 Main St.; 945-4040. Assorted antiques.
- *Spyglass Nautical Antiques,* 618 Main St.; 945-9686. Marine antiques and nautical instruments.
- *Wayne's Antiques,* 1300 Main St.; 945-4265. Assorted antiques.
- *Windsor Antiques,* 400 Main St.; 945-4343. English antique furniture and accessories; handmade Windsor chairs a specialty.
- *Yankee Ingenuity,* 525 Main St.; 945-1288. Brass, copper, and assorted antiques.

EASTHAM

- *The Birches Antiques,* Depot Rd.; 240-1936. Assorted antiques, furniture.
- *Quail Song Antiques,* by appointment only; 255-4968. China, lamps, assorted antiques.

HARWICH

- *The Carriage Shop,* Parallel St.; 432-0201. Gifts, gallery, assorted antiques.
- *Ralph Diamond Antiques,* 103 Main St.; 432-0634. Assorted antiques; by appointment.
- *Mariner House Antiques,* 457 Lower County Rd.; 432-9400. Assorted antiques.
- *New-to-You Shop,* 543 Main St.; 432-1158. Assorted antiques.
- *Poor Ginnie's Cache,* 27 Main St.; 432-6979. Assorted antiques.
- *Seven South Street Antiques,* 7 South St.; 432-4366 or 432-1525. Antique silver, jewelry, china.
- *Patti Smith Antiques,* 51 Parallel St.; 432-3927. Decorated stoneware.
- *Windsong Antiques,* 245 Bank St.; 432-8281. Formal and country antiques, silver, jewelry.
- *House of Morgan,* 546 Main St.; 432-0595. Assorted antiques.

ORLEANS

- *Continuum,* 7 Rte. 28; 255-8513. Antique lamps and lighting.
- *Countryside Antiques,* 6 Lewis Rd.; 240-0525. Assorted antiques.
- *Lilli's Antique Emporium,* Rte. 6A; 255-8300. Bayberry Square, glassware, assorted antiques.
- *Lilac Hedge Antiques,* 12 West Rd.; 255-1684. Assorted antiques.
- *Peacock Alley Antiques,* 35 Rte. 28; 240-1804. Victorian arts as well as 50's paraphernalia.
- *Pleasant Bay Antiques,* 540 Chatham Rd.; 255-0930. Assorted antiques, early American.

WELLFLEET

- *Farmhouse Antiques,* Rte. 6 and Village Lane; 349-1708. Multi-dealer shop, 2000 plus square feet.

WELLFLEET (continued)

- *Mortar & Pestle Antiques,* Rte. 6 (next to Bay Sails); 349-2574. Country furniture, early American, microscopes.
- *Dorothy Watson Antiques,* 17 School St.; 349-9207. Jewelry, silver, china.
- *Trading Post,* E. Commercial (opposite Gull Pond Rd.); 349-6006. Assorted antiques.

Sports & Recreation

Boating

Each town has numerous landings, some with parking available. Call town halls (phone numbers listed on Page 171) for locations.

Here is a listing of places where you can rent boats, sailboards, and surfboards:
- *Arey's Pond,* 43 Arey's Lane, South Orleans; 255-0994. Sailing instructions, full-service boat yard.
- *Art Gould's Boat Livery*—"The Water Taxi," Chatham Fish Pier; 430-2346. Rides to North Beach, South Beach or Monomoy Island. Harbor tours and seal tours, can fit your schedule.
- *Bay Sails Marine,* Rte. 6, Wellfleet; 349-3840.
- *Chatham Harbor and Pleasant Bay Tours,* Chatham Fish Pier; 255-0619. Narrated tours out of Chatham, complimentary steamers.
- *Chatham Sailing Club,* Stage Harbor Rd., Chatham; 945-1899.
- *Cinnamon Rainbow Surf Company,* 9 Rte. 6A, Orleans; 255-5832 or 800-540-5832.
- *Jack's Boat Rental and Aqua Ventures,* Brewster; 896-8556 or Wellfleet; 349-7553.
- *Jasper's Surf Shop,* Rte. 6, Eastham; 255-2662.
- *Monomoy Sail & Cycle,* Orleans Rd., Chatham; 945-0811.
- *Nauset Sports,* Rte. 6A (Jeremiah Square near the Orleans Rotary), Orleans; 255-4742.
- *Offshore Water Sports,* Chatham Fish Pier; 945-5700. Waverunner and sea-doo rentals.
- *Small Boat Service,* Wellfleet Town Pier, Wellfleet; 349-9680.
- *Yankee Deep Sea Fishing Parties,* Saquatucket Harbor, Harwich Port; 432-2520.
- *Wellfleet Marine,* Wellfleet Town Pier, Wellfleet; 349-2233.
- *Cape Cod Paddle Adventures,* Brewster; 896-2610. Guided canoe and kayak tours into habitats of wildlife on Cape Cod.
- *Cape Cod Museum of Natural History,* 896-3867. The Museum offers Nauset Marsh cruises aboard a glass-bottom boat and an on-board aquarium, as well as various trips out to Monomoy Island. Canoe trips around the Cape are also run by the museum. Call for more information and reservations.
- *Cape Water Sports,* Rte. 28, Harwich Port; 432-7079. Rentals of sailboats, wind surfers, canoes, Hobie Cats and power boats; lessons available.
- *Seashore Park Boat Tours,* 240-3100. Tours through the coves, creeks and marshes of Cape Cod National Seashore.
- *"Sabbatical,"* out of Saquatucket Harbor; 432-3416. Sunset trips, half- or full-day trips aboard this 31-foot sailboat.

• *"Tiger Too,"* out of Stage Harbor; 945-9215. Fishing for bass and blues, tackle furnished.

Fishing

The Outer Cape offers some of the best salt- and freshwater fishing in the country. Anglers have their choice of the Atlantic, Cape Cod Bay, Nantucket Sound, Pleasant Bay, Cape Cod Canal, and scores of fresh- and saltwater rivers and ponds.

For deep-sea charter fishing we recommend the *Rock Harbor Charter Boat Service* in Rock Harbor, Orleans, 255-9757 or 800-287-1771 (the service represents all the charter boats in the harbor), and *Yankee Deep Sea Fishing Parties* in Harwich Port's Saquatucket Harbor, 432-2520.

If you're looking to buy a new rod and reel or you just want to look, we suggest the following fishing tackle dealers:
• *Black Duck Sports Shop*, off Rte. 6, S. Wellfleet; 349-9801.
• *Cliff's Bait & Tackle*, off Rte. 28, Chatham; 945-3228.
• *Goose Hummock Shop,* Rte. 6A, Orleans; 255-0455.
• *"Luau,"* N. Eastham; 255-4527. Fiberglass sport fisherman, bluefish and stripers.
• *MacSquid's,* 85 Lowell Square, Orleans; 240-0778. Fishing tackle.
• *Nauset Tackle & Hardware,* Rte. 6, Eastham; 255-7158.
• *"Navigator,"* Wellfleet Town Pier; 349-6003. Fishing as well as sunset cruises and special charters.
• *"Nekton,"* Rock Harbor, Orleans; 255-1289. Sport fishing charters.
• *"Osprey,"* Rock Harbor, Orleans; 255-1266.
• *Wellfleet Marine,* Town Pier, Wellfleet; 349-6578.

Golf

BREWSTER
• *Captains' Course,* 1000 Freeman's Way; 896-5100. Par 72, 6794 yards; *Golf Digest* called it the best new public course in America the year it opened.
• *Ocean Edge,* off Rte. 6A; 896-5911. Par 72, 6581 yards; challenging course; New England PGA Championships held here.

CHATHAM
• *Chatham Seaside Links,* Seaside St., next to Chatham Bars Inn; 945-4774. Public 9-hole course, lessons, magnificent views.

HARWICH
• *Cranberry Valley,* off Oak St.; 430-7560. Par 72, 6745 yards; every bit as good as the Captains' Course!
• *Harwich Port Golf Club,* off Forest Rd.; 432-0250. Nine holes, par 35, 2643 yards.

TRURO
• *Highland Golf Links,* off Highland Rd.; 487-9201. Nine holes, par 36, 3069 yards; like Chatham Bars and Chequessett, play this one for the scenery. Ocean views!

WELLFLEET
• *Chequessett Yacht & Country Club,* Chequessett Neck Rd.; 349-3704. Nine holes, par 35, 3000 yards; pretty course.

Biking

Most of these bike shops are on or near the Rail Trail and there are convenient stores or sandwich shops to stop at for a snack. Be sure to try the Brewster Express on the trail.

BREWSTER
- *Brewster Bike,* 442 Underpass Rd.; 896-8149.
- *Idle Times Bike Shop,* Rte. 6A; 896-9242.
- *Rail Trail Bike Shop,* 302 Underpass Rd.; 896-8200. Next to Mano's Pizza where you can pick up lunch or a snack.
- *Palmer Bicycle Shop,* 454 Main St.; 385-9044.

CHATHAM
- *Bert and Carol's*, 347 Orleans Rd.; 945-0137. Bike rentals.
- *Bikes and Blades*, 195 Crowell Rd.; 945-7600. Bikes, inline skates, biking apparel and accessories.

EASTHAM
- *The Little Capistrano Bike Shop,* Salt Pond Rd.; 255-6515.
- *Idle Times Bike Shop,* Rte. 6; 255-8281.

HARWICH
- *Harwich Port Bike Co.*, Rte. 28 next to the 400 Club; 430-0200. Bike and inline skate rentals.

ORLEANS
- *Orleans Cycle,* 52 Main St.; 255-9115.

WELLFLEET
- *Idle Times Bike Shop,* Rte. 6; 349-9161.

Hiking & Nature Trails

- *Nickerson State Park,* Rte. 6A, Brewster; 896-4615. Trails, camping, swimming (see listing under *Campgrounds*).
- *Cape Cod Museum of Natural History,* Rte. 6A, Brewster; 896-3867. Marsh and beach trails, workshops and exhibits (see listing under *Museums & Historic Sites*).
- *Cape Cod National Seashore,* 349-3785 (headquarters). See listing under *National Seashore.*

Also, pick up a copy of *Short Walks on Cape Cod and the Vineyard* by Hugh and Heather Sadlier, published by Globe Pequot Press; it's one of the best hiking books on the market.

Spectator Sports

Cape Cod is home to the *Cape Cod Baseball League*, one of the top college summer leagues in the country. It is financed, in part, by the major leagues. Orleans, Chatham, Harwich, and Brewster have teams. For times and places of the games, check the *Cape Codder* sports pages and the *Cape Cod Times.*

Cape Cod is home to the *Cape Cod Amateur Soccer League*, a top summer college league; and the *Cape Cod Lacrosse League*. Check the newspapers for game schedules.

Tennis

Most towns have public tennis courts. We suggest you call the various town halls for locations. Here is a list of recommended private courts:
- *Bamburgh House,* off Rte. 6A, Brewster; 896-5023.
- *Chequessett Yacht & Country Club,* Chequessett Neck Rd., Wellfleet; 349-3704.
- *Brewster Courts,* Rte. 6A; 896-7110.
- *Manning's Tennis Courts,* off Rte. 28, W. Harwich; 432-3958.
- *Melrose Tennis Center,* 792 Main St., Harwich Port; 430-7012. Some clay courts, instruction.
- *Norsemen Athletic Club,* Rte. 6, N. Eastham; 255-6370.
- *Oliver's Clay Courts,* Rte. 6, Wellfleet; 349-3330.
- *Provincetown Tennis Club,* 286 Bradford St., Provincetown; 487-9574.
- *Provincetown Tennis & Yacht Club,* off Rte. 6, Provincetown; 487-0157.
- *Wellfleet Tennis Courts,* Kendrick Ave., Wellfleet; 349-0330.

Annual Outer Cape summer tennis tournaments include the following:
- *Chatham Junior Tournament,* in Chatham toward end of the summer; for more information, call 945-3163.
- *Mid Cape Open,* Mid Cape Racquet Club in Yarmouth, middle of the summer; for more information, call 394-3511.
- *Lower Cape Open,* Eldredge Park in Orleans, toward end of the summer; for more information, call 255-1921.
- *Year Rounders Tournament,* Provincetown Tennis Club, around July 4; for more information, call 487-9574.

Beaches

Public Beaches

Cape Cod National Seashore beaches are listed separately (starting on page 213). While all Seashore beaches provide lifeguards, most town beaches on the bay and on freshwater ponds do not.

BREWSTER

Beach stickers, available at Town Hall, are required for parking at all Brewster public beaches, with the exception of beaches on Nickerson State Park ponds. Summer visitors can purchase either daily stickers, weekly stickers, or seasonal stickers. Brewster residents, as in other Cape towns, are charged a nominal fee to use the beach and town dump. The beaches have toilets, but no lifeguards or food stands. Snack vans visit the beach regularly. For more information, call Town Hall at 896-3701.

Bay Side Beaches

These bay side beaches are all off Route 6A:
- *Breakwater Beach,* Breakwater Rd.
- *Crosby Landing,* Crosby Ln.

BREWSTER (CONTINUED)

- *Ellis Landing,* Ellis Landing Rd.
- *Linnell Landing,* Linnell Landing Rd.
- *Paine's Creek Beach,* Paine's Creek Rd.
- *Saint's Landing,* Robbins Hill Rd.
- *Robbins Hill Beach,* Robbins Hill Rd. Ext.

Freshwater Pond Beaches

- *Flax Pond, Cliff Pond, and Little Cliff Pond*, all in Nickerson State Park off Rte. 6A.
- *Long Pond,* Crowell's Bog Rd., off Rte. 124 near the Harwich line.
- *Sheep Pond,* off Rte. 124.
- *Slough Pond,* near the intersection of Slough and Red Top rds. (off Setucket Rd.).
- *Upper Mill Pond,* dirt parking area and a landing, end of Run Hill Rd.
- *Walkers Pond,* off Slough Rd. beyond Slough Pond.

CHATHAM

You have your choice in Chatham of beaches on the ocean, Nantucket Sound, Chatham's inner harbor, and fresh- and saltwater ponds. Beach stickers are required and can be purchased at Town Hall or at some of the beaches. Visitors can purchase daily, weekly, and seasonal stickers. For more information, call Town Hall, 945-2100. All town beaches have lifeguards, with the exception of Chatham Lighthouse Beach.

Ocean Beach

- *North Beach* spit, across from Chatham Lighthouse. Ferry service across Chatham Harbor located at the end of nearby Andrew Harding Lane.

Nantucket Sound

- *Hardings Beach,* Hardings Beach Rd., off Rte. 28 (the beach separates Oyster Creek and Stage Harbor, toilet facilities available.
- *Ridgevale Beach,* Ridgevale Beach Rd., off Rte. 28 (toilet facilities and snack bar).
- *Cockle Cove Beach,* Cockle Cove Beach Rd., off Rte. 28 (toilet facilities).

Inner Harbor

- *Chatham Lighthouse Beach,* Main St., across from the Coast Guard Station; plenty of parking, but current is dangerous; not a good beach for the children.

Saltwater Pond

- *Oyster Pond Beach,* off Stage Harbor Rd., not far from the center of town (Oyster Creek runs Nantucket Sound into pond); parking and toilet facilities nearby; swimming lessons available.

Freshwater Pond

- *Schoolhouse Pond Beach,* off Sam Ryder's Rd. and Old Comers Rd. (parking and restroom facilities available).

EASTHAM

All of Eastham's ocean beaches belong to the Cape Cod National Seashore (see separate listing), but the town has many beaches on the bay side and on freshwater ponds. Parking stickers, available at Town Hall, are required at town-run bay side and pond beaches. Visitors can purchase daily stickers, weekly stickers, two-week stickers, three-week stickers, four-week stickers, and seasonal stickers. For more information, call Town Hall, 255-0333.

Bay Side Beaches

These bay side beaches are all off Route 6 (see maps):
- *Campground Beach.*
- *Cooks Brook Beach* (toilet facilities).
- *First Encounter Beach.*
- *Sunken Meadow Beach.*
- *Thumpertown Beach.*
- *Cole Road Beach.*
- *Kingsbury Beach.*
- *Boat Meadow Beach.*
- *Herring Brook Landing.*

Freshwater Ponds

- *Herring Pond,* off Herring Brook Rd.
- *Great Pond,* off Great Pond Rd.
- *Wiley's Pond,* off Herring Brook Rd. (toilet facilities, picnic area, lifeguards).

HARWICH

With more than four uninterrupted miles of shoreline on Nantucket Sound, Harwich is a great place for swimming and sunbathing. The water here is warmer and calmer than the ocean; the Sound is sheltered by Monomoy Island, off the southern tip of Chatham, and by Nantucket, a little more than 20 miles off Harwich's coast. The town also has a beach on Pleasant Bay in East Harwich, and beaches at several of the ponds. Parking stickers, available at Brooks Academy in Harwich Center, are required at all the beaches. Summer visitors can purchase weekly stickers, two-week stickers, or seasonal stickers. One-day permits are available for *Red River Beach*. Red River is at the end of Uncle Vernie's Road or Old Wharf Road. For more information, call Town Hall, 432-0145. Other town beaches are as follows.

Nantucket Sound Beaches

- *Bank Street Beach,* at the end of Bank St. (within walking distance from Harwich Port Center; toilet facilities; one of the town's most popular beaches).
- *Pleasant Road* and *Earle Road* beaches, W. Harwich (both off Rte. 28). Pleasant Road Beach has toilet facilities.

Pleasant Bay

- *Pleasant Bay Beach,* off Rte. 28, E. Harwich (good beach for the children, but limited parking).

Freshwater Pond Beaches

There are two freshwater beaches on the 740-acre *Long Pond* (off Rte. 124); one on Long Pond Drive called *Fernandez Bog Beach* (with toilet facilities); and another on Cahoon Drive (off Long Pond Drive) called *Wixen Beach*.

There is also a freshwater beach at *Bucks Pond* on Bucks Pond Road (off Rte. 39) in East Harwich and one at *Sand Pond* off Great Western Road near Harwich Center.

ORLEANS

If you're looking for a good ocean beach outside the Cape Cod National Seashore, head to *Nauset Beach* on Beach Road in East Orleans. The parking here is ample, the access is easy, and there's a great clam shack (Liam's). Get there early. There are also public beaches on the bay and two freshwater pond beaches. For nonresidents, there's a daily parking fee at Nauset Beach. But visitors can purchase weekly stickers, two-week stickers, or seasonal stickers. Stickers are not required for the ponds. For more information, call Town Hall, 255-0900.

ORLEANS (CONTINUED)
Ocean Beach
• *Nauset Beach,* on Beach Rd., E. Orleans. Parking, snack bar, and toilet facilities available.
Bay Side Beach
• *Skaket Beach,* on Skaket Beach Rd. Parking, snack bar, and toilet facilities available.
Freshwater Ponds
• *Meetinghouse Pond,* on Barley Neck Rd. (also off Main St., not far from the Barley Neck Inn).
• *Pilgrim Pond,* on Monument Rd. (off Main St.).

TRURO
Beach stickers, available at the chamber of commerce building off Route 6, are required at all ocean, bay, and pond beaches run by Truro. *Head of the Meadow* is the only ocean beach in Truro run by the Cape Cod National Seashore. There are no lifeguards on the town's beaches. Visitors can purchase two-week stickers, four-week stickers, and seasonal stickers. For more information, call Town Hall, 349-3635.
Ocean Beaches
Ocean beaches (all off Rte. 6) are *Ballston; Longnook; Coast Guard.*
Bay Side Beaches
Bay side beaches listed below are off Route 6:
• *Corn Hill Beach,* off Corn Hill Rd.
• *Great Hollow Beach,* off Great Hollow Rd.
• *Fisher Beach,* off Fisher Rd.
• *Ryder Beach,* off Ryder Rd.
• *Beach Point.*
• *Pond Village.*

WELLFLEET
Unlike Eastham, all of Wellfleet's ocean beaches (ironically some of Cape Cod's prettiest) are run by the town, not the Cape Cod National Seashore, with the exception of *Marconi Beach.* Stickers are required for most of Wellfleet's ocean, bay, and pond beaches. Visitors can purchase daily permits for ocean beaches and for Mayo Beach on the bay. Summer visitors can purchase weekly stickers, two-week stickers, and seasonal passes. Wellfleet also has some of the prettiest ponds on the Cape. For more information, call Town Hall, 349-3707.
Ocean Beaches
• *Maguire's Landing,* (also called Lecount Hollow Beach) off Lecount Hollow Rd.
• *White Crest Beach* (also called Four Mile Beach, the surfers' beach), off Ocean View Dr. (lifeguards, snack bar, rest rooms).
• *Cahoon Hollow Beach,* off Ocean View Dr. (lifeguards, snack bar, rest rooms).
• *Newcomb Hollow Beach,* off Ocean View Dr. (lifeguards, snack bar, rest rooms).
Bay Side Beaches
Bay side beaches are all near the harbor:
• *Duck Harbor,* toilet facilities.
• *Indian Neck.*
• *Mayo Beach,* toilet facilities.
• *Powers Landing.*

Freshwater Ponds
- *Great Pond,* off Cahoon Hollow Rd. (no public parking available).
- *Gull Pond,* off Gull Pond Rd. (no public parking available).
- *Long Pond,* off Long Pond Rd. (no public parking available).

Cape Cod National Seashore

PROTECTED BEACHES

There are six protected ocean beaches within the Cape Cod National Seashore—all with parking and bathhouse facilities. Nominal parking fees are charged. All of the beaches are located off Route 6. Maps are available at the visitor centers. The beaches are as follows:

Eastham
Coast Guard Beach, at the end of Doane Rd.; *Nauset Light Beach,* at the end of Cable Rd.

Provincetown
Race Point Beach, at the end of Race Point Rd.; *Herring Cove Beach,* off Province Lands Rd.

Truro
Head of the Meadow Beach, at the end of Head of the Meadow Rd.

Wellfleet
Marconi Beach, beyond the Cape Cod National Seashore headquarters.

VISITOR CENTERS

There are two visitor centers at the Cape Cod National Seashore equipped with brochures, exhibits, slide presentations, and rangers to answer all your questions. The two centers are the *Salt Pond Visitor Center* in Eastham off Route 6 at the Seashore's front gate (255-3421); and the *Province Lands Visitor Center* off Race Point Road in Provincetown (487-1256).

BICYCLE TRAILS

There are three marked bicycle trails within the Seashore—the 1.6-mile Nauset Trail in Eastham, the 2-mile Head of the Meadow Trail in Truro, and the 5-plus-mile Province Lands Trail in Provincetown. Maps are available at the visitor centers.

Something about the trails:

• The *Nauset Trail* starts at the Salt Pond Visitor Center parking area in Eastham and runs down to Coast Guard Beach. You can also gain access at the Doane Rock picnic area, the halfway point. The trail takes you up hills and through meadows where the Nauset Indians once lived.

• The *Head of the Meadow Trail* starts on High Head Road in Truro and runs along a salt marsh toward Head of the Meadow Beach. You can also gain access at Head of the Meadow Beach parking area. Not far from the trail is Pilgrim Lake and Pilgrim Spring where the Pilgrims in 1620 drank their first fresh water in the New World.

• The *Province Lands Trail* starts at the Province Lands Visitor Center parking area, loops around a series of kettle ponds, and runs down to the Old Harbor Station at Race Point Beach and out toward Herring Cove Beach. You can also gain access at the Beech Forest parking area, the Race Point Beach parking area, the Herring Cove Beach parking area, and Race Point Road, not far from Route 6. You don't have to peddle the full five miles.

RANGER-GUIDED ACTIVITIES

The Cape Cod National Seashore offers a number of ranger-guided activities and self-guiding nature trails, ranging from a quarter mile to four miles. The trails are open year-round. (The following information was provided by the Cape Cod National Seashore.)

Eastham

Call Salt Pond Visitor Center, 255-3421, for times and starting places of the following activities:

• *Birds of the Beach,* three hours, three miles. Introduction to terns, plovers, and other birds of the beach and their nesting habits. Bring binoculars. Reservations necessary.

• *Early Bird Walks,* two hours, one mile. An introduction to the birds of Cape Cod and their habitats. Bring binoculars. Reservations necessary.

• *Great Beach Walk,* one and one-half hours, one mile. Walk along the outer beach with a park ranger. Learn about the geology of Cape Cod and factors that limit plant and animal life at the edge of the sea.

• *Outermost Walk,* three hours, three miles. Follow along Nauset Marsh in the footsteps of Henry Beston to a land that has inspired writers for generations.

• *Penniman House Tour,* one and one-half hours. Explore the interior of this historic structure and learn about a whaling captain and his family.

• *Shellfishing Demonstration,* one hour. Learn about the life history of some local shellfish and how to harvest them.

• *Children's Hour,* one hour. Varied seashore activities: scavenger hunts, sea stories, children's games. Fun while learning. For ages five and up. Parents must be present.

• *Salt Pond Walk,* two hours, one mile. A delightful afternoon walk! Discover the beauty of the salt marsh environment. Here is a chance to exercise your senses.

• *Sunset Beach Walk,* two hours, one-half mile. An evening walk with a campfire program alongside the Atlantic Ocean. Just plain fun.

• *Evening Program,* three-quarters of an hour. Slide-illustrated talks or special events about the many features of Cape Cod. Meet at Salt Pond Visitor Center amphitheater (or auditorium). Weekly list of topics available at visitor centers.

Provincetown

Call Province Lands Center, 487-1256, for times and starting places:

• *Storms, Shipwrecks, and Surfmen.* Visit Old Harbor Museum, an 1897 station (open two hours) to discover the story of the 19th-century lifesaving. Learn of the heartbreak of shipwrecks on Cape Cod and the heroic work of the men of the U.S. Life Saving Service. A short walk from Race Point Beach parking lot along the boardwalk. Small parking fee charged.

• *Seashore Surprise: The Children's Hour.* One hour. Cape Cod beaches are special places to have fun; learn about sea creatures and the forces that shape the margin between land and sea. Various activities for children 6–12 years old. Meet at Race Point Beach. Small parking fee. Parents must be present.

• *Cape Cod Whales,* one hour. Whales are fantastic creatures; learn why the largest animals in the world concentrate in the fertile waters surrounding Cape Cod. Meet at Province Lands Visitor Center.

• *Province Lands Dunes–Manmade Land.* A one-hour walk from Province Lands Visitor Center reveals the striking effect of various human influences on the Provincetown dunes, from forest burial to successful revegetation. Shoes are a must (sneakers preferable), and a hat is recommended for protection.

• *Native Cranberry-Dune Walk,* one hour, one-half mile. Explore the wild dune bogs where the native cranberry lives a sheltered life. Meet at Province Lands Visitor Center for a hike into the valley below.

• *Tidal Flats Walk,* two hours, three-quarters mile. Cape Cod's coastline is a dynamic setting. Wet your feet while visiting sand flats, a rocky shore, and salt marsh to view the multitude of creatures that await your discovery. Make reservations at Province Land Visitor Center (487-1256). Starting time depends on tides.

• *Sunset Beach Walk,* one and one-half hours, three-quarters mile. Stories around the campfire are timed with the sunset across Cape Cod Bay. Meet at northern end of Herring Cove Beach (north) parking lot. Turn right at traffic lights at end of Route 6.

• *Evening Program,* three-quarters to one hour. Illustrated talks on stories of Cape Cod. Meet at Province Lands Visitor Center amphitheater (or auditorium). Weekly list of topics available at the visitor center.

Truro

Call Province Lands Visitor Center, 487-1256, for times and starting places:

• *Pilgrim Lake Dunes Hike,* two hours, one and one-half miles. Venture through the great dunes of Cape Cod. Learn about their history and discover their charm. Route 6 to High Head Road. Take left fork onto dirt road and meet in parking lot.

• *Beach–Dune Walk,* two hours, one mile. Wander the margins of ocean, wind, and sand as we view the action of beach–dune–human dynamics at the origin of the Province Lands hook. Meet at Head of the Meadow parking lot, North Truro. Small parking fee charged.

• *Life and Times of a Duneland Bog,* two hours, one and one-half miles. Orchids and insect-eating plants are among the beautiful and unusual wildflowers in this fleeting world. Turn east off Route 6, North Truro, onto High Head Road (first road south of Pilgrim Lake), left off this road onto dirt road.

• *Cranberry Connection,* one and one-half hours, one-half mile. A lovely place to learn about the Cape Cod cranberry story. View restoration of the Pamet Bog. Route 6 to North Pamet Road, Truro. Meet at Youth Hostel parking lot.

• *Historic Beach Apparatus Drill,* one hour. Surfmen demonstrate the methods once used to rescue shipwrecked mariners along the dangerous coastline of Cape Cod. The Lyle gun is fired and the breeches buoy is used in this special program at Old Harbor Station, a short walk from Race Point Beach parking lot. Small parking fee is charged.

Wellfleet

Call Salt Pond Visitor Center, 255-3421, for times and starting places:

• *Tide Flats,* two hours, two miles. Discover marine life in the tidal flats. Wear sneakers or boots. Starting time depends on tides.

• *Atwood-Higgins House Tour,* one and one-half hours. Explore the interior and surroundings of a circa 1740 Cape Cod house. Tour provided by shuttle bus. Purchase tickets at Salt Pond Visitor Center.

SELF-GUIDING NATURE TRAILS

There are nine self-guiding trails at Cape Cod National Seashore. Self-guiding leaflets are available at trailheads for each trail except the Buttonbush Trail, which has large text and Braille labels. To enjoy these trails, here are some suggestions from the Cape Cod National Seashore:

• Flat-soled shoes, such as sneakers, are recommended. It is advisable in hot weather to wear a hat and use insect repellent.

SELF-GUIDING NATURE TRAILS (CONTINUED)

- *Poison ivy* grows abundantly on Cape Cod. *Ticks* live in tall grass and shrubs. Stay on the trails. There are no poisonous snakes along the trails.
- Only fruit may be picked in the National Seashore. As some berries are poisonous, be sure you know what you are picking. Do not pick wildflowers or other plant material.
- For your safety, do not walk the bicycle trails.
- Please do not litter. Preserve these trails so that others may enjoy them, too.
- Pets are prohibited from all self-guiding trails year-round.

Directions given below are from Eastham by way of Route 6.

Eastham

- ### Fort Hill Trail (includes Red Maple Swamp)
  Length: about one and a half miles. Allow at least one hour for entire walk.

  Access: turn left (east) at Fort Hill sign on Governor Prence Road. Continue on Fort Hill Road one-quarter mile to parking area on left, across from the Captain Edward Penniman House.

  Moderate walking difficulty, solid surface. Some log steps on slopes. Tree roots in Red Maple Swamp protrude above ground. Part of this trail is boardwalk.

- ### Buttonbush Trail
  Length: one-quarter mile.

  Access: near Salt Pond Visitor Center amphitheater. Trail begins where you see the sign and white guide rope.

  Special Features: texts in Braille and large print; guide rope.

  Easy; some log steps, moderate grade. Part of this trail is boardwalk.

- ### Nauset Marsh Trail
  Length: one mile.

  Access: outside the Salt Pond Visitor Center to the right of the outdoor amphitheater. Trail winds along edge of Salt Pond and Nauset Marsh, crosses fields, and returns to visitor center. Be careful when crossing bicycle trail.

  Easy; some log steps, moderate grade.

Provincetown

- ### Beech Forest Trail
  Length: one mile.

  Access: turn right (north) at traffic light on Race Point Road. Proceed about one-half mile to the Beech Forest parking lot on the left side of the road.

  More difficult; steep log steps, mostly soft sand.

Truro

- ### Cranberry Bog Trail
  Length: one-half mile.

  Access: turn right (east) on North Pamet Road, Truro. Park at the Environmental Education Center (a youth hostel in the summer) near the end of North Pamet Road. Trail begins at the parking lot.

  Easy; some log steps, moderate grade. Part of this trail is boardwalk.

- ### Small Swamp Trail
  Length: three-quarters mile.

  Access: turn right (east) at the Pilgrim Heights area sign. Walk begins at interpretive shelter.

  Easy; many log steps, steep grade.

  - ### Pilrgim Spring Trail
    Length: three quarters mile.

Access: interpretive shelter, Pilgrim Heights area. Path leads to site of spring where Pilgrims may have drunk their first water in New England.

Easy; some log steps, moderate grade.

Wellfleet

• *Atlantic White Cedar Swamp Trail*

Length: one and one-quarter miles.

Access: turn right (east) into Marconi Station area at traffic light on Route 6, South Wellfleet, 5.2 miles north of Salt Pond Visitor Center, Eastham. Follow signs to Marconi Site and White Cedar Swamp.

Moderate difficulty; some steep stairs, return route is one-half mile in soft sand. Part of this trail is boardwalk.

• *Great Island Trail*

Length: four miles, *one way.*

Access: turn left (west) into Wellfleet center; left again onto Commercial Street. Turn right at town pier, on Kendrick Road, and left on Chequessett Neck Road. Trail begins at Great Island parking lot. Head covering, sturdy footgear, and drinking water are advisable.

The National Seashore's most difficult trail; mostly soft sand. Some log steps.

 # Churches

BREWSTER

• *Brewster Baptist Church,* Rte. 6A; 896-3381.
• *Cape Cod Bible Alliance,* Rte. 6A (near Orleans line); 896-6151 (nondenominational).
• *First Church of Christ, Scientist,* corner of Rte. 6A and Foster Rd.; 896-5250.
• *First Parish Church,* corner of Rte. 6A and Breakwater Rd.; 896-5577 (Unitarian Universalist).
• *Immaculate Conception,* Rte. 6A; 385-2535 (Catholic).
• *Our Lady of the Cape,* Stony Brook Rd.; 385-2535 (Catholic).
• *Trinity Lutheran Church,* corner of Rte. 6A at Lower Rd.; 896-3396 or 896-7946.

CHATHAM

• *First Church of Christ, Scientist,* 613 Main St.; 945-9534.
• *South Chatham Community Church,* Rte. 28; 432-4248 or 432-4417.
• *First Congregational Church,* 650 Main St.; 945-0800.
• *Chatham Baptist Church,* Rte. 137 (near Rte. 28 intersection); 432-8022 (Southern Baptist Association).
• *St. Christopher's Episcopal Church,* 625 Main St.; 945-1033.
• *First United Methodist Church,* 16 Cross St.; 945-0474.
• *Holy Redeemer Church,* 57 Highland St.; 945-0760.

EASTHAM

• *Nauset Baptist Church,* Great Pond Rd.; 255-2709.
• *Eastham United Methodist Church,* Rte. 6A; 255-4724.
• *Nauset Fellowship,* Chapel-in-the-Pines; off Rte. 6A near town windmill.
• *Our Lady of The Visitation,* Massasoit Rd.; 255-6588 (Catholic).

HARWICH

- *Christ Church Episcopal,* Main St., Harwich Port; 432-1787.
- *First Baptist Church of West Harwich & Dennisport,* 60 Main St., W. Harwich; 432-2792.
- *First Church of Christ, Scientist,* 648 Main St. (Rte. 28), Harwich Port; 432-1997.
- *First Congregational Church,* Main St.; 432-1053.
- *Harwich United Methodist Church,* One Church St., E. Harwich; 432-3734.
- *Holy Trinity Roman Catholic Church,* Main St.; 432-0650 or 432-4000.
- *Pilgrim Congregational Church,* Main St., Harwich Port; 432-1668.
- *St. Peter's Lutheran Church,* Rte. 137; 432-5172.
- *Kingdom Hall of Jehovah's Witnesses,* corner of Rte. 39 and Church St.; 432-5957.

ORLEANS

- *Church of the Holy Spirit,* corner of Rte. 28 and Monument Rd.; 255-0433.
- *Federated Church of Orleans,* corner of Main St. and Meetinghouse Rd.; 255-3060.
- *Kingdom Hall of Jehovah's Witnesses,* Pine Ridge Ln., E. Orleans; 255-3054.
- *St. Joan of Arc,* Bridge Rd.; 255-0170 (Catholic).
- *United Methodist Church,* corner of Rte. 28 and Main St.; 255-0622.

TRURO

- *Christian Union Church,* off Rte. 6, N. Truro.
- *First Congregational,* Rte. 6A, N. Truro.
- *Lady of Perpetual Help,* N. Truro (Catholic).
- *Sacred Heart Church,* Truro (Catholic).

WELLFLEET

- *Grace Assembly of God,* corner of Rte. 6A and Lt. Island Rd.; 349-9323.
- *First Congregational Church,* Main St.; 349-6877.
- *Our Lady of Lourdes,* Main St.; 349-2222 (Catholic).
- *St. James the Fisherman,* off Route 6 (Episcopal).
- *Wellfleet United Methodist,* Main St.; 349-2202.

Odds & Ends

Laundromats

CHATHAM

- *Acme Laundry Center,* 22 Queen Anne Rd.; 945-4122.
- *Frog Pond Launderette,* 1274 Main St.; 945-3831.

HARWICH

- *Harwich Port Speed Wash & Coin Laundry,* corner of Rte. 28 and Doane Rd.; 432-0552.

ORLEANS

- *Acme Laundromat,* Main St. (behind Fleming's Donut Shack); 255-0361.
- *Maytag Laundromat,* Rte. 6A (next to bowling alley near Rte. 6A and West Rd. intersection).

Laundries

CHATHAM
- *The Clothes Clinic,* Rte. 28, W. Chatham; 945-2584.
- *Hopkins Cleaners,* Rte. 28; 945-1937.

ORLEANS
- *Hopkins Cleaners,* 120 Rte. 6A; 255-0163.

Farm Stands

BREWSTER
- *Satucket Farm Stand,* Rte. 124 (near Rte. 6A intersection). Fresh produce, gourmet items, native corn.
- *Namskaket Farm,* off Rte. 6A. Strawberries only (pick your own). Large strawberry farm with view of the bay, bring the children, come early, opens at 8 A.M. in June and early July.

CHATHAM
- *Fancy's Farm Stand,* 1286 Main St. (Rte. 28), W. Chatham; 945-1949. Complete line of fruits and produce.

EASTHAM
There's a small farm stand (no name or phone) that sells sweet native corn off Route 6, just up from the Orleans Rotary.

HARWICH
- *Ring Brothers,* Rte. 28; 432-9827. Fresh produce, fruit, corn, and more.

ORLEANS
- *Fancy's Farm Stand,* Main St. (on the way to Nauset Beach); 255-1949. Complete line of fruits and produce.
- *Log Cabin Farm Stand,* Rte. 6A; 255-6919. Fresh produce, native corn (some of the Cape's sweetest).
- *Phoenix Fruit and Vegetables,* Orleans Marketplace Plaza; 255-5306. Along with fresh produce, you can find delicious homemade breads, jams and jellies here.

TRURO
- *Hillside Farm Stand*, Rte. 6; 487-9765. Fresh vegetables, fruit, eggs, and Portuguese breads.

Fish Markets

BREWSTER
Breakwater Fish and Lobster, 235 Underpass Rd.; 896-7080. Smoked seafood and fish market next to Brewster Express and the bike trail.

CHATHAM
- *Chatham Fish & Lobster Co.,* 1297 Main St. (Rte. 28); 945-1178 (retail), 432-7180 (wholesale). Fresh Chatham haddock, scallops, shellfish, lobsters; year-round.
- *Nickerson Fish & Lobster,* Chatham Fish Pier; 945-0145. Fresh fish right off the boat; open spring, summer, fall.

CHATHAM (CONTINUED)

• *Old Harbor Fish Co.,* 1082 Main St. (Rte. 28); 945-1223. Fresh ground fish (cod, haddock, flounder), lobsters, scallops, shrimp, and clams; open year-round.

EASTHAM

• *Cape Cod Seafood Smokers,* Rte. 6; 255-4697. Assortment of fresh fish.
• *Eastham Lobster Pool,* Rte. 6A; 255-9706. Assortment of fresh fish.
• *Friendly Fishermen's Fish Market,* Rte. 6; 255-3009. Assortment of fresh fish.

HARWICH

• *George's Place,* Kildee Rd., Harwich Port; 432-5493. Fresh fish and lobsters daily, retail and wholesale; year-round.

ORLEANS

• *Capt'n Elmer's Seafood,* 18 Old Colony Way; 255-7221. One of the best assortments of fresh fish and shellfish on the Cape, editor's favorite.
• *Nauset Fish & Lobster Pool,* Rte. 6A; 255-1019. Fresh lobsters, haddock, halibut, swordfish, flounder, smelts, shellfish; open year-round.
• *Young's Fish Market,* Rock Harbor Rd. (next to marina); 255-3366. Assortment of fresh fish and shellfish; seasonal.

TRURO

• *Cape Cod Fish Market,* Rte. 6 (near Hillside Farm Stand); 487-2199. Assortment of fresh fish.

WELLFLEET

• *The Boathouse Fish Market,* Holbrook Ave.; 349-7377. Assortment of fresh fish.
• *Harbor Freeze Seafood Market,* Town Pier; 349-9611. Assortment of fresh fish.
• *Hatch's Fish Market,* Main St. (behind Town Hall); 349-2810. Assortment of fresh fish, fruits, and vegetables.

Clambakes

• *America's Greatest Clambake,* Chatham; 432-4200.
• *Clambake Celebrations,* 9 West Rd., Skaket Corners, Orleans; 255-3289 or 800-423-4038. Pick up for local enjoyment or ship to friends at home. Store also carries aprons, pots, platters, and utensils with a lobster-fish-clam theme.
• *Cape Cod Seafood Specialties,* Truro; 349-9591.

Ice Cream Parlors

BREWSTER

• *Brewster Express,* Underpass Rd. (just off bicycle trail); 896-6682. Great ice cream and sandwiches.
• *Brewster Scoop,* Rte. 6A at the Brewster General Store; 896-7824.
• *Captain Fudd's,* Underpass Rd. next to Brewster video; 896-4467. Small miniature golf, fried seafood and 4 Seas Ice Cream—often named the best on Cape Cod.

- *Exclusive Scoop,* 2655 Main St.; 896-3322. Outdoor deck, ice cream and coffees.
- *Kate's,* corner of Rte. 6A and Paine's Creek Rd.; 896-9517. Ice cream and sandwiches.

CHATHAM

- *Ben & Jerry's,* 10 Chatham Bars Ave.; 945-5959.
- *Buffy's Ice Cream Shop,* 456 Main St.; 945-5990.
- *Chatham Cookie Manor,* 459 Main St.; 945-1152. Ice cream.
- *Chatham Creamery,* 1221 Main St.; 945-5811.
- *Emack & Bolio's*, 2 Kent Place; 945-5506.
- *Chatham Ice Cream Shoppe,* 470 Main St.; 945-4360. Homemade ice cream and deli sandwiches.
- *Friendly's,* Rte. 28; 945-2040. Ice cream, breakfast, lunch, dinner.

EASTHAM

- *Ben & Jerry's,* off Rte. 6 at Brackett Rd.; 255-2817. Vermont's finest homemade ice cream, fresh-baked cookies, brownies, and muffins. Ice cream cakes custom decorated and made to order while you wait; open year-round.

HARWICH

- *Dairy Queen,* 441 Main St., Harwich Port; 432-3340. Soft ice cream.
- *Nick & Dick's,* 594 Main, Harwich Port; 430-1239.
- *Friendly's,* Rte. 28, W. Harwich; 432-6388. Ice cream, breakfast, lunch, dinner.

ORLEANS

- *Emack & Bolio,* Rte. 6A (Oracle Square); 255-5844. Ice cream for the connoisseur.
- *Dairy Queen,* Rte. 6A (near Orleans Rotary). Soft ice cream.
- *Friendly's,* Canal Rd. (off Rte. 6A near Orleans Rotary); 255-5342. Ice cream, breakfast, lunch, dinner.
- *The Hot Chocolate Sparrow,* 85 Rte. 6A; 240-2230. Go in here for more than just ice cream, like: coffee and candies.
- *Ice Cream Café,* 5 S. Orleans Rd.; 240-0003. Homemade ice cream and espresso bar.
- *Sundae School,* Main St. (next to Fancy's Farm Stand); 255-5473. Great ice cream.

WELLFLEET

- *A Nice Cream Shop,* Main St. Ice cream.
- *Just Dessert,* off Commercial St.; 349-6333. Ice cream.

Bakeries

BREWSTER

- *Fleming's Donut Shack,* Rte. 6A. Assortment of fresh donuts and baked goods, great coffee, room to sit.
- *Hopkins House Bakery,* 2727 Main, 896-3450. Next door to the Hopkins House Shop, great scones!

CHATHAM

- *Amara's Italian Pastry and Specialty Shop,* 637 Main; 945-5777. Wonderful pastries as well as a good selection of gourmet items.

CHATHAM (CONTINUED)

- *The Bread Harbor,* 410 Main St.; 945-4556. Breads, pastries, gourmet pizza, pasta, cappuccino and espresso.
- *Marion's Pie Shop,* Rte. 28; 432-9439. Homemade pies and assorted baked goods.
- *Old Harbor Bakery,* Old Harbor Rd.; 945-3433. Coffee shop, baked goods, restaurant.

EASTHAM

- *Arturo's Pasta to-go and Bakery,* Massasoit Rd.; 240-7828. Ready-to-eat homemade pasta dishes and hard-crust breads.
- *Fleming's Bakery and Deli,* Rte. 6. Fresh donuts, good coffee, great sandwiches.
- *Hole in One Donut Shop,* Rte. 6; 255-9446. Great donuts.

HARWICH

- *Bonatt's Home Bakery,* Rte. 28, Harwich Port; 432-2713. Assortment of baked goods.
- *The Stewed Tomato,* 707 Main St.; 432-1203. Assorted baked goods and restaurant (excellent breakfast place).

ORLEANS

- *Cottage Street Bakery,* 2 Cottage St. (off Rte. 28 near intersection with Rte. 6A); 255-2821. Assorted baked goods.
- *Fleming's Donut Shack,* Main St. (in town center). Assorted baked goods.
- *Hole-in-One,* Rte. 6A (near Main St. and Rte. 6A intersection); 255-3740. Assorted baked goods, great coffee (by the cup or fresh beans). Also fine selection of wines and cheeses, as well as a reasonably priced lunch menu (take-out and sit down).
- *Brown Bag Bakery,* at intersection of West Rd. and Old Colony Way (behind Brown Bag Restaurant); 255-8144. Assorted baked goods.

TRURO

- *First Landing Bakery & Coffee Shop,* Highland Rd., N. Truro; 487-2118. Assorted baked goods, coffee.

WELLFLEET

- *Christine's Oasis,* Cove Corner; 349-0000. Assorted baked and gourmet goods. Try it!
- *Lighthouse Bakery,* Wellfleet Center; 349-1600. Bagels, cakes, pies, donuts and pastries.

Libraries

BREWSTER

- *Brewster Ladies Library,* Rte. 6A; 896-3913. Books and children's activities.

CHATHAM

- *Eldredge Library,* Main St.; 945-5170. Special programs.

EASTHAM

- *Eastham Public Library,* Samoset Rd.; 255-3070. New addition.

HARWICH

- *Brooks Free Library,* Main St.; 430-7562. Summer reading program.

- *Chase Library*, Rte. 28, W. Harwich; 432-2610.
- *Harwich Public Library*, Main St.; 432-1799.

ORLEANS

- *Snow Library*, Main St.; 240-3760. Children's story hour.

TRURO

- *Cobbs Memorial Library*, Truro Rd.; 349-6895.
- *Pilgrim Memorial Library*, Rte. 6A, N. Truro; 487-1125.

WELLFLEET

- *Wellfleet Public Library*, Main St. (old candle factory); 349-0310. Weekly story hour.
- *South Wellfleet Public Library*, upstairs in S. Wellfleet Neighborhood Association Hall.

Best of Outer Cape

BEST COUNTRY INNS

- *Captain Freeman Inn*, 15 Breakwater Rd., Brewster; 896-7481.
- *High Brewster*, Satucket Rd., Brewster; 896-3636.
- *Isaiah Clark House*, 1187 Main St. (Rte. 6A), Brewster; 896-2223.
- *The Whalewalk Inn*, 169 Bridge Rd., Eastham; 255-0617.

BEST RESORTS

- *Chatham Bars Inn*, Shore Rd., Chatham; 945-0096.
- *Ocean Edge Resort & Conference Center*, off Rte. 6A, Brewster; 896-2781; or toll-free 1-800-221-1837 (outside Massachusetts) or 1-800-626-2688 (in Massachusetts).
- *Wequasett Inn*, Rte. 28, Chatham; 432-5400.

BEST BREAKFAST

- *Bittersweet Café*, 352 Main St., Chatham; 945-9123.

BEST LUNCH

- *Land Ho! Tavern*, corner of Rte. 6A and Cove Rd., Orleans; 255-5165.
- *Chatham Squire*, 487 Main St., Chatham; 945-0945.

BEST DINNERS (MODERATELY PRICED)

- *Beechcroft Inn*, Rte. 6A, Brewster; 896-9534.
- *Brewster Fish House*, 2208 Main St. (Rte. 6A), Brewster; 896-7867.
- *Jailhouse Tavern*, West Rd., Orleans; 255-5245.
- *Nauset Beach Club*, Main St., E. Orleans; 255-8547.
- *The Sea Grille*, 31 Sea St., Harwich; 432-4745.

BEST DINNERS (EXPENSIVE)

- *Bramble Inn*, Rte. 6A, Brewster; 896-7644.
- *Captain Linnell House*, Skaket Rd., Orleans; 255-3400.
- *Chillingsworth*, Rte. 6A, Brewster; 896-3640.
- *High Brewster*, 964 Satucket Rd. (near herring run), Brewster; 896-3636.

BEST FRIED SEAFOOD

- *Arnold's,* Rte. 6, Eastham; 255-2575.
- *Bayside Lobster Hutt,* Commercial St., Wellfleet; 349-6333.
- *Eastham Lobster Pool,* Rte. 6, Eastham; 255-9706.

BEST ENTERTAINMENT (CASUAL)

- *Chatham Band Concerts,* Kate Gould Park, Main St., Chatham. Every Friday night at 8 P.M.
- *The Irish Pub,* Rte. 28, Harwich; 432-8808. Irish music.

BEST ENTERTAINMENT (STAGE)

- *Academy of Performing Arts,* Main St., Orleans; 255-1963.
- *Monomoy Theatre,* Main St., Chatham; 945-1589.

BEST MUSEUM & HISTORIC SITE

- *Cape Cod Museum of Natural History,* Rte. 6A, Brewster; 896-3867.

BEST ART GALLERIES

- Browse through the town centers of Wellfleet, Chatham, Brewster and Orleans!

BEST CRAFT & SPECIALTY SHOPS

- *The Artful Hand,* Main St. Square, Orleans; 255-2969.
- *The Christmas Tree Shop,* intersection of Rte. 6A and Rte. 28, Orleans; 255-8494.
- *Oceana,* One Main St. Square, Orleans; 240-1414.
- *Tree's Place,* at corner of Rtes. 6A and 28, Orleans; 255-1330.
- *Wayside Gallery,* 512 Main St. at the Wayside Inn, Chatham; 945-0749.

BEST ANTIQUE SHOPS

All along Route 6A in Brewster.

BEST PUBLIC GOLF COURSES

- *Captains' Course,* Freeman's Way, Brewster; 896-5100.
- *Cranberry Valley,* off Oak St., Harwich; 432-6300.

BEST PUBLIC BEACHES

- *Cape Cod National Seashore,* ocean beaches.
- *Nauset Beach,* Beach Rd., E. Orleans. Town beach, parking charged, facilities available.

BEST HIKING OR NATURE TRAIL

- *Nickerson State Park,* Rte. 6A, Brewster; 896-3491.
- *Fort Hill Trail,* off Rte. 6 in Eastham. Look for signs.
- *John Wing Trail,* Rte. 6A, Cape Cod Museum of Natural History.

BEST CAMPING

- *Nickerson State Park,* Rte. 6A, Brewster; 896-3491.

BEST CHILDREN'S ACTIVITIES

- *Bassetts Wild Animal Farm,* Tubman Rd., Brewster; 896-3224.
- *Cape Cod Bay*—walking the flats in Brewster and Eastham at low tide.
- *Cape Cod Museum of Natural History,* Rte. 6A, Brewster; 896-3867.

BEST FARM STANDS

- *Fancy's Farm Stands,* Orleans and Chatham.
- *Satucket Farm Stand,* Rte. 124 (near Rte. 6A intersection), Brewster.

BEST FISH MARKETS

- *Breakwater Fish and Lobster,* 235 Underpass Rd., Brewster; 896-7080.
- *Capt'n Elmer's Seafood,* 18 Old Colony Way, Orleans; 255-7221.
- *Nauset Fish & Lobster Pool,* Rte. 6A, Orleans; 255-1019.

PROVINCETOWN

Provincetown: Viewpoints

by Hamilton Kahn

While neighboring Wellfleet and Truro offer a slice of Cape life, Provincetown will give you the whole loaf. Likening this cornucopia of humanity to Noah's Ark, a chamber of commerce brochure boasts that in the summer you will find "at least two of everything" here—from a trendy New York art crowd to weatherbeaten fishermen; from gay men in pastel pink tank tops to bikers in boots and black leather; from midwestern families in rumpled madras to the literati in work shirts and faded jeans; and from tour bus types with cameras at the ready to Boston's social elite.

Combine all this with seaport charm, old European flair, and some of the best restaurants in New England, and you have one of the most intriguing places in all of America.

Though undeniably a part of the Outer Cape, Provincetown is separate, set off by itself—a highly independent community with its own character, history, and life-style. It is, at times, as much a state of being as a point on the map. Thrust out into the Atlantic Ocean at the Cape's tip, Provincetown draws residents and visitors from all walks of life and for a variety of reasons. Fishermen, for one, have long valued Provincetown's large, protected harbor, located not far from one of the world's richest fishing grounds. Locals see the town in the off season as the ultimate refuge from civilization, yet they welcome the annual influx of summer visitors, who in turn love Provincetown's combination of seashore casualness and urban sophistication.

Precisely what makes Provincetown special and separate from other Cape and Island towns is hard to say. It may be the special light reflected off its waters, which has inspired artists and writers. It may be the beaches and open vistas, which are among the most beautiful the Cape has to offer. It may be the look of its old wooden buildings nestled along its narrow, European-style streets or the sight of its fishing fleet unloading a day's catch at the end of MacMillan Wharf. It may be the atmosphere of freedom and tolerance that welcomes those who feel out of place elsewhere, but at home in Provincetown.

Put it all together and you have a town with a feel, an ambience, all its own. In the summer months, Provincetown crackles with energy, with visitors from all over the East Coast and beyond. The town swells from a village of 3000 to a booming minicity of nearly 30,000 during July and August; by contrast, the town in the winter has an eerie, desolate tranquility that is reminiscent of nineteenth-century small town America.

Provincetown is many things to many people. It is a Portuguese fishing port, tourist town, literary and artistic colony, natural paradise, and a gathering place for gay men and women—all rolled into one. But for some, Provincetown is simply a place to go, somewhere to walk around, a spot to see and be seen. But as crowded as the town often gets, it is a place where individuality—be it physical or philosophical—is encouraged to thrive.

Even Provincetown's shape supports this image of the town going its own way. While the rest of the Outer Cape—from Harwich to Truro—heads north toward the peninsula's tip, Provincetown curves sharply to the west, then south, then east—forming what appears to be a tightly clenched fist. The sheltered harbor created by this natural semicircle has provided safe haven for centuries of seafarers and a fleet of 30 fishing boats that still fills its nets 12 months a year on rich Georges Bank, about 50 miles to the northeast.

As any careful reader of history knows, it was Provincetown, not Plymouth, where the Pilgrims first dropped the anchor of the *Mayflower* on November 11, 1620. The ship remained anchored off Provincetown in Cape Cod Bay for six weeks while Pilgrim men explored the area. Before they chose to settle in Plymouth (because of its safer harbor and less sandy soil), the Pilgrims established two fundamental principles they were to live by. One came with the signing aboard the *Mayflower* of the Mayflower Compact, which outlined the Pilgrims' commitment to self-government. "Thus was executed in Cape Cod Harbor, the first instrument probably that the world ever saw, recognizing true republican principles, intrusting all powers in the hands of the majority," wrote historian Frederick Freeman in his book *History of Cape Cod*, which was published in 1858. The same day the compact was signed, John Carver was unanimously chosen to serve as governor of the Pilgrims' new settlement for one year. Another, less democratic declaration was the designation of Mondays—the day the Pilgrims first came ashore in Provincetown—as "wash day." This was prompted by the Pilgrims' immediate need for clean clothes in the New World.

The place the Pilgrims first set foot in Provincetown—the West End of what is now Commercial Street—is marked by a bronze plaque attached to a boulder (see map). Locals look upon this as the real "Plymouth Rock." Historians, pressed on the issue, might have to agree. Other memorials to the Pilgrims worth taking in are the 253-foot (77 meters), all-granite Pilgrim Monument off Bradford Street behind Town Hall, and the bas-relief plaque beneath it that depicts the signing of the Mayflower Compact. The Pilgrim Monument, a long climb, offers a panoramic view of the entire Cape and, for you trivia buffs, is the tallest all-granite building in the United States.

The Pilgrims, however, weren't the first Europeans to set foot in Provincetown. "The first discovery of Cape Cod by a European is generally conceded to Bartholomew Gosnold, the intrepid mariner of the west of England," writes Freeman of the man who named Cape Cod. In 1602, Gosnold (captain of the bark *Concord*) and members of his crew explored the headland from Race Point to Wood End. "Near this cape within a league of land, he came to anchor, in fifteen fathoms, and his crew took a great quantity of cod-fish, from which circumstance he named the land Cape Cod," adds Freeman, noting the name at first referred only to the Provincetown headland. It took a hundred years for the name to spread south to other towns.

Legend, though, has it that Provincetown was actually visited 598 years earlier by Viking Leif Ericson's brother, Thorvald. According to the legend, Thorvald came ashore in the year 1004 to fix the damaged keel on his boat, and named the area "Cape of the Keel." While there is no monument to Thorvald, the legend has inspired much speculation.

Provincetown, or Cape Cod as it was then called, continued to serve as a way station, of sorts, until the 1700s when it was incorporated under the name "Province Lands," a reference to the land's value to Plymouth Colony as a shipping port.

All of Provincetown's early settlers made a living from the sea, fishing for mackerel and cod. Whaling—both beach whaling and deep-water whaling—was also a mainstay. Fishermen built their homes around the harbor's perimeter and used the beach as their main road. As the fishing industry grew, so did the town, and by the mid-1800s more than 50 wharves jutted into its harbor, then one of the busiest in the country. Processing plants also lined the shore; mackerel and cod were flaked in those days—a process that involved salting, pickling, and drying the filets in the sun for several days. Whaling was also an important part of the town's economy; Stellwagen Bank, seven miles northeast of Provincetown, was (and still is) a rich feeding ground for the mammals, whose oil was used to fuel lamps. By 1900, the practice was rare—the victim, though, of a changing economic climate rather than moral outrage. While electricity put an end to whaling, whale-watching boats still leave Provincetown Harbor in the spring, summer, and fall to view the gentle giants during their annual migration south.

It was whaling, as well as good ground fishing, that attracted the Portuguese here. They now make up a sizable portion of the town's year-round population. Portuguese fishermen began coming to Provincetown in the 1800s, having heard about the town and its fishing from Cape Cod whale captains who stocked up on supplies at the Azores and Cape Verde islands during trips around the world. Many members of these families still man the town's fishing boats, while others are key players in the real estate and tourist industries. Portuguese cooking, music, and traditions—most notably the annual Blessing of the Fleet which we discuss later—are hallmarks of Provincetown and contribute greatly to its European allure.

Among the many benefits that resulted from the Outer Cape's prosperity in the 1800s was the construction of the Cape Cod and Old Colony Railroad, which made its first run to Provincetown in 1873. The railroad made it possible, for the first time, for city dwellers to get to the town without having to take a long, arduous overland route. It also signaled the beginning of a new era, almost a redefinition of the town, which now began attracting artists, actors, and writers who found inspiration and solace in Provincetown's quaint beauty.

Among them was impressionist Charles W. Hawthorne, who led groups of aspiring artists to paint in the Provincetown dunes at the turn of the century. His Cape Cod School of Art, which has been carried on in a small building near the town center by successors Hans Hoffman and Henry Hensche, marked the beginning of Provincetown's art colony, the first of its kind in the country. The Provincetown Art Association, founded in 1914, still shows many of Hawthorne's paintings and has a collection of more than 500 works. It continues to be one of the building blocks of this creative art colony.

Another artist attracted to Provincetown during this period was a young playwright named Eugene O'Neill. O'Neill found Provincetown a more relaxed showcase for his early playwriting efforts than Manhattan, and with the help of George Cram "Jig" Cooke and a small troupe, O'Neill's *Bound East for Cardiff* was produced in the town's tumbledown Wharf Theater in 1916. It was to launch his career. Provincetown, at one time or another, has also been home to writers such as Sinclair Lewis, John Dos Passos, Tennessee Williams, Stanley Kunitz, and Norman Mailer, who directed the film version of his book *Tough Guys Don't Dance* on location here in 1986.

Not only has Provincetown been a magnet for those involved in the arts, it also has drawn those who patronize the arts, many of them gay men and women. There is now a large, politically powerful gay population in town that owns many of Provincetown's businesses and controls its own chamber of commerce, the Provincetown Business Guild, which promotes the town in gay-oriented national publications to attract gay visitors. While both the Provincetown Business Guild and the Provincetown Chamber of Commerce, the town's other information bureau, stress that the town is open to all types, the guild's brochure helpfully lists all businesses owned by gays. This does not, of course, mean that the businesses are for gays only.

Equally a part of Provincetown's character is the town's layout. There are four main sections of Provincetown, each with a distinct setting and flavor: the East End, where art galleries, inns, and restaurants are mixed among the Victorian and Cape-style homes; the Town Center, where you'll find the fish pier and most of the town's shops; the West End, the far end of town, which is relatively quiet and less-traveled, but includes several fine inns and restaurants nonetheless; and the Province Lands, an undeveloped area of sand dunes and sparse vegetation just to the north of the town proper. Although it is within the town's boundaries, the Province Lands are owned by the federal government and are a part of the Cape Cod National Seashore. The area offers guided trails for hikers, bikers, and horseback riders, as well as two superb beaches—Race Point and Herring Cove—and a visitor center.

Despite Provincetown's isolated location, getting there is not difficult, but there are times when traffic will try your patience. Provincetown has its own airport near Race Point, which offers regular flights to and from Boston. There is also regular bus service in and out of the center of town, and a cruise ship makes a round trip once a day in the summer from Boston Harbor to MacMillan Wharf. But most choose to come by car. It is by far the most direct and accommodating method (just follow Route 6), even if parking is a problem once you get there. More on that later.

Approaching Provincetown from Truro on Route 6, you catch your first glimpse of the town as you reach the top of a bluff called Pilgrim Heights. The view is striking from here. To the right is Pilgrim Lake, a freshwater pond with a supply of pickerel, perch, and black bass. The lake is bordered on three sides by lofty, white sand dunes. To the left is Truro's magnificent Beach Point, which sits on the edge of Cape Cod Bay; matchbox cottages line the shore. Across the bay is Provincetown, its town center curving in a fist. Provincetown's skyline is dominated by the massive Pilgrim Monument and the town's baby-blue water towers, which hold a drinking water supply from Truro well fields.

This long view of Provincetown is particularly beautiful at night when the lights of the town reflect off the bay, giving Provincetown the look of a miniature metropolis. At Christmastime, the Pilgrim Monument is strung from its base to its turret with white lights—an impressive scene that can be viewed for miles.

As you drive closer to the town, you will notice that the varied roof lines of Provincetown's buildings start at the shoreline and progress up into the small, wooded hills just to the north. You will also notice the waterfront and inner harbor. They are protected by a long breakwater that runs parallel to the beach. Smaller breakwaters, piers, and the town's two main wharves—MacMillan and Marina—jut out from the shoreline. In the summer, scores of small sail- and motorboats are moored in the harbor, which empties out at low tide, leaving the boats stranded on a sandy bottom. The tightly packed buildings and streets of Provincetown, as well as its colorful shops and sidewalk cafés (all of which are not far from the wharves) give the town Old World charm.

There are three main exits off Route 6 into Provincetown, but in high winds it is advisable to cross over to Route 6A at Beach Point in North Truro to avoid flying sand that can take years off the life of a windshield. Route 6 at this point is bordered on the east (ocean side) by migrating sand dunes that tend to creep across the highway.

But if the wind isn't blowing, we suggest you take one of the main exits. The first one, Snail Road, will lead you into the East End.

East End

Snail Road will take you from Route 6 to Route 6A, a distance of about a quarter mile. On Route 6A turn right, then left at the fork about 200 yards up the road. This is Commercial Street, the town's main drag. You may want to stop near the town center at an art gallery operated by one of the town's leading impressionists, Anne Packard. This is just one of the many outstanding galleries in the East End. Over on nearby Bradford Street, which runs the length of the town proper and parallel to Commercial Street, the Provincetown Group Gallery also shows the works of many of the town's best young artists. Founded in 1964, it is one of the oldest cooperative galleries on the Cape. It represents 29 artists, among them Betty Bodian and Jim Forsberg. Adjacent to the gallery is the Provincetown Tennis Club, which rents clay and all-weather courts by the hour and sponsors open tournaments for players of all levels.

Back on Commercial Street, just up from Anne Packard's gallery, you'll pass the multistory Surfside Inn and the attractive St. Mary of the Harbor Episcopal Church, both of which have a view of the bay. Not far from here is the Howland Street intersection where you'll find the American Legion Hall, home to the Long Point Gallery in the summer. Many distinguished American artists show their works here—among them, Robert Motherwell, Budd Hopkins, and Sidney Simon. Howland Street, by the way, will take you through Bradford Street and out onto Route 6, heading toward Truro.

Coming up over a slight rise on Commercial Street you will pass the Ice House Apartments (an old icehouse converted into attractive living quarters). The building, like most in Provincetown, has a view of the bay. Just up the road and to your right you will see the Provincetown Art Association and Museum. Established in 1914, this institution keeps itself at the forefront of the local art scene by involving artists of all ages and styles with its exhibits and events. The museum's three galleries are open year-round, showing works from its impressive permanent collection (reflecting the best of the town's artistic heritage) and from touring exhibits and exhibits of local art organizations. The Provincetown Theatre Company, a 25-year-old amateur troupe, used to perform there in the winter but has found a new year-round home at the Provincetown Inn in the West End.

Across the street is Bryant's Market, owned by former Selectman George Bryant, a member of one of Provincetown's oldest families. The store offers a fine variety of wines and liquors, in addition to groceries reasonably priced.

One block up from here is Kiley Court, a small alleyway that conceals the basement location of one of the town's finest restaurants, Ciro & Sal's. The Italian food here is as good as or better than in Boston's famed North End. The restaurant is a favorite among locals. Across the street is the Studio Shop, also located in a basement, where many of the town's artists and fledgling artists buy their supplies.

The East End is a good place to linger for a cool drink or a complete meal. There are several waterfront establishments. Pucci's Harborside, a summertime favorite of many locals, offers brunch, lunch, dinner, and late-night snacks in a light-filled indoor setting or on an outside deck. Another excellent waterfront restaurant in the East End is Mews, farther up the road on Commercial Street, not far from the town center area.

Nearby are several other fine galleries. We recommend you visit the Eva DeNagy Gallery, one of the town's oldest. Here you will find paintings and pastels, as well as crafts and artifacts from around the globe. Harvey Dodd, a year-round resident skilled at line drawings and watercolors, also operates a gallery in the vicinity.

If you're looking for a great place to stay in the East End, we have two suggestions: the Cape Codder Guest House, owned by a scientist from the renowned Provincetown Center for Coastal Studies, is a cozy retreat off Commercial Street. The Watermark Inn at 603 Commercial Street is a bit more posh; it offers fireplaces in each room and private decks on the water's edge.

Town Center

While the focus is on art in the East End, the center of town is a place where commerce and the crush of humanity are more visible, although the center is certainly not lacking in redeeming cultural qualities. The most direct route off the highway to the center of town is by way of Conwell Street, the second Provincetown exit. Conwell Street will take you by the town's only chain supermarket, the A&P, past the intersection of Cemetery Road and Harry Kemp Way (named after Provincetown's "Poet of the Dunes"). When you get to Bradford Street, take a right, then a left on Standish Street. That will bring you to Commercial Street and MacMillan Wharf, the town pier. There is a large public parking lot at the town pier, as well as public rest rooms. Parking is a primary consideration when visiting the center; it can cost you time and money, and cause much aggravation. If the main lot is full, we suggest you park at the Bradford Street public lot, which is next to the high school and within walking distance of Town Hall (see map). There are several smaller public and privately owned lots around town, most of them on Commercial Street, but they will cost you more money. Provincetown police, you should know, will ticket and tow illegally parked cars, especially those that shouldn't be in spaces reserved for the handicapped.

Once you have parked, you're prepared to explore the town center in the manner for which it was designed—on foot. In addition to the map we have provided here, we suggest you pick up a town map prepared by Provincetown's Historical Society. They are available at most gift shops and often cost less than 50 cents. They will help you pick and choose; there's so much to see. The town center is filled with shopping, dining, and entertainment options, as well as several points of historical interest.

At first glance, it may seem as though commercialism has run amok on aptly named Commercial Street (and it has to some extent); but that impression may be tempered on closer inspection. The big name chain stores and restaurants have been kept out of the center, even Burger King, which was denied a downtown franchise after a long, local protest. The Burger King controversy typifies the town's resolve against outside exploitation. Despite zoning laws that seemed to permit the fast-food chain to move in, residents tried in every way to block its arrival. In the end, Burger King lost out, not having it—as their old commercial touts—their way.

More typical of downtown Provincetown's eating establishments is the Café Edwige, a cozy upstairs restaurant offering reasonably priced, carefully prepared food, and the emphasis is on healthful, fresh natural ingredients. Exhibits of work by local artists are also displayed here. And nearby is the brash Café Blasé, with its large outdoor seating area, varied menu, and late-night hours. This is a prime spot to view the passing pedestrians.

If you're overwhelmed by choices of how to spend your time upon your arrival, here are some sure bets:

We recommend you visit the Provincetown Heritage Museum at the corner of Commercial and Center streets. Built in 1860 (a registered national landmark), it originally housed a church, then the Chrysler Art Museum, which featured pop and traditional art. The larger-than-life-sized sculpture of two comical tourists by Chaim Gross that still stands in front of the building, serves as a reminder of the museum's past. The town bought the building in 1976, and it is now home to a collection of artifacts and art recalling the town's maritime history. On display is a model of the Grand Bank Indian Head fishing schooner *Rose Dorothea*, winner of the Lipton Cup in 1907.

Sir Thomas Lipton (1850–1931) was a Scottish merchant and yachting enthusiast who made five attempts to win the America's Cup, but never succeeded. (He was given a trophy by that race's sponsors for his persistence.) The Lipton Cup was donated by him for a race of fishing schooners in Boston Harbor in 1907, which the *Rose Dorothea* won. The cup itself is on display at the Provincetown Monument Museum.

For entertainment, we suggest you try the Pilgrim House, one block up from the Heritage Museum. The Pilgrim House offers fine dining and some of Provincetown's most sought-after entertainment—ranging from female impersonators, to rock bands, to the renowned puppetry of Wayland Flowers.

We also recommend Napi's Restaurant off nearby Freeman Street. A rustic drinking and dining spot that offers a varied menu, it is also a gathering place for the town's artistic and literary community.

One spot in the town center you shouldn't miss is MacMillan Wharf, named after Admiral Donald Baxter MacMillan, a Provincetown native and Arctic explorer. The wharf offers a plethora of activities; boats regularly depart here for harbor sightseeing, charter fishing, and whale watching, a favorite of many visitors. You have your pick of whale-watching boats, among them the *Dolphin Fleet*, the *Portuguese Princess*, and *Ranger V.* All have naturalists or scientists on board to answer your questions.

Summertime music billows out of the nearby Governor Bradford, at the corner of Standish and Commercial streets. This club and restaurant has been presenting New England's best rhythm and blues acts for 15 years—including Rhode Island's Roomful of Blues and Duke Robillard—and although it is leaning toward Top 40 bands these days, the blues are still featured Monday nights through the summer. For those looking to get away from it all—including the music—there are video games and pool tables in a large room downstairs.

Now if you have an incurable sweet tooth, there's no place like the Provincetown Penny Candy Store, on Commercial Street near the wharf, or Cabot's Candy Store, which is across the street. Homemade fudge and saltwater taffy are specialties here.

Not far from the candy stores you'll find Provincetown Town Hall, an imposing white clapboard structure built in 1866. The building's spacious auditorium is sometimes used for musical and theatrical presentations. Paintings by well-known Provincetown artists grace the building's halls, and its high ceilings, dark wood paneling, and large windows are all worth a quick look. Public rest rooms are located on the second floor.

Behind the building, across Bradford Street, is another sight worth taking in: the recently refurbished Pilgrim Bas Relief, located in a small, shady park where art exhibits and craft shows are occasionally presented, and the towering Pilgrim Monument overhead.

Modeled after the larger Torre del Mangia in Siena, Italy, the monument was built in 1907 from granite blocks brought to the Cape from Stonington, Maine. President William Howard Taft dedicated the structure on August 5, 1910, and it remains to this day one of the most impressive public monuments in the country. The Pilgrim Monument has its own private parking lot, on Winslow Street off Bradford, and houses a museum at its base.

For those with strong legs, the climb to the monument's turret is worth the view. To the northwest, looking across the bay, you can see the mainland and Boston's skyscrapers in the distance. To the southeast, you look out over the Province Lands to the Atlantic where only the curved horizon divides the sea from the sky.

Don't tarry in the turret; there is still plenty to see in the town center. Heading west on Commercial Street past Town Hall, you will run into more shops and studios. For those on the go, dune tours depart regularly from Standish Street, and horse 'n buggy rides through town leave from Town Hall. Look for the Provincetown Horse and Carriage Company sign.

The Universalist Meeting House, at 236 Commercial Street, is also worth visiting for its impressive trompe l'oeil interior—painted details that represent three-dimensional columns and molding—as well as for the religious services and occasional concerts presented there. Set slightly off the street in the heart of the town's busiest district, it is a noncommercial oasis.

If you just want to read, we suggest you browse through the cozy Provincetown Bookstore, which offers an outstanding range of hard- and softcover selections. This store also happens to be one of the bigger publishers of recorder (wooden flutelike wind instrument) music in the United States. Farther up Commercial Street, you'll find an intriguing shop called Outer Cape Kites where the emphasis is on originality as well as aerodynamics.

Another favorite stop, especially on a rainy day, is Marine Specialties, a large warehouse where military surplus goods run from clothing to unidentifiable doodads of dubious purpose. With its offering of everything from pith helmets to paraffin candles, this store will cause you to buy things you couldn't possibly anticipate but at prices that won't make you regret your impetuousness.

Still farther west on Commercial Street is the New Art Cinema, the town's only movie theater. But don't be fooled by its bourgeois name; it shows popular Hollywood releases, not art films.

The town center also offers a number of night spots geared for gay men and women. The Crown & Anchor, with its Back Room dancing club, is a popular gathering place.

But if you're just looking for a great place to eat, we recommend you try

Front Street, on Commercial Street near the post office (the recipes here are so intricate the chef often feels obliged to explain them in person).

When the bars close at 1 A.M. (a state law), a popular after-hours gathering spot is Spiritus Pizza, which also sells espresso and ice cream.

West End

If the center of Provincetown is where most of its businesses and nighttime establishments are located, the West End is where you can enjoy the harborside architecture of the town without having to deal with crowds. Because of its location (on the way to almost nowhere), the West End is the quietest part of Provincetown. The most direct access to the West End from Route 6 is on Shank Painter Road, the third exit off the highway.

Commercial Street heads west from the town center past the U.S. Coast Guard Station and curves left at Tremont Street. Several blocks beyond, at the corner of Soper Street, is the Seth Nickerson House, the town's oldest, circa 1746. It is open to the public from 10 A.M. to 5 P.M., daily from June through October. Across the street is the Center for Coastal Studies, a private non-profit organization conducting important research on whale migration and coastal geology. (Cetacean researchers from the Center accompany the Dolphin Fleet whale-watch cruises offered at MacMillan Wharf.) Stories about the center's work have been featured in the *New York Times* and on ABC's "20/20."

Heading toward the end of Commercial Street, you pass Land's End Inn on the right, which features a beautiful tulip garden and antique collection housed in an old captain's house, and the Red Inn on the left, which has the best view of any restaurant in Provincetown, and is open year-round.

At the end of Commercial Street is the Provincetown Inn, a sprawling resort that gained national recognition several years ago because middleweight boxing champ Marvelous Marvin Hagler trained there. He no longer does, but the inn is still worth a visit if only to see its series of murals depicting key moments in Provincetown's history. (The Provincetown Theater Company now makes its home here.)

Nearby is the long breakwater that stretches out to Wood End. It is a great place to visit at sunsets and low tide, though sneakers are recommended for those trying to negotiate the breakwater's boulders on foot. The barnacles can be murder.

Commercial Street ends at the rotary, but the road continues, curving to the north into the Province Lands. At the intersection with Bradford Street, which heads back into town, is the Moors, a restaurant offering outstanding Portuguese cooking and a unique jazz brunch (with live music) on Sundays. Next to the restaurant you will find the town's other public-access tennis courts.

But the best place, we think, to eat not only in the West End but in all of Provincetown is Sal's Place, which offers great Italian food and a water view. It is located on Commercial Street, not far from the Coast Guard Station.

Province Lands

The Province Lands, which make up most of the town's land mass, are home to scrub pines, shifting sand, some wildlife, and miles of beautiful beaches—all of which are part of the Cape Cod National Seashore. The most direct access to this area is on Race Point Road, a right-hand turn off Route 6 at the Conwell Street traffic lights. Passing the town "sanitary landfill"—the modern-day euphemism for "dump"—you come upon the Beech Forest Area on the left, which offers marked trails through a varied environment of woodland, ponds, and open dunes. This area is of particular interest to bird-watchers, who may be interested to know that the prime area for seeing rare species during the spring and fall migration is this area's parking lot, of all places.

Race Point Road continues through a lovely wooded area, then rises up over a bluff where the Province Lands Visitor Center offers a great view stretching from the Atlantic to the bay. Exhibits, films, and lectures are scheduled here nine months a year and offered free of charge. From the center's observation deck, binoculars can provide the keen-eyed visitor with the sight of whales splashing off Race Point.

The Province Lands has three horseback riding trails: Sunset Trail, West Trail, and Herring Cove Trail, each of which takes about two hours to cover. (The Provincetown Horse and Carriage Company offers guided rides for those who didn't ride their own steed into town). An eight-mile paved bicycle path through the Province Lands is another way to enjoy the scenery and get some exercise at the same time.

As Race Point Road heads north, you pass Provincetown Airport.

At the end of the road is Race Point Beach, where another U.S. Coast Guard Station is located. Just to the north is the National Seashore's Old Harbor Museum, housed in what used to be a U.S. Life Saving Service Station, which was moved here on a barge from Chatham. The Park Service floated it across the bay in 1978, refurbished it, and now it houses several fascinating exhibits relating to that service's storied past.

Both Race Point Beach and Herring Cove Beach, to the west off Province Lands Road, are unequaled white-sand Atlantic beaches, open to the public for a small fee. As is the case with all Cape beaches, those who arrive before noon have their pick of the parking. At the height of the season, there may be a wait to gain access to the parking lot, but bear in mind that there is no special treatment afforded locals.

Yearly Calendar of Events

There is a great contrast between the natural beauty of the Province Lands and the inhabited area of Provincetown, and the same is true of the pace of life during a typical year. While the rest of the Cape is developing a year-round economy, Provincetown remains a place that is hauntingly quiet in the winter and jarringly busy for two months of the summer. The off-season population is small, energetic, and fiercely devoted to the town, but efforts to extend the season beyond its normal parameters—Memorial Day to Labor Day—have been, for the most part, unsuccessful. Because of this, however, the best times to visit are the spring and the fall, when the weather is good (often better than during July and August), and the prices are lower. The residents tend to be friendlier as well.

The calendar year may begin in January, but in Provincetown the year really begins in April, when business owners return to their closed-up shops and begin to prepare for summer. Most open up during Memorial Day weekend, and then there is a lull during June, which ends abruptly with the annual Blessing of the Fleet celebration during the last weekend of that month. This unique celebration, which draws many visitors to the town, is a high-spirited mixture of the secular and sacred. The streets are colorfully decked out, and the town takes on a party atmosphere (though drinking in the streets, it must be mentioned, is strictly prohibited). The climax is a procession of boats past MacMillan Wharf where a visiting bishop dispenses holy water and blessings for safe passage and bountiful catches during the coming year. After the floating parade, the fishing fleet heads for Long Point, the absolute tip of the Cape (inaccessible by car), where a joyous feast and further good cheer end the day. Whatever the religious significance of the event, there is no denying that it is one heck of a party.

A week later, the Fourth of July is marked with a parade down Commercial Street and then a spectacular fireworks display over Provincetown Harbor, which can be seen from other Outer Cape towns across the bay.

The last big weekend of the season, Labor Day weekend, is often the busiest of the year, though the reality can fall short of expectations because of early departures, bad weather, and late-season burnout. In any case, the drop off in intensity in Provincetown following these three days is immediate, and the town breathes a collective sigh of relief.

The Provincetown Festival of Arts, which began in Provincetown under a different name in 1978, has been expanded in recent years to become a month-long celebration held each September in all eight Outer Cape towns. Artists open their studios to the public, and galleries show special exhibits and sponsor demonstrations. Other cultural events are scheduled by various local groups during this period, and a catalog including complete schedule and biographies of local artists is published by the festival's sponsor, Lower Cape Arts and Humanities Council.

Fall weather in Provincetown is superb. The water in the bay and ocean remains warm enough for swimming, and traveling around town is hassle-free. Many of Provincetown's stores and art galleries remain open until Christmas, offering reduced prices that make Provincetown a bargain hunter's paradise for finding unique Christmas gifts.

Following the holidays, things get really quiet. Those who choose to stick out the winter gather together in early February for the annual Year Rounders' Festival, a day-long celebration at Town Hall that includes an exposition by nonprofit organizations, a free banquet, talent show, and dancing till the wee hours. It signals both the end and beginning of another year in Provincetown and gives residents a chance to become reacquainted with each other.

From February to April, the weather can be as dismal as it is beautiful in the summer, though New England can wreak havoc on these assumptions. But this time of year is also one that many people enjoy the most—when neighbors can be visited, conversations can linger, and nature can be enjoyed without having to be concerned about where one is supposed to be in the next 15 minutes. Locals know it won't be long before the boards come off the windows, as Provincetown prepares for another summer season.

For over a century, the best source of information in Provincetown was the town crier, who walked around town announcing the time and other news accompanied by the ring of a large handbell. Although a costumed town crier can still be found roaming the summer streets, a greater wealth of information is available these days from other sources.

The oldest newspaper in town is the *Advocate*, founded in 1869. Published each Thursday, it offers news of town government, legal notices, arts and entertainment features, and classified ads. Also published weekly is the new *Provincetown Banner*, which provides an equally broad range of news, features and events. The twice weekly *Cape Codder* is also a good source for news and events.

Some of the best and most up-to-date information about Provincetown is on WOMR-FM, 91.9 on the radio dial, the town's unique community radio station with studios located at the corner of Bradford and Center streets. Founded six years ago by an eclectic collection of local residents, it has become an important voice of the Outer Cape, in spite of the technical imperfections that come from having a staff of volunteer DJs. Classical, folk, jazz, blues, and rock music, along with news interviews and weather information, is offered in a commercial-free format from 6 A.M. to 2 A.M. daily, year-round. Its monthly program guide, *Airwaves*, is available for free at many locations and is mailed to contributors.

One final word of advice: If you are going to stay in Provincetown at a hotel, inn, cottage, or campground, we urge you to plan ahead, especially if you're coming in July and August. Reservations are a must. And besides, why be distracted with such concerns once you get here? Provincetown's blend of casual living, unspoiled nature, and civilized luxury make for a spectacular place to vacation. It's no small wonder so many people return each year.

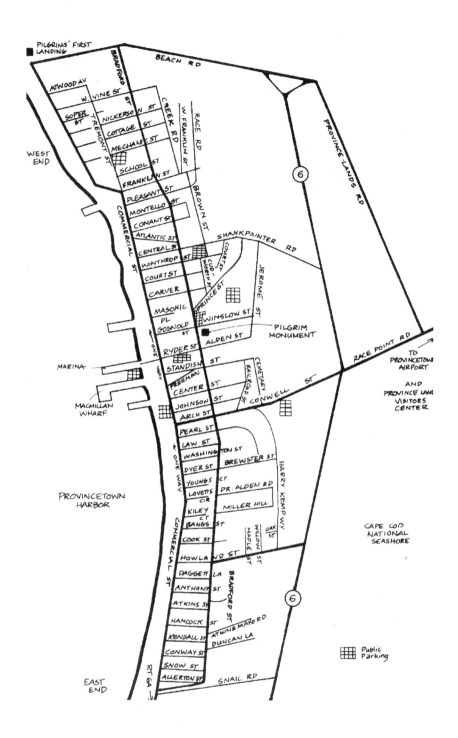

PROVINCETOWN

Provincetown: Essentials

 ## Important Public Information

Municipal Services

Town Hall: 487-7000
Police: 487-1212
Fire: 487-0345

Medical Services

Cape Cod Hospital, 27 Park St., Hyannis; 771-1800.
Outer Cape Health Services, Harry Kemp Way, Provincetown; 487-9395.

Veterinarians

Provincetown Animal Hospital, 140 Commercial St.; 487-2191.

Weather

The Cape Codder Weatherphone, 255-8500.

Tourist Information Services

Provincetown Chamber of Commerce, 307 and 309 Commercial St.; 487-3424.
Provincetown Reservations System, 487-6400. Call for tickets and information about Provincetown's summer theater, concerts, and shows.

243

Lodging

B&Bs & Guest Houses

RESERVATIONS SERVICES & DIRECTORIES

• *House Guests Cape Cod and the Islands* is the Cape and Islands' original and most varied bed and breakfast reservation service. More than 300 guest rooms are available; year-round service. Offers accommodations for singles, doubles, and families; water views and wooded locations. All accommodations have been inspected and approved; reasonable rates. For a directory covering Cape Cod and the Islands, write Box 1881, Orleans, MA 02653, or call 896-7053 or 1-800-666-HOST; Visa, MasterCard, American Express cards welcome.

• *Bed and Breakfast Cape Cod,* Box 341, West Hyannis Port 02672; 508-775-2772. Select from 60 host homes, country inns, and sea captains' houses on Cape Cod and the islands of Nantucket and Martha's Vineyard. Beaches, great seafood restaurants, whale watches, and summer theater are all a part of the local attractions. Modest/deluxe rates, private or shared baths. Write or call for free selection information.

We suggest for all Provincetown bed and breakfast establishments and guest houses you check to see if they are gay oriented.

• *Admiral's Landing Guest House,* 158 Bradford St.; 487-9665. Expensive. Open year-round. Walk to beach, color cable TV in common room, private baths, continental breakfast. Off-season rates; reservations required. Major credit cards accepted.

• *Ampersand Guest House,* 6 Cottage St.; 487-0959. Private bath. Major credit cards; reservations required.

• *Anchor Inn,* 175 Commercial St.; 487-0432. Expensive. Open year-round. Private beach, maid service in Victorian waterfront building. TV, private baths, off-season rates. Major credit cards accepted, suites available.

• *Asheton House,* 1 Cook St.; 487-9966. Open all year. Reservations required.

• *Bed 'n Breakfast,* 44 Commercial St.; 487-9555. Continental breakfast. Major credit cards; reservations required.

• *Bradford Gardens Inn,* 178 Bradford St.; 487-1616. Expensive. Fireplaces, gardens, long season from spring to fall. Maid service, reservations only. TV, breakfast available. Major credit cards accepted.

• *The Cape Codder Guest House,* 570 Commercial St.; 487-0131. Moderate to expensive. Antique captain's house in East End, shared baths, long season from spring to fall. Some efficiencies, breakfast available. Off-season rates, major credit cards accepted. Private beach. Reservations only.

• *The Captain & His Ship,* 164 Commercial St.; 487-1850. Expensive; moderate to expensive off-season. Victorian sea captain's home, now year-round guest house. Some private baths, TV, heat, continental breakfast. Off-season rates, maid service. Major credit cards accepted.

• *Captain Lysander Inn,* 96 Commercial St.; 487-2253. Private bath, reading room. Major credit cards accepted.

• *The Chicago House,* 6 Winslow St.; 487-0537. Private bath. Major credit cards; reservations required.

• *Dyer's Beach House,* 171 Commercial St.; 487-2061. On beach and near shopping, 5 rooms, seasonal.

• *1807 House,* 54 Commercial St.; 487-2173. Private bath. Major credit cards; reservations required.

• *The Elephant Walk,* 156 Bradford St.; 487-2543. Expensive. Country inn open year-round. Refrigerators, maid service, TV. Morning coffee. Off-season rates. Private baths. Major credit cards accepted.

• *Gabriel's,* 104 Bradford St.; 487-3232. Expensive. Guest rooms and apartments, open year-round. Near Town Center, cable TV, private baths, some efficiencies. Reservations only. Hot tub, sun deck, maid service. Off-season rates.

• *Gull Walk Inn,* 300-A Commercial St.; 487-9027. Reservations required.

• *Haven House,* 12 Carver; 487-3031. Private bath. Continental breakfast. Major credit cards; reservations required.

• *Heritage House,* 7 Center St.; 487-3692. Enjoy bayviews from the veranda of this 19th century home; residential neighborhood but close to town.

• *The Lamplighter Inn Guest House & Cottage,* 26 Bradford St.; 487-2529. Close to town, continental breakfast, waterviews and roof top deck.

• *Lands End Inn,* 22 Commercial St.; 487-0706. Beautiful gardens, great location.

• *Lotus Guest House,* 296 Commercial St.; 487-4644. Seasonal. Off-season rates. Major credit cards accepted; reservations suggested.

• *Masthead Cottages & Motel,* 31 Commercial St.; 487-0523. Expensive. Spacious West End waterfront location. Private baths, some efficiencies. Year-round, free mooring for yachts. Sun Decks. Reservations only. Off-season rates. Major credit cards accepted.

• *Ocean's Inn,* 386 Commercial St.; 487-0358. Expensive. Year-round, harbor view, restaurant, lounge. Some private baths, maid service. Major credit cards accepted.

• *Richmond Inn,* 4 Conant St.; 487-9193 or 487-1921. Open year-round. Restored captain's home. Common room. Water view. Maid service. Reservations required; major credit cards.

• *Rose & Crown Guest House,* 158 Commercial St.; 487-3332. Off-season rates.

• *Sea Drift Inn,* 80 Bradford St.; 487-3686. Inexpensive to moderate. Lounge, and full bar. Airport pick-up, open year-round. Major credit cards accepted.

• *Six Webster Place,* 6 Webster Place; 487-2266 or 800-6WEBSTER. Restored 1750's Cape with working fireplaces, luxury apartments available.

• *Somerset House,* 378 Commercial St.; 487-0383. Private bath. Major credit cards; Victorian inn across from the beach.

• *Sunset Inn,* 142 Bradford St.; 487-9810. Off-season rates. Continental breakfast.

• *Trade Winds Inn,* 12 Johnson St.; 487-0138. Victorian home, private bath, continental breakfast. Major credit cards; reservations required.

• *Twelve Center Guest House,* 12 Center St.; 487-0381. Victorian house, private bath, TV, continental breakfast. Major credit cards; reservations required.

• *Watermark Inn,* 603 Commercial St.; 487-0165. Expensive. Harbor views, private beach, elegant suites with decks, maid service, some efficiencies. Private baths, open year-round. Off-season rates. Major credit cards accepted.

• *White House Inn,* 500 Commercial St.; 487-1790. TV, private bath. Reservations required.

• *White Wind Inn*, 174 Commercial St.; 487-1526. Victorian guest house, TV, maid service. Open year-round. Off-season rates; reservations required; major credit cards.

• *Windamar House,* 568 Commercial St.; 487-0599. Private bath, continental breakfast. Reservations required.

Resorts, Hotels, Motels, Condominiums, & Selected Cottages

- **Blue Sea Motor Inn,** Rte. 6A; 487-1041. Private beach; view of Cape Cod Bay, across from National Seashore. Color TV, heated indoor pool. May and September, lower rates. Maid service. Major credit cards; reservations required.
- **The Boatslip,** 161 Commercial St.; 487-1669 or 800-451-7547. Seasonal hotel on the water; pool.
- **Bradford House and Motel,** 41 Bradford St.; 487-0173. Expensive. Near beach and shopping.
- **Breakwater Motel,** Rte. 6A; 487-1134. Moderate to expensive. Near beach and shopping, water view.
- **Chateau Motor Inn,** Bradford St. W.; 487-1286. Moderate to expensive. Centrally located.
- **Crown & Anchor Motor Inn,** 247 Commercial St.; 487-1430. Expensive. In town center, close to beach and shopping.
- **Dexter's Country Inn & Resort,** 6 Conwell St.; 487-1911. Rooms, suites, cable TV, greenhouse, pool.
- **Dingby Dock,** 71 Commercial St.; 487-0075. Moderate. Apartments on the beach.
- **Dunes Motel,** Bradford St. W.; 487-1956. Moderate to expensive. Near beach and shopping.
- **Dyer's Beach House,** 171 Commercial St.; 487-2061. Expensive. On the beach and near shopping, water view, 5 rooms, seasonal.
- **The Fairbanks Inn,** 90 Bradford St.; 487-0386. Private baths; fireplaces, lounges, and sun decks. Open year-round; reservations required.
- **The Heritage House,** 7 Center St.; 487-3692. Off-season rates, continental breakfast. Reservations preferred.
- **Holiday Inn,** Rte. 6A; 487-1711 or 800-422-4224. Near beach and shopping, water view.
- **The Masthead,** 31-41 Commercial St.; 487-0523 or 800-395-5095. Cottages, apartments, efficiencies or rooms overlooking Provincetown Harbor, sundecks, moorings and launch service.
- **Meadows Motel,** Bradford St. Ext.; 487-0880. Private bath; major credit cards.
- **Moors Motel,** Beach Highway; 487-1342. Expensive. Close to beach and shopping.
- **Pilgrim Colony Motel & Cottages,** Rte. 6A; 487-0455. Moderate to expensive. Close to beach and shopping, water view.
- **Provincetown Inn & Conference Center,** 1 Commercial St.; 487-9500. Moderate to expensive. Beautiful water views, attractive rooms.
- **Sandcastle Condominiums,** rentals and time-share, Rte. 6A; 487-9300. Indoor and outdoor pools, restaurant, and lounge.
- **Shamrock Motel, Cottages,** 49 Bradford St.; 487-1133. Color cable TV, private baths, maid service. Reservations required; major credit cards.
- **Ship's Bell Inn & Motel,** 586 Commercial St.; 487-1674. Expensive. Close to beach and shopping, water view.
- **Surfside Inn,** 543 Commercial St.; 487-1726. Expensive. Close to beach and shopping, water.
- **Sutton Place East,** Rte. 6A; 487-9420. Moderate. Cottages, apartments and houses, private beach.

• *The Tides Motor Inn,* Rte. 6A, Shore Rd.; 487-1045. Swimming pool, cable TV, maid service. Reservations required; major credit cards.
• *Victoria House,* 5 Standish St.; 487-4455. Private baths, cable color TV, refrigerators. Open year-round.
• *Westwinds on Gull Hill,* 28 Commercial St.; 487-1841. Private beach.
• *White Sands Motel,* Rte. 6A; 487-0244. Waterfront resort with private beach, pools, efficiencies available, continental breakfast.

Campgrounds

• *Coastal Acres Camping Court,* W. Vine St.; 487-1700. Wooded sites, electricity, and water. Telephones, laundry, gas, grocery, trailer hookups. April through October, three-day minimum. Reservations recommended in peak season.
• *Dunes Edge Camp Ground,* off Rte. 6; 487-9815. Rustic sites, sanitary facilities. Brochure upon request, reservation suggested, spring through fall.
• *Outermost Hostel,* 28 Winslow St.; 487-4378. Youth hostel, May–Oct.

Dining

• *Billy Bones Raw Bar,* 16 MacMillan Wharf; 487-3688. At the end of the wharf, this new restaurant has gourmet sandwiches and a raw bar, all enjoyed on a wraparound deck overlooking the harbor.
• *Boatslip Restaurant,* 161 Commercial St.; 487-2509. Moderate to expensive. American cuisine, three separate dining areas decorated with the work of local artists. Water view; breakfast, lunch, and dinner. Specials include lobster with red pepper and shallot butter. Full liquor license, extensive wine list. Sunday brunch. Major credit cards, reservations suggested. Seasonal.
• *Bubala's By the Bay,* 183 Commercial St.; 487-0773. Moderate. Innovative dining, serving breakfast (Huevos Rancheros!), lunch (Foccacia sandwiches), and dinner (seafood and vegetarian specialties).
• *Cactus Garden,* 186 Commercial St.; 487-6661. Southwestern cuisine.
• *Café Blasé,* 328 Commercial St.; 487-9465. Moderate. Imaginative French and American cuisine served on a spacious patio under umbrellas, with a great view of the passing street scene. Breakfast, lunch, and dinner seasonally. Full liquor license, major credit cards.
• *Café Edwige,* 333 Commercial St.; 487-2008. Moderate to expensive. Simple, elegant dining in a spacious upstairs loft or on outdoor deck. Fresh breakfast from 8 A.M. Nouvelle cuisine dinners from 6 P.M. Full liquor license, year-round. Closed Tuesdays. Exhibits of work by local artists. Reservations suggested for dinner. MasterCard and Visa accepted.
• *Carreiro's Tips for Tops'n*, 31 Bradford St.; 487-1811. Inexpensive to moderate. Straightforward family dining and Portuguese specialties. Seasonal. Generous portions, modest prices, nautical decor, free parking. Wine and beer license. Visa and MasterCard accepted.
• *Ciro & Sal's,* 4 Kiley Court; 487-0049. Moderate to expensive. Elegant dining in a rustic basement setting rich with atmosphere. Fine Italian cuisine and fresh seafood; specials include Vitello Scalloppine alla Marsala, Lasagna Verdi. Full liquor license, extensive wine list, upstairs lounge. Year-round (weekends off-season). Major credit cards accepted, reservations recommended. Dinner only, from 5:30 P.M.

DINING (CONTINUED)

- *Dairyland,* Shank Painter Rd.; 487-1724. Inexpensive. The freshest fried seafood, as well as burgers, fries, onion rings. Soft ice cream, ample seating. Free parking. Seafood market on premises.
- *Dancing Lobster,* 9 Ryder St.; 487-0900. Moderate. Mediteranean cuisine, fresh seafood, pasta. Dinner only. Beer/wine license. No reservations taken. Seasonal—April to late Nov.
- *Dodie's Diner,* 401 Commercial St.; 487-3868. Inexpensive. New York-style pizza, pasta specialties, deli salads, spinach pies. Homemade desserts, cakes, and cannoli. Open from 11:30 A.M. to 2 P.M. Seasonal. Take-out service.
- *Fat Jack's Café,* 335 Commercial St.; 487-4822. Inexpensive. Breakfast, lunch, and dinner, simple fare including soups, appetizers, sandwiches, salads, and Mexican dishes. Full bar. Open from 11 A.M. to 1 a.m., seasonal. MasterCard and Visa accepted.
- *Front Street,* 230 Commercial St.; 487-9715. Expensive. Gourmet dining in a dark, casual atmosphere. Menu changes weekly, including innovative seafood, fowl, and meat dishes for the discriminating palate. Full bar and wine list. Dinner from 6 to 11 P.M. Saturday and Sunday brunch from 11:30 A.M. to 3 P.M. Major credit cards. Reservations recommended.
- *Gallerani's Café,* 133 Commercial St.; 487-4433. Moderate. Good food, pleasant atmosphere in the remodeled location of the former Cookie's Tap, a legendary local bar and restaurant. Full bar; breakfast, lunch, and dinner; bar open until 1 A.M. Some parking, major credit cards accepted. Open year-round, reservations recommended for dinner during peak season. Take-out service.
- *Gloria's,* 269 Commercial St.; 487-0015. Italian-Portuguese food, waterfront dining.
- *Governor Bradford,* 312 Commercial St.; 487-9618. Moderate. No frills fare, generous portions, served indoors or on patio in the heart of downtown, with view of street scene. Children's menu. Saloon atmosphere, with nightly entertainment (rock, rhythm and blues) during summer. Game room downstairs. Major credit cards accepted. Reservations not necessary.
- *Landmark Inn Restaurant,* 404 Commercial St.; 487-9319. Moderate. Varied menu emphasizing rich, imaginative seafood dishes and indulgent desserts. Full bar. Candlelit antique decor. No children's menu. Major credit cards accepted, reservations recommended. Dinner only, April through November.
- *Lobster Pot,* 321 Commercial St.; 487-0842. Moderate to expensive. Exhaustive seafood menu, generous portions, and authentic, fresh recipes. Outstanding chowder. Lunch and dinner. Full liquor license. Seasonal. Open at noon. Water view, downtown location. Major credit cards accepted. Reservations suggested.
- *Martin House,* 157 Commercial St.; 487-1327. Housed in a 1750's captain's house, the fare is international. Fireplaced rooms, harbor views, afternoon tea on Sundays Sept.–June.
- *Mayflower Café,* 300 Commercial St.; 487-0121. Inexpensive. Basic American food and Portuguese specialties offered year-round for lunch and dinner. Full liquor license. Informal family restaurant, gathering place for locals as well, casual atmosphere. Major credit cards. No reservations.
- *The Mews,* 429 Commercial St.; 487-1500. Expensive. Continental gourmet cuisine, gourmet seafood and vegetarian dishes and meat specials in elegant courtyard setting with water view. Dinner from 6 P.M., Sunday brunch from 11 A.M. Full liquor license, extensive wine list. Major credit cards accepted, reservation recommended.

• *Mojo's,* 5 Ryder St. Ext.; 487-3140. Inexpensive. Quality fast food including shellfish and seafood, chowder, burgers, homemade chili, hot dogs, juices, and ice cream shakes. Outdoor seating. Open 11:30 A.M. to 2 A.M., summer only.

• *The Moors,* Bradford St. W.; 487-0840. Moderate. Portuguese and American cuisine served in attractive driftwood-decorated setting with many nautical touches. Specials include full Lobster Clambake and Parrichada de Mariscos, a kind of Portuguese bouillabaisse. Lunch and dinner, full liquor license. Lounge with piano entertainment on weekends. Reservations suggested. Seasonal. Major credit cards accepted.

• *Napi's Restaurant,* 7 Freeman St.; 487-1145. Moderate. Excellent, eclectic menu, striking casual atmosphere (exposed wood and stained glass), a favorite of locals and visitors. Specials include Brazilian, Middle Eastern, oriental, and Portuguese offerings, as well as vegetarian entrées. Open year-round, with upstairs art gallery, full bar. Breakfast, lunch, and dinner. Major credit cards accepted. Reservations for dinner during July and August.

• *Ocean's Inn,* 386 Commercial St.; 487-0358. Moderate. Elegant atmosphere and varied cuisine, including seafood, duck, prime rib, homemade desserts. Water view. Full bar and lounge; lodging available. Breakfast and lunch from 11 to 3 P.M. (on outdoor deck); dinner from 5:30 P.M. on. Year-round. Major credit cards accepted. Reservations for dinner during summer.

• *Pepe's Wharf,* 371 Commercial St.; 487-0670. Moderate to expensive. Superb international cuisine emphasizing fresh seafood, served in romantic waterfront setting. Specials include bouillabaisse au Pernod, barbecued shrimp. Raw bar, upstairs deck, full bar. Lunch from 11:30 A.M., dinner from 6 to 11 P.M. Major credit cards accepted, reservations suggested. Seasonal.

• *Post Office Café,* 303 Commercial St.; 487-3892. Moderate. Breakfast, lunch, and dinner in small, casual pub atmosphere in the heart of downtown. Generous portions, full bar. Major credit cards accepted. Year-round. Entertainment in upstairs lounge. Reservations not necessary.

• *Provincetown Inn Harborview Restaurant,* One Commercial St.; 487-9500. Moderate; inexpensive early-bird specials. American fare, generous portions, tasteful atmosphere. Children's menu, breakfast buffet, lunch, dinner. Entertainment in lounge. Major credit cards accepted. Reservations suggested. Free parking. Water view.

• *Pucci's Harborside Restaurant & Bar,* 539 Commercial St.; 487-1964. Moderate. Tastefully prepared brunch, lunch, and dinner, with seafood specialties including grilled swordfish and bass. Outdoor deck, casual bar. Reservations suggested for dinner. Seasonal. Major credit cards accepted. Commanding view of harbor.

• *The Red Inn,* 15 Commercial St.; 487-0050. Moderate to expensive. Superb atmosphere in a spacious historic building on the waterfront. New England country cooking with shellfish and other seafood specialties. Breakfast from 9 A.M., lunch, and dinner from 5 P.M. Open year-round. Parking available. Full bar and lounge. Major credit cards accepted. Dinner reservations recommended.

• *Sal's Place,* 99 Commercial St.; 487-1279. Moderate to expensive. Superb homestyle Italian cuisine and seafood specialties, including Scampi alla Marinara, and outstanding wine list. Dinner indoors or on deck with harborfront view. Seasonal (weekends through fall). Reservations recommended at all times.

• *Sea View Restaurant,* 183 Commercial St.; 487-0773. Moderate. Family-style dining, with water view. Seafood specialties, prime rib. Lunch and dinner, summer only. Major credit cards accepted, full liquor license. Parking on premises. Reservations at peak season recommended.

DINING (CONTINUED)

- **Sebastian's Long and Narrow Restaurant,** 177 Commercial St.; 487-3286. Moderate. Waterfront dining with excellent view of harbor. Greenhouse atmosphere. Seafood, poultry, meats, and rack of lamb among specialties. Dinner only, summer only. Major credit cards accepted. Reservations recommended.
- **Spiritus,** 190 Commercial St.; 487-2808. Inexpensive to moderate. Pizza, ice cream, espresso at premium prices, open until 2 A.M. Breakfast sweet rolls, danish, and croissants with fresh juice and coffee. Seasonal.
- **Stormy Harbor Restaurant,** 277 Commercial St.; 487-1680. Inexpensive to moderate. Simple, well-prepared Portuguese and American cuisine. Breakfast, lunch, and dinner, with children's menu available. Major credit cards accepted. Reservations not necessary.
- **Surf Restaurant, Inc.,** 315A Commercial St.; 487-1367. Open every day, serving food and liquor.
- **The Town House Restaurant,** 291 Commercial St.; 487-0292. Moderate to expensive. Breakfast, lunch, and dinner served year-round. Tasteful decor, full bar, lounges, entertainment. Banquet facilities available. Major credit cards accepted. Reservations for dinner at peak season.
- **Vorelli's,** 226 Commercial St.; 487-2778. Moderate. Steaks, seafood, Italian specialties. Casual, dark atmosphere with brass, leather, and booths. Full bar. Lunch from 11 A.M. on, dinner at 5:30 P.M. Major credit cards accepted. Reservations at peak season recommended. Closed Mondays. Seasonal.

Entertainment

Music & Stage

- **Music series** include the Muse Series, sponsored by the Provincetown Playhouse, Inc., and the Beach Plum Music Series, produced by Erwin Frankel and Ellen Rafel. Top-name folk and jazz performers in concert at Town Hall and the Universalist Meeting House. Summer only.
- **Provincetown Art Association,** 460 Commercial St.; 487-1750.
- **Provincetown Theater Co.,** 14 Center St.; 487-3466. A 25-year-old amateur theater group; performs off-season only.
- **Provincetown Repertory Theatre,** 487-6400. Call for schedule and ticket information.

Nightlife

- **Conrad's Pilgrim House,** 426 Commercial St.; 487-0319. Topical musical reviews, female impersonators in Madeira Room, jazz groups and lounge singers in upstairs lounge, nightly. Summer only. Reservations suggested.
- **The Crown & Anchor,** 247 Commercial St.; 487-1430. Lounge pianist-singer in bar weekends, summer only. Occasional performances (music, drama) in Back Room.
- **Different Ducks,** 135 Bradford St.; 487-9648. Female impersonators, acoustic folk rock groups, lounge singers in upstairs lounge. Nightly in summer. Weekends year-round.

- *Governor Bradford,* 312 Commercial St.; 487-9618. Rock, Top 40, blues, and reggae bands nightly, summer only.
- *The Moors,* Bradford St. W.; 487-0840. Lenny Grandchamp, local favorite on piano, vocal and repartee, weekends during summer.
- *Post Office Cabaret,* 303 Commercial St.; 487-3892. Lounge singers, female impersonators, nightly summer only. Reservations suggested.
- *Provincetown Inn,* One Commercial St.; 487-9500. Seasonal entertainment.
- *Surf Club,* 315A Commercial St.; 487-1367. The Provincetown Jug Band, eclectic folk-rock-jazz-novelty band, six nights during summer. Dinner and lunch available, seasonal.
- *Town House,* 291 Commercial St.; 487-0295. Lounge singers in bar, rowdy puppetry in comedy room, occasional rock band in downstairs bar. Reservations suggested.

Movie Theater

- *New Art Cinema,* 214 Commercial St.; 487-9222. First-run pictures; daily in summer; weekends off-season.

Museums

- *Old Harbor Museum,* owned and operated by the Cape Cod National Seashore at Race Point, off Race Point Rd. Exhibits of memorabilia from U.S. Life Saving Service. Open daily spring through fall. No fee.
- *Pilgrim Memorial Monument and Museum,* Monument Hill; 487-1310. Impressive exhibits concerning the Pilgrims, Provincetown's artistic and literary heritage, and memorabilia of Admiral Donald MacMillan, Arctic explorer and Provincetown native. Open 9 A.M. to 5 P.M. in season, reduced hours year-round. Admission.
- *Provincetown Art Association and Museum,* 460 Commercial St.; 487-1750. Permanent collection of art by famed Provincetown painters, past and present. Open year-round; weekends off-season. Changing exhibits, special events.
- *Provincetown Heritage Museum,* 356 Commercial St.; 487-0666. Town-owned collection of art, nautical artifacts and other exhibits of the town's fishing heritage, antique fire equipment, and environmental displays. Open 10 A.M. to 10 P.M. daily, summer only. Admission.

Historic Sites

- *First Landing Place of the Pilgrims,* near breakwater at beginning (West End) of Commercial St. Bronze plaque on boulder marks where the *Mayflower's* passengers first set foot in the New World in 1620. No fee.
- *Seth Nickerson House,* 72 Commercial St., the oldest house in Provincetown, built around 1746 by a ship's carpenter. Authentic full Cape. Open to public from 10 A.M. to 5 P.M., daily June through October. Admission.
- *Pilgrim Bas Relief,* Bradford St., behind Town Hall. Large bronze work set in grassy knoll depicts Pilgrims signing the Mayflower Compact, the first democratic document signed in North America. No fee.
- *Pilgrim Monument,* Town Hill. Granite public monument built in 1910. 225 ft., ramps to top, open year-round. Museum at bottom. Admission.

Seasonal Events

- *Annual Year Rounders' Festival.* Late January or early February, day-long exhibits and feast at Town Hall.
- *Blessing of the Fleet.* Last weekend of June, procession of boats past Bishop on MacMillan Wharf, townwide celebrations and events.
- *Provincetown Business Guild "Carnival."* Festive celebration of gay lifestyle, arts and entertainment events, early August.
- *Provincetown Craft Guild Annual Shows.* July and August at Bas Relief Park. Before Christmas at Provincetown Art Association and Museum. Labor Day. The finale to the summer season, with many special events planned.

Tours/Whale Watching

Whale-watching tours are available on the following:
- *Dolphin Fleet,* MacMillan Wharf; 349-1900 or 1-800-826-9300. Capacity 150 per cruise, departures morning, afternoon, and sunset. Spring through fall, weather permitting. Researchers from Center for Coastal Studies on board. Food, cocktails available. MasterCard, Visa accepted.
- *Portuguese Princess,* MacMillan Wharf; 487-2651 or 1-800-442-3188. Naturalists lead cruises, 150 capacity. April to November. Food and full bar on board.
- *Ranger V,* MacMillan Wharf; 487-3322, 487-1582, or 1-800-992-9333. Three trips daily, naturalists on board.
- *Cape Cod Whale Watch Hot Line,* 487-2600.

Dune tours are available at the corner of Commercial and Standish streets; here are some other touring opportunities:
- *Art's Dune Tours,* 487-1950. Lecture tours along the beach and through the dunes.
- *Provincetown Trolley, Inc.,* leaves from Commercial St. outside Town Hall; 487-9483. Narrative tour of Provincetown; about 40 minutes.
- *Nelson's Riding Stables,* 43 Race Point Rd.; 487-1112. Guided trail rides through the Cape Cod National Seashore, sunset ride available for more advanced riders.
- *Sea Faris*, MacMillan Wharf; 48-SHARK or 1-800-923-8773. A lively tour with Capt. Mike Orbe aboard his R/V *Tiger Shark.* This is a 40-year-old wooden research boat that gives the visitor a glimpse into marine geology, knot tying, marine history, sea creatures, and a few yarns about pirates. A nauralist is on board.

Shops

Art Galleries

- *Berta Walker Galleries,* 208 Bradford St.; 487-6411 and 153 Commercial St.; 487-8794. Represents many Provincetown artists.
- *Robert Clibbon Gallery,* 120 Commercial St.; 487-3563. Summer only. 10 A.M. to 6 P.M. Color etchings of marine and animal life, and landscapes by Robert Clibbon and Melyssa Bearse.
- *Cortland Jessup Gallery,* 432 Commercial St.; 487-4479. Works by Ron Bauer, Bruce Cratsley.

- *East End Gallery,* 432 Commercial St.; 487-4745. Contemporary art by artists from Boston and New York as well as Provincetown.
- *Elements,* 338 Commercial St.; 487-4351. Jewelry, pottery, metalworks, wood sculpture by local artists.
- *Halcyon Gallery,* 371 Commercial St.; 487-9415. Handmade clothing and jewelry.
- *Eva DeNagy Gallery,* 427 Commercial St.; 487-9669. Open days and evenings in summer; by appointment year-round. Showing carvings and pastels by Eva DeNagy, African and Japanese imports.
- *Harvey Dodd Gallery,* 437 Commercial St.; 487-3329. Seasonal. Showing paintings, prints and drawings by Harvey Dodd of local sights and architecture.
- *Eye of Horus Gallery,* 7 Freeman St.; 487-9162. Open year-round, showing work by Provincetown artists. Framing services. Upstairs from Napi's Restaurant.
- *Fine Arts Work Center Hudson D. Walker Gallery,* 24 Pearl St.; 487-9960. Contemporary works in all media by past and present fellows at the center, a state- and federally-endowed residential program for artists and writers. Open year-round.
- *Ellen Harris Gallery,* 355 Commercial St.; 487-1414. Fine arts and crafts from around the country. Outstanding young artists featured in shows through summer. Open days and nights, seasonally.
- *Julie Heller Gallery,* 2 Gosnold St.; 487-2169. Featuring early Provincetown painters and printmakers, folk art, Americana and contemporary art. Days and evenings, summer only.
- *Impulse,* 188 Commercial St.; 487-1154. Daily, 10 A.M. to 11 P.M. Summer only. Provincetown artists, including Hensche, Knaths, and Griffel. Also crafts and kaleidoscopes.
- *Kiley Court Gallery,* 445 Commercial St.; 487-4496. Cape Cod artists.
- *The Little Gallery,* 227 Commercial St.; 487-0208. Gayle Lovett Prints. The Little Store.
- *Long Point Gallery,* 492 Commercial St.; 487-1795. Paintings and sculptures by nationally renowned artists including Bultman, Cicero, Hopkins, Motherwell, and Simon. Days and evenings, summers only.
- *Massimo Gallery,* 416 Commercial St.; 487-0265. Contemporary paintings by local artists, sculpture, ceramics, antique glass. Individual exhibits, artist-owned.
- *The Packard Gallery,* 418 Commercial St.; 487-4690. Days and evenings in summer, by appointment year-round. Showing contemporary impressionist paintings by Anne and Cynthia Packard, as well as the work of other artists.
- *Provincetown Art Association and Museum,* 460 Commercial St.; 487-1750. Three galleries showing work by Provincetown artists of today, works from an important permanent collection, touring exhibits and members' cooperative shows. Music and drama also presented. Open year-round; weekends off-season.
- *Provincetown Group Gallery,* 286 Bradford St.; 487-0275. Upstairs, open daily, summer only, weekends, evenings. The best young artists from Provincetown, Boston and New York, as well as established names including Richter, Shahn, and Wells.
- *Rising Tide Gallery,* 494 Commercial St.; 487-4312.
- *Star Gallery,* 432 Commercial St.; 487-4100. Gallery of Rock 'n Roll, emphasis on John Lennon.

ART GALLERIES (CONTINUED)

• *Tennyson Gallery,* 237 Commercial St.; 487-2460. Sculpture, art glass, ceramics, and jewelry by leading Provincetown artists. Days and evenings, summer only.

• *Wenniger Graphics Gallery,* 445 Commercial St.; 487-2452. Prints, watercolors, etchings, and handmade paper. Individual shows throughout the season. Summer only, days and evenings, Wednesday to Monday.

Craft & Specialty Shops

Take a walk from the east end of Commercial Street to the west. You'll find scores of craft and specialty shops.

Antiques

• *Remembrances of Things Past,* 376 Commercial St.; 487-9443. Antiques and memorabilia, gifts. Open year-round, credit cards accepted.

• *September Morn,* 385 Commercial St.; 487-9092. Oriental antiques.

 # Sports & Recreation

Biking

• *Arnold's Bicycle Rental,* 329 Commercial St.; 487-0844. Seasonal.

• *Nelson's Bike Rental,* Race Point Rd.; 487-0034. Horseback rentals, lessons. Guided tours of Province Lands.

• *Province Lands Bicycle Trail.* No fee.

• *Provincetown Bikes,* 42 Bradford St.; 487-8735.

Boating

• *Flyer's Boat Rental,* 131A Commercial St.; 487-0898. Power- and sailboats by the hour, day or week. Skippers for hire. Mooring available.

• *Provincetown School of Sailing,* 235 Commercial St.; 487-1764. Sail- and powerboat rentals, marine store. Seasonal, weather permitting, through September.

Fishing

• *The Shady Lady,* MacMillan Wharf; 487-1700. Full- or half-day charters for bass, blues, tuna.

Hiking & Nature Trails

• *Beech Forest Area.* Self-guided and ranger-guided walks and trails, prime birding site, varied terrain.

• *Cape Cod National Seashore,* Province Lands Visitor Center, Race Point Rd.; 487-1256. Exhibits, talks, guided trails. Open spring through New Year's. No fee. Outdoor amphitheater.

• *Center for Coastal Studies,* 59 Commercial St.; 487-3622. A non-profit environmental organization that offers walks, lectures and educational programs year-round.

Tennis

• *Bissell's Tennis Court,* Bradford St. W.; 487-9512. Clay courts, rented by the hour. Reservations. Summer only.

• *Provincetown Tennis Club,* 286 Bradford St.; 487-9574. Hourly rental, spring to late fall. Clay and all-weather. Racket restringing, open tournaments. Reservations.

Beaches

• *Cape Cod National Seashore, Herring Cove,* and *Race Point beaches.* Lifeguards on duty, daily fees. Toilet facilities, parking.

For detailed information on Provincetown beaches in the National Seashore, see special section starting on page 213.

Churches

• *St. Mary of the Harbor,* 517 Commercial St.; 487-0199. (Episcopal).
• *St. Peter the Apostle,* 15 Prince St.; 487-0095 (Roman Catholic).
• *United Methodist Church,* 10 Shank Painter Rd.; 487-0584.
• *Universalist-Unitarian Meeting House,* 236 Commercial St.; 487-9344.

Odds & Ends

Laundries

• *Don's Pick Up & Delivery Service,* 506 Commercial St.; 487-0991.
• *Mama's Laundry Service,* 487-4941.

Farm Stands

• *J&E Fruit & Produce,* Provincelands Rd.; 487-3627.

Fish Markets

- *Cape Cod Fish Company,* 27 Court St.; 487-0085.
- *Long Wharf Fish Market,* 30 Conwell St.; 487-1634.
- *The Missing Link,* 3 Standish; 487-2589.
- *Provincetown Seafood Market,* Shank Painter Rd.; 487-9184.

Ice Cream Parlors

- *Dairy Queen of Provincetown,* Bradford St.; 487-1574.

Bakeries

- *Provincetown Portuguese Bakery,* 299 Commercial St.; 487-1803.

Library

- *Provincetown Public Library,* 330 Commercial St.; 487-7094.

 # *Best of Provincetown*

BEST COUNTRY INN
- *Watermark Inn,* 603 Commercial St.; 487-0165.

BEST GUEST HOUSE
- *The Cape Codder Guest House,* 570 Commercial St.; 487-0131.

BEST RESORT
- *Provincetown Inn & Conference Center,* 1 Commercial St.; 487-9500.

BEST BREAKFAST
- *The Boatslip Restaurant,* 161 Commercial St.; 487-2509.

BEST MEAL
- *Dancing Lobster,* 9 Ryder St.; 487-0900.
- *Front Street,* 230 Commercial St.; 487-9715.
- *The Mews,* 359 Commercial St.; 487-1500.
- *Sal's Place,* 99 Commercial St.; 487-1279.

BEST FRIED SEAFOOD
- *Mojo's,* 5 Ryder St. Ext.; 487-3140.

BEST ENTERTAINMENT
- *Walking Commercial Street;* the show is continuous, and it's free.

BEST MUSEUM AND HISTORIC SITE
- *The Provincetown Art Association and Museum,* 460 Commercial St.; 487-1750.

BEST GALLERY, CRAFT, SPECIALTY & ANTIQUE SHOPS

Take your pick; we suggest you browse up and down Commercial Street.

BEST SEASONAL EVENT

• *The Blessing of the Fleet,* MacMillan Wharf the last weekend in June.

BEST WHALE WATCHING

• *Dolphin Fleet,* MacMillan Wharf; 1-800-826-9300.

BEST BEACHES

• *Race Point* and *Herring Cove* (both National Seashore beaches).

BEST TENNIS

• *Provincetown Tennis Club,* 296 Bradford St.; 487-9574.

BEST HIKING OR NATURE TRAIL

• *Province Lands,* inside the Cape Cod National Seashore.

BEST CAMPING

• *Coastal Acres Camping Court,* W. Vine St.; 487-1700.

THE ISLANDS

*Martha's Vineyard, Nantucket,
Elizabeth Islands*

The Islands: Viewpoints

by Mark Alan Lovewell

Martha's Vineyard, Nantucket, and a collection of smaller islands called the Elizabeth chain stretch out upon the sea off the backside of Cape Cod like a string of jewels. These jewels were formed more than 30,000 years ago during the last glacial period as ice from the huge glacier that covered most of North America receded—leaving behind precious deposits of sand.

Nowhere else along the Massachusetts coast is the shoreline so uninterrupted by development, and nowhere else have communities—descendants, for the most part, of whalers, Indians, shellfishermen, and farmers—remained so closely tied to the land.

Accessible only by air and sea, these isolated communities have been slow to change, and that in itself attracts hundreds of thousands of visitors each year to these island retreats to bask on pristine beaches, view the early American architecture, or stroll in protected woodlands.

There are no high-rise buildings here, no swank motels to speak of—just stately inns and sea captains' homes. And although the landscape has changed over the years (less open space), the character of the islands has remained intact.

But despite similarities, each island is different and has its own tradition, history, and charm. In a word, Martha's Vineyard is quaint; Nantucket is rustic; and the Elizabeth Islands—named after the Queen of England or, as some historians suggest, the sister of discoverer Bartholomew Gosnold—are truly insular.

The difference can also be seen in geographies. The Vineyard is a collection of lush plains, steep cliffs, thick forests, and rocky farmland. Nantucket is more uniformly flat; you can sense the presence of the ocean everywhere— "an elbow of sand, all beach without a background," Herman Melville wrote of the island. The Elizabeth chain is more a combination of the two, with its moors, meadows, thick woodlands, and peaceful sandy beaches.

The islands themselves have contrasts within, which make them all the more enticing. On Martha's Vineyard, for instance, Vineyard Haven (or Tisbury, as it is also called) seems worlds apart from Edgartown, which is in reality less than 10 miles away. Edgartown is considered more upscale, more highbrow and conservative, while Vineyard Haven is thought to be more liberal—a gathering place for New York and Washington intellectuals and literati.

On Nantucket, the town of Nantucket bustles with activity; its trendy galleries, shops, and boutiques are filled with vacationers and "day-trippers" (visitors who have come over on the ferry for only the day). But just six miles to the east in subdued Siasconset (called 'Sconset), a thriving actors' colony in the early 1900s, the pace is slower. Here you'll find residents and visitors playing a leisurely round of tennis at Siasconset Casino, dining on Nantucket-raised hen pheasant at the pricey Chanticleer Inn, or browsing in the 'Sconset Market—one of a handful of stores in 'Sconset Center.

Nowhere else, though, is the contrast more dramatic than within the Elizabeth Islands. Cuttyhunk, the outermost of the chain, is the only island fully open to the public, and the only one served by a seaplane or a public ferry (out of New Bedford). Cuttyhunk has one church, one general store, three gift shops, and a magnificent marina. If you're looking to "get away," this is the place. All of the other islands in the chain are privately-owned, virtually uninhabited, and accessible only by private boat. The chain's harbors and coves—such as Tarpaulin Cove, on the south side of Naushon Island and Hadley Harbor, which lies between Uncatena and Nonamesset islands—are spectacular. Swimming is even allowed in certain designated areas, but no one is permitted to explore the islands without permission from the owners.

What the islands—Martha's Vineyard, Nantucket, and the Elizabeth chain—do share in common is a rich maritime history, one you can feel the minute you arrive.

When visitors, for instance, step off the ferry at Nantucket dock, they take a step backward into the nineteenth century. The village, with its cobblestone streets, red brick buildings, and sea captains' homes, remains almost as it was in the late 1800s, when Nantucket was one of the whaling centers of the world.

Whaling was first conducted from island shores by Indians long before the arrival of white settlers in the 1600s; colonists upon their arrival on Nantucket were quick to realize the importance of oil products derived from whales. The demand, though, exceeded the immediate supply, and even before the Revolutionary War, large ocean-fit ships were built and equipped to sail around the world in search of whales.

Nantucket whalers, together with men from Martha's Vineyard and New Bedford, made millions from such ventures. This money was used, among other things, to build Nantucket's ornate Victorian center and the port of Edgartown, whose streets are lined with white clapboard and shingled homes.

The more isolated Elizabeth Islands do not have the whaling histories of Nantucket and Martha's Vineyard, but they have played a key role in the region's maritime history, nonetheless. Cuttyhunk was first used as an important ship rescue outpost. Many a ship has been lost along the island's treacherous southern shores—even to this day boaters are warned of the dangerous currents and hidden reefs. Many houses on the island have been built with timbers from wrecked vessels.

This respect for the sea literally put the fear of God in island residents, who built great churches that have stood the test of time. Evidence of this devotion can be seen in Edgartown at the Old Methodist Whaling Church and at the Federated Church. These two tall white churches dominate the town's skyline and are the first landmarks seen from the outer harbor. Whale oil lamps are still used inside. On Nantucket, the Unitarian Church, built in 1809, is also open to the public and worth a visit.

Island residents share, in addition, a concern about their future. This, after all, is their home. With more and more people visiting these islands each year (populations increase five-fold in the summer), residents are concerned about preserving what these visitors have come to see. Tough new building and zoning codes have been put in place, and innovative land acquisitions have been executed. What sets island residents apart from people who live in other summer resorts is their dogged determination to keep commercial development in perspective—an attitude the locals hope is contagious.

Martha's Vineyard

Martha's Vineyard, the largest island in New England, is just a few miles south of Nobska Point off Cape Cod's Woods Hole, a village of Falmouth. The island is 24 miles long and 10 miles wide, and has a year-round population of less than 10,000, which swells to five times that in the summer.

The island, simply called "the Vineyard" by locals, offers a geological and architectural diversity that surpasses other areas in the region. From cornfields, to the gingerbread cottages that occupy the center of Oak Bluffs, to the fishing shanties along the harbor in picturesque Menemsha, to the aristocratic white-shingled, black-shuttered homes that frame the island's narrow, tree-lined streets, Martha's Vineyard has something for every visitor.

The island has seven townships: Vineyard Haven, Oak Bluffs, Edgartown, Gay Head, Chilmark (which includes Menemsha), and West Tisbury. It also has been conveniently divided by local parlance into "Up-Island," which is the western part of the Vineyard and is dominated by Vineyard Haven, and "Down-Island," which is east and refers to the Edgartown area. (On sailing charts, we should note, degrees of longitude drop or "go down" as the lines move east.)

The island has a diverse human landscape, too—one that includes fishermen, farmers, celebrities, and distinguished statesmen. The Vineyard, for instance, is home to fishermen and farmers who can trace their heritage back to the Vineyard's original settlers, and it provides summer relief to people such as columnist Art Buchwald, and television newsmen such as Mike Wallace and Walter Cronkite—not to mention all the famous and not-so-famous novelists and painters who spend time here. Each summer, Martha's Vineyard Community Services holds a "celebrity auction" where celebrities auction off their time and personal effects to raise money for the Vineyard's needy, who often find winters here financially harsh. The auction, usually held in August, is open to the public; call the Chamber of Commerce for more information.

But more than an island of celebrities, the Vineyard is indeed a special place—a spot of land, of hills, meadows, and cliffs in a moving sea. The east side of the island (Edgartown) stretches for miles with hardly a ripple, while the west side has hills and valleys with large woodlands separating farmland blessed with rich, fertile soil. At a few roadside spots, there are sweeping lookouts over ponds and natural harbors below. The highest lookout is Gay Head Cliffs, which rise 150 feet above Vineyard Sound. The view is worth the drive out; parking is available.

The natural boundaries of Martha's Vineyard are set by its lighthouses. On a foggy night, the sound of the surf pounding on the beach or a deep-sounding foghorn is never too far away.

It is a 45-minute trip from Woods Hole to the Vineyard on the Steamship Authority ferries. In summer there are additional carriers. The Hy-Line ferries shuttle passengers (no cars) between Hyannis and the Vineyard. Another passenger carrier is the *Island Queen,* which runs from Falmouth to Oak Bluffs. There is also passenger ferry service running between New Bedford and Vineyard Haven and scheduled service from Boston.

When making landfall in Vineyard Haven, you can easily pick out two of the island's lighthouses: the white West Chop lighthouse of Tisbury with its flashing white light, and the brown-colored East Chop lighthouse of Oak Bluffs with its green light.

In the summer, ferry service on the Steamship Authority stops at both Vineyard Haven and Oak Bluffs, and ferry service on the Hy-Line stops at Oak Bluffs.

Oak Bluffs

Oak Bluffs is the preferred summer port of entry, especially for those heading on to Edgartown. The harbor is small but cozy, and the town harbor-master says he has never had to turn away any boat. There always seems to be room for one more.

Surprisingly, Oak Bluffs is the only town on the Vineyard designed as a summer colony. It is a town with wide-open green parks and colorful summer cottages. The island's second busiest port, Oak Bluffs has its large hotels right near the ferry dock. Today, the Wesley House, built in 1879, on Lake Avenue, looks much as it did in the age of steamboats and petticoats. As the town's most prominent building, it is not easily missed.

Making a two-minute walk from the ferry wharf, children can visit America's oldest operating carousel, the Flying Horses, built in 1876. The restored old-fashioned merry-go-round, originally from Coney Island, is owned and operated by the Martha's Vineyard Historical Preservation Society. Twenty-two original 100-year-old wooden horses speed around in a circle carrying children and grownups on a ride that has become a tradition for many old families on the island.

Riders must grasp the steel rings that are just a child's arm length from the speeding horses. At each turn around, horsemen grab anxiously, hoping that one of the rings is brass. With a brass ring one earns a free ride.

On Circuit Avenue, the town's main street, it is still possible to buy saltwater taffy. And on some Sunday evenings, music lovers gather at the foot of the town gazebo in the wide-open Ocean Park to listen to the Vineyard Haven Town Band play music by John Philip Souza.

On two evenings during the summer, Oak Bluffs rewards residents and visitors with a fireworks display and a unique Japanese lantern display. Both events, randomly scheduled, are tied closely to town history.

The largest and strongest settlement to take place in Oak Bluffs was a result of a strong Methodist movement—a call for summer religious camp meetings. As early as 1835 a group of Vineyarders chose an open grove and set up tents for a religious meeting and retreat. In years that followed, the numbers of tents increased and again were multiplied with the arrival of visitors from the mainland.

Later, tent floors made of wood were laid to keep their inhabitants off the ground. By the country's centennial, tiny buildings were replacing the tents. Cottages took on the shapes of the earlier tents and reflected the ornamental architecture of the period.

Thus the Vineyard gingerbread house was born.

In 1879, an open-air tabernacle was constructed of iron in the center of the camp to shelter its participants. Today, just as in the days before, community sings are still held on warm summer evenings.

Once a year in excess of 500 visitors from afar crowd into the tabernacle on Illumination Night to sing and celebrate another good summer. After singing, every gingerbread house on the campground is lit with antique Japanese lanterns. Thousands of yellow, red, blue, and green lanterns wave in the gentle air. And though the date of this event is announced but a week in advance, thousands make a point not to miss it. For more information, we suggest you contact the Campground Meeting Association in Oak Bluffs or the Chamber of Commerce in Vineyard Haven.

Vineyard Haven (Tisbury)

Vineyard Haven is the island's largest port of entry. Sheltered from the worst of winter storms, Vineyard Haven Harbor is open for ferry service year-round. This is the busiest end of the island; large fuel oil and gasoline tanks stand at the edge of the harbor. But don't be fooled. There's plenty to see here, and the landscape outside the town center is as nice as just about any place you'll find on the island—hefty elms, wild roses, white picket fences, and old, weathered homes.

Vineyard Haven has two boatyards, two gasoline stations (gas up here because service stations are hard to find on the island), two drugstores, and a variety of shops and restaurants. It is also home to the Martha's Vineyard Chamber of Commerce, located on Beach Street. The chamber will assist you in finding lodgings, restaurants, shops, stores, beaches, and historic sites. People who work there are pleasant and knowledgeable.

There are no liquor stores here; the town, by its own preference, is dry. You can buy liquor only in Edgartown and Oak Bluffs, although many restaurants on other parts of the island allow you to bring your own liquor and will provide set ups. We suggest you call to inquire.

The real measure of Vineyard Haven's value is not its fine restaurants and shops, but the fact that of all other ports in the Northeast, the town has the largest collection of resident wooden boats. Vineyard Haven Harbor is also home to the 108-foot topsail schooner *Shenandoah*, owned by Captain Robert S. Douglas. *Shenandoah*, launched in February 1964 at a Maine boatyard, is the town's official mascot. When it is not sailing, the white steel-hulled vessel can be seen moored a short distance away from the ferry wharf. If you're in luck, you can see her under full sail in Vineyard or Nantucket sounds.

Passengers aboard the *Shenandoah* never know precisely where they are going when they leave the harbor. But they are always assured as chartered guests that their quiet, motorless trip beneath the large wind-filled canvas will be memorable. The captain's love for sail can take the vessel as far east as Nantucket and as far west as Block Island.

Stepping off the ferry at the dock (there are plenty of places to rent bicycles, mopeds, and cars near here), visitors to Vineyard Haven will first see the home of the Seaman's Bethel, a combination chapel and museum, on their left as they leave the wharf. The bethel served in the age of sail, when many coastal schooners visited the harbor en route to Boston or New York. Its mission was to provide crewmen with free transportation to shore, free newspapers and magazines, and religious counsel while they visited.

Walking 200 yards east along the beach from the Steamship Authority Wharf, visitors will arrive at the Black Dog Tavern, a restaurant that is set a few feet from the beach. On its open porch, in a relaxed atmosphere, patrons slowly eat their meal and watch the ferry head back to the mainland or look at the photographs of old ships. It's a great spot for breakfast; the menu is unusual.

The town has two summer museums, in addition to the Seaman's Bethel.

The Jirah Luce House, formerly called the Ritter House, is off Beach Road and a five-minute walk from Steamship Wharf. The house was built in the late 1700s and is considered one of the oldest houses in downtown Vineyard Haven. Inside, the Dukes County Historical Society has installed an exhibition of Vineyard land and sea memorabilia. Guides will take visitors through the exhibition rooms and explain the history of the town and island. It is an excellent first stop for anyone wanting an orientation of island history.

The other museum is the Old Schoolhouse Museum on upper Main Street, formerly the DAR (Daughters of the American Revolution) Building. The little white schoolhouse built in 1828 has one of the finest collections of whaling scrimshaw on the island. The museum is operated by the Martha's Vineyard Historical Preservation Society. Not far from the museum is Owen Park, one of the best sites overlooking all of Vineyard Haven Harbor.

Edgartown

From a tourist's point of view, Edgartown is perhaps the most interesting Vineyard town. It is the island's fastest growing commercial center, and yet it is rich in history (Edgartown is the island's oldest town). In the 1800s, Edgartown was an important whaling port, rivaled only by Nantucket. Whaling ships that sailed as far away as the Bering Sea off Alaska's shores once unloaded their whale oil at Osborn Wharf—a site today occupied by the affluent and exclusive Edgartown Yacht Club.

Throughout all of Edgartown, there is evidence of great wealth derived from the sea. The tallest buildings—the Edgartown Whaling Church built in 1843 and the Federated Church built in 1828—were constructed by a community rich from whaling profits. Elsewhere, there are magnificent sea captains' homes, each one in the Greek Revival type of architecture. The most elaborate houses have white wooden columns near the front entrance.

Edgartown each summer attracts bus loads of visitors, making it the busiest island town from June to September; ironically, it is the quietest in winter because most of the shops close shortly after Labor Day. To escape the summer crush, we suggest you stroll through the neighborhoods and view the many gardens of this town, made famous or infamous several years ago by Hollywood. To some moviegoers, Edgartown will always be thought of as "Amity," the quaint island community in the thriller *Jaws*. The movie and its sequels were filmed here. But as far as anyone can remember, no one in Edgartown has ever been bitten by a shark.

On Main Street in Edgartown, one can buy a wide range of goods—from fine clothes to Vineyard gifts and souvenirs and from fashion jewelry to works of art by local artists. It also has its share of great inns and restaurants, which are mentioned in the Essentials section.

The town also has its share of fine museums and historic sites. We recommend you visit the Dukes County Historical Society Museum and Library on Cooke Street. The society maintains the restored 1765 house of Thomas Cooke where you'll find antique furnishings, period clothes, and equipment used by Edgartown whalers. The adjacent Gale Huntington Library of History displays other island memorabilia and provides detailed records of early island life. It contains the island's richest archives. Here you can also view the lens used atop Gay Head lighthouse from 1854 to 1952. The lens has 1008 prisms and is capable of taking light from a whale oil lamp and generating a beacon that can be seen for 20 miles. The lens, built by Augustin Fresnel and Henry Lepaute of France, was given to the historical society in 1952.

On the walls of the library hang the charts of Edgartown's prominent whaling captains. One important Edgartown whaler, Captain Valentine Pease, captained the only whaling ship Herman Melville sailed on as a youth. Though it still can't be proved, islanders believe that Captain Ahab of the novel *Moby Dick* was based on their Edgartown captain.

Melville—while serving under Captain Pease—jumped ship in the Pacific, it is said, because of difficulties aboard. After their whaling days together and after the novel was published, the captain and the writer became good friends.

Another museum on Main Street you should see is the Vincent House and the Old Whaling Church, owned by the Martha's Vineyard Historical Preservation Society. The Vincent House, built in 1672, is believed to be the oldest house on the island, and the Whaling Church, used recently as the island's Performing Arts Center, is a good example of Greek Revival architecture.

Perhaps the biggest attraction in Edgartown is its county-and-town-managed South Beach. Thousands visit the beach every sunny summer day, attracted by the island's finest sands and promise of good-sized (two-to-three foot) swells. The surf is excellent for body surfing, but because the waves break close to the beach, South Beach is not a good place for board surfing.

The town of Edgartown offers public transportation from downtown to South Beach, five miles away. Bicycling the trip is easy; there are no hills. The beach, you should know, offers no facilities, just parking and, in some places, lifeguards.

Another big attraction in the area is the island of Chappaquiddick, an Indian word meaning "the separated island." The island, across Edgartown Harbor, was inhabited by Indians long before white settlers took an interest in the 1750s in living there.

Because of its limited access, Chappaquiddick, or "Chappy," as the locals call it, remained virtually undeveloped until the 1970s when the building boom began. The island also received some unwanted national notoriety as a result of the well-publicized tragedy involving Senator Edward Kennedy.

To get to Chappy, drive to the end of Dock Street—a winding road that runs a few hundred yards along the Edgartown waterfront. There you'll find Memorial Wharf, a structure built solely for the purpose of allowing the public a good view of the activities of the harbor. Sometimes special events are held here, but its primary purpose is to allow young and old a place to sit or stand and watch the great sailing yachts enter and exit the harbor. The fishing here is fairly good.

Beside Memorial Wharf is the landing for the Chappaquiddick ferry, which can take four cars at a time across the narrow channel to the small island. The trip takes a few minutes and costs little, but the lines can be long. Be patient.

Once on the other side, see the wooden Cape Pogue lighthouse, which is located on the northernmost spit of land and marks the most isolated beach area on the island. On this piece of land 489 acres of seldom-disturbed grasslands and bluff and beachgrass-covered dunes belong to the Trustees of Reservations and are protected from development. The public is discouraged from walking through the lands, as many threatened seabirds use the area for nesting.

Wasque Point, on the southeastern tip of the small island, is another 200-acre reservation of protected lands for wild flora and fauna. Crossing currents from the ever-changing tides make Wasque the fishing spot surf fishermen dream about. When the fish are biting, as much as several hundred pounds of fish may be reeled in in a day by the scores of fishermen that line up on the quarter mile of beach.

Getting to Edgartown and Chappaquiddick can be as much fun as being there. The most scenic road between Vineyard Haven and Edgartown is by way of Oak Bluffs—whether you're going by car, moped, bicycle, or on foot. The road winds by spectacular shoreline. A more direct route is by way of County Road, which runs inland and is the best way to get to Edgartown if you're in a hurry. But if you have time on your hands, as most vacationers do, take the shore road route. Between Oak Bluffs and Edgartown is the popular Joseph Sylvia State Beach. Known simply as State Beach, it stretches for about three miles with its creamy white sand and calm seas. If you're driving, finding a parking space here in the summer can be difficult, but not impossible.

Since the beach faces Nantucket Sound, the water is always warm and seldom rough and attracts a young family crowd. Terns, herring gulls, and black-backed gulls continually fly over this barrier beach. Schools of small fish regularly swim in the area, and the shellfishing is excellent. In the spring and fall, fishermen gather at dawn and dusk to fish for bluefish and striped bass at the "big bridge" and "small bridge" jetties. At these jetties, bait fish can sometimes be seen jumping out of the light surf while under chase by larger fish.

Across the road from the main section of State Beach is the warm and shallow Sengekontacket Pond, also a popular spot for young families and fledgling windsurfers. In the early summer months, the pond is bordered by a blanket of the pink and red flowers of *Rosa rugosa*, a rose that complements the deep-green color of nearby brush. The bright red tart fruit from these flower blossoms (rose hips) is picked in late fall and made into a rich jelly. If you have proper permits (available at Town Hall), the pond is also a good place to dig for quahogs (large clams) in the summer and dredge for tasty bay scallops in the winter.

On the southern side of Sengekontacket Pond the Massachusetts Audubon Society supervises a 350-acre reserve called the Felix Neck Wildlife Sanctuary. It offers a number of trails for nature walkers; the public is also encouraged to walk barefoot in the water and look for tiny flounders and other marine life.

Felix Neck is the home of the returning osprey, one of the largest predatory birds in the nation. Up until a decade ago, ospreys, which feed on fish, were suffering a major decline in southeastern New England. They are now coming back. Efforts by Vineyard bird lovers to put up osprey pole nests across the island have given the bird a second chance to recover. Gus Ben David, director of the sanctuary, said the bird's natural nesting home used to be dead trees. But with more trees being cut down and utility poles being dangerous, the bird has had no place to build its nest. New specially designed nesting poles have helped the bird on the Vineyard, and now poles are being introduced on Cape Cod and Nantucket with similar success.

One of the many pluses of State Beach, Sengekontacket Pond, and Felix Neck Wildlife Sanctuary is that you can bike to them, avoiding unpleasant summer traffic congestion. It is easier, in fact, to bike to State Beach than to any other beach on the island. Whether you leave from Oak Bluffs or Edgartown, there is a separate bicycle path, and the two-mile trip from either direction takes but a few minutes.

Menemsha (in Chilmark)

The good Lord had a fishing village in mind when he created Menemsha Harbor and Menemsha Pond on the west end of the island in the township of Chilmark. Few would argue that the port of Menemsha, with its weathered shanties, rustic dock, and no-nonsense fish markets where you buy the day's catch, is one of the most authentic fishing villages in all of New England and for that matter the entire country. The fishing boats here are owned by families affiliated with the island for more than 300 years.

Not far from the fish markets is the popular seafood restaurant, Home Port, which has a magnificent view of the harbor and offers a simple menu of freshly caught seafood. The restaurant has been serving New England-style cooking since 1931. Dinner reservations that coincide with sunsets are often filled days in advance—sunsets are a special event in Menemsha. Each evening at dusk, summer visitors gather at nearby Menemsha Beach facing Vineyard Sound just to observe daylight's finale. It takes but a few days to become an expert in the art of sunset watching here.

Although Menemsha is a popular harbor among boating enthusiasts, services and space are limited. For those arriving by land, Menemsha is a 15-mile drive from Vineyard Haven and about an equal distance from Edgartown. No public buses are allowed here. The roads are winding and go past acres of scrub oak and fields bordered by stone walls. On North Road, just up from Menemsha Harbor, you'll find two fine inns and restaurants: the Beach Plum Inn, which overlooks Vineyard Sound and offers comfortable rooms and a restaurant worthy of four stars; and the Menemsha Inn, which also has a view of the sound, attractive rooms and cottages and more casual fare.

West Tisbury

If you take South Road from the Gay Head–Menemsha area, you drive through West Tisbury, and as the saying goes, "If you blink, you will miss the center of town."

It takes about a minute to bicycle through the center of West Tisbury. First on your right is Alley's General Store, which except for the removal of a wood stove, has remained unchanged for decades. Shoppers can buy nails as easily as a fresh loaf of bread. The bare wood floors still squeak, and crowds gather on the porch for Sunday morning conversation and a newspaper. Nearby is West Tisbury Town Hall, built in 1833 as an academy. Later it served as a town school.

The annual country fair is held next door at the Agricultural Society Fairgrounds. For one weekend in August, jam makers and vegetable growers from across the island compete for blue ribbons. Participants can win prizes for a variety of skills, including quilt making, axe throwing, and fiddle playing. And children have easy access to cotton candy and carnival rides.

If you miss the fair there is always the farmer's market, which is held every Saturday morning at the same site—the Agricultural Hall. The best vegetables and flowers grown on the island in summer are brought together just in front of the hall. It is an age-old tradition. Farmers collect their freshest produce and assemble them on the backs of pickup trucks. The best is brought early, so come no later than 10 A.M.

In season, the farmers and backyard gardeners show up with flowers, sweet corn, broccoli, lettuce, melons, tomatoes, and even fresh honey from a local beehive. Bakers often show up with home-baked cookies and breads.

Gay Head and Other Sights

Some of the island's prettiest sights are seen on the road from Chilmark to the Gay Head Cliffs. The weaving road, dangerous for bicyclists, rises and falls. At times the Atlantic Ocean to the south and Vineyard Sound to the north can be seen by turning one's head. At one scenic vista, Quitsa and Menemsha ponds and a tiny little cluster of Sailfish boats that race twice a week in the ponds are seen far below.

Gay Head is home of the Gay Head Indians. Indians populated the entire island (they called it *Noe-pe*) prior to the arrival of the white man. They fished, farmed, and did some whaling. They taught many of their skills to the newest settlers, with whom they lived harmoniously. Eventually the Indians sold what land they owned and settled in two places: the island of Chappaquiddick and Gay Head.

Herman Melville in *Moby Dick* wrote of the Gay Headers: "Next was Tashtego, an unmixed Indian from Gay Head, the most westerly promontory of Martha's Vineyard, where there still exists the last remnant of a village of red men, which has long supplied the neighboring island of Nantucket with many of her most daring harpooneers."

Besides Melville's Tashtego, maritime history tells of heroism displayed by the tribe. In the Revolutionary War, an Indian, a Gay Header named Anthony Jeremiah, was highly regarded by his captain, John Paul Jones, when they engaged the British in the new country's first naval battle. Gay Headers also served in the Civil War and in World Wars I and II. Through succeeding generations, the Gay Head Indians remained close while others scattered.

Up into this century, a few have distinguished themselves by fashioning clay from the Gay Head Cliffs into highly prized pottery. However, conservationists, concerned about the fast erosion of the national landmark cliffs, moved to make the gathering of clay illegal, subsequently ending the making of Gay Head Indian pottery.

With a rich lore and heritage behind them, today's Indians of Gay Head are tied into the modern ways of the twentieth century. Some shellfish for scallops in winter. Others are engaged in island trades. But they all struggle to preserve what is left of their heritage.

It is at the top of the Gay Head Cliffs that the frailty of these islands is apparent. The cliffs rise 150 feet above the shore, and yet even on a calm day, one can see that the eroding clay colors the sea water that washes up on the shore. Generations of Vineyarders have watched as one storm after another has taken much of the colorful clay cliffs away.

The explorer Verrazano in 1524 called the cliffs Claudia. In 1602 Gosnold called them the Dover Cliffs after the white cliffs he knew at home.

In February 1799 the first lighthouse was erected on the cliffs. Despite its presence, the cliffs have seen their share of shipwrecks. Extending away from the cliffs is what has long been called Devil's Bridge—a dangerous reef. In the stormy early morning hours of January 17, 1884, the steamer *City of Columbus*, having left Boston the previous day, ran up upon the rocks at Devil's Bridge and partially sank.

A total of 121 men, women, and children drowned in the hours that followed the sinking. Despite a heroic effort by Vineyarders in the daylight hours to rescue the survivors still alive on the vessel, only 29 people were saved. The sinking of the *City of Columbus* is considered the worst of maritime accidents in Vineyard history.

From atop the cliffs, you can see Cuttyhunk to the north, the Buzzards Bay light tower to the west, and Noman's Land, a wildlife preserve used by the navy as a bombing target, to the south. Sometimes in winter, you may be able to see spouting whales and hundreds of pelagic birds in flight or adrift in the water.

Cedar Tree Neck is the Vineyard's most special sanctuary. Protected from man, Cedar Tree Neck on the north shore of the Vineyard is 250 acres of unaltered woodlands and beach off Indian Hill Road in North Tisbury. Though parking is provided, visitors must walk a mile-long path to get to the entirely isolated part of the reserve.

Following a lengthy nature trail through tall oaks, you come upon a small saltwater pond. A sand and stone beach faces Vineyard Sound. Picnickers can watch fishing boats drag for fluke and flounder in the Sound. Or they can watch the terns dive bomb the water in their own more efficient way of fishing. There are birds seldom found so easily elsewhere: red-tailed hawk, great blue heron, and sometimes a snowy egret.

Whatever is seen or heard is done to the quiet music of an island sanctuary.

To learn more about the Vineyard and its offerings, we suggest you pick up a copy of the *Vineyard Gazette*, the island's weekly newspaper. Its late publisher and editor, Henry Beetle Hough, wrote *Country Editor*, a book about the insular struggles of his small newspaper. The book earned Mr. Hough and his newspaper national acclaim. Today the newspaper publishes 17,000 copies at the height of summer. It is sent to 20 foreign countries and all 50 states.

Visitors can walk through the newspaper's offices, which are inside a restored pre-revolutionary captain's house located on South Summer Street in Edgartown. The original Seth Adams press that printed the first issues of the *Vineyard Gazette* is on exhibit. On the wall is the first issue of the paper printed —Vol. 1, No.1, dated May 14, 1846. The masthead reads: "A family newspaper—neutral in politics, devoted to general news, literature, morality, agriculture and amusement."

Nantucket

From the air, the 50 square miles that make up the island of Nantucket look like a mere spit of sand rising up from a silver sea.

By ferry, the island, 14 miles long and 3 1/2 miles wide, first appears out of the water as an unassuming landscape; there are neither large hills nor cliffs, just long stretches of sandy beaches that run without a break for miles.

But perhaps the best way to describe the shape of Nantucket is to say that it looks like a pork chop. The village of Nantucket, on the west edge of the harbor, is the meaty part; Great Point, north of Wauwinet, is the bone.

Nantucket is one of the East Coast's outermost islands. Its year-round residents, like its shores, are seasoned. Their culture and native stamina are enriched by the island's isolation and its affinity with the sea.

Wrote Herman Melville in *Moby Dick*: "What wonder, then, that these Nantucketers, born on a beach, should take to the sea for a livelihood! They first caught crabs and quahaugs in the sand; grown bolder, they waded out with nets for mackerel; more experienced, they pushed off in boats and captured cod; and at last, launching a navy of great ships on the sea, explored this watery world [for whales]."

Small Island

On Nantucket, despite the presence of cars and trucks, there are no traffic lights. Because of the island's size, visitors shouldn't feel compelled to bring their cars. You can travel extensively by bicycle and get a better appreciation for the flora and the fauna. And it is easier to travel by foot on the clean beaches.

A visitor coming off the ferry is first greeted by the nineteenth-century village that at one time was the third largest city in Massachusetts. Upon further investigation of the island, visitors will find many open spaces framed by salt-seasoned, cedar-shingled houses.

Some houses are clustered, while others stand alone surrounded by oak and evergreen. Other mansionlike houses overlook the sea and stand upon slowly eroded bluffs, looking down to changing beaches.

Along the south shore roll in large waves created in the deep sea by a prevailing southwest wind. Surfers gather at Surfside Beach. On the north shores the waters are much smoother, and in the inshore bays, water at sunrise can appear in stillness as smooth as a cobalt-blue–tinted pane of glass. It is even possible to spend a day out on the moors and spot a rare white heron hiding on a salt marsh.

One thing visitors always find confusing is that the town of Nantucket on Nantucket Harbor and the island of Nantucket bear the same name. Other island communities, all of them residential (few have shops), are villages. To the east of Nantucket Center are Monomoy, Shimmo, Quaise, Polpis, Pocomo, Squam, Quidnet, Siasconset (perhaps the loveliest spot of all on Nantucket), and Tom Nevers. To the south are Surfside and Cisco, both on the Atlantic. To the east are Dionis and Madaket, which has the second-best harbor on the island.

Visitors to Nantucket Center are first amazed at the orderliness of the town with its variety of buildings and trimmed rose bushes and hedges. Within walking distance there are at least 100 houses, each at least a century old. And because Nantucket was in the early 1800s a wealthy community, mansions reflect the styles of early America: Greek Revival with its white-pillared mansion homes, Georgian, and Federal.

And not far away from the center of town on Sunset Hill Lane is the island's oldest house, the Jethro Coffin House. Built in 1686, it resembles the old gray-shingled farmhouses of England. The house represents an early, austere Nantucket, when most of the settlers arriving at the island were Quaker exiles from Boston.

To the south, a half mile from the Steamboat Wharf, is yet another island landmark, the Old Mill, built in 1746 and now maintained by the Nantucket Historical Association. The 50-foot-high Old Mill was constructed out of hickory and old timbers. Some of the posts and beams were obtained from shipwrecks on the island's beaches. Four arms extending out 30 feet from the center give a total span of 60 feet. In its time, when it was powered with wind, the mill ground the grains grown by farmers.

It is told that during the Revolutionary War, a cannonball shot from a British man-of-war entered through the east wall and exited on the other side—nearly hitting the miller.

The island's early prosperity came and went with the whaling industry. At the Nantucket Whaling Museum on Broad Street, close to Steamboat Wharf, you can learn all about whaling. This is one of the best museums on the subject. Visitors can have an opportunity to see original whaling gear and models of fitted-out whaling ships and boats. Whale oil, whale products from bone, and a number of keepsakes from distant lands were brought to Nantucket from as far away as the Pacific and Indian oceans. The museum itself was originally a spermaceti candle factory built in 1847.

Next door, the Peter Foulger Museum—named after the highly regarded Nantucketer and grandfather of Benjamin Franklin—is devoted to the entire history of the island from the time of the Indians up until the beginning of the twentieth century. The museum, which opened in 1971, includes a comprehensive library of Nantucket literature, history, and genealogy.

The old seafarers' organization, the Pacific Club (formed in 1854), is located on lower Main Street. The unmistakable red-brick three-and-a-half-story building overlooking the cobblestone square was built in 1771 for Captain William Rotch, a highly regarded Nantucket whaler. The building's roof is adorned with a widow's walk—a lookout where one could watch as the ships of another age came in.

Founded as an organization for beached whaling captains, today members of the club spend their time gamming (conversing) and playing cribbage and pinochle. "Gamming," as the patrons call it, is a term from whaling times; when two whaling ships met at sea during their years-long voyages, they exchanged news and letters.

In the quiet of winter, members meet on Thursday nights for serious cribbage tournaments. They keep themselves warm seated on ancient chairs next to an old wood stove converted to oil. On the walls are illustrations of great whaling ships and portraits of a few of its seafaring members. Though the club is private and membership is exclusive, the public is allowed to view the premises when the club is open.

On Broad Street, the Jared Coffin House has treated visitors to the island with opulent hospitality for 140 years. Built in 1845 by Jared Coffin to suit his homesick wife, two years later is was turned into an inn. Though the inn has kept up with the times in services, antique furniture in large open rooms with working fireplaces makes the mansion a place to which all other inns on the island are compared.

On Main Street, you can still sit at an old-fashioned soda fountain and spin around on one of the stools that face the counter at Congdon's Pharmacy, established back in the nineteenth century.

There are plenty of restaurants, shops, and galleries to choose from in the center of town, which we detail in Essentials.

While you're in the vicinity of Nantucket Harbor, you should also take a look at the bright-hulled Nantucket Lightship, the last of the floating live-in lighthouses that marked one of the offshore shipping channels and warned of dangerous shoals.

The lighthouse ship, built in 1936, was stationed 50 miles southeast of Nantucket and marked the edge of the Nantucket Shoals, well known as a shallow and treacherous area. The lightship, like her predecessors, had a live-in crew who kept the beacon lit and the radios working.

The Nantucket lightship basket owes its origins to the painstaking work done by crews who were often knocked about in 20-foot seas. In quiet times, to alleviate boredom, crew members took up basket weaving and scrimshaw. The work of these men earned wide recognition, hence the familiar Nantucket lightship basket. Onshore, the baskets and work brought a good second income.

Though the lightship has since been replaced by an automated buoy, imitation lightship baskets are still a popular item in town and can be found for sale. The in port lightship, though quiet, is a "living" museum, and with its restored diesel engines now working, the ship has traveled to other ports in summer.

East Side of the Island

From Nantucket center it is a downhill, six-mile bicycle ride on Milestone Road to the easternmost town, Siasconset (pronounced "Sconset"). It is smaller than the town of Nantucket and is made up of little old doll house cottages, former fishing shacks that over time have been enlarged.

Siasconset, on the southeast side of the island, has its own small center with a post office, a gas station, and some fine restaurants—many visitors have enjoyed the Chanticleer Inn on New Street, the 'Sconset Café, and the Summer House on South Bluff. There's also a place in 'Sconset Center called Claudette's that prepares take-out food for the beach, a picnic, or a clambake.

In the 1800s, the town's principal business was fishing. Later, in the early 1900s, came the mansions as the town became an attractive spot for thespians from New York City. The change earned the little town the nickname "Actors' Colony." And as a colony it remains, a little off step from the center of the island.

On the beach road—Ocean Avenue—a visitor discovers the natural beauty that makes this part of the island different. Looking east, you see the

Atlantic Ocean with all its unencumbered strength—with large waves regularly rolling in. To the west of the road lie the large summer mansions that line the road; each resident cherishes his or her spectacular panorama of the sea long after the house has closed for the season.

The beach from Siasconset to Tom Nevers Head and including the Coast Guard Loran Station is separated from east access by bluffs, which rise up as much as 70 feet. In some places, the violent storms of winter erode the beach by as much as a foot a storm.

'Sconset Beach is open to public bathing, but not all beaches on the eastern side of Nantucket are public.

Offshore is what the boating fishermen call the backside of Nantucket, with excellent fishing at such places as Old Man Shoal, Bass Rip, and Southern Shore Ground. Depending on the time of year, bluefish, mackerel, striped bass, codfish, false albacore, bonito, and even blue shark and mako fill the waters. Known more formally as Nantucket Shoals, this area is but a small portion of the much larger fishing ground called Georges Bank to the south and southeast.

A visitor must ride six miles north to find the island's next small community, Wauwinet, where public bathing is allowed. From Wauwinet four miles northward stands the Great Point lighthouse, a special place for angler, naturalist, and beach stroller.

North of Wauwinet, those with four-wheel drive must have an appropriate beach sticker on their vehicle before proceeding. There is considerable concern about excessive erosion created by such vehicles on this barrier beach. Those who walk need only check in at the entrance and make sure they are briefed about how to make their visit safe.

Walking northward, you see the Atlantic Ocean to the east and the Head of the Harbor, an inland saltwater pond, to the west. In the Head of the Harbor in winter Nantucket shellfishermen drag for bay scallops, the highly regarded seafood delicacy. Bay scalloping is the largest off-season industry on the island. Half of all the bay scallops harvested in the state come from these clean Nantucket waters.

On this barrier beach the separation between the ocean and the bay may be as narrow as a few hundred yards of sand. Only tall-growing beach grass acts as a protector from extensive wind and water erosion. In early summer tern colonies nest and raise their young. The public is warned to stay clear of the colonies, as the young can die easily if their parents are forced away from their simple sand nests for too long.

At Great Point stands the 70-foot-high light-gray lighthouse, Great Point Light. A winter storm in March of 1984 toppled the original stone lighthouse; it was rebuilt in 1986.

Though it is a difficult spot to reach, when the bluefish are in season (spring and fall), the beach is crowded with surf fishermen. Hundreds of pounds of the fish have been brought in by one fisherman in a single day.

On the Nantucket Sound side of the beach extending southward is Coskata (see map), where the most vigorous bathers go to get away from the summer crowds and have the calm Nantucket Sound waters to themselves.

On the ocean side, the beach is smooth and soft underfoot. On the inshore side, the area is marshy, attracting a different type of wildlife. Tall windblown cedar trees mark the area's landscape and offer shelter for birds such as the red-winged blackbird. Watch out for poison ivy hidden in the tall grasses, but listen for the bobwhite, also in the grass, calling out its name repeatedly. Elsewhere there are marsh hawks, and egrets can be found near the cattails.

From this beach you can look back down toward the Nantucket Harbor entrance more than six miles away. And you can watch as the ferry and a number of other boats enter and leave.

From Wauwinet back to town, take the Polpis Road. En route you will come upon the Windswept Cranberry Bog on the left where you can see a functioning bog owned and operated by the Nantucket Conservation Foundation. Visitors are welcome, but they must leave their automobiles in the parking lot. In addition to cranberries, there are in excess of 200 acres of forest, ponds, marshes, bogs, and open meadows. Pale-pink tiny flowers cover the cranberry bushes from June through early July. Each little flower has a yellow and red stamen. When the flowers are blossoming, you can stand at the edge of the bog and see the subtle floral colors extend far into the bog.

In fall the bogs are flooded and the little tart-flavored berries are thrashed from the plants by machinery. Workers crowd the floating berries to one section of the bog where they are harvested. These cranberries, together with those from other bogs held by the foundation, are harvested and exported off-island to Ocean Spray. As much as 3,000 one-hundred-pound barrels are shipped off-island a year.

En route, you'll also come upon the Nantucket Life Saving Museum, an authentic re-creation of the original Surfside Beach Station built in 1874. On display are old lifesaving boats, rescue equipment, and other lifesaving memorabilia.

West Side of the Island

To reach the west side of the island take Madaket Road from Nantucket center. Along the way, you'll come across the 300-acre Sanford Farm. The landscape, again restricted to pedestrian traffic, is a combination of rolling fields and plains, commonly called moors. Once a dairy farm, the land has returned to its natural state. At the edge of the grasslands is the traditional shrubbery of scrub oak.

Following trails heading southward, pass into the Ram Pasture, an additional piece of land protected from development. It is a three-and-a-half mile walk from Madaket to the ocean, and there's not a noisy automobile to be heard. In the early history of the island, sheep raising was an important livelihood for an island limited in resources. With a growing need for wool on the mainland, many Nantucketers got into the act—so many that in 1790 there were too many sheep. Without adequate fencing, the numbers became uncontrolled, and the situation unhealthy.

Looking across the Sanford Farm heartland it is easy to imagine why sheep are so easy to raise on the island.

In late summer, wildflowers come to bloom uncontrolled on the land: there are the bright yellows of black-eyed Susan and the white embroidery of Queen Anne's lace. You shouldn't be surprised to see a bobwhite quail flushed from the grass or a red-tailed hawk circle above.

On the westernmost edge of the island is Madaket Bay, a highly regarded boating and fishing community. Quahogs from Madaket Bay are precious, as are the fish caught off of Eel Point. Madaket Bay is a popular fishing and boating haven, and there is a small grocery store for the needy boater.

Madaket Beach, by the way, is one of the best island beaches. This ocean beach is located south of the harbor at the end of Madaket Road.

South Side of the Island

To reach the south side of Nantucket, take Surfside Road from Nantucket Center. It will lead you to Surfside Beach on the Atlantic, one of the island's better beaches. There's a youth hostel located out there, as well as some beautiful countryside.

Elizabeth Islands

The Elizabeth Island chain, consisting of about 16 small islands stretching from Woods Hole southwest toward Buzzards Bay, represents the town of Gosnold, the smallest town in the Commonwealth with slightly more than a hundred voters. From Cuttyhunk, the outermost of the chain, you can look across Vineyard Sound and see Martha's Vineyard.

The Indians called the whole chain *Nashanow*, and many of the islands still bear Indian names. Heading away from Woods Hole, the islands are Nonamesset; Uncatena (also called Onkatonka); the tiny Weepecket Islands, named after the Indian who once owned land in the area; Naushon, the largest island in the chain; Pasque; Nashawena; Penikese; and Cuttyhunk. There are additional islands, ones that represent either a boulder, a patch of land at low tide, or a few acres. They are the Veckatimest Islands, Fisherman's Island, Pine Island, Cedar Island, Bull Island, and Little Bachelor's Island.

The highest number of islands documented is 16, but erosion has eliminated a few. Cuttyhunk, while not the largest of the chain, is the most populated. From 25 residents in winter, the population in the summer rises to more than 300. Its name is an Indian word meaning "a thing that lies out in the water."

Each morning in summer, the 60-foot *Alert*, a tugboat-like vessel, leaves from New Bedford Pier Three and travels almost due south to make the 14-mile trip across Buzzards Bay to the tiny island. In winter the trips are less frequent, and in July and August there are two trips a day on Sundays.

The island is three-quarters of a mile wide by two and a half miles in length. Those who choose to live on or visit Cuttyhunk also choose to leave the urgencies of modern living behind. Once on the island, there are few amenities relating to the twentieth century. There is electricity, but no movie theater or nightclub. Movies are shown occasionally at the Town Hall, and because cars are scarce, no full-service gas station has been built.

The landscape is rolling, and the properties that make up the island are well manicured. There are grassy lands—each sparse tree is allowed to have its special place.

A small saltwater pond, called Gosnold Pond, is named after the island's first visitor, Bartholomew Gosnold. A special monument to the explorer was erected on the island in September of 1902 on the tricentennial of his first visit.

Above the pond and all other landmarks is a gigantic hill that overlooks the red roofs of the village below and the waters that surround the island. The hill is simply called Lookout, and during the war, the Coast Guard maintained a station on its top. A tower was erected to keep an eye out for ships in distress. The top of the hill commands a full 360 degree view.

Atop the hill is a failed 80-foot-high wind generator. Though Cuttyhunk gets its power from a diesel-powered generator, back in 1973 one of the island's residents thought of wind power as another source for electricity. The generator worked for only a short time.

To the south is Vineyard Sound with Martha's Vineyard seven miles away. There once was a regular boat service from the Vineyard to Cuttyhunk. But these days the only way to get to Cuttyhunk—other than chartering a boat—is by way of New Bedford.

On the northeast side of Cuttyhunk is the protected bay where all vessels arrive and leave. Cuttyhunk Marina has 60 berths and 40 moorings. It is a good idea to call ahead to get reservations.

Since the age of great coastal schooners and large square-sailed ships, Cuttyhunk has marked one of the most dangerous ports. For ships bound between Boston and New York, before the Cape Cod Canal was cut, many large ships had to navigate the narrow Vineyard Sound. Maritime history at the Cuttyhunk Historical Society is filled with shipwrecks.

In the days before radar, ships ran aground on Sow and Pigs Reef, just southwest of the island. Cuttyhunk history abounds with tales of Cuttyhunk men braving stormy seas to rescue passengers aboard ships awash on the reef.

George W. Eldridge, a chartmaker and a founding publisher of the *Eldridge Tide and Pilot Book*, was well aware of the dangerous waters along the Elizabeth Islands. His first book was published in 1854, and his observances of the waters are still printed in the current issues of the book. Today the book is considered the navigator's Bible for these waters:

"Do you know, Captain and mates, of a place on the Atlantic Coast that is called The Graveyard? I propose to tell you something about it and do what I can to keep vessels out of it. The Graveyard, so called, is that part of the coast which lies—between Sow and Pigs Rocks and Naushon Island. This place has been called The Graveyard for many years, because many a good craft has laid her bones there, and many a captain has lost his reputation there also."

As recently as July 28, 1985, the 190-foot cruise ship *Pilgrim Belle* with

85 passengers and 23 crew aboard ran aground and nearly sank on Sow and Pigs Reef. Coast Guard officials estimate that at least one fishing boat or pleasure boat runs aground on the underwater reef each year.

Many homes on this tiny isle are made from shipwrecks. A.P. Tilton, former selectman and the island's longest-residing resident, lives in a house that was built from a damaged ship. His kitchen was a mess hall. Mr. Tilton, one of the island's 25 permanent residents, inherited his house from his parents many years ago. His family originally emigrated in 1918 from the Vineyard, where he was born.

On Cuttyhunk, telephones are at a premium. There are fewer than a dozen lines from New Bedford. Visitors familiarize themselves with the pay telephone at the Marina.

Naushon, the largest island in the chain, is owned by the wealthy Forbes family. It is also a most private island with an impressive bight on the south side of the island, known as Tarpaulin Cove.

Tarpaulin Cove is five miles west southwest from Nobska Point and Woods Hole and is visited by sailors from the Cape and Vineyard. Though it is stretching the nautical dictionary to describe the spot as a cove, for centuries it has been recognized as a haven for coastal captains seeking a moment's peace from an unwelcome storm and adverse sea. For the experienced Vineyard sailor, Tarpaulin Cove is an excellent day-trip destination if there is a good summer wind and a favorable tide.

For many Vineyard day sailors, it is an exhilarating trip requiring good sea sense. A sailor who leaves either Lake Tashmoo or Vineyard Haven on a favorable tide in the early morning can make a two-hour sail to the bight in time for a noontime lunch and swim.

A small 30-foot-high white lighthouse marks the bight, and it is a pleasant spot to explore once the visitor is ashore. The land surrounding the beach is grassy with a variety of oaks and evergreens.

Though Tarpaulin Cove is private property, the free acceptance of boaters has been due to the public's good behavior. Visitors are permitted to anchor their boats—water is but 14 feet deep and the bottom makes a good anchorage. There are no public facilities. The public is allowed to use the beach and walk to the lighthouse.

The Forbes family has had title to the island since 1842, and they have done little to change its natural character. The wildlife (which includes deer) is tame in comparison to anywhere else. As on the other islands, sheep were once raised for their wool and traveled across the island unthreatened by any natural predators. Naushon wool was highly prized years ago.

On a good summer day, it is not unusual to see the grand white 108-foot topsail schooner *Shenandoah* sail into Tarpaulin Cove for the night after a day-long cruise in Vineyard Sound. The *Shenandoah* hails from Vineyard Haven and either ends or begins a week-long charter with a stop here.

One of the smallest of the Elizabeth Islands, Penikese is but a mile north of Cuttyhunk. In the early part of this century, the island was a leper colony. In 1925 it became a bird sanctuary, and later still a few structures were built and the island was used for a short time as a school for delinquent boys.

The Elizabeth Islands, either by boat or on the shore, are fun to fish—that is, when fish are moving through the sound. Cuttyhunk once ran its own fishing tournament in celebration of its good fishing.

Off Season on the Islands

Like its residents, the islands of Nantucket and Martha's Vineyard use the off season as an opportunity to recover from the summer popularity. Rain water refills the aquifer. Bays and salt marshes are flushed with the rise and fall of the tide. Footprints are cleared from the beaches.

In mid-September, Martha's Vineyard has its annual Striped Bass and Blue-fish Derby. For a month 2,000 fishermen from all over the country compete for daily and weekly prizes for the largest bluefish, flase albacore, bonito, and weakfish. Because of concerns for its survival, the striped bass has been removed from the competition.

Later in the fall residents shift to commercial bay scalloping. Restaurants that remain open offer a variety of bay scallop delicacies to patrons.

In the weeks just before Christmas, both islands have an end-of-the-year surge of activity. Nantucket leads with its Christmas Stroll, a weekend of special events early in December. The downtown takes on an old-time festive appearance. The public is encouraged to stroll along the cobble streets and stop in and visit the various shops. The streets are decorated with Christmas trees adorned with ornaments made by the island's school children. Santa Claus makes a visit and carolers and instrumentalists join in the stroll.

There are public Christmas parties, antique auctions, and church fairs. Chamber music and traditional Christmas music is performed in the various churches.

On Martha's Vineyard, similar events are held in Vineyard Haven and Edgartown though on separate weekends.

Cuttyhunk pretty much shuts down after Labor Day. There is not much activity on the island until the following June.

The season begins again in late April when Nantucket holds its annual Daffodil Festival—a rite of spring. Most island restaurants and lodgings open up for the festivities, which include an antique car parade, a gourmet picnic and a Daffodil Ball. Shops decorate their windows and displays with the long-stem yellow flower.

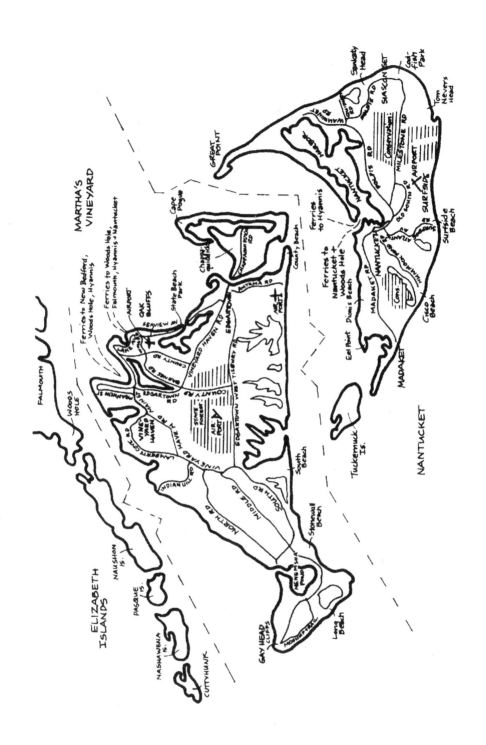

THE ISLANDS

Martha's Vineyard: Essentials

 ## Important Public Information

- *Chilmark Town Hall;* 645-2100.
- *Edgartown Town Hall;* 627-6100.
- *Gay Head Town Hall;* 645-9915.
- *Oak Bluffs Town Hall;* 693-5511.
- *Vineyard Haven (Tisbury) Town Hall;* 696-4200.
- *West Tisbury Town Hall;* 693-9659.
- *Martha's Vineyard Commission* (land use and zoning regulations); 693-3453.
- *Massachusetts State Police;* 693-0545.
- *U.S. Coast Guard, Menemsha Base;* 645-2611.
- *Massachusetts SPCA;* 627-8662.
- *Weather forecast;* 771-5522.
- *Martha's Vineyard Chamber of Commerce;* Beach Rd., Vineyard Haven; 693-0085.
- *Martha's Vineyard Hospital;* Lincoln Ln., Oak Bluffs: 693-0410.
- *Animal Health Care Associates;* Martha's Vineyard Airport, W. Tisbury; 693-6515.
- *Vineyard Medical Services,* State Rd., Vineyard Haven; 693-6399. Walk-in medical care.

 # Lodgings

Major credit cards are accepted at most B&Bs, guest houses, inns, motels, resorts and cottages listed here, and many places offer off-season rates. Call to inquire.

RESERVATION SERVICES & DIRECTORIES

- *House Guests Cape Cod and the Islands* is the Cape and Islands' original and most varied bed and breakfast reservation service. More than 300 guest rooms are available; year-round service. Offers accommodations for singles,

283

doubles, and families; water views and wooded locations. All accommodations have been inspected and approved; reasonable rates. For a directory covering Cape Cod and the Islands, write Box 1881, Orleans, MA 02653, or call 896-7053 or 1-800-666-HOST; Visa, MasterCard, American Express cards welcome.
• *Dukes County Reservation Service,* Box 2370, Oak Bluffs, 627-4779 or 800-732-7435.
• *House Guests of Cape Cod,* Box A-R, Dennis 02638; 398-0787. Offers accommodations in private homes, inns, and guest houses all over the Cape and Islands.
• *Bed and Breakfast Cape Cod,* Box 341, West Hyannis Port 02672; 508-775-2772. Select from 60 host homes, country inns, and sea captains' houses on Cape Cod and the islands of Nantucket and Martha's Vineyard. Beaches, great seafood restaurants, whale watches, and summer theater are all a part of the local attractions. Modest/deluxe rates, private or shared baths. Write or call for free selection information.
• *Martha's Vineyard & Nantucket Reservations,* Box 1322C, Lagoon Pond Rd., Vineyard Haven; 693-7200 or 800-649-5671. Individual and corporate reservations.

CHILMARK

• *Breakfast at Tiasquam,* off Middle Rd.; 645-3685. Expensive. This B&B is set among farms, woodlands, and ponds; comfortable, quaint rooms; great country breakfast (that's how the inn got its name); menu varies but never disappoints. Some of the special qualities: lots of decks and skylights, pottery sinks, cherry spiral staircase.
• *Captain D. Larsen House,* Beetlebung Corner; 645-3484. Moderate. Weekly rental units, television, private baths, off-season rates.
• *Captain R. Flanders' House,* North Rd.; 645-3123. Great location, near pond.
• *The Inn at Blueberry Hill,* North Rd.; 645-3322 or 800-356-3322. Moderate. Suites and cottages on 56 acres with access to nature trails, pool; continental breakfast.
• *North Bend Cottages,* North Rd.; 645-2234. Moderate. Weekly rental units, private baths, off-season rates.
• *Rivers Guest Cottage,* State Rd.; 645-2511. Expensive, double occupancy, private baths, continental breakfast.

EDGARTOWN

• *The Arbor,* 222 Upper Main St.; 627-8137. Moderate to expensive. Turn-of-the-century guest house; attractive setting; continental breakfast; close to beaches and town center, one bedroom cottage available.
• *The Ashley Inn,* 129 Main St.; 627-9655 or 800-477-9655. Expensive. TV and air-conditioning in some rooms, private baths, continental breakfast. Open year-round, off-season rates, major credit cards accepted.
• *Captain Dexter House,* 35 Pease's Point Way; 627-7289. Moderate to expensive. Sea captain's home, continental breakfast, located in town.
• *Chadwick Inn,* Winter and Pease's Point Way; 627-4435. Moderate to expensive. This attractive 1840 inn is two blocks from the harbor; rooms furnished with antiques or reproductions; many rooms have private baths; breakfast served in dining room; recommendations offered on what to see and do on the island.
• *The Charlotte Inn,* 27 S. Summer St.; 627-4751. Expensive. One of the island's best inns, featured in *Country Inns and Back Roads*; the *Saturday*

Review called it, "one of the most exquisite of all New England country shelters." Built in 1860, the inn offers elegantly decorated rooms; ask about the carriage house; credit cards accepted.

- *Colonial Inn,* N. Water St.; 627-4711 or 800-627-4701. Expensive. Continental breakfast, some rooms with private bath, off-season rates, major credit cards accepted.
- *The Daggett House,* 59 N. Water St.; 627-4600 or 800-946-3400. Expensive. One of the island's best B&Bs; completely restored; continental breakfast; close to beaches and town center shopping.
- *Edgartown Commons,* Pease's Pt. Way; 627-4671. Expensive. Heated apartments, TV, private baths, pool, off-season rates, major credit cards accepted.
- *Edgartown Heritage Hotel,* 227 Upper Main St.; close to town center; 627-5161 or 800-922-3009. Expensive. 34-room hotel, large rooms, private baths, color TV, air-conditioning, hair salon, game room, hotel shops; restaurant on premises (Beeftender); continental breakfast.
- *Edgartown Inn,* N. Water St.; 627-4794. Expensive. Seasonal, off-season rates, public dining room.
- *The Edgartown Lodge,* off Church St.; 627-9444 or 203-839-2828. Moderate to expensive. Six 2-room suites designed to accommodate four guests each; fully equipped kitchenette, living-dining area, full bath; close to beaches and town center shopping.
- *The Dr. Daniel Fisher House,* 99 Main St.; 627-8017 or write: Box 5277, Edgartown, 02539. An 1840 Federal style house that is available for special events. Features a grand foyer with a winding staircase, ballroom and porch overlooking the lawn.
- *The Governor Bradford Inn,* 128 Main St.; 627-9510. Moderate to expensive. Gracefully restored mid-19th-century home; guest rooms decorated with antiques and reproductions, all with private baths and ceiling fans; breakfast served in sun room; beaches, shopping, tennis, and golf nearby.
- *The Harbor View Hotel,* N. Water St. (across from Lighthouse Beach); 627-7000 or 800-225-6005. Expensive. This 1891 restored hotel-resort offers one of the best water views on the island; large, comfortable rooms (some with decks), great restaurant and lounge, entertainment offered, pool, music room, game room, tennis; golfing and boating nearby; credit cards accepted; a Regency Inn.
- *The Harborside Inn,* 3 S. Water St. (at town dock); 627-4321 or 800-627-4009. Expensive. Waterfront resort; restaurant, lounge, pool, large rooms with water views, boating nearby; credit cards accepted.
- *Katama Guest House,* 166 Katama Rd.; 627-5158. Moderate. Heated rooms, continental breakfast. Open year-round, off-season rates available.
- *Katama Shores Inn,* 272 Katama Rd. facing South Beach; 627-4747. Moderate to expensive. 67 guest rooms, tennis courts, pool with decks and garden terrace, recreation room, shuffleboard, barbecue area, guest bicycle rentals, volleyball; dine at the Dunes Restaurant; Visa, MasterCard, and American Express accepted.
- *The Kelley House,* Kelley St.; 627-7900 or 800-225-6005. Expensive. One of the oldest inns in the country; completely restored, located in town center, view of Edgartown Harbor; 55 rooms, each with color TV, air-conditioning, and telephone; sheltered pool, brick terrace, close to tennis and shopping; credit cards accepted; a Regency Inn.
- *Mattakesett Homes,* Katama Rd.; 627-4432. Expensive. Eight privately owned homes. Seasonal operation, off-season rates.

EDGARTOWN (CONTINUED)

- *Meeting House Inn,* 40 Meeting House Way; 627-6220 or 800-627-2858. Moderate. A 1750 colonial home on 58 acres of wooded land, but just 3 miles from Edgartown center. Provides coolers, towels, and blankets for the beach.
- *Jonathan Munroe House,* Main St.; 627-5536. Expensive. Six guest rooms with private baths, some with whirlpools and fireplaces; separate garden cottage available.
- *Ocean View Homes,* South Beach; 203-659-1932. Moderate. Weekly house rentals, some with TV, heated, off-season rates.
- *Point Way Inn,* Main St. and Pease's Point Rd.; 627-8633 or 800-942-9569. Moderate to expensive. A 150-year-old sea captain's house with 14 rooms and eight fireplaces; beautiful setting; close to shopping and beaches. Enjoy breakfast by the fire, in the gazebo or in the garden.
- *Seaspray Vacation Homes,* South Beach; 203-658-2628. Moderate. Weekly house rentals, seasonal, off-season rates, contemporary designs on Katama Point.
- *The Shiretown Inn,* N. Water St.; 627-3353. Moderate to expensive. Inn consists of two restored sea captains' homes and a group of carriage houses; try the Shiretown Restaurant, one of the island's great dining spots, and the Shiretown Pub (great for before- or after-dinner drinks); Visa, MasterCard, and American Express cards accepted.
- *The Shiverick Inn,* Pent Lane; 627-3797 or 800-723-4292. Expensive. Graceful country inn built in 1840 for Dr. Clement Shiverick; all rooms have private baths; continental breakfast offered; Visa and MasterCard accepted.
- *The Tuscany Inn,* 22 N. Water St.; 627-5999 or 627-8999. Expensive. A truly exceptional inn. Formerly the Captain Fisher House, has recently been restored and renovated by one of the innkeepers, a native of Tuscany. Laura Scheuerhas combined her talents in art, interior design and culinary arts to transform this inn into a special place.
- *The Victorian Inn,* S. Water St.; 627-4784. Expensive. This 1820s inn is listed in the National Register of Historic Places. A restored whaling captain's home; all rooms have private baths and are decorated with family furniture and antiques. Complimentary gourmet breakfast offered.
- *Vineyard Preferred Properties,* Box 1104; 693-9451. Moderate. Weekly house rentals, TV.

GAY HEAD

- *Duck Inn,* off State Rd.; 645-9018. Moderate to expensive. Ocean view, full breakfast.
- *Leastway Cottage,* 693-7987. Expensive. Three-bedroom cottage overlooking Atlantic Ocean, private beach, sleeps 6, laundry room.
- *Up Island Country Inn,* Lobsterville Rd.; 645-2720. Near the shoreline.

MENEMSHA

- *The Beach Plum Inn & Restaurant,* on the road to Menemsha Harbor; 645-9454. Expensive. Small, cozy inn overlooking Vineyard Sound; excellent restaurant, one of the island's best; inn located on 10 acres, formal gardens; highly recommended.
- *Menemsha Inn and Cottages,* on the road to Menemsha Harbor; 645-2521. Moderate to expensive. Many rooms in the inn have water views; complimentary breakfast offered. Each cottage has its own kitchen, bath, and screened porch. Restaurant on premises offers fresh native seafood, milk-fed veal, and prime beef.

OAK BLUFFS

• *The "Admiral Benbow" Inn,* of the Black Dog Tavern Company, a short walk from Oak Bluffs Harbor, 520 New York Ave.; 693-6825 or 800-331-1787. Moderate to expensive. A classic island inn, complimentary gift certificate redeemable toward any meal at the Black Dog Tavern or any purchase at the Black Dog Bakery; Visa, MasterCard, and American Express accepted.

• *Arend's Samoset on the Sound,* Seaview Ave.; 693-5148 or 693-3878. Moderate to expensive. Bed and breakfast inn with water view, continental breakfast, some rooms with private baths. Seasonal, off-season rates, Visa and MasterCard accepted.

• *Attleboro House,* Lake Ave.; 693-4346. Moderate. Bed and breakfast with water view, continental breakfast, seasonal, off-season rates.

• *The Beach House,* Pennacook and Seaview aves., walking distance from ferry landing; 693-3955. Moderate. Seven bedrooms available; guests have access to large sitting room and front porch facing waterfront. Complimentary coffee and pastry served each morning; Visa and MasterCard accepted.

• *Capricorn House,* Seaview Ave.; 693-2848. Moderate. Bed and breakfast with water view, continental breakfast, seasonal.

• *Coming Home Cottage,* Colonial Ave.; 693-5499 or 986-5277. Moderate. Year-round, TV.

• *David's Island House,* Circuit Ave.; 693-4516. Moderate. Hotel, restaurant (breakfast, lunch, and dinner), lounge; 17 large rooms available.

• *The Dockside Inn,* on Oak Bluffs Harbor, Lower Circuit Ave.; 693-2966. Moderate to expensive. Close to beaches, shopping, restaurants, theaters, and summer concerts; comfortable rooms, continental breakfast; Visa, MasterCard, and American Express accepted.

• *East Chop Landing Apartments,* 21-23 East Chop Dr.; 696-0009. Moderate to expensive. One- and two-bedroom apartments with decks with a view of Oak Bluffs Harbor. Grills, linens, and fully equipped kitchens.

• *Island Inn,* Beach Rd.; 693-2002 or 800-462-0269. Expensive. Single and two-bedroom suites; one- to three-room units and a cottage available, all with kitchens or kitchenettes; pool, 18-hole Farm Neck Golf Course adjacent; conference center; Visa, MasterCard, American Express, Diners Club, and Carte Blanche accepted.

• *Lucille's Guest House,* Circuit Ave.; 693-1944. Moderate. Water view.

• *Martha's Vineyard Surfside Motel,* Oak Bluffs Ave.; 693-2500 or 800-537-3007. Moderate to expensive. Motel, TV, air-conditioning, private baths, continental breakfast. Seasonal, off-season rates, major credit cards accepted.

• *Narragansett House,* Narragansett Ave.; 693-3627. Moderate. Bed and breakfast, continental breakfast, efficiencies. Seasonal, off-season rates, Visa and MasterCard.

• *Nashua House,* Kennebec Ave.; 693-0043. Moderate. Bed and breakfast, seasonal, Victorian guest house.

• *Oak Bluffs Inn,* Circuit Ave. at the corner of Pequot Ave.; 693-7171 or 800-955-6235. Expensive. Victorian style inn, private baths, breakfast, afternoon tea in off-season, package deals.

• *The Oak House,* Seaview and Pequot aves.; 693-4187. Moderate to expensive. Built in 1872, this rustic but elegant Victorian summer house has 10 bedrooms, ornate tin ceilings and turn-of-the-century lamps; across from beach; Visa and MasterCard accepted.

• *Pequot House Hotel,* Pequot Ave.; 693-5087. Moderate. Seasonal, Visa and MasterCard, private baths.

OAK BLUFFS (CONTINUED)

- *Sengekontacket Condos,* off County Rd.; 693-2810. Moderate. Weekly condo rentals, TV, tennis, seasonal.
- *Shearer Cottages,* Rose Ave.; 693-4735 or 693-2634. Expensive. Efficiency units.
- *The Ship's Inn,* 14 Kennebec Ave.; 693-2760 or 800-564-2760. Moderate. Most rooms have private baths, some with private entrances; in town center area, close to beach; Visa, MasterCard, and American Express accepted.
- *The South Wind Guest House,* near the intersection of Circuit and Pequot aves.; 693-5031. Moderate. Turn-of-the-century Victorian home; within walking distance to shops and harbor, beaches and tennis courts; continental breakfast served.
- *Titticut Follies,* Naragansett Ave.; 693-4986. Moderate. Guest house, efficiencies, seasonal.
- *Tivoli Inn,* 222 Circuit Ave.; 693-7928. Moderate. Breakfast, wrap around porch, shared and private baths.
- *The Towers,* Pequot Ave.; 693-9894. Moderate. Guest house, seasonal.
- *Wesley Hotel,* One Lake Ave.; 693-6611. Moderate to expensive. In town center, one of the island's oldest hotels, completely restored Victorian setting; close walk to beaches; Visa, MasterCard, American Express, and Diners Club accepted.

VINEYARD HAVEN

- *Aldworth Manor,* 26 Mt. Aldworth Rd.; 693-3203. Moderate to expensive. Recently restored inn on secluded 2 acres, walk to VIneyard Haven, fireplaces, homemade breakfast.
- *Captain Dexter House,* 100 Main St.; 693-6564. Moderate to expensive. Built in 1843, this inn used to be the home of sea Captain Rodophus Dexter; restored and nicely furnished; each room has a private bath, and several have working fireplaces, period reproduction wallpaper; Visa and MasterCard accepted.
- *Causeway Harborview,* Skiff Ave.; 693-1606. Moderate. 24 individual apartments and cottages with fully equipped kitchens, full baths, color TVs, and linens. Complex sits on the crest of a hill overlooking Vineyard Haven Harbor and Nantucket Sound; pool, picnic areas, and barbecues; no credit cards.
- *Crocker House Inn,* Crocker Ave.; 693-1151 or 800-772-0206. Expensive. Inn with private baths, heat, some with air-conditioning. Year-round, Visa and MasterCard.
- *Deux Noisettes,* 114 Main St.; 693-0253. Expensive. Gracious residence features 4 guest rooms, rose-covered porch, 8 fireplaces and a gourmet breakfast.
- *Hanover House,* 10 Edgartown Rd.; 693-1066 or 800-339-1066. Moderate to expensive. Large, old inn offers much chrm and convenience; all rooms have private baths, color TVs, many with air-conditioning; kitchenettes.
- *Harbor Landing,* Beach Rd.; 693-2600. Moderate to expensive. Motel, private baths, TV, air-conditioning. Off-season rates. Visa and MasterCard.
- *High Haven House,* Summer St.; 693-9204 or 800-232-9204. Moderate. Bed and breakfast, some rooms with TV, private baths. Continental breakfast in season, pool, efficiencies, gas grills, year-round, off-season rates available, major credit cards accepted.
- *The Look Inn,* 13 Look St.; 693-6893. Moderate. An 1806 farmhouse, shared baths, continental breakfast.

- *The Lothrop Merry House,* Box 1939; 693-1646. An 18th-century guest house overlooking Vineyard Haven Harbor, most rooms have a harbor view, private beach, continental breakfast.
- *Ocean Side Inn,* two acres of waterfront property overlooking Vineyard Haven Harbor, Main St.; 693-1296. Moderate to expensive. Private beach, peaceful grounds, private baths; complimentary continental breakfast; Visa and MasterCard accepted.
- *Pierside*, Box 1951; 693-5562. Moderate to expensive. On Lake Tashmoo, red brick paths, gardens, full breakfast.
- *The Ribarik House,* N. William St.; 693-0544. Moderate. Bed and breakfast inn, continental breakfast.
- *1720 House,* 130 Main St.; 693-6407. Expensive. Historic home built in 1720 offers complimentary European style breakfast and afternoon tea.
- *Singer's Rentals,* Box 2216; 693-3097. Moderate. Seasonal rentals.
- *Thorncroft Inn,* on the road to West Chop, Main St.; 693-3333. Moderate to expensive. One of the best B&Bs of the Cape and Islands; written up in the *Boston Herald, Cape Cod Life,* and the *Cape Cod Times.* Inn located on three and a half acres of landscaped grounds; guest rooms authentically and elegantly decorated; gourmet breakfast offered in a sunny, formal dining room setting. Innkeepers Lynn and Karl Buder personally assist guests in offering recommendations on everything from museums and restaurants to beaches and back roads.
- *The Tisbury Inn,* Main St.; 693-2200. Expensive. Established in 1794; located in town center; 31 newly renovated rooms; private baths, color TVs, and ceiling fans; quaint and convenient; Visa, MasterCard, and American Express accepted.
- *The Tuckerman House,* 45 William St.; 693-0417. Expensive. Private beach, continental breakfast, close to town on two acres on the waterfront.
- *Twin Oaks Inn,* 8 Edgartown Rd.; 800-696-8633. Moderate. Dutch colonial styled inn, complimentary continental breakfast and afternoon tea served on the porch or in the gazebo.
- *Vineyard Harbor Motel,* Beach Rd.; 693-3334. Moderate to expensive. Rooms with view of the harbor, private beach, sun decks, close to town center; Visa and MasterCard accepted.
- *Wave's Edge Motel,* 32 Beach Rd.; 693-9695. Moderate to expensive. Motel rooms and two efficiency units available. Each unit has private bath with shower, equipped kitchenette and individually controlled heat; units overlook harbor. Close to town center; Visa and MasterCard accepted.

WEST TISBURY

- *The Bayberry,* Old Courthouse Rd.; 693-1984. Expensive. Year-round, some private baths, full breakfast available. Off-season rates, Visa, MasterCard accepted.
- *The Blue Goose,* Old Courthouse Rd.; 693-3223. Moderate. B&B, in a rural section of town, renovated farmhouse built in the 1700s on land that can be traced back to Indian owner. The inn is located on 45 acres of rolling pasture and surrounded by farms and woodlands; continental breakfast served.
- *Cove House & Studio House,* Runner Rd.; 693-9199. Moderate. Weekly rental efficiencies, seasonal.
- *The Farmhouse,* State Rd.; 693-5354. Moderate. Seasonal operation.
- *The House at New Lane B&B,* New Lane; 693-4046. Moderate. Shared bath, continental breakfast, children welcome.
- *Lambert's Cove Country Inn,* Lambert's Cove Rd.; 693-2298. Expensive. Year-round inn. Private baths, continental breakfast, tennis. Major credit cards.

Campgrounds

- **Martha's Vineyard Family Campground,** Edgartown Rd., Vineyard Haven; 693-3772 (in season) or 784-3615 (during off season). A mile from the Vineyard Haven ferry; wooded sites with picnic tables, fireplaces, hookups to accommodate tents or RVs, modern restrooms, laundromat, store, recreation hall, and playground; affordable; run by the Feeney family.
- **Webb's Camping Area,** Barnes Rd., at the head of Lagoon Pond, about three miles from both the Vineyard Haven and Oak Bluffs steamship landings; 693-0233 or write to RD#3, Box 100, Vineyard Haven, 02568. Campground offers 90 acres of woods and meadows, 150 campsites, 25 trailer hookups, some private campsites, and a separate area for cyclists and backpackers. Two-minute walk to Lagoon Pond, which offers boating, fishing, and swimming; hot and cold showers, picnic area, laundry, a general store, and fireplaces.

Youth Hostels

- **American Youth Hostel,** Box 158, W. Tisbury Rd., W. Tisbury, 02575; 693-2665. Five dormitories, double occupancy, seasonal.

Dining

CHILMARK

- **Feasts of Chilmark,** 645-3553. Moderate. Casual dining for lunch and dinner; Sunday brunch, 10:30 A.M.–2 P.M.; BYOB; Visa, MasterCard accepted; reservations suggested.

EDGARTOWN

- **Among the Flowers Café,** Mayhew Lane; 627-3233. Inexpensive. Serving breakfast, brunch and lunch; homemade chowder, crêpes, salads; outdoor dining.
- **Andrea's,** Upper Main St.; 627-5850. Moderate. Italian cuisine; overlooking the lawn and garden; dinner 6–10 P.M. Closed Sunday and Monday; parking available; reservations suggested.
- **The Beeftender Restaurant,** Upper Main St.; 627-8344. Moderate. Charcoal-broiled steaks and salad bar; open nightly 5–10 P.M. Cocktails till 11 P.M. Credit cards accepted; reservations suggested.
- **The Daggett House,** 59 N. Water St.; 627-4600. Moderate. Serves breakfast, brunch and dinner in a historic inn, views of Edgartown Harbor.
- **David Ryan's,** 11 N. Water St.; 627-4100. Moderate. Extensive menu includes pastas, seafood, sandwiches and burgers.
- **Edgar's Bar & Grill,** South Beach; 627-8972. Moderate. Serving lunch and dinner; open daily noon to 1 A.M. Reservations suggested; MasterCard, Visa, American Express, Diners Club accepted.
- **Edgartown Inn,** N. Water St.; 627-4794. Moderate. Serves country breakfast daily; reservations suggested.
- **L'Etoile,** S. Summer St.; 627-5187. Expensive. Gourmet French dining in the garden of the Charlotte Inn; open daily for dinner; Sunday brunch; reservations suggested.

- *Lawry's Seafood Restaurant,* Upper Main St.; 627-8857. Moderate. Open for lunch, Monday–Saturday 11 A.M.–2 P.M.; dinner 5 P.M.–9 P.M.; casual dining; American Express, MasterCard, Visa, Diners Club accepted.
- *Main Street Diner,* Main St., Old Post Office Square; 627-9337. Inexpensive. Breakfast, lunch, dinner; good for the children.
- *The Navigator Restaurant,* Main St.; 627-4320. Expensive. Serves lunch and dinner; overlooks Edgartown Harbor.
- *Savoir Fare,* Post Office Square; 627-9864. Moderate. Open daily; serving Sunday brunch.
- *Sandcastles,* 71 Main St., 627-8446. Moderate to expensive. Creative cuisine in a cozy atmosphere; breakfast, lunch, dinner and Sunday brunch.
- *The Shiretown Inn,* N. Water St.; 627-6655. Moderate. Grilled seafood and other entrées; dine by candlelight in a pleasant garden setting; desserts a specialty; open daily for dinner 6–10 P.M. American Express, MasterCard, Visa accepted; reservations suggested.
- *Square Rigger Restaurant,* at the Triangle; 627-9968. Moderate. Charbroiled entrées and seafood specialties; pleasant dining with a nautical flavor; open daily for dinner 6–10 P.M.; MasterCard, Visa accepted; reservations suggested.
- *Starbuck's/Harbor View Hotel,* N. Water St.; 627-7000. Expensive. Open daily for breakfast, lunch, and dinner; elegant dining overlooking Edgartown Harbor; American Express, MasterCard, Visa accepted; reservations suggested.
- *Warriner's,* Post Office Square; 627-4488. Expensive. Enjoy classic cuisine in the atmosphere of an English drawing room; dinner; American Express, MasterCard, Visa accepted; reservations suggested.
- *The Wharf Pub,* Lower Main St.; 627-9966. Inexpensive. Casual dining in a comfortable pub atmosphere; open daily for lunch and dinner; American Express, MasterCard, Visa accepted.
- *Your Market,* Triangle Market; 627-4000. Inexpensive. Delicatessen.
- *Zacariah's/Kelley House,* Kelley St.; 627-4394. Moderate to expensive. Serves breakfast, lunch and dinner; Sunday brunch; American Express, MasterCard, Visa accepted. Reservations suggested.

GAY HEAD

- *The Aquinnah,* at the cliffs; 645-9654. Moderate. Casual dining inside and outside on deck overlooking the Atlantic; open for breakfast, lunch, and dinner.

MENEMSHA

- *The Beach Plum Inn,* North Rd.; 645-9454. Expensive. Elegant dining; overlooking Menemsha Harbor; Sunday brunch; reservations suggested.
- *The Bite,* Basin Rd.; 645-9239. Moderate. Fried seafood.
- *The Galley,* 645-9819. Moderate. Take it out or sit on the porch; open daily from 11 A.M.–9 P.M.
- *Home Port,* 645-2679. Moderate. Casual dining while watching sunsets; seafood specialty; BYOB; serves dinner nightly from 5 P.M.; reservations required; MasterCard, Visa accepted.
- *Menemsha Deli,* 645-9902. Inexpensive. Delicatessen.
- *Menemsha Inn & Restaurant,* North Rd.; 645-2521. Moderate. Peaceful country setting; serving dinner; MasterCard, Visa accepted; reservations suggested.

OAK BLUFFS

- *Atlantic Connection,* Circuit Ave.; 693-7129. Moderate. Restaurant and dance club; charbroiling specialty; open daily 11:30–midnight; serving lunch and dinner.

OAK BLUFFS (CONTINUED)

- *David's Island House,* Circuit Ave.; 693-4516. Moderate. Comfortable dining in a Victorian setting; piano music; serving lunch and dinner; lounge; open daily; MasterCard, Visa, Diners Club accepted; reservations suggested.
- *Giordano's Restaurant,* Circuit Ave.; 693-0184. Inexpensive. Italian fare and seafood; open daily; serving lunch and dinner.
- *Linda Jean's,* Circuit Ave.; 693-4093. Inexpensive. Home-style cooking; open daily for breakfast, lunch, and dinner.
- *Lola's,* Beach Rd.; 693-5007. Moderate. Food with a taste of New Orleans.
- *The Lost Pelican Bistro,* Lake Ave.; 693-3101. Moderate. Across from the harbor, 1860's Gingerbread-style café, take out, daily pasta and seafood specials.
- *Ocean View Restaurant,* Chapman Ave.; 693-2207. Moderate. Open daily for lunch and dinner; lunch served in tavern 11:30 A.M.–2 P.M., except Sunday; dinner, dining room 6–9 P.M. Casual dress.
- *The Oyster Bar,* Circuit Ave.; 693-3300. Moderate. "An American Bistro," fresh fish and raw bar; beer and wine only.
- *Papa's Pizza,* Circuit Ave.; 693-1400. Inexpensive. Family restaurant; Italian menu; full dinners; pizza and salads.
- *Pilot House Restaurant,* Circuit Ave.; 693-9850. Inexpensive. Casual; serves breakfast and lunch.
- *Whales Rib,* Circuit Ave.; 693-2627. Inexpensive to moderate. Specializing in Cajun seafoods, salads, burgers, and subs; open for breakfast at 8 A.M.; lunch and dinner late till 12:45.
- *Zapotec,* 10 Kennebec Ave.; 693-6800. Inexpensive to moderate. Featuring authentic Mexican south-of-the-border specialties; beer and wine.

VINEYARD HAVEN

- *Artcliff Diner,* Beach Rd.; 693-1224. Inexpensive. Open daily for breakfast and lunch; home-style cooking.
- *Black Dog Tavern,* Beach Rd. Ext.; 693-9223. Moderate to expensive. Casual dining in a rustic atmosphere, on the beach overlooking Vineyard Haven Harbor; breakfast, lunch and dinner; BYOB.
- *Le Grenier French Restaurant,* Main St.; 693-4906. Expensive. Intimate dining atmosphere, balcony dining available; open evenings at 6 P.M.; American Express, MasterCard, Visa accepted; reservations suggested.
- *Louis' Tisbury Café & Take Out,* State Rd.; 693-3255. Inexpensive. Italian menu. Open seven days. Take-out Monday–Saturday, 11:30 A.M., Sunday, 4 P.M.; dining room nightly from 5:30 P.M.
- *Patisserie Francaise,* Main St.; 693-8087. Moderate. French café-style; sidewalk café sitting; open daily for breakfast, lunch, and dinner. Sunday brunch; MasterCard, Visa accepted.
- *Sandy's Fish & Chips,* State Rd.; 693-1220. Inexpensive. Fried seafood.
- *Tisbury Inn Café,* Main St.; 693-3416. Moderate. Open seven nights for dinner; lunch, Wednesday–Monday from 11:30 A.M.; Sunday brunch from 10 A.M. Grilled seafoods and steaks; outdoor café.

WEST TISBURY

- *Lambert's Cove Country Inn,* Lambert's Cove Rd.; 693-2298. Expensive. Intimate dining by candlelight in an old country estate; serves dinner and Sunday brunch; BYOB; American Express, MasterCard, Visa, Diners Club accepted; reservations suggested.

Entertainment

Music & Stage

- *Center for the Performing Arts,* Old Whaling Church, Main St., Edgartown; 627-8017. Variety of concerts and shows held each summer for all age groups.
- *Chilmark Chamber Concerts,* 645-9606. Chamber music.
- *Island Theater Workshop,* Box 1893, Vineyard Haven; 693-4060. Provides theater productions year-round.
- *MV Campmeeting Association Tabernacle,* Oak Bluffs; 693-0525. Art shows, concerts by entertainers such as Arlo Guthrie and many others.
- *Nathan Mayhew Seminars,* N. William St., Vineyard Haven; 693-6603. This organization sponsors music and film festivals throughout the summer and offers educational services year-round.
- *Martha's Vineyard Chamber Music Society,* Old Whaling Church in Edgartown and at the Chilmark Community Center; 645-9446.
- *The Vineyard Playhouse,* 10 Church St., Tisbury; 696-6300. Year-round theater, summer theater can be enjoyed outdoors at the Tashmoo overlook.
- *Wintertide Coffeehouse,* 5 Corners, Vineyard Haven; 693-8830. Folk, jazz, comedy and instrumental music offered in this coffeehouse that has been rated among the top ten in the nation. Food and dessert available.
- *The Yard,* Beetlebung Corner in Chilmark; 645-9662. Original dance and art; workshops and classes.

Nightlife

- *Atlantic Connection,* Circuit Ave., Oak Bluffs; 693-7129. Music; dancing; live entertainment.
- *The Harbor View Hotel,* N. Water St., Starbuck's Neck, overlooking Edgartown's outer harbor, Lighthouse Beach, and Chappaquiddick; 627-7000. Live entertainment offered in this grand 1890 hotel-resort; excellent musical reviews!
- *Hot Tin Roof,* Martha's Vineyard Airport; 693-1137 and Lake Ave., Oak Bluffs; 693-6767. Music, dancing, live entertainment.
- *David's Island House,* Circuit Ave.; 693-4516. Piano.

Movie Theaters

- *Edgartown Town Hall,* Main St. (upstairs). For more information, call 627-3788.
- *Vineyard Theaters,* Main St., Edgartown; 627-8044.
- *Island,* Circuit Ave., Oak Bluffs; 627-3788.
- *Strand,* Oak Bluffs Ave., Oak Bluffs; 627-3788.
- *Capawock,* Main St., Vineyard Haven; 627-8044.

Museums & Historic Sites

- *Cottage Museum,* 1 Trinity Place, Oak Bluffs. Tour one of the gingerbread cottages and see how they were furnished 100 years ago, open June–September.

- **Dukes County Historical Society Museum & Library,** Cooke St., Edgartown; 627-4441. Varied historical exhibits on island life; the museum has 12 rooms of antique furniture, scrimshaw, ship models, costumes, and gear used by early settlers; also visit the adjacent Gale Huntington Library of History.
- **Jirah Luce House,** located in the old Ritter House, Beach Rd., Vineyard Haven (opposite fire station); 693-5353. An eight-room 1796 Federal home with exhibits of island life from 1800 to 1900; adults $1, children 50 cents; open mid-June until mid-September, from 1 P.M. until 5:30 P.M. (closed Sundays).
- **Mayhew Chapel** and **Old Indian Burial Ground,** at the corner of Christiantown and Indian Hill rds., W. Tisbury. Also a wildflower sanctuary; chapel named after the Reverend Thomas Mayhew Jr., who converted many of the Indians to Christianity in the 1600s.
- **Old Schoolhouse Museum,** 110 Main St., Vineyard Haven; 693-3860. The original Tisbury School, now owned and maintained by the Vineyard's preservation society; artifacts and exhibits depicting early island life.
- **The Old Whaling Church** and **Vincent House,** Main St., Edgartown; 627-4440. Both museums are owned by the Vineyard Historical Preservation Society. The Vincent House, built in 1672, is thought to be the oldest house on the Vineyard. The Old Whaling Church, a magnificent, white-pillared structure, was built in 1843 and is a fine example of Greek Revival architecture. The preservation society recently converted the old church into a performing arts center.
- **Seaman's Bethel, Museum and Chapel,** Union St., Vineyard Haven; 693-9317. The structure was built in 1893 as a church for seamen whose ships were anchored in the harbor. The chapel is now a maritime museum; open daily, from 10 A.M. until 4 P.M.
- **Windfarm Museum,** on Edgartown–Vineyard Haven Rd., Vineyard Haven; 693-3658. Solar-heated, wind-powered house; fish pond with "underwater windows"; farm animals; historic and modern windmill exhibit. Great for the family; children's program offered; call for more information.

Seasonal Events

The island has a variety of entertaining happenings throughout the season—everything from children's fairs and yard sales to luncheons and lectures. Some are annual events; others are new each year.

EDGARTOWN

- **A Taste of the Vineyard,** on the lawn of the Old Whaling Church, 627-4440. Each June; benefit for the Martha's Vineyard Historical Preservation Society. Eating, dancing, gourmet stroll (a sampling of some of the fine foods the island has to offer).
- **Celebrity Hat Auction.** Sponsored by the Martha's Vineyard Hospital Day Care Center; held annually; auction off various choice items from some of your favorite celebs.
- **Evening under the Stars,** on the lawn of the historic Vincent House; 627-8017. Sponsored by the Martha's Vineyard Historical Preservation Society. Musical event held in June.
- **Edgartown Regatta,** from the harbor in Edgartown; call the Edgartown Yacht Club; 627-4361. Sailboat races in July.
- **First Night Martha's Vineyard,** 693-4486. Events in Oak Bluffs, Edgartown and Vineyard Haven, fireworks at Vineyard Haven Harbor.

- *Possible Dreams Auction.* Benefit for Martha's Vineyard Community Services; for more information, call 693-4460.
- *Christmas on the Vineyard.* Activities throughout the island; starts second weekend in December. For more information, call Chamber of Commerce at 693-0085. Christmas sales, open houses, craft fairs, chowder contest, children's activities.
- *Striped Bass and Bluefish Derby.* Annual event usually held in mid-September to mid-October; for more information, call Chamber of Commerce at 693-8342.

OAK BLUFFS

- *Annual fireworks,* Ocean Park. For more information, call Oak Bluffs Town Hall at 693-5511.
- *Illumination Night.* Unique light display; for more information, call Chamber of Commerce or Campground Meeting Association.
- *Tivoli Day.* Held in September; fishing derby for kids, street fair, bike race, blessing of fishing fleet. For more information, call Chamber of Commerce.

VINEYARD HAVEN

- *Tisbury Street Fair,* Main St. Held in July; crafts, food, music, family fun. For more information, call Chamber of Commerce at 693-0085.

WEST TISBURY

- *Annual County Fair,* Agricultural Society Fairgrounds. Held in August; call Chamber of Commerce for more information.

Tours

The island's three bus companies offer regular tour and shuttle services around the Vineyard. The narrated tours run two to two and a half hours. For more information, call the following: *Gay Head Sightseeing*, Oak Bluffs, 693-1555; *Island Transport*, Vineyard Haven, 693-0058; *Martha's Vineyard Sightseeing*, Oak Bluffs, 627-8687.

- *The Winery at Chicama Vineyards,* Stoney Hill Rd., W. Tisbury; 693-0309. Visit the Vineyard's own winery, allow a half hour for the tour; 35 acres of vineyards produce wines such as chardonnay, chenin blanc, cabernet sauvignon, Riesling, merlot, and Pinot noir, among others.
- *Holly Tours,* 627-9201. Walking tours.

Children's Activities

In addition to the activities listed here, we suggest you check our listings for public beaches, hiking and nature trails, camping, ice cream parlors, farms, and museums.

- *Band concerts.* Check with town halls or local papers for schedule of outdoor band concerts in Vineyard Haven and Oak Bluffs.
- *Dreamland Fun Center,* across from the Flying Horses Carousel, Oak Bluffs; 693-5163. Video games, bumper cars, skeeball.
- *Edgartown Public Library,* 58 North Water St.; 627-4221. Story hour each Wed. morning at 10:30.
- *Felix Neck Wildlife Sanctuary,* 627-4850. Programs for children of all ages.
- *The Flying Horses,* Oak Bluffs; 693-9481. The oldest working carousel in the country.

- *Gymnastics Day Camp and Tumble Bugs Day Camp,* run by the U.S. Academy of Gymnastics; 203-847-4994. Camps held in Vineyard Haven. Gymnastics Day Camp for children grades one through high school. Tumble Bugs Day Camp for preschoolers (one of the most innovative preschool programs). Call for more information.
- *Horseback riding,* W. Tisbury, 693-3770; Pond View Farms, New Lane, W. Tisbury, 693-2949; Misty Meadows Farm, Old County Rd., W. Tisbury, 693-1870.
- *Island Mini Golf Cove,* State Rd., Vineyard Haven; 693-2611.
- *The Lobster Hatchery,* Oak Bluffs; 693-0060. Learn all about lobsters.
- *Spinnaker Lanes,* State Rd., Vineyard Haven; 693-9691. Bowling and billiards.
- *Sketch Art and Theater Camp,* Box 2676, Vineyard Haven; 696-8257. Weekly programs that offer drama or painting.
- *Summer Adventure Programs,* 627-3303. Boys and Girls Club of Martha's Vineyard.
- *Teenprov!,* Vineyard Playhouse; 693-6450. Theater games, classes, improv for ages 13-18.
- *Thimble Farm,* 693-6396. Pick your own strawberries or raspberries.
- *Tabernacle,* Oak Bluffs; 693-0525. Evening programs throughout summer for family; community sings.
- *Tisbury Healthworks,* Beach Rd., Vineyard Haven; 693-4796. Indoor pool, swimming lessons, kids' exercise classes.
- *Vineyard Museum Art Makers,* Box 11, Vineyard Haven; 693-5353. Weekly programs that provide adventures in lobstering, drama, sculpture and various crafts.

Shops

Art Galleries

- *Martha's Vineyard Art Association,* Edgartown; 627-4881. Local artists, lessons, workshops.
- *Edgartown Art Gallery,* 27 S. Summer St., Edgartown; 627-5991. Assorted offerings.
- *The Granary Gallery at the Red Barn Emporium* (next to Nip 'n' Tuck Antiques); Old County Rd., W. Tisbury; 693-0455. Frequent shows featuring a variety of works.
- *Red Barn Emporium,* Old County Rd., W. Tisbury; 693-0455. Good selection of antiques and an art gallery.
- *Scott Studio-Gallery,* South Rd., Chilmark; 645-9577. Assorted offerings.
- *Travis Tuck,* Main St., Vineyard Haven; 693-3914. Assorted offerings.
- *Vineyard Vignettes,* Winter St., Edgartown; 627-8794. Variety of art.

Craft & Specialty Shops

- *Bowl & Board,* Main St., Vineyard Haven; 693-9441. Wood items, baskets, and housewares.
- *Bunch of Grapes Bookstore,* Main St., Vineyard Haven; 693-2291. One of the best bookstores in all of New England.

- *Calico Sue's Country Store,* Menemsha Harbor; 693-6252. Assorted crafts.
- *Crispin's Landing,* corner of Main St. and Union St., Tisbury; 693-6758. A collection of craft shops.
- *Essence,* Tisbury Market Place, Vineyard Haven; 693-1369. Fragrances made to order and other items, jewelry, etc.
- *The Heath Hen Quilt Shop,* Tisbury Market Place, Vineyard Haven; 693-6730. Assorted items.
- *Fligors',* N. Water St., Edgartown; 627-8811. Gifts, classic clothing, quality toys, Christmas shop.
- *Claudia,* Main St., Edgartown; 627-8306. Leather goods and fine jewelry.
- *Tori Togs,* State Rd., Vineyard Haven; 693-6383. Children's clothing, maternity clothes, toys, books; cribs, car seats and strollers for rent.
- *Menemsha General Store and Post Office,* Menemsha Harbor.
- *The Menemsha Trader,* Menemsha Harbor; 645-9984. Assorted crafts.
- *Menemsha Wood Shop,* Menemsha Harbor; 645-3417. Assorted crafts.
- *Oversouth Antiques and Collectibles,* Menemsha Harbor; 645-3348. Assorted crafts.
- *Pandora's Box,* Menemsha Harbor; 645-9696. Clothes.
- *Peaceable Kingdom,* off Kennebec Ave., Oak Bluffs; 693-7716. Stuffed animals, jewelry, collectibles.
- *Secret Garden,* Circuit Ave., Oak Bluffs; 693-4759. China, linen, lace, and gifts.
- *Tashtego,* Main St., Edgartown; 627-4300. Carefully selected household items, from lamps, to rugs, to spoons and glasses.
- *The Tisbury Market Place,* Beach Rd., Vineyard Haven; across from New Bedford ferry slip. Collection of shops.
- *Rags,* Dock St., Edgartown; 627-8160. Nice clothing store.
- *Nevin Square,* off Winter St., Edgartown. A new area of shops.
- *Peacock Papers,* at the Colonial Inn Shops, Edgartown. A good shop to pick up fun gifts for children.
- *Sioux Eagle Designs,* Crispin's Landing, Main St., Vineyard Haven; 693-6537. Handmade jewelry.
- *The Vermont Shop,* Edgartown; 627-8448. Pottery, special foods, and gifts.

Antiques

- *Aunties' Attic,* Edgartown–Vineyard Haven Rd., Edgartown; 627-9833. Estate sales, country and formal furnishings, other offerings.
- *Bramhall & Dunn,* Main St., Vineyard Haven; 693-6437 and in West Tisbury at 693-5221. English country antiques, home furnishings.
- *Clocktower Antiques,* N. Summer St., Edgartown; 627-8006, 693-3507 or 693-9155. Jewelry, silver, porcelain, rugs, other offerings.
- *Chilmark Flea Market,* Chilmark church grounds; End of June to first of Sept., hundreds of dealers.
- *Coal Wharf Antiques,* Dock St., Edgartown; 627-8342 or 627-3019. Assorted nautical offerings, furniture.
- *Cove Hollow Antiques,* 20 Summer St., Edgartown; 627-9293. Assorted offerings.
- *C.W. Morgan Marine Antiques,* Beach Rd.; 693-3622. Nautical items, scrimshaw.

- *Early Spring Farm Antiques,* 93 Lagoon Rd., Vineyard Haven; 693-9141. American country antiques, folk art.
- *The Edgartown Art Gallery and Antique Shop,* at the Charlotte Inn, 27 S. Summer St., Edgartown; 627-5991. One of the best art and antique exhibits on the island.
- *Elegant Crow,* 6 S. Water St., Edgartown; 627-8232. One of a kind items in this one of a kind shop, a delight.
- *Island Antiques,* Oak Bluffs; 693-0202. Assorted offerings.
- *Nip 'n' Tuck Antiques,* Old County Rd., W. Tisbury; 693-4338. 18th- and 19th-century country furniture and house items.
- *Now and Then Shop,* Circuit Ave., lower end, Oak Bluffs; 696-8604. Collectibles, china, glassware, other offerings.
- *Old Barn Antiques, Inc.,* Lagoon Rd., Vineyard Haven; 693-3425. Jewelry, furniture, other offerings.
- *Oversouth,* Menemsha Harbor, Basin Rd., Chilmark; 645-3348. Assorted offerings.
- *Past and Presents,* 12 N. Water St. and 37 Main St., Edgartown; 627-3992. Antiques and gifts.
- *Pyewackets,* 63 Beach Rd., Vineyard Haven; 696-7766. Over 20 Island artisans display their wares in this restored gallery.
- *Red Barn Antiques,* Old County Rd., W. Tisbury; 693-5221. Island art and collectibles.
- *The Red Pony,* South Rd., Chilmark; 645-3003. Antique furniture from England, America, Orient and Eastern Europe.
- *Soulanet Collection,* Winter St., Edgartown; 693-9812 or 627-7759. Afghans, folk art, and Americana.
- *Traditions,* 43 Main St., Edgartown; 627-4500. New England antiques and contemporary accessories.
- *Vintage Jewelry,* Summer St., Edgartown; 627-5409. Art Deco, Nouveau, and Victorian gold jewelry; other offerings.

Sports & Recreation

Biking

Just about everyone, it seems, who has vacationed on the Vineyard has rented a bicycle or moped at one time. This is often the best way to tour the island, especially during busy summer months. The Vineyard offers something for every biking or moped enthusiast—from flat, easy-to-pedal stretches on the bike path along State Beach to the steep valleys and challenging hills of Chilmark and Gay Head that require some huffing and puffing.

For the casual biker or day tripper, we suggest pedaling along Beach Road from Vineyard Haven or Oak Bluffs (where the ferries dock) to Edgartown—an easy ride. You can stop off at the beach along the way or take in such places as magnificent Sengekontacket Pond. You can also take the inland route along Edgartown–Vineyard Haven Road. Marked bicycle trails also run through West Tisbury.

Here is a town-by-town listing of island bicycle and moped rentals:

- *R. W. Cutler Bike,* One Main St., Edgartown; 627-4052. Rents bikes.
- *DeBettencourt's Bike Shop,* Circuit Ave. Ext., Oak Bluffs; 693-0011. Rents bikes and mopeds.
- *King's Bike & Moped,* Circuit Ave. Ext., Oak Bluffs; 693-1887. Rents bikes and mopeds.
- *Martha's Vineyard Scooter and Bike,* Union St., Vineyard Haven; 693-0782. Rents bikes and mopeds.
- *Quawk Cycle Tours,* 73 Lagoon Rd., Vineyard Haven; 693-1188 or 800-694-1188. Will plan a 2–3 hour bike tour or an entire cycling vacation.
- *Ride-on-Mopeds,* Circuit Ave. Ext., Oak Bluffs; 693-2076 or 800-564-2076. Moped rentals.
- *Sun 'n' Fun.* Lake Ave., Oak Bluffs; 693-5457. Rents bikes and mopeds.
- *Vineyard Bike and Moped,* Oak Bluffs; 693-7886.
- *Vineyard Vehicle Rentals,* Vineyard Haven; 693-1185. Bike rentals.
- *Wheel Happy,* 8 South Water St., Edgartown; 627-5928.
- *Edgartown Bicycles,* 190 Upper Main St.; 627-9008.

Boating

EDGARTOWN

- *Edgartown Harbor Tours,* 627-4388 or 627-7295. Departs from bottom of Main Street, near the yacht club.
- *Gale Force Charters,* out of Edgartown Harbor; 627-3091. Day sails and sunsets aboard the *Claire*, a Kaiser Gale Force 45-foot ketch.
- *Harborside Inn,* S. Water St. (near Edgartown Yacht Club); 627-4321. Day sailers and outboards for rent.
- *Island Windsurfing,* Dock St.; 627-5886. Sailboarding lessons at Lighthouse Beach; from novice to would-be pro.
- *Mad Max Sailing Adventures,* 31 Dock St., Edgartown; 627-7500. Take a ride on this state-of-the-art catamaran.

GAY HEAD

- *Gay Head Boat Rentals,* Menemsha Pond; 645-9746. Day sailer and Sunfish rentals.

MENEMSHA

- *Dogfish Sea Kayaking Company,* Menemsha, next to the Homeport Restaurant.

OAK BLUFFS

- *Vineyard Boat Rentals,* Circuit Ave., Oak Bluffs; 693-8476.

VINEYARD HAVEN

- **Ayuthia *Charters*,** Beach St. Ext.; 693-7245. 48-foot classic gaff ketch for charter half day, full day, overnight, or longer; full-day charters explore Elizabeth Island area; overnights to Newport, Block Island, Cuttyhunk, or Nantucket.
- **Laissez Faire *Charter*,** out of Vineyard Haven Harbor; call John and Mary Clarke at the Lothrop Merry House, 693-1646. 54-foot Alden ketch; half-day sails, day sails, overnights to Nantucket and Cuttyhunk, winter Caribbean charters.

VINEYARD HAVEN (CONTINUED)

- **Shenandoah *Charters*,** Vineyard Haven Harbor; 693-1699. 108-foot iron-hulled, square-topsail schooner for charter.
- ***Wind's Up*,** 95 Beach Rd., Vineyard Haven; 693-4340. Canoes, kayaks, surfing items, lessons, beach and snorkel gear.

For other charters on other vessels, call 693-1646 or 693-5689.

Fishing

If you like to fish, you've come to the right place. The Vineyard boasts of some of the best fresh- and saltwater fishing in all of New England. In the ocean surf, anglers go for striped bass and bluefish in season (spring, early summer, and early fall are the best times). Sport fishermen also troll for swordfish, tuna, mackerel, and white marlin. You can also land your share of cod, flounder, pollock, tautog, and fluke in island waters.

Here is a list of fishing tackle and supply stores:
- ***Big Eye Charters*,** Edgartown Harbor; 627-3649.
- ***Brickman's*,** Main St., Vineyard Haven; 693-0047.
- ***Capt. Porky's Bait & Tackle*,** Edgartown; 627-7117. Charter boat and fishing supplies.
- ***Coop's Bait & Tackle*,** 147 W. Tisbury Rd.; 627-3909.
- ***Larry's Tackle Shop*,** dock at Edgartown; 627-5088.
- ***Locals Only*,** Tisbury; 627-6040. Fishing adventures for the novice or beginner, rod demonstrations, instruction.
- ***Reel Adventures*,** Oak Bluffs Harbor; 693-7926.

CHARTER FISHING

- ***Clyde's Beach Charter*,** 135 W. Tisbury Rd., Edgartown; 627-8181.
- ***Patriot Party Boats*,** Oak Bluffs Harbor; 548-2626. Charter fishing aboard the *Minuteman*.
- ***Ranger*,** Main St., Edgartown; 627-9840.
- ***Ruddy Duck Marine*,** Main St., Edgartown; 627-4709.
- ***The Skipper*,** Oak Bluffs Harbor; 693-1238 or 627-0219.

Golf

- ***Farm Neck Golf Club*,** County Rd., Oak Bluffs (overlooking State Beach and Sengekontacket Pond); 693-3057. 18 holes, par 72, 6700 yards.
- ***Mink Meadow Golf Club*,** off Franklin St., West Chop; 693-0600. 9 holes, par 35, 3069 yards.

Hiking & Nature Trails

- ***Felix Neck Wildlife Sanctuary*,** located about three miles outside Edgartown Center on the Vineyard Haven–Edgartown Road; 627-4850. More than 200 acres of woods, salt marshes, and a pond; sanctuary offers exhibits, a library, and six miles of trails. It is run by the Felix Neck Wildlife Trust, which is affiliated with the Massachusetts Audubon Society. A $1 admission fee is charged for adults, 50 cents for children; open year-round.
- ***Cedar Tree Neck*,** on the north shore of the Vineyard off Indian Hill Road, all the way to the sharp left-hand curve; take dirt road downhill to the right—it leads

to a parking lot. About 250 acres of meadows and headland; abundant plant and wildlife; follow marked trail; area is run by Sheriff's Meadow Foundation.

• *Long Point*, W. Tisbury. 580 acres with frontage on Tisbury Great Pond, Middle Point Cove, Long Cove, and a half mile of South Beach (on the Atlantic). Admission free; fishing; swimming, and picnics allowed. Parking lot located about three miles off the Edgartown–West Tisbury Road—take Deep Bottom Road for about two miles until you come to the Long Point sign. Deep Bottom Road is located exactly one mile west of Martha's Vineyard Airport entrance. Area is run by the Trustees of Reservations.

• *Cape Pogue and Wasque Reservation,* on Chappaquiddick Island. Cape Pogue Wildlife Reservation (489 acres) and the adjacent Wasque Reservation (200 acres) offer dunes, beaches, and salt marshes. A good part of the area is accessible only by four-wheel drive—vehicle permit, obtained through the Trustees of Reservations, is required; for more information, call the Martha's Vineyard Chamber of Commerce at 693-0085.

For more on Vineyard walks and nature trails, we suggest you pick up a copy of *Short Walks on Cape Cod and the Vineyard* by Hugh and Heather Sadlier. The book is published by the Globe Pequot Press.

Sporting Goods Stores

• *Brickman's,* Main St., Vineyard Haven; 693-0047; Edgartown; 627-4700.
• *Larry's Tackle Shop,* at the Edgartown dock; 627-5088.
• *Vineyard Sport Center*, 243 Vineyard Haven Rd., Edgartown; 627-3933. All sports equipment, rollerblade rentals.

Tennis

As in most Cape Cod communities, there are private and public tennis courts on Martha's Vineyard—more than 30 courts in all. You'll find private or public courts in every island town. Here is a sampling:

CHILMARK
• *Beach Plum Inn,* Menemsha; 645-9454. Courts for guests.
• *Tea Lane Courts.* For reservations, call 645-9712.

EDGARTOWN
• *Harbor View Hotel,* Starbuck's Neck; 627-4333. Great courts for guests.
• *Town courts,* Robinson Rd. Reservations made at courts; for more information, call 627-8594.

OAK BLUFFS
• *Farm Neck Club,* off County Rd.; 693-9728.
• *Island Country Club Tennis Court,* Beach Rd.; 693-6574.
• *Martha's Vineyard Regional High School,* on Vineyard Haven–Edgartown Rd. Reservations made at court.
• *Town courts,* at Niantic Park. Reservations made at court.

VINEYARD HAVEN
• *Clark Leland & Clark Tennis Courts,* Boxbury Ave.; 693-3888.
• *Town courts,* on Church St. Reservations made at court.

WEST TISBURY

• *Lambert's Cove Inn,* off Cove Rd.; 693-2298.
• *West Tisbury Elementary School,* Old County Rd. Reservations made at court a day in advance.

Beaches

If there's one thing Martha's Vineyard has, it's plenty of beaches.

The island is bounded by the Atlantic, Nantucket Sound, and Vineyard Sound— not to mention its numerous coves and fresh- and saltwater ponds. While many beaches are open free of charge to the public, some require resident or summer visitor parking stickers (available for a reasonable fee at town halls throughout the island). Here is a town-by-town list of Vineyard beaches.

CHAPPAQUIDDICK

• *Chappy Point,* a short ferry ride (about 100 yards) from Edgartown Center. Ferry ride costs about $1.50 a car and 35 cents per person; ferry runs continually from 7:30 A.M. until midnight during the summer. Chappy Point beaches (there are two—one facing inner harbor, one facing outer harbor) are within walking distance of ferry landing.
• *East Beach/Cape Pogue Wildlife Refuge and Wasque Reservation.* Open to public. The two adjacent beaches on the east side of the island are run by the Trustees of Reservations (see listing under Hiking & Nature Trails); no sticker required.

CHILMARK

• *Menemsha Public Beach,* at Menemsha Harbor on Vineyard Sound, not far from the famous fishing shanties. Open to public, no sticker required.
• *Squibnocket Beach,* on the Atlantic near Squibnocket Pond. For year-round and summer residents of Chilmark only; sticker required.
• *Lucy Vincent Beach,* on the Atlantic. Open to Chilmark year-round and summer residents only; sticker required.

EDGARTOWN

• *Bend-in-the-Road Beach,* on Nantucket Sound near town center. Good family beach; open to the public; no sticker required.
• *Lighthouse Beach,* Edgartown Harbor beach at Starbuck's Neck (in front of attractive Harbor View Hotel resort). One of the island's prettiest beaches; views of harbor and nearby Chappaquiddick Island; old lighthouse located on the beach; within walking distance of Edgartown Center by way of North Water Street; no on-site parking available.
• *South Beach* (Katama Beach), ocean beach along the south shore of Edgartown off Katama Road, a few miles from town center. County beach, open to public, no sticker required; limited parking (get there early); good surf.

GAY HEAD

Two-hour parking limits are often enforced at Gay Head beaches.
• *Gay Head Beach,* on Atlantic. For Gay Head year-round and summer residents only; stickers required.

• *Gay Head Clay Cliffs Beach,* on the Atlantic at Gay Head Cliffs. Open to the public; park in town lot at the top of cliffs and take Moshup's Trail to the beach; don't climb the cliffs; no sticker required.

• *Lobsterville.* There are two beaches here, one private, the other public. *Lobsterville Road Beach,* for residents only, is located off Lobsterville Road on Vineyard Sound; *Lobsterville Beach,* a public beach, is located at the end of Lobsterville Road (public access to Menemsha Pond).

• *Philbin Beach,* on the Atlantic. Open only to year-round and summer residents of Gay Head; sticker required.

• *West Basin Beach,* off West Basin Road. Open to public, no sticker required.

OAK BLUFFS

• *Eastville Point Beach,* off Beach Road on Vineyard Haven Harbor near East Chop. County-run beach; open to public, no sticker required; great view of harbor.

• *Oak Bluffs Town Beach,* between East Chop and Sengekontacket Pond along Beach Road on Nantucket Sound. Open to public, no sticker required.

• *Joseph A. Sylvia State Beach,* on Nantucket Sound off Beach Road between Oak Bluffs and Edgartown. Spectacular stretch of sandy beach; great family beach; perfect for swimming; limited parking; open to public; bike trail runs by the beach; no sticker required.

VINEYARD HAVEN

• *Lake Tashmoo Beach,* at the end of Herring Creek Road on Lake Tashmoo (out toward West Chop). The lake empties out into Vineyard Sound; sandy beach; warm and brackish water; beware of boaters; beach open to the public, no sticker required.

• *Owen Park Beach,* not far from the steamship dock. Good place for children to swim; adjacent to park; open to public, no sticker required.

• *Lagoon Bridge Park,* along the road to Oak Bluffs just outside Vineyard Haven. Beach open to public, no sticker required; watch out for boats and *don't* dive off bridge!

WEST TISBURY

• *Lambert's Cove Beach,* off Vineyard Sound. Beautiful beach, but restricted to year-round and summer residents of West Tisbury only; sticker required.

• *Uncle Seth's Pond,* freshwater pond off Lambert's Cove Road (easy to miss). Open to public, no sticker required.

• *West Tisbury South Shore Town Beach.* For year-round and summer residents of West Tisbury only; sticker required.

 # Churches

• *Apostolic House of Prayer,* Pequot Ave., Oak Bluffs; 693-8485.
• *Assembly of God,* State Rd., Vineyard Haven; 696-7576.
• *First Baptist Church,* Vineyard Haven; 693-1539.
• *Community Baptist Church,* Gay Head; 693-1539.
• *Christian Science,* Christian Science Society, Oak Bluffs. Christian Science Reading Room, Vineyard Haven; 693-6464.
• *West Tisbury Congregational Church,* W. Tisbury; 693-2842.
• *Grace Church,* Vineyard Haven; 693-0332 (Episcopal).

- *St. Andrew's,* Edgartown; 627-5330.
- *Federated Church,* Edgartown; 627-4421 or 627-4662.
- *New Life Christian Fellowship,* Meeting House Way, Edgartown; 627-8975 or 693-3767 (Independent).
- *The Tabernacle Church,* Oak Bluffs (Interdenominational) seasonal; 693-0525.
- *Union Chapel,* Oak Bluffs, seasonal; 693-9010, summer; 693-2426.
- *Kingdom Hall,* Pine Tree Rd., Vineyard Haven; 693-3932 (Jehovah's Witnesses).
- *Martha's Vineyard Hebrew Center,* Centre St.,Vineyard Haven; 693-0745.
- *Christ United Methodist Church,* Vineyard Haven; 693-0476.
- *Edgartown United Methodist Church,* Old Whaling Church, Edgartown; 645-3100.
- *Lambert's Cove United Methodist Church,* Lambert's Cove Rd.; 693-0476.
- *Trinity Methodist Church,* Oak Bluffs; 693-0589.
- *New Life Mennonite Church;* 693-3767.
- *Quaker Meetings.* June through September at Mayhew Chapel off Indian Hill Rd., W. Tisbury; September through May at 24 William St., Vineyard Haven; 693-1834 or 693-0512.
- *Our Lady Star of the Sea,* Oak Bluffs; 693-0342 (Catholic).
- *St. Augustine's Church,* Vineyard Haven; 693-0103 (Catholic).
- *St. Elizabeth's Church,* Edgartown; 627-5017 (Catholic).
- *Seventh Day Adventist.* Church meetings held in Cottager's Building, Oak Bluffs.
- *Unitarian Universalist,* Vineyard Haven; 693-8982.

Odds & Ends

Laundromats

- *Airport Laundromat,* Martha's Vineyard Airport; 693-5005.
- *Bluffs Laundry Center,* Kennebec Ave., Oak Bluffs; 693-9821.
- *Merchant's Mart,* State Rd.,Vineyard Haven; 693-7389.
- *Takemmy Laundry,* Martha's Vineyard Airport; 693-5005.

Laundry

- *Takemmy Laundry & Linen,* Martha's Vineyard Airport, Vineyard Haven; 693-2788. Linen rental.

Farms

- *Hillside Farm,* State Rd., N.Tisbury; 693-5851.
- *Meadow View Farm,* off W.Tisbury Rd.; 627-4666.
- *Morning Glory Farm,* W.Tisbury Rd.; 627-9003.
- *Seven Gates Farm,* N.Tisbury; 693-0016.
- *Thimble Farm,* Stoney Hill Rd., Tisbury; 693-6396.

Fish Markets

- *John's Fish Market,* State Rd., Vineyard Haven; 693-1220.
- *Larsen's Fish Market,* Menemsha Harbor; 645-2680.
- *Menemsha Basin Seafood,* Pine St., Edgartown; 627-7676, (wholesale).
- *The Net Result,* Beach Rd., Vineyard Haven; 693-6071.
- *Poole's Fish,* Menemsha, Chilmark; 645-2282.
- *Edgartown Seafood Market,* 138 Cook St., Edgartown; 627-3791. Lobsters cooked to order, raw bar, homemade chowders.

Clambakes

- *New England Clambake Co.,* Edgartown; 627-7462.
- *Bill Smith,* Edgartown; 627-8809. Clambakes to go.
- *Lobster Tales,* Edgartown; 627-5933.

Ice Cream Parlors

- *Dairy Queen,* Upper Main St., Edgartown.
- *Galley Snack Bar,* Menemsha Harbor; 645-9819.
- *Ice Cream & Candy Bazaar,* 45 Dock St., Edgartown; 627-8735.
- *Mad Martha's,* N. Main St., Edgartown (627-9768), Vineyard Haven Center (693-9856), and Oak Bluffs (693-9151).

Bakeries

- *Black Dog Bakery,* Water St. (across from A&P near Steamship Authority parking lot), Vineyard Haven; 693-4786. Year-round; great breads, desserts, donuts, "chewies," coffee, teas, and juices.
- *Patisserie Francaise,* Main St., Vineyard Haven; 693-8087. Excellent assortment of freshly baked goods.
- *Old Stone Bakery,* on the Mini-Mall, Oak Bluffs (693-3688) and on N. Water St., Edgartown (627-5880).
- *Scottish Bakehouse,* State Rd., Vineyard Haven (a half mile up from Vineyard Haven Center); 693-1873.
- *Mrs. Miller's Muffins,* 3 Dock St., Edgartown; 627-9608.

Libraries

- *Chilmark Public Library,* Chilmark Center, Chilmark; 645-3360.
- *Dukes County Historical Society Museum & Library,* Cooke St., Edgartown; 627-4441.
- *Edgartown Public Library,* 58 N. Water St., Edgartown; 627-4221.
- *Gay Head Public Library,* at the corner of State Rd. and Church St.; 645-9552.
- *Oak Bluffs Public Library,* Circuit Ave., Oak Bluffs; 693-9433.
- *Vineyard Haven Public Library,* Main St., Vineyard Haven; 696-4210.
- *West Tisbury Public Library,* Music St., W. Tisbury; 693-3366.

Best of the Vineyard

BEST COUNTRY INNS
- *The Charlotte Inn,* S. Summer St., Edgartown; 627-4751.
- *The Tuscany Inn,* 22 N. Water St., Edgartown; 627-5999.

BEST RESORT INN
- *The Harbor View Hotel,* N. Water St., Edgartown; 627-7000 or 800-225-6005.

BEST BED & BREAKFASTS
- *The Shiverick Inn,* Pease Point Way, Edgartown; 627-3797.
- *Thorncroft Inn,* on the road to West Chop, Vineyard Haven; 693-3333.

BEST BREAKFAST
- *Black Dog Tavern,* Beach St. Ext., Vineyard Haven; 693-9223.

BEST LUNCH
- *The Aquinnah,* Gay Head Cliffs; 645-9654.
- *David Ryan's,* N. Water St.; 627-4100.

BEST DINNERS
- *The Beach Plum Inn,* Menemsha; 645-9454. Water view.
- *The Home Port,* Menemsha Harbor; 645-2679. Water view.
- *L'Etoile,* at Charlotte Inn, S. Summer St., Edgartown; 627-5187.
- *Lambert's Cove Country Inn,* Lambert's Cove Rd., W. Tisbury; 693-2298.
Close to cove.

BEST DELI
- *Martha's Vineyard Deli,* Main St., Edgartown (693-1943) and in Menemsha (645-9902).

BEST ENTERTAINMENT
- *Center for Performing Arts,* Old Whaling Church, Main St., Edgartown; 627-8017.
- *Harbor View Hotel,* N. Water St., Starbuck's Neck, Edgartown; 627-4333.
- *Hot Tin Roof,* Martha's Vineyard Airport; 693-1137.

BEST MUSEUM
- *Dukes County Historical Society Museum & Library,* Cooke St., Edgartown; 627-4441.

BEST CRAFT, SPECIALTY, & ANTIQUE SHOPS
- *The Edgartown Art Gallery and Antique Shop,* at the Charlotte Inn, S. Summer St., Edgartown; 627-5991.
- *Elegant Crow,* 6 S. Water St., Edgartown; 627-8232.
- *Tashtego,* Main St., Edgartown; 627-4300.
- *The Tisbury Market Place,* Beach Rd., Vineyard Haven, next to Lagoon Pond.

BEST SEASONAL EVENTS
- *Oak Bluffs fireworks.* For more information, call 693-5511.
- *Tisbury Street Fair,* Main St. In July; for more information, call the Chamber of Commerce at 693-0085.

BEST PUBLIC BEACHES

- *Menemsha Public Beach,* at Menemsha Harbor on Vineyard Sound. Open to public.
- *South Beach* (Katama Beach), on the Atlantic off Katama Road, a few miles outside Edgartown Center. Open to public.
- *Joseph A. Sylvia State Beach,* on Nantucket Sound, off Beach Road between Oak Bluffs and Edgartown. No sticker required, but limited parking.

BEST GOLF

- *Farm Neck Golf Club,* Oak Bluffs (overlooking State Beach and Sengekontacket Pond); 693-3057.

BEST HIKING OR NATURE TRAIL

- *Cape Pogue and Wasque Reservation,* on Chappaquiddick (take short ferry ride from Edgartown). Cape Pogue Wildlife Reservation is 489 acres; Wasque Reservation is 200 acres; both are run by the Trustees of Reservations; for more information, call Chamber of Commerce at 693-0085.

BEST CAMPING

- *Martha's Vineyard Family Campground,* off Edgartown Rd., Vineyard Haven; 693-3772 or 784-3615.
- *Webb's Camping Area,* on Barnes Rd., at the head of Lagoon Pond, between Vineyard Haven and Oak Bluffs.

BEST CHILDREN'S ACTIVITIES

- *Band concerts,* in Vineyard Haven and Oak Bluffs. Call town halls.
- *The Flying Horses,* Oak Bluffs; 693-9481. Oldest working carousel in America.

BEST FISH MARKETS

- *Larsen's Fish Market,* Menemsha Harbor; 645-2680.
- *Poole's Fish,* Menemsha Harbor and Chilmark; 645-2282.

BEST ICE CREAM PARLORS

- *Mad Martha's,* N. Main St., Edgartown (627-9768) and in Vineyard Haven Center (693-9856).

Nantucket: Essentials

Important Public Information

- *Town Hall:* 228-6800.
- *Police:* 228-1212.
- *Fire:* 228-2323, 228-2324.
- *Information Bureau:* 228-0925.
- *Nantucket Island Chamber of Commerce:* Main St., 2nd floor of Pacific Club Bldg.; 228-1700.
- *Nantucket Cottage Hospital:* 228-1200.
- *MSPCA:* 228-1491.
- *Weather:* 771-5522.

Lodgings

Major credit cards are accepted at most of the following establishments, and many places offer off-season rates. Call to inquire.

RESERVATION SERVICES & DIRECTORIES

- *Accommodations Et Al,* 11 India St.; 228-0600 or 800-673-4559. Six 18th century inns, B&Bs, and cottages owned and operated by the O'Reilly family. The accommodations include: The Robert's House Inn, 228-3052; Periwinkle Guest House & Cottage, 228-9754 or 228-9725; Linden House, 228-6722. Call for additional information or brochures on the various inns.
- *Heaven Can Wait,* Siasconset; 257-4000. A unique reservation service, specializing in honeymoon planning. Planning includes setting up accommodations, restaurants, entertainment, sports and beach information. Also plans small weddings. Call Dorothy Vollans.
- *House Guests Cape Cod and the Islands* is the Cape & Islands' original and most varied bed and breakfast reservation service. More than 300 guest rooms are available; year-round service. Offers accommodations for singles, doubles, and

families; water views and wooded locations. All accommodations have been inspected and approved; reasonable rates. For a directory covering Cape Cod and the Islands, write Box 1881, Orleans, MA 02653, or call 896-7053 or 1-800-666-HOST. Visa, MasterCard, American Express cards welcome.

• *Nantucket Accommodations,* Box 217; 228-9559. Guest houses and hotels.

• *Nantucket and Martha's Vineyard Reservations,* Box 1322, Vineyard Haven, 02568; 693-7200 or 800-649-5671. Inns, hotels, cottages, guest houses and B&Bs.

• *Nantucket Reservations,* 62 Old South St.; 228-6612 or 1-800-NANTUCKET.

• *Nantucket Vacation Rentals,* Box 426; 228-3131. Apartments, cottages, and houses.

• *Bed & Breakfast Cape Cod,* Box 341, West Hyannis Port 02672; 508-775-2772. Select from 60 host homes, country inns, and sea captains' houses on Cape Cod and the islands of Nantucket and Martha's Vineyard. Beaches, great seafood restaurants, whale watches, and summer theater are all a part of the local attractions. Modest/deluxe rates, private or shared baths. Write or call for free selection information.

All B&Bs, guest houses, inns, resorts, and cottages listed below are in Nantucket Village unless otherwise specified.

• *A-Cottage in Town,* Box 179; 228-6964. One- and two-bedroom cottages located close to town.

• *The Anchor Inn,* 66 Centre St.; 228-0072. Moderate to expensive. Once the home of whaling captain Archaelus Hammond, this attractive inn offers ten guest rooms, all with private baths; centrally located in the historic district next to the Old North Church; walk to shops, ferries, beaches, theaters, and museums; no credit cards.

• *Ayers House,* 6 Union St.; 228-0245. Moderate. Seasonal, shared baths.

• *Barntucket,* Cliff Rd.; 228-4835 or 617-367-6033. Expensive. Antique carriage house with 5 bedrooms, 3 baths, common areas on both floors with full kitchens. A great place for family reunions or meetings.

• *Beachside at Nantucket,* N. Beach St.; 228-2241 or 800-322-4433. Moderate to expensive. Located in the heart of the beach district on Brant Point; motel units and three efficiency apartments available, private baths; no credit cards.

• *Brass Lantern Inn,* 11 N. Water St.; 228-4064 or 800-377-6609. Moderate to expensive. Rebuilt in 1846, inn offers 20 rooms; located on a quiet, cobblestone street a few blocks from town center; Nantucket Yacht Club, Whaling Museum, Children's Beach, and Steamship Wharf are a three-minute walk from the inn; complimentary continental breakfast offered.

• *Capizzo Cottages,* Box 225; 228-2273. Moderate. At Surfside Beach, ocean views, open spring to late fall, TV, linens supplied.

• *Captain's Corners,* 89 Easton St.; 228-0313. Moderate. Full breakfast, seasonal, credit cards accepted.

• *The Carlisle House Inn,* 26 N. Water St.; 228-0720. Expensive. Built in 1765, the inn has 14 rooms and offers a variety of accommodations, from single rooms to elegant master bedrooms with canopied beds and working fireplaces; considered one of the island's top inns; highly recommended.

• *The Carriage House,* Five Ray's Ct.; 228-0326. Moderate. This B&B offers seven bedrooms and a sheltered patio; close to beaches, tennis, and shopping.

• *Carroll Cottages,* Mrs. James E. Carroll, Box 2227; 228-2948, 617-257-9889, or 203-388-2602. Moderate. Four modern homes located in different areas, fully equipped, linens supplied.

• *The Centerboard,* 8 Chester St.; 228-9696. Moderate. Guest house in a 100-year-old Victorian home, continental breakfast, private baths, year-round, off-season rates, credit cards accepted.

• *Century House,* 10 Cliff Rd.; 228-0530. Moderate. Continental breakfast, cottage available, private baths, year-round, off-season rates.

• *The Chestnut House,* 3 Chestnut St.; 228-0049. Moderate. Sleeps four, comfortable setting, private and semiprivate baths; close to beaches and shopping; Visa and MasterCard accepted.

• *Cliff House,* 34 Cliff Rd.; 228-2154. Moderate. Some water views, private baths, breakfast served on the lawn, open May through October, credit cards accepted.

• *Cliff Lodge,* 9 Cliff Rd.; 228-9480. Moderate. Bed and breakfast inn, private baths, barbecue area, efficiencies, year-round, credit cards accepted.

• *Cliffside Beach Club and Hotel,* Jefferson Ave.; 228-0618. Moderate. On the beach, rooms and apartments available, TV, continental breakfast, seasonal.

• *The Cobblestone Inn,* 5 Ash St.; 228-1987. Moderate to expensive. Close to Main Street, five guest rooms with private baths, continental breakfast of homemade breads and muffins.

• *Jared Coffin House,* 29 Broad St.; 228-2400 or 800-248-2405. Expensive. Located in the heart of historic district, the three-story main brick structure was once the home of wealthy ship owner Jared Coffin. The inn is comprised of six structures; three are connected, and three surround the main complex. Without a doubt, one of the best inns on the Cape and Islands; private baths; excellent restaurant and lounge; Visa, MasterCard, American Express, and Diners Club accepted.

• *The Corner House,* 49 Centre St.; 228-1530. Moderate to expensive. Historic B&B, wide-board pine floors, paneling and fireplaces, private baths, screened porch, continental breakfast; afternoon tea.

• *Deb Mar Cottages,* 16 Meadow Court, Fairfield, CT 06430; 203-255-3192. Cottages located a few miles from town, fully equipped, outdoor showers, grills.

• *Dionis Beach Cottages,* 121 Main St.; 228-4524. Moderate. Water views, TV, off-season rates, linens supplied.

• *Dolphin Guest House,* 10 N. Beach St.; 228-4028. Moderate. Private baths and TV, common kitchen for guests, continental breakfast, seasonal.

• *Eighteen Gardner Street,* 18 Gardner St.; 228-1155 or 800-435-1450. Moderate to expensive. Built in 1835, this guest house is located in the historic district a few minutes' walk from Main Street; nine double-occupancy rooms, several with fireplaces, all with private baths; two-bedroom suite and two-bedroom apartment with full kitchen also available, free bikes.

• *Elegant Dump,* 56 Union St.; 228-4634. Moderate. Bed and breakfast, water views, TV, shared baths, year-round, full breakfast.

• *Fair Gardens,* 27 Fair St.; 228-4258 or 800-377-6609. Moderate to expensive. Cozy guest house, double rooms, triple rooms, private baths, light breakfast.

• *Fair Winds,* 29 Cliff Rd.; 228-1998. Moderate. B&B in Colonial home, private baths, some water views, continental breakfast, efficiencies available, seasonal.

• *The Folger House,* Easton St.; 228-0313 or 800-FOLGER-1. Moderate. Hotel with restaurant on premises (The Whale), continental breakfast, suites and cottages.

• *Four Ash Street,* 228-4899. Moderate. Bed and breakfast, shared baths, open mid-April through December.

• *The Four Chimneys,* 38 Orange St.; 228-1912. Expensive. Private baths, continental breakfast, seasonal, credit cards accepted.

NANTUCKET (CONTINUED)

- *The Gray Goose,* 24 Hussey St.; 228-6597. Moderate. Private baths, decorated in antiques, private garden for barbecues, no children under eight.
- *Great Harbor Inn,* 31 India St.; 228-6609 or 800-377-6609. Moderate to expensive. Built in 1790, inn offers large comfortable rooms; located in historic district; private baths, rooms have canopy and four-poster beds; complimentary breakfast; Visa and MasterCard accepted.
- *The Grey Lady,* 34 Centre St.; 800-245-9552 or 228-9552. Moderate. Victorian style guest house, newly renovated suites and apartments.
- *Halliday's Nantucket House,* 2 East York St.; 228-9450. Moderate. Continental breakfast, seasonal.
- *Hamilton House,* 78 Orange St.; 228-9364. Moderate. Guest house, private baths, seasonal.
- *Harbor House,* near town center; 228-1500 or 800-ISLANDS. Expensive. More than 100 years old, the inn offers attractive rooms, great dining, entertainment lounge, breakfast on the patio; outdoor swimming pool, close to beaches; credit cards accepted.
- *The Hawthorn House,* 2 Chestnut St.; 228-1468. Moderate. Guest house, private baths, year-round, canopy beds, antiques and personal artwork decorate this 1850s house, full breakfast.
- *Holiday Inn,* 78 Centre St.; 228-0199 or 800-298-0199. Expensive. A few minutes from town this Holiday Inn is in a house built circa 1742.
- *The House of Orange,* 25 Orange St.; 228-9287. Moderate. Private and semiprivate baths, gardens, some rooms with fireplaces. 1810 whaling captain's home, year-round.
- *House of Seven Gables,* 32 Cliff Rd.; 228-4706. Expensive. Guest house overlooks mouth of Nantucket Harbor; short walk to beaches, shopping, tennis courts, restaurants, and museums; private and semiprivate baths; some rooms have fireplaces; complimentary breakfast; credit cards accepted.
- *Hussey House,* 15 N. Water St.; 228-0747. Moderate. Built in 1795, guest house is located in historic district; furnished with antiques, fireplace in every room, private baths; close to shopping and beaches.
- *Hutchison House,* 47 Centre St.; 415-837-8326. House available in the spring, fall and during the holidays, but not rented during July and August. Four bedrooms, modern kitchen, laundry, outside shower, decks, private yard.
- *India House,* 37 India St.; 228-9043. Moderate. Cozy inn with a gourmet restaurant on the premises, private baths, private garden and fireplace, reading room, seasonal.
- *The Island Reef,* 20 N. Water St.; 228-2156. Moderate. Guest house, private baths, continental breakfast, year-round, built in 1717.
- *Ivy Lodge,* 2 Chester St.; 228-7755. Moderate. Guest house, cottages available, seasonal, located across from the White Elephant Hotel, grounds suitable for cookouts or relaxing.
- *La Petite Maison,* 132 Main St.; 228-9242. Moderate. Rooms, suites or apartments available, breakfast, year-round.
- *Le Languedoc Inn & Restaurant,* 24 Broad St.; 228-4298 or 228-4682. Expensive. Inn named for a province in the south of France; located in the historic district; comfortable accommodations; fine restaurant with intimate bar and patio; lunch and dinner served; owners maintain two other lodgings (the Hussey Street Guest House and the Grey Lady Apartments; 228-4682, 228-4298, or 228-4715).

• *Lowell Cottages,* Main St. at New Lane; 228-1182. Moderate. TV, year-round, one- or two-bedroom cottages.

• *Maiden Lane House,* 6 East York St.; 228-4362 or 800-838-9267 (Jan.–May). Moderate. Located in a quaint neighborhood close to town, continental breakfast.

• *Martin's Guest House,* 61 Centre St.; 228-0678. Moderate. Built in 1803 as a mariner's home, inn offers spacious rooms, country setting; great breakfast; American Express accepted.

• *Nantucket Inn,* 27 Macy's Lane at Nobadeer near Surfside Beach on the island's south side; 228-6900 or 800-321-8484. Expensive. A self-contained resort offering cottage suites, swimming pool, conference facilities, tennis, rooftop restaurant (the Windsong), lounge; credit cards accepted.

• *Nantucket Landfall,* 4 Harbor View Way; 228-0500. Moderate. Six guest rooms with private baths, located at Children's Beach, continental breakfast, lawn and veranda provide harbor view, seasonal.

• *Nantucket Roosts,* Cliff Rd. (not far from Children's Beach); 228-9480 or 228-6071. Moderate to expensive. Guests have their choice of the Cliff Lodge (a quaint B&B guest house built in 1771) or the Still Dock Apartments (completely furnished one- and two-bedroom apartments); one of the best lodgings of its kind on the island; innkeepers very knowledgeable about the island.

• *Nantucket Settlements,* Box 1337; 228-6597 or 800-462-6882. Historic 19th-century guest houses and seven cottages with kitchens, grills, daily maid service. Some with decks and ocean views.

• *Nesbitt Inn,* 21 Broad St.; 228-0156 or 228-2446. Moderate. Victorian-style inn, continental breakfast, year-round, credit cards accepted.

• *The Parker Guest House,* 4 E. Chestnut St.; 228-4625 or 228-4886 or 800-248-4625. Moderate. Close to shopping, beaches, and dock; rooms come with private and semiprivate baths.

• *The Overlook Hotel,* 3 Step Lane; 228-0695. Moderate. Some rooms with views of Nantucket Harbor, continental breakfast.

• *Quaker House,* 5 Chestnut St.; 228-0400. Inexpensive. Furnished in antiques, seasonal.

• *Safe Harbor,* 2 Harbor View Ln.; 228-3222. Moderate to expensive. Guest house, water views, private baths, continental breakfast.

• *76 Main Street,* Main St.; 228-2533. Moderate. A captain's home built in 1883, located in the heart of Nantucket's cobblestone streets, buffet breakfast, suites available.

• *Sherburne Inn,* 10 Gay St.; 228-4425. Moderate to expensive. Located in Nantucket's historic downtown, elegant inn with 8 rooms with private baths.

• *Ships Inn,* 13 Fair St.; 228-0040. Moderate. Whaling captain's house, private baths, continental breakfast, seasonal, credit cards accepted.

• *Spring Cottage,* 98 Orange St.; 325-4644. Expensive. Romantic B&B suites, full breakfast in your sitting room or on outside garden deck.

• *Still Dock Apartments,* Still Dock; 228-6071. Moderate. One- and two-bedroom apartments overlooking Old North Wharf, TV, washer/dryer, year-round, credit cards accepted.

• *Stumble Inne,* 109 Orange St.; 228-4482. Moderate to expensive. Built in 1704, the inn is near shopping and beaches; 6 of the inn's 12 rooms are located at the Starbuck House, just across the street (94 Orange St.); highly recommended for the price. Ask about three-bedroom saltbox cottage ("Wester") for rent in village of Madaket.

NANTUCKET (CONTINUED)

- *The Summer House,* village of Siasconset; 255-4577. Expensive. Great summer hideaway in an English country setting; cozy rooms; great restaurant (the Summer House Restaurant); credit cards accepted.
- *The Taylor Cottages,* 152 Main St.; 228-0519. Moderate. Two- and three-bedroom cottages with ocean views, sailboats available, seasonal.
- *Ten Hussey Street,* Mrs. Edward Grennan; 228-9552. Moderate. Rooms, suites and a two-bedroom waterfront cottage available, private baths, seasonal, open Easter through the Christmas Stroll.
- *Ten Lyon Street,* 10 Lyon St.; 228-5040. Moderate to expensive. 1850 bed and breakfast, private baths.
- *The Tuckernuck Inn,* 60 Union St.; 228-4886 or 1-800-228-4886. Moderate to expensive. A handsome B&B about a 10-minute walk from Main Street; just outside the hustle and bustle; close to beach; view of Nantucket Harbor; continental breakfast included; lawn croquet available; Visa, MasterCard, and American Express accepted.
- *Paul West House,* 5 Liberty St.; 228-2495. Moderate. Continental breakfast, year-round with off-season rates.
- *The Wade Cottages,* off Shell St., Siasconset; 257-6383. Moderate to expensive. Guest rooms, apartments, cottages, water views.
- *Wauwinet,* 800-426-8718. Expensive. This inn is located outside of town in a spectacular setting on the water, elegant, superb dining, sailing and tennis.
- *Westmoor Inn,* Cliff Rd.; 228-0877. Moderate to expensive. 1917 mansion located on two acres, gourmet breakfast, clay tennis court next door, close to the beach, lots of special touches, seasonal, credit cards accepted.
- *The Wharf Cottages,* New Whale St.; 800-ISLANDS. Expensive. Located on the docks of Nantucket Boat Basin; beautiful, convenient setting; one-, two-, and three-bedroom cottages with fully equipped kitchens; ideal for families or small groups.
- *While-Away Guest House,* 4 Gay St.; 228-1102. Moderate. Private and semi-private baths, some have fireplaces, family unit available, seasonal.
- *The White House,* 48 Centre St.; 228-4677. Moderate. Guest house, family suite available, private baths, year-round, off-season rates.
- *The White Elephant,* on the harbor waterfront; 800-ISLANDS. Expensive. Luxury rooms with water view and freshly cut flowers; complimentary champagne, wine, cheese, and mixers in private refrigerators; elegant dining, swimming pool; credit cards accepted.
- *The Woodbox,* 29 Fair St.; 228-0587. Moderate. Built in 1709, suites available, private baths, some fireplaces, gourmet restaurant on premises.

Campgrounds

There are no campgrounds on Nantucket, and sleeping in the open or in any vehicle is not allowed and is subject to a fine.

- *Hostelling International–Nantucket,* 31 Western Ave., Nantucket 02554; 228-0433. Historic life saving station across from Surfside Beach.

Dining

All restaurants listed here are in the village of Nantucket unless otherwise specified.

- *Arno's,* 41 Main St.; 228-7001. Moderate. Serves breakfast, lunch and dinner. Local seafood, burgers, salads, lobster.
- *Atlantic Café,* 15 S. Water St.; 228-0570. Inexpensive. Water view; lunch and dinner; a favorite local hangout, publike lounge area; nautical design; varied menu, some Mexican food offered; highly recommended. You'll probably have to wait in line, but it's worth the wait if you're looking for a great, casual meal. Visa, MasterCard, and American Express accepted.
- *Beach Plum Café,* 11 West Creek Rd.; 228-8893. A short distance from town, this café serves breakfast, brunch and dinner; the menu changes monthly.
- *The Boarding House,* 12 Federal St.; 228-9622. Moderate. Lunch and dinner; proper dress required; reservations accepted; Visa, MasterCard, and American Express accepted.
- *Broad Street Grill,* Steamboat Wharf; 228-4746. Inexpensive, good family restaurant.
- *The Brotherhood,* 23 Broad St.; no telephone listed. Inexpensive. Another local favorite; casual, rustic atmosphere; varied menu of seafood and meat; lunch and dinner; no reservations. Visa, MasterCard, and American Express accepted.
- *Cambridge Street,* 12 Cambridge St.; 228-7109. Moderate. Menu with lots of innovation, cozy.
- *Capt'n Tobey's Chowder House,* Straight Wharf; 228-0836. Inexpensive to moderate. Lunch and dinner; seafood a specialty here; lounge area; Visa, MasterCard, and American Express accepted.
- *The Chanticleer,* New St., Siasconset; 257-6231 or 257-9756. Expensive. Formal atmosphere; lunch and dinner; classic and nouvelle cuisine; rose-covered setting; reservations; Visa, MasterCard, and American Express accepted.
- *Jared Coffin House,* 29 Broad St.; 228-2400. Moderate to expensive. Lunch and dinner; elegant dining in 1845 whaling mansion; pub, outdoor patio, entertainment; varied menu; jackets requested; reservations; Visa, MasterCard, and American Express accepted.
- *Company of the Cauldron,* 17 India St.; 228-4016. Moderate. Informal atmosphere; varied menu; reservations accepted.
- *De Marco Restaurant,* 9 India St.; 228-1836. Moderate. Informal atmosphere, but jackets requested; dinner; northern Italian cuisine, great pastas along with seafood; chicken, lamb, and veal are also on the menu; reservations; Visa, MasterCard, and American Express accepted.
- *Easy Street Café,* Steamboat Wharf; 228-5824. Moderate to expensive. Lunch and dinner; waterfront atmosphere (near ferry terminal); great seafood and lobster, Cajun and California nouvelle cuisines are also on the menu; late meals offered; major credit cards accepted.
- *Espresso Café,* 40 Main St.; 228-6930. Serving breakfast, lunch or dinner for eat-in or take-out; baked goods, gourmet pizza, sandwiches, soups, ice cream and yogurt.
- *Evergreen Café at Congdon's Pharmacy,* 47 Main St.; 228-0020. Inexpensive.
- *Food for Here and There,* 149 Orange St.; 228-4291. Inexpensive. Subs, quiche, pizza.

NANTUCKET (CONTINUED)

- *The Galley,* at Cliffside Beach Club on Jefferson Ave.; 228-9641. Expensive. Lunch and dinner served; jackets requested for dinner; great water view; varied menu; reservations; Visa, MasterCard, and Diners Club accepted.
- *The Hearth at the Harbor House,* S. Beach St.; 228-1500. Moderate. Informal atmosphere; breakfast (on an outdoor terrace), lunch, and dinner; varied menu; reservations; Visa, MasterCard, and American Express accepted.
- *Henry's Sandwiches,* Steamboat Wharf; 228-0123. Inexpensive.
- *Hutch's,* Nantucket Airport; 228-5550. Inexpensive. Good family spot.
- *India House,* 37 India St.; 228-9043. Expensive. Dinner; gourmet breakfast and dinner; continental and nouvelle American; reservations; Visa and MasterCard accepted.
- *Le Languedoc,* 24 Broad St.; 228-2552. Moderate. Lunch and dinner; Continental and American cuisine, café menu; reservations; Visa, MasterCard, and American Express accepted.
- *Lobster Trap,* 23 Washington St.; 228-4041. Emphasis on fresh seafood and lobsters; will prepare clambakes for your home, boat or at the beach.
- *Morning Glory Café,* Old South Wharf; 228-2212. Breakfast, lunch and dinner. Indoor and outdoor seating.
- *Nantucket Inn at Nobadeer,* near Surfside Beach; 228-6900. Expensive. See listing under Lodgings.
- *Obadiah's,* 2 India St.; 228-4430. Inexpensive to moderate. Lunch and dinner; varied menu, mostly seafood; reservations requested; Visa, MasterCard, and American Express accepted.
- *Quaker House,* 5 Chestnut St.; 228-0400. Moderate. Breakfast and dinner; seafood, pasta, great breakfasts; no reservations; Visa and MasterCard accepted.
- *Raffels,* One Straight Wharf; 228-7171. Moderate to expensive. Lunch and dinner; indoor and outdoor dining; on the waterfront; varied menu; reservations requested; Visa and MasterCard accepted.
- *The Regatta at the White Elephant,* Easton St.; 228-2500. Expensive. Jacket required; elegant dining on waterfront; lunch and dinner; reservations required; Visa, MasterCard, and American Express accepted.
- *Rose & Crown Café,* 23 S. Water St.; 228-2595. Moderate. Lunch and dinner; seafood and blackboard specials; entertainment; Visa and MasterCard accepted.
- *'Sconset Café,* at the circle in Siasconset. Small, casual, but impressive food. No liquor license, but you are welcome to bring your own beer or wine.
- *SeaGrille,* 45 Sparks Ave.; 325-5700 or 228-5700. Moderate. Casual, seafood.
- *The Summer House,* South Bluff in Siasconset; 257-9976. Expensive. Lunch and dinner; water view; varied and excellent menu; reservations requested; Visa, MasterCard, and American Express accepted.
- *Surfside Snack Bar,* Surfside Beach; no telephone. Inexpensive.
- *Tacos Tacos,* Steamboat Wharf; 228-5418. Even out in the middle of the Atlantic Ocean you can still get a taco, burrito or nachos!
- *Toppers,* at the Wauwinet; 228-8768. Expensive. This restaurant has received stunning reviews from *Travel & Leisure, Bon Appetit* and *New York* magazine ... need we say more?
- *Twenty-one Federal Street,* 21 Federal St.; 228-2121. Moderate. Lunch and dinner; varied menu; reservations requested; Visa, MasterCard, and American Express accepted.
- *Vincent's Restaurant,* 21 S. Water St.; 228-0189. Moderate. Breakfast, lunch, and dinner; casual atmosphere; varied menu.

- *The Whale,* 89 Easton St.; 228-0313. Breakfast and dinner; New England cuisine, salad bar.
- *White Dog Café,* N. Union St.; 228-4479. Inexpensive. Breakfast, lunch, and dinner; varied menu.
- *The Woodbox,* 29 Fair St.; 228-0587. Moderate to expensive. Nantucket's oldest inn; varied menu, great food; reservations required; no credit cards.
- *Westender,* 326 Madaket Rd., Madaket; 228-5100. Views of Madaket Harbor and the ocean, American Grill cuisine.

Entertainment

Music & Stage

- *Actor's Theatre of Nantucket,* Gordon Folger Hotel on Easton St.; 228-6325 (box office), 228-4840 or 228-0313 (information). Professional summer theater (they sponsor a Sock Hop on Columbus Day weekend featuring "Oldies But Goodies").
- *Band concerts,* Harbor Square starting at 7 P.M. Every night during July and August in the gazebo.
- *Nantucket Chamber Music Center,* 11 Centre St.; 228-3352.
- *Nantucket Musical Arts Society,* Box 897; 228-1287. Concerts in July and August, brochures available.
- *Theatre Workshop of Nantucket,* Bennett Hall, Box 1297; 228-4305. Year-round performances by an amateur community group.
- *Thursday Noonday Concerts,* Unitarian Church, 11 Orange St., just off Main St.; 228-0738 or 228-2730. Feature a variety of music at noon from July to September. Music varies from string quartets, to spirituals, to classical guitar.

Nightlife

- *The Brotherhood,* 23 Broad St. Folk music.
- *The Club Car,* 1 Main St.; 228-1101. Piano bar.
- *Jared Coffin House,* 29 Broad St.; 228-2400. Piano music.
- *The White Elephant,* Easton St.; 228-2500. Summer months, dancing.

Movie Theaters

- *Dreamland,* 19 Water St.; 228-5365. Movies.
- *Gaslight Theatre,* N. Union St.; 228-4435. Films.
- *Siasconset Casino Stage,* New St., Siasconset; 257-6585. Movies.

Museums & Historic Sites

- *The African Meeting House on Nantucket,* 46 Joy St.; 228-4058. A small house that dates from around 1827, first served as a church, then a school for African children and a meeting house.

- The historical buildings in Nantucket are operated by the Nantucket Historical

NANTUCKET (continued)

Association (228-1894). There is a small admission charge for most museums or sites, but you may purchase a Visitor's Pass that lasts all season.

• *1800 House,* Mill St. The house of Nantucket's High Sheriff around the 1800s, furnishings give a peek at early 19th-century life of the Island, $1 admission.

• *Fair Street Museum,* Fair St. Changing exhibits offer views of Nantucket's 300-year history of culture and arts, $1 admission.

• *Fire Hose Cart House,* Gardner St., between Liberty and Main sts. A neighborhood fire station of the 1800s, firefighting equipment.

• *Peter Foulger Museum,* Broad St., next to the Whaling Museum. Details Nantucket's history; information about Indians, Quakers, and whaling captains; $1.50 admission.

• *Abiah Folger Franklin Memorial,* one-half mile out Main St. Site of Benjamin Franklin's mother's birthplace and home of his grandfather.

• *Greater Light,* Howard St., between Gardner and Main sts. 1930s livestock barn that was converted into a summer cottage by two Quaker sisters; $1.50 admission.

• *Hawden House,* corner of Pleasant and Main sts. An 1844 Greek Revival mansion that shows the elegance of Nantucket at its peak during the whaling days; gardens are maintained by the Nantucket Garden Club; $1.50 admission.

• *Nantucket Historical Association,* 228-1894. Passes available to visit several of the historic buildings that are open to the public. The Association also publishes a brochure for a self-guided walking tour of the historic sights, homes, and buildings in Nantucket; pick one up at the Chamber of Commerce on Main Street.

• *Nathaniel Macy House,* corner of Liberty St. and Walnut Ln. Early 1700s house that has been restored; accessories, arts, furnishings and household items of the 18th and 19th century; $1.50 admission.

• *Old Gaol,* Vestal St., near Quaker Rd. An 1805 prison.

• *Old Mill,* Mill Hill, Prospect St. Built in 1746, the only remaining mill of four that once stood west of town; the mill operates in season; $1 admission.

• *Oldest House,* Sunset Hill, off W. Chester St. The Jethro Coffin House, built in 1686, is on its original site and reflects life of families who first settled Nantucket.

• *Quaker Meeting House,* Fair St. Used as a gathering place for Quakers since 1838; $1 admission.

• *Sankaty Light House,* near Siasconset. Built in 1849. The original lens can be seen at the Whaling Museum.

• *Thomas Macy Warehouse,* Straight Wharf. This building used to equip whaling ships; now it is the headquarters for the Artists Association of Nantucket.

• *Whaling Museum,* Broad St., head of Steamboat Wharf. Originally a factory to refine whale oil, now the museum has collections of artifacts chronicling the whaling era; $2.50 admission.

• *The First Congregational Church,* 62 Centre St. The best view of the town from the church's tower. Open to visitors.

• *Nantucket Life Saving Museum,* 228-1885. Just outside of Nantucket Center. An authentic re-creation of Nantucket's original Surfside station built in 1874; museum displays old Life Saving Service boats and rescue equipment as well as other artifacts. Because of the many shipwrecks off its shores, Nantucket was called the "Graveyard of the Atlantic." Open June 15 to October 15 from 10 A.M. to 5 P.M. Admission charge.

• *The Maria Mitchell Association* operates the birthplace of Maria Mitchell (an early-19th-century Quaker home), two observatories, a science library, and the Hinchman House (museum of natural history; bird, wildflower, and nature walks; lectures also), all on Vestal St., just off Main St. The association also runs an aquarium at 28 Washington St. Maria Mitchell was a 19th-century astronomer who became famous by providing at the age of 14 astronomical calculations for Nantucket's whaling captains and later discovered a comet. As an adult she taught at Vassar College.

Seasonal Events

• The island's *Daffodil Festival* is held toward the end of April and is well attended by "off-islanders." The shops decorate their windows and displays with daffodils. The town center is brimming with the yellow flowers, and there are contests for the best daffodil arrangements. There is also an antique car parade, a gourmet picnic in Siasconset, and a Daffodil Ball.

• Memorial Day brings the *Figawi Race* with boats sailing from Hyannis to Nantucket. There are many social events planned around this race, including a clambake and a dance. Call 778-1691 for more information.

• *Chamber of Commerce Bike Race,* held in May. Contact the chamber about dates and registration at 228-1700.

• *Fourth of July* is busy on the island with bike races, an antique car parade, fireworks, and a windsurfing regatta.

• If you are on Nantucket in the summer, among the striking sights are the beautiful, rambling roses. The Congregational Church on Centre Street has a *Rose Sunday* in July when the church is decorated with these flowers that thrive on the island.

• In August there are several special events: *Nantucket Garden Club* sponsors a house tour of private homes; *Billfish tournament,* sponsored by the Nantucket Angler's Club; *sandcastle contest,* at Jetties Beach, sponsored by the Chamber of Commerce. There are antique shows, fairs, and other races; contact the Chamber of Commerce for updates.

• *Seafest* is held in September at Children's Beach and is sponsored by the Fisherman's Association of Nantucket. Try different kinds of fish; call 228-9556 for information.

• *Columbus Day Road Race,* requires advance registration with the Chamber of Commerce.

• One of the most popular seasonal events on Nantucket is the annual *Christmas Stroll* held the first weekend in December. Main Street is lined with Christmas trees that have been decorated by the schoolchildren with everything from Queen Anne's lace spray-painted white to scallop shells. There are carolers strolling the streets singing seasonal favorites; the shops are festive and offer goodies, eggnog, hot cider, and music; Santa arrives by a horse-drawn carriage; and the Christmas tree at the foot of Pacific Bank is lit about 4 P.M., along with all the smaller trees along Main Street. This event is a charming way to begin your Christmas Season, but it is very well attended and requires some thoughtful planning. If you are making it a day trip, get to the boat early. If possible, try to get to the island on Friday night and stay at one of the inns or guest houses—you may be able to avoid the crowds and have more room to move in the shops before the ferry arrives around noon. Many Cape towns have duplicated this idea, but none, so far, comes close to the enchantment of Christmas on Nantucket.

Children's Activities

• *Maria Mitchell Scientific Library,* Vestal St.; 228-0898. Science and nature classes for children.
• *Nantucket Atheneum,* India St.; 228-1110. Town library; children's room downstairs; story hours.
• *Aquarium,* 28 Washington St.; 228-5387. Displays of fish and a "touch me" tank of marine life.
• *J.J. Clammp's,* Nobadeer Farm Rd.; 228-8977. Miniature golf, free shuttle van from town.
• *Nantucket Parks and Recreation,* Jetties Beach; 228-7213. Tennis clinics, swimming lessons, tie dying clinics and Lacrosse camp.
• *Ice Cream Cruises,* Straight Wharf; 228-1444. Aboard the "Anna W II."
• *Pinwheel Toys,* 38 Centre St.; 228-1991. Demonstrations in rubber stamps, balloon twisting, storytelling and juggling.
• *Murray Camp Kids Night Out;* 325-4600. Evening outings for ages 5–13, includes crabbing expeditions, miniature golf, pool and pizza parties.

Tours

• *Ara's Tours,* Box 734; 228-1951 or 352-1512. Guided tours of Nantucket or take a four-wheel drive tour to Great Point.
• *Barrett's Tours, Inc.,* 20 Federal St., across from the Information Bureau; 228-0174. Six different tours offered each day, year-round.
• *Betty's Tours,* Lower Main St.; 228-5786. Personal tours of Nantucket's sights and history.
• *Gail's Tours, Inc.,* 257-6557. Personal tours of Nantucket by this native will pick you up.
• *Harbor Cruises,* Straight Wharf; 228-1444. Lobstering, sunset cruises, shoreline sightseeing.
• *Hy-Line Cruises,* Straight Wharf; 228-3949. Take a day trip to Martha's Vineyard during your stay on Nantucket.
• *Nantucket Island Tours,* Straight Wharf; 228-0334. May 1–November 1.
• *Nantucket Jeep Rental,* across from airport on Macy Ln.; 228-1618.
• *Sea Tabby,* 385-3322 or 228-1333. (June to September) Motor yacht can be chartered for luncheons, cocktails, dinner; for the day, half day, or week.
• *Nantucket's Golden Age Walking Tour.* Sponsored by the Nantucket Historical Association; 228-1894.
• *The Nantucket Carriage Company,* Gordon Folger Hotel; 228-0313. Horse-drawn carriage rides.
• *Beach Excursions, Ltd.,* One Old North Wharf; 228-3728. Beach picnics to Great Point, surf fishing, jeep picks you up at your lodging.
• *Nantucket Whalewatch,* Straight Wharf, Hy-Line dock; 1-800-322-0013. End of July to October 1; reservations suggested.
• *Nantucket Whaleboat Adventures,* Box 64; 228-5585. Take an educational and adventurous journey aboard the *Wanderer* to learn what it was like for whalers to pursue whales.
• *Points of View;* 228-0529. Guided beach tours, sunrise or sunset.
• *Strong Wings' Saturday Adventure Series,* Box 2884; 228-1769. Various tours include mountain biking, sea kayaking, naturalist-guided hikes through wildflowers, berries, and bogs.

• *Trustees of Reservations,* 228-6799. Naturalists will take you on a 3-hour trip to Coskata-Coatue Wildlife Refuge. Pre-registration required.
• *Roger A. Young Walking Tour,* 228-1062. Historical tour through the paths and lanes of Nantucket.

Shops

Art Galleries

• *Artists Association of Nantucket, Inc.,* Straight Wharf; 228-0722.
• *Eric Holch Gallery,* 22 Old South Wharf; 228-7654. Oils, posters, puzzles, notecards by Eric Holch.
• *Jas Hunt Barker Galleries,* 1 Pleasant; 228-0878.
• *The Gallery at Four India St.,* 4 India St.; 228-8509.
• *Hill's of Nantucket,* Straight Wharf; 228-1353.
• *Hostetler Gallery,* 2 Old Wharf; 228-5152.
• *Debbie Henry Johnston, Art Studio,* 91 Hummock Pond Rd.; 228-1452.
• *Krebs Studio,* S. Warren Krebs, 57 Union St.; 228-4655. Impressionist paintings and Nantucket drawings; year-round.
• *Main Street Gallery–Nantucket Inc.,* 50 Main St.; 228-2252 or 228-4027. Sculpture, graphics, paintings.
• *Mielko & Hostetier Gallery,* 4 Old Wharf; 228-0014.
• *Nantucket Gallery,* 23 Federal St. (228-1943) and 1 Shimmo Surfside Rd. (228-5603).
• *One New Street Gallery,* Barbara Kaufmann-Locke, Siasconset; 257-9842.
• *Sailor's Valentine Gallery,* 40 Centre St.; 228-2011. Weekly featured exhibitions, catalog available.
• *Sleight-Hallam Gallery,* Old South Wharf; 228-5778 or 228-2100.
• *South Wharf Gallery,* Shanty 21, Old South Wharf; 228-0406.
• *Spectrum of American Artists and Craftsmen,* 26 Main St.; 228-4606.
• *Teryl Townsend Speers,* 16 Old South Wharf; 228-1506 or 228-9497.
• *Spindrift Gallery,* 11 Old South Wharf,; 228-5173.
• *Stephen R. Swift Woodworking Gallery,* Old Quidnet Milk Rte.; 228-0255.
• *Kenneth Taylor Gallery,* Artists Association, Straight Wharf; 228-0722.
• *Tonkin of Nantucket,* 33 Main St.; 228-9697.
• *William Welch Gallery,* 14 East St.; 228-0687. Good selection of paintings and prints of Nantucket.

Craft & Specialty Shops

When you get off the boat in Nantucket, you will find the majority of the shopping is within easy walking distance. The following list is not comprehensive of all the fine shops, but it is just enough to give the visitor a taste of the treasures you can find on Nantucket!
• *Cold Noses,* Straight Wharf; 228-KISS. Do you love your pet? You'll love this shop.
• *Coffin's Gift Shop,* 51 Main St.; 228-4662. Gifts.
• *Craftmasters of Nantucket,* Lower India St.; 228-0322. Leather goods, jewelry, scrimshaw.

NANTUCKET (CONTINUED)

- *The Crafts Centre,* 4 Quaker Rd.; 228-1572. Yarns and basket-making supplies.
- *Crabtree & Evelyn,* 14 Centre St.; 228-0062. Fragrances, soaps, lotions.
- *Eagle's Eye,* Candle and Salem St.; 325-4219. Save on clothing from Eagle's Eye, 40–70% off retail prices.
- *Four Winds Craft Guild,* Straight Wharf; 228-9623. Nantucket baskets, ship models, prints, decoys, shore birds, gifts.
- *Force Five,* 37 Main St., Jetties Beach; 228-0700 or 228-5358. Sportswear, jams; also instructions and rentals for boardsailing.
- *The Golden Basket,* 44 Main St.; 228-4344. Jewelry.
- *Gumballs,* 8 Washington St.; 228-4546. Children's cotton clothing.
- *Handblock,* 42 Main St.; 228-4500. Women's and children's clothing, pottery, giftware and stationery.
- *Heburn,* 3 Salem St.; 228-1458. Unique women's clothing.
- *Hills of Nantucket,* Straight Wharf; 228-1353. American and Nantucket-made gifts.
- *Island Pursuit,* Main St.; 228-5117. Nautical sportswear, shoes.
- *Kennedy Studios,* Federal and Broad sts.; 228-9784. Nantucket prints, sweatshirts, T-shirts.
- *The Lion's Paw,* Zero Main St.; 228-3837. A fine collection of various items.
- *Made on Nantucket,* 58 Main St.; 228-0110. Over 60 local artists display their work here.
- *Michael Kane Carvers Guild,* Shanty 22, Old South Wharf; 228-3552. Bird carvings, prints.
- *Michael Kane's Nantucket Lightship Baskets,* 18 1/2 Sparks Ave.; 228-1548. Decoys, shorebirds.
- *Nantucket Fragrances.* Items for sale in several shops on the island, or write for a free catalog to: The Perfume Company of Nantucket, Box 875, Nantucket 02554; 228-3936.
- *Nantucket Sports Locker;* 228-5669. Sportswear for men, women, and children.
- *Nesting Feather,* 20 Old South Wharf; 228-1300. Antiques, gifts, painted furniture.
- *Nobby Clothes Shop,* 17 Main St.; 228-1030.
- *Old South Wharf,* Old South Wharf; 228-0406. 20 shops, art galleries, outdoor café.
- *Pinwheels,* 7 S. Beach St.; 228-1238. Children's clothing.
- *The Seven Seas Gifts,* 46 Centre St.; 228-0958. Gifts. Kids love this store!
- *Stephen Swift, Inc.,* Old Quidnet Milk Rte.; 228-0255. Woodworking, furniture.
- *R & M Schlesinger,* 45 India St.; 228-2006. Handmade silver objects.
- *Seldom Scene,* 17 N. Beach St. at Brant's Place; 325-7010. The word here is "eclectic" for the collectibles for home, boat, or yourself.
- *Tonkin of Nantucket,* 33 Main St.; 228-9697. Nantucket Lightship baskets, antiques, gifts.
- *The Toy Boat,* Straight Wharf; 228-4552. An original toy store that offers many additional services, such as Camp "care" packages, rare or antique toy search, party planning.
- *Wolfhound,* 21 Main St.; 228-3552. European and domestic clothing for the entire family.
- *Zero Main,* Zero Main St.; 228-4401. Contemporary women's clothing.

Antiques

- *Antiques Depot,* 14 Easy St.; 228-1287. Duck and fish decoys, decorative accessories.
- *Forager House Collection,* 20 Centre St.; 228-5977. Americana and folk art, open Daffodil Weekend to the Christmas Stroll.
- *Frank F. Sylvia Antiques,* 6 Ray's Ct.; 228-0960.
- *Nina Hellman,* 22 Broad St.; 228-4677. Marine antiques including ship models, naval instruments, and whaling memorabilia.
- *Val Maitino Antiques,* 31 N. Liberty St.; 228-2747. Weather vanes, marine artifacts, accessories, English and American furniture, open year-round.
- *Paul Madden Antiques,* 5 N. Water St.; 228-0112. Americana, year-round.
- *Modern Arts,* 44 Main St.; 228-2358. Antiques, arts and crafts, 50's and 60's memorabilia, home accessories.
- *Nantucket Bay Auction,* 95 Washington St.; 325-4219. Antiques, folk art.
- *Nantucket House Antiques,* 1 South Beach St.; 228-4604. French, English and American country antiques and accessories.
- *Old English Pine,* 118 Lower Orange St.; 228-4755. Continental and British pine.
- *Puss-n-Boots,* 18 Federal St.; 228-5167. Sterling, jewelry, accessories.
- *Rafael Osona Auctions,* 21 Washington St.; 228-3942. Monthly sales, call for schedule.
- *Tranquil Corner Antiques,* 38 Centre St.; 228-0848. Large scrimshaw selection; American, Canadian, and English accessories and furniture; open from Easter to Christmas or by appointment.
- *Tranquil Corner II,* 228-6000. Paintings, silver, large furniture such as beds and dining room tables, open Easter to Christmas or by appointment.
- *Tonkin of Nantucket,* 33 Main St.; 228-9697. Marine and medical antiques, English antiques, year-round.
- *Lynda Willauer Antiques,* 2 India St.; 228-3631. Folk art, quilts, American and English furniture, porcelain, paintings.
- *Wayne Pratt, Inc.,* 28 Main St.; 228-8788. Assorted antiques.

Sports & Recreation

Biking

- *Cook's Cycle Shop,* 6 S. Beach St.; 228-0800. Bicycles and surreys for rent.
- *Holiday Cycle,* 4 Chester St.; 228-3644. Bike and moped rentals.
- *Island Adventures,* John Simms, 228-2703. Mountain biking trips through Nantucket.
- *Nantucket Bike Shop,* Steamboat Wharf; 228-1999. Bike and moped rentals.
- *Young's Bicycle Shop,* Steamboat Wharf; 228-1151. Bike, moped, and car rentals, year-round.

Boating/Fishing

- *All-Over-It,* 325-2550. Surf fish Nantucket's beaches with Mike Cody in a 7-passenger Land Cruiser.
- *Albacore,* Straight Wharf; 228-5074. Charter fishing.
- *Captain Marc J. Genther's "Just Do It" Sportsfishing,* Straight Wharf, Slip 13; 228-7448.
- *Custom Sailing Charters,* 152 Main St.; 228-3464. Sail Nantucket Sound with your own group.
- *Dan Ropitzky,* 228-8460 or 325-1820. Surf cast off the beaches, 4-wheel drive, will pick up.
- *Endeavor,* Straight Wharf; 228-5585. Charter—sail to nearby Coature for a day or enjoy a sunset or moonlight cruise, or sail with a fiddler playing seafaring tunes, a storyteller or take a pirate adventure.
- *Flicka Sport Fishing,* Straight Wharf; 325-4000. Charter fishing.
- *Harbor Cruises,* Straight Wharf; 228-1444. Rental and charter.
- *Herbert T,* Straight Wharf; 228-6655. Charter sportfishing.
- *Madaket Marine,* Madaket Harbor; 228-9086. Complete line of boats.
- *Nantucket Community Sailing,* Polpis Harbor, Wauwinet Rd.; 228-6600. Lessons.
- *Nantucket Harbor Cruises,* Straight Wharf; 228-1444.
- *Nantucket Harbor Sail,* Petrel Landing, Swain's Wharf; 228-0424. Rentals, outboards and sailboats available.
- *Nantucket Boat Rental,* 59 Old South Rd.; 325-1001. Rentals out of Straight Wharf.
- *Sea Nantucket,* Washington St. amd Francis St.; 228-7499. Family kayak rentals and tours.
- *Whitney Mitchell Surffishing,* 228-2331. Hop on this Jeep Wagon to the outer beaches, gear included.

Fishing Tackle & Supplies

- *Bill Fisher Tackle,* New Ln.; 228-2261.
- *Hardy's Inc.,* 13 S. Water St.; 228-0058.
- *Nantucket Tackle Center,* 41 Sparks Ave.; 228-4081.
- *Ship's Chandlery,* New Whale St.; 228-2300.
- *Sunken Ship,* corner Broad and S. Water sts.; 228-9226.
- *Barry Thurston's,* Harbor Square; 228-9595.

Hunting

Deer, waterfowl, rabbit, and game birds can be hunted on Nantucket. Permits are available through the town clerk's office, 228-6800.

Golf

- *Miacomet,* off Somerset Rd.; 228-9764. Nine holes, public.
- *Sankaty Head,* Siasconset; 257-6391. 18 holes, private.
- *Siasconset Golf Club,* Milestone Rd.; 257-6596. Nine holes, semiprivate.

Tennis

- *Brant Point Racquet Club,* 48 N. Beach; 228-3700. Nine clay courts, racket rentals, lessons.
- *Jetties Beach Public Tennis Courts,* N. Beach; 325-5334.
- *Miacomet Tennis Courts,* Somerset Rd.; 228-4546.
- *Nantucket Tennis Club,* Westmoor Ln.; 228-3611.
- *Nantucket Racquet & Squash Club,* Young's Way off Old South Rd.; 228-0155.
- *Sea Cliff Tennis Club,* Tennis Club Drive, off North Beach St.; 228-0030 or 228-4734. Lessons as well as rentals.
- *Tristam's Landing Tennis Courts,* 228-4588.

Windsurfing

- *Indian Summer Sports,* 6 Broad St.; 228-3632. Also at Jetties Beach (228-9401) and at Madaket; rentals, lessons, sales.
- *Upper Deck–Sailways,* 19 N. Beach; 228-7088. Beach chair and raft rentals too.

Beaches

You must get a permit from the Fire Department for any cookouts on the beach. The fire house is located on Sparks Avenue. There are areas for four-wheel-drive vehicles, but you must have a permit. Contact the Nantucket Conservation Foundation, Box 13, Nantucket 02554; 228-2884. Permits available in the summer at Refuge Reception Station, Wauwinet; 228-0006.

Like Martha's Vineyard, Nantucket has miles of sandy beaches. All beaches on Nantucket are open to the public, and there are no stickers required or any charge for parking. The beaches are either on Nantucket Sound (where the water is gentler and great for children) or the Atlantic Ocean, where the waves are great for swimming or surfing.

NORTH SHORE/NANTUCKET SOUND

- *Brant Point.* Close to town, no bathhouse or lifeguard.
- *Children's Beach.* Close to town, park and playground, lifeguard, concessions and rest rooms.
- *Dionis.* Another good beach for children, lifeguard, rest rooms.
- *Jetties Beach.* Food service, rest rooms, lifeguards and bathhouse for a fee.

SOUTH SHORE/ATLANTIC OCEAN

- *Cisco.* Good for surfing, lifeguard, no facilities.
- *Madaket.* Good surf, lifeguard, toilets, a favorite spot for watching the sun set.
- *Siasconset,* on the east side of the island. This beach is also good for surfing. There is a lifeguard and a playground. Siasconset is about seven miles from town.
- *Surfside.* Lifeguard, rest rooms, food service, bathhouse, and as the name suggests, lots of surf.

Churches

- *Christian Science;* 228-0452.
- *Congregational,* 62 Centre St.; 228-0950.
- *First Baptist,* Summer St.; 228-4930.
- *Friends Meeting,* 7 Fair St.; 228-0316.
- *Jehovah's Witnesses,* Milk St. Ext.; 228-1153.
- *Lighthouse Baptist,* Hooper Farm Rd.; 228-3380.
- *Methodist,* Centre Street at Main; 228-0810.
- *St. Mary's Roman Catholic,* Federal St.; 228-0100.
- *St. Paul's Episcopal,* 16 Fair St.; 228-0916.
- *Union Chapel,* Siasconset; 257-6616 (summer only). Catholic and Protestant services.

Odds & Ends

Laundromats

- *Holdgate's Island Laundry,* 4 Vesper Ln.; 228-0750.
- *Nantucket Laundromat Inc.,* Washington St.; 228-4597.

Farm Stands

- *Bartlett's Ocean View Farm,* Bartlett Farm Rd.; 228-9403.
- *Mt. Vernon Flowers & Plant,* Hummock Pond Rd.; 228-3205.

Fish Markets

- *The Fish Market,* 19 N. Beach; 228-0577. Local fresh fish as well as clambakes, fish-and-chips, local eggs and bread, deliveries.
- *Glidden's Island Seafoods,* Steamboat Wharf; 228-0912.
- *Island Seafoods,* Steamboat Wharf; 228-0912.
- *Sayles Seafoods,* Washington St.; 228-4599.
- *Souza's Seafood,* 19 Trotter Ln.; 228-9140. Fresh fish, homemade chowders; lobsters and scallops for travel or shipping.
- *Straight Wharf Fish Store,* Straight Wharf; 228-1095.

Clambakes

- *Claudette's Catering,* Main St., Siasconset; 257-6622.
- *Nantucket Clambake Co.,* 228-9283. Clambakes prepared for the beach or for your backyard.

Ice Cream Parlors

- *Crazy Quinn's,* 75 Water St.; frozen yogurt.
- *Fratellis,* East St., gourmet Italian ice, old-fashioned custard.

- *The Juice Bar,* 12 Broad St.; 228-5799.
- *Yogurt Plus,* 6 Oak St.; 228-6616. Yogurt, sandwiches, bagels.

Bakeries

- *Nantucket Bake Shop,* 79 Orange; 228-2797.
- *Something Natural,* 50 Cliff Rd.; 228-0504.
- *Nantucket Bagel Company,* 5 West Creek Rd.; 228-6461. Bagels, pies, cakes, sandwiches, homemade soup and cappuccino and espresso.
- *Daily Breads,* 147 Orange; 228-8961. Breads, muffins, cookies, coffee.

Libraries

- *Maria Mitchell Association,* 2 Vestal; 228-9198.
- *Nantucket Atheneum,* Lower India; 228-1110.

Best of Nantucket

BEST COUNTRY INN
- *The Summer House,* Siasconset; 255-4577.

BEST BED & BREAKFAST
- *Cliff Lodge,* 9 Cliff Rd.; 228-9480.

BEST RESORT
- *The Wauwinet,* 120 Wauwinet Rd.; 228-0145 or 800-426-8718.

BEST RESTAURANT (CASUAL)
- *The Atlantic Café,* 15 S. Water St.; 228-0570.

BEST RESTAURANTS (FORMAL)
- *The Chanticleer Inn,* New St., Siasconset; 257-6231.
- *India House,* 37 India St.; 228-9043.
- *The Woodbox,* 29 Fair St.; 228-0587.

BEST ENTERTAINMENT
- *Actor's Theatre of Nantucket,* Easton St.; 228-6325.
- *Band concerts,* at Harbor Square. During July and August; call Chamber of Commerce for more information.

BEST ART GALLERY
- *Artists Association of Nantucket,* Straight Wharf; 228-0722.

BEST CRAFT, SPECIALTY, & ANTIQUE SHOP
- *The Lion's Paw,* Zero Main St.; 228-3837.

BEST GOLF COURSES
- *Sankaty Head,* Siasconset; 257-6391. Private; 18 holes.
- *Siasconset Golf Club,* 257-6596. Semiprivate; nine holes.

BEST BEACHES

You can't really miss with any beach on Nantucket, but we suggest you try *Siasconset Beach*, *Madaket Beach*, *Surfside Beach*, and *Cisco Beach*—all on the Atlantic—and *Jetties Beach* (great for windsurfing) on Nantucket Sound, not far from Nantucket Center.

Cuttyhunk: Essentials

Cuttyhunk, outermost in the chain, is the only one of the Elizabeth Islands with any sort of commercial development. The other islands are privately owned. But commercial development Cuttyhunk-style is far different from what you'll find on Nantucket, Martha's Vineyard, and the Cape.

First of all there are no private telephones here—just six pay phones to be exact (so be patient when the line is busy and be prepared to let it ring if the line is free). An assortment of quaint cottages and apartments is available. Don't despair, what Cuttyhunk lacks in quantity, it more than makes up for in quality. For those who really want to "get away," this one-mile wide, two-mile long island is nothing short of paradise. In the summertime, there are usually no more than 400 people on Cuttyhunk; in the winter, there are about 30.

To get here, you have three choices: you can come by private boat and tie up, for a reasonable fee, at Cuttyhunk Marina; you can take a ferry from New Bedford; or you can take a seaplane from New Bedford.

Here is a listing of what the island has to offer; everything is in walking distance from the marina. The streets, trails, and paths on Cuttyhunk have no names.

Beaches

- *Barges Beach,* on Vineyard Sound. Open to public.
- *Churches Beach,* on Buzzards Bay. Open to public.
- *Jetty Beach,* on Buzzards Bay. Open to public.

Churches

- *Cuttyhunk Church.* Roman Catholic Mass offered here on Sunday mornings in the summer. Methodist services offered Sunday nights.

Odds & Ends

Hiking & Nature Trails

All throughout the island; consult map or explore on your own.

Bakeries

- *Vineyard View Bakery,* Cuttyhunk Center.

Marina Services

Moorings and dock tie-ups offered at reasonable fees; write Cuttyhunk Wharfinger, Cuttyhunk Island 02713 for fee schedule and reservations.

Transportation

• New Bedford ferry the *Alert,* leaves from New Bedford Pier Three. Runs daily from June 15 until September 15; from September 15 until June 15 runs only on Tuesday and Friday.
• *The Island Shuttle,* seaplane, leaves from New Bedford waterfront; 997-4095. Cessna five-seater.

INDEX